BASIC PROBLEMS
OF THE
EUROPEAN COMMUNITY

Edited and Introduced by

P. D. Dagtoglou

*Professor for Public Law and European Community Law
at the University of Regensburg*

BASIL BLACKWELL · OXFORD · 1975

Set in Monotype Times (text) and Gill Sans (display)
Printed in Great Britain by
Burgess & Son (Abingdon) Ltd.
and bound by
Mansell Bookbinders Ltd., Witham

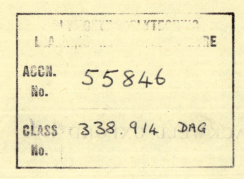

J. C. B. Mohr (Paul Siebeck) (Tübingen), and the editors of the periodicals *Europa-Archiv* (Bonn), *Europarecht* (Munich–Hamburg) and *Integration* (Brussels), and the editors of the series *Kölner Schriften zum Europarecht*, for their kind permission to reprint the contributions to this volume.

The idea of this collection occurred to me, and much of the editorial work was done, during a Visiting Fellowship at All Souls College, Oxford, in the academic year 1972/73. Not least for this I am very much indebted to the College.

Notes

1. For reasons of simplicity 'European Community' stands here for the three legally separate Communities which, however, share the same organs or institutions. This simplification may be also justified by the fact that the discussion of Community problems mostly refers to the European Economic Community, by far the most important of the three Communities.

2. Walter Hallstein's *Der unvollendete Bundesstaat-Europäische Erfahrungen und Erkenntnisse* (Düsseldorf-Vienna 1969), is obviously written with this in mind. Cf. now id. *Die Europäische Gemeinschaft* (Düsseldorf/Vienna 1973).

3. Cf. Ernst Forsthoff, in: *Veröffentlichungen der Vereinigung der Deutschen Staatsrechtslehrer,* vol. 18 (Berlin 1960), p. 177.

4. William N. Hogan, *Representative Government and Integration* (Lincoln/Nebraska 1967): p. 207: 'Power which does not exist does not need an external control in order to be consistent with "democracy" '; cf. also id. 'Political representation and European integration', in: *Integration*, 1970, p. 294.

5. J.O. no. 79 25 April 1967; J.O. L129 30 May 1969; J.O. L49 1 March 1971.

6. Cf. Ernst B. Haas, *The Uniting of Europe and the Uniting of Latin-America,* 5 (1966/67), p. 315 *et seq.* at p. 330: 'And the technical decisions always incorporated in the major choices must be made by technocrats; indeed, the leading role of the technocrat is indispensable in a process as close to the heart of the industrial economy as is the formation of common markets'.

7. Case 22/70, 3 March 1971, *CMLR* (1971) 335.

8. Cf. *Le Monde* of 27 April 1971 (S. 19/20): 'La Cour de Justice de Luxembourg a-t-elle outrepassé ses compétences?'

importance and also the limitations, of the legal structure of the Community and its development towards a European union.

After these more specific papers we come back to a general appreciation of the constitutional problems of the Community offered by the next and largest contribution: Professor Ipsen's last chapter from his recent work on European Community law, the most comprehensive textbook on this subject in any language. Professor Ipsen draws together the constitutional perspectives of the Community and makes some forecasts about its development. He reviews the aim of European integration and analyses the role of people, the dimensions of space and time, and the procedural methods and institutional means of the Community. The fundamental fact that the European Community is a community of people leads him to the basic problems of democratic consensus and legitimacy and the search for an adequate form for the Community in the future.

The last essay, contributed by the editor, examines what could with some reason be called 'the last question' namely how 'indissoluble' is the Community. The purpose is certainly not to put wrong ideas in people's heads (as if they needed that!) but to emphasize that it is not the denial of a right to withdrawal from the Community which promotes integration, but an advanced stage of integration excludes the right of withdrawal.

The essays are certainly too individual to allow any general conclusion. Despite their sometimes considerable differences, they agree on the fundamental 'openness' of the integration process in the sense that it cannot and should not be prejudiced by fixed ideas and premature decisions. They agree basically on the indispensable value of the legal and institutional factor in the process of European integration but also on its inability to replace political backing in the *really* important questions. To be sure, there is some varying interaction between these two factors, which should not be ignored, and the borderline between them is uncertain and controversial—not least throughout this collection. But the time for an emotional and almost metaphysical approach to European integration is behind us and an unprejudiced, down-to-earth discussion about needs, aims, ways and means of European integration is well under way. This volume offers some contributions to this discussion.

Much of the work for this book is done by three English translators: Rosaleen Ockenden, Gordon Adlam, Christopher J. Wells. I thank all three of them—especially as their task was sometimes very arduous indeed.

I should like to thank the publishers and especially their Managing Director, Jim Feather. The publication of this volume owes much to his friendly efficiency. I also thank the publishers: Verlag C. H. Beck (Munich), Carl Heymann Verlag KG (Cologne–Berlin–Bonn–Munich), Verlag für Internationale Politik GmbH (Bonn), R. Piper & Co Verlag (Munich), writings. There is also a third reason: German scholarship has ways of expression which sometimes differ considerably from those of English scholarship. This volume forms no exception to that rule. It is hoped that the reader will see here a fruitful intellectual challenge.

All nine essays are concerned with 'basic' problems of the Community, in the sense of questions relating to the degree of present and future political stability and viability of the Community and the process of European integration. The first contribution by Professor Schwarz asks the simple but difficult question *how* to unite ('federate') Europe. In his comprehensive analysis he examines the different kinds of 'federators', i.e. combinations of forces which initiate, co-ordinate and provide the impetus for political integration. He describes and evaluates the experience gained by mobilizing these different federators in the course of the history of European integration. The results of this methodological study hardly call for a celebration of the United States of Europe, but they do something very valuable: they put events, trends and concepts back in their right proportions.

Professor Scheuner's essay does the same from the legal and institutional point of view. The plans for an economic and monetary union and their failure hitherto give him the framework for a general review of the constitutional problems of the Community, its present powers and those legally and politically attainable in the future, the sense and the weakness of its organization and institutions. Professor Sasse, a former legal adviser and deputy chief of cabinet to the Vice-President of the Commission, concentrates on the analysis of the delicate relations between the Commission and the Council, the causes of friction and frustration, also the possibilities of co-operation. He appeals, finally, for the preservation of the federal features in the constitution of the Community. Professor Zuleeg is concerned with the relations of the Council and the Commission to the European Parliament. He examines the suitability of the parliamentary system of government for the Community. He comes to some interesting though, inevitably, controversial conclusions. Some of his thoughts can also be found in the report of the Vedel group published soon after his essay. Professor Frowein who, together with Professor Scheuner, belonged to this group, comments on the report and the communiqué of the Paris Summit conference and summarizes his suggestions on the constitutional development of the Community. The Vedel Report is also analysed by Professor Fuss. His argument, again inevitably controversial, is that the so-called 'democratic deficit' of the Community is partly overrated and partly compensated by the rule of law in force in Brussels so that priority should be given to the efficiency of the Community institutions.

Unlike the permanent controversy about the political institutions of the Community the European Court of Justice enjoys a relatively high degree of acceptability. Professor Nicolaysen's critical review of the Court's work and contribution to European integration demonstrates once again the mainly lacks is a political basis. There can be little doubt that the concept of the Commission cannot be fully understood without relating it to the belief that there are important decisions which are mainly technical, not political—and must therefore be taken by technocrats, not by politicians[6]—in other words, administration can replace the constitution. The frustration of the Commission (the Council not often approbates reform proposals of the Commission—and quite frequently simply ignores them) is not unconnected with this imbalance. And yet, the integrating role of the Commission can hardly be underrated.

The European Court of Justice, finally, seems to be the only Community institution which has been created with a good sense of balance and taken as a whole, has also hitherto acted correspondingly. Its integrating capacity is more important than observers unused to the interaction of law and government on the Continent and in the Community would probably expect. But it also has its limits, as the reaction to the Court's judgment in the *European Road Transport Agreement* case[7] has shown[8]. Again legal argument cannot replace basic political decisions.

There is certainly no lack of problems touching the very existence of the Community. Though present circumstances justify little optimism about the future, Oscar Wilde's words, a little varied, would be appropriate: 'There is only one thing in Europe worse than to live with the Community, and that is to live without it'.

The only realistic alternative to the Community is a better Community.

This volume includes nine contributions which try to go behind the façade, and present some basic problems, relate them to each other, evaluate them and, sometimes, suggest solutions or alternatives. The reader will easily infer that these essays have been neither written nor selected with the intention of presenting a harmonious set of opinions. Whenever they have been brought up to date for the purpose of this collection there was no coordination of opinions. As a matter of fact, there are not only great disparities in the size and style of the different contributions but also not inconsiderable disagreements between them—both with regard to particular questions and in the general tendency, though all authors accept in principle and welcome European integration through the Community.

All nine essays have been originally published in German. This limitation should be explained—especially as the object of this collection is a Community of several nations. There are three reasons, and rather simple ones at that. A selection from writings in all European languages about such a basic subject could come up against difficulties regarding the proportion of contributions from each nation. It would also certainly require a much larger volume. The second reason is that essays in German are in Britain, for linguistic reasons, much less accessible than, say, French

Centrifugal and centripetal forces in Europe are thus not only based on emotion and ideology but also on reason and rationality.

Another basic problem of the European Community is therefore how to combine integration with decentralization, that is how to strengthen the political will towards European integration and at the same time direct Community politics towards a more devolutional way of thinking—and that not only for reasons of temporary expediency but as a basic policy.

Political will towards integration on the side of the Member States and an attitude orientated towards decentralization on the side of the Community—neither does nor should lead to a devaluation of the Community institutions. Though they by themselves cannot achieve integration, no integration is possible without them. This means that they must be given the powers to bring about the degree of integration which is backed by the declared political will of the Member States. But demanding—or even expecting in the foreseeable future—the development of the Commission into a European Government 'invested' by a directly elected European Parliament, and the retreat of the Council to a second class power level, is wishful and harmful thinking, disregarding political realities and, by positing unreachable aims, inhibiting more modest, but possible achievements.

The institutional problem is, indeed, a very complicated one. The Council enjoys both powers and, indirectly, democratic legitimacy but operates all too often at a level which, far from being supranational, can only be described as traditionally diplomatic. Its working methods can hardly be called efficient. But it is by far the most powerful Community institution. Nevertheless it is, at Community level, subject to practically no control.

The European Parliament is democratically (though not directly) elected but still powerless. It is true that under the Luxembourg Treaty of 22 April 1970 it has been given some limited, though not negligible, powers of budgetary control. For all that—and this is usually overlooked—it will always, even if directly elected, suffer under the severe handicap that, since it is not divided into groups supporting and opposing the current policies of Council and Commission, it cannot fulfil its controlling function with the impetus, commitment and temperament secured by the constant confrontation of Government and Opposition. This does not mean that a simple transplantation of the parliamentary system to the Community would be wise or even possible. But since no control mechanism has yet been found which can fully replace oppositional control, a parliament without opposition is, as a control instrument, doomed to minor significance. This remains basically true with regard to a participation of Parliament in the decisions of the Council as recommended by the Vedel Report, though an enlargement of the powers of Parliament would not fail to influence its means of action.

The position of the Commission is even more extraordinary: What it

Hans-Peter Schwarz

FEDERATING
EUROPE—BUT HOW?

*A critical essay on the
methods of European Integration*

'*Voyez-vous, quand on évoque les grandes affaires, eh bien! on trouve agréable de
rêver à la lampe merveilleuse qu'il suffisait à Aladin de frotter pour voler au-dessus
du réel. Mais il n'y a pas de formule magique qui permette de construire quelque
chose d'aussi difficile que l'Europe unie.*'
General de Gaulle (Press conference of 15 May 1962)

'*The judgments of many must unite in the work; experience must guide their labour;
time must bring it to perfection, and the feeling of inconvenience must correct the
mistakes which they inevitably fall into in their first trials and experiments.*'
David Hume (*The Ways of Arts and Sciences*)

1. Methodology: The Cinderella of Research on Integration

By comparison with the lavish proliferation of work on European integration, the number of studies dealing *systematically* with the methods of
integration is small indeed. Of course, there are the odd isolated statements and studies treating individual problems, but what is missing are
detailed analyses that present basic concepts in all their aspects and discuss
their capabilities critically. The lack of such work is a truly remarkable
phenomenon considering the prominent position of European integration
on the list of priorities of western European politics.

The outline that follows lays no claim to filling this gap. The spade-work
which is the prerequisite for such an ambitious undertaking is lacking; and
it would also be necessary to go into details much more thoroughly than is
possible here. All that is intended is a preliminary mapping-out of the field

1

of research and a rough draft of a number of highly provisional propositions.

Needless to say, a comprehensive discussion of methodology could not be limited to the politics of European integration alone. History places a whole treasure trove of widely scattered material at the disposal of any systematic study. The evaluation of these historical paradigms is still in its infancy. Karl Deutsch and his school have shown in several studies how sociological theories of integration can be developed on the basis of historical data.[1] Etzioni's case-studies are equally orientated towards a historical comparative approach. So is Lipset's analysis of the genesis of the United States, which still constitutes the prime example of a successful federation.[2] But it is too early as yet to speak of an even tolerably thorough investigation of relevant historical examples that are further removed in time. For this reason it would now be highly appropriate to undertake a comparative analysis of the paradigms Belgium, Switzerland, Germany, Italy, Canada and Australia in the nineteenth century, and of the founding of the Republic of South Africa, Czechoslovakia and Yugoslavia in the twentieth.

By contrast, any methodological discussion concerned with *contemporary* processes of integration would be able to build on extensive preliminary studies. This holds good for the 'nation-building' of those states which were created from the disintegrating colonial empires as well as for the many and varied attempts at regional integration, which we are experiencing at the present time.[3]

However, these paradigms will be largely disregarded in the following study, which will limit itself to discussing the methods of integration that have been discussed and tried out in Western Europe since the First World War.

The European initiatives of the inter-war period and, above all, the course of European history since the Second World War, have left an extremely rich deposit of empirical material that has as yet hardly been worked over systematically—at least, not with anything like the thoroughness one might wish, considering the importance of the subject.

There are various reasons for this. Some are connected with the idiosyncrasies of the European social sciences, which Karl Kaiser recently circumscribed in the pointed proposition: '*L'Europe des savants*' corresponds to '*L'Europe des patries*'.[4] Political studies are—in Europe at least—generally orientated along national lines; intergovernmental relations are considered first, if indeed other states are discussed at all. This basic attitude is equally a feature of historical studies on the Continent—and this is not restricted to German historians, either.[5] Thus, disregarding American research for the moment, the most important contributions to the question of European integration have been made by lawyers and economists, for whom the social and political aspects of the alliances are naturally not the prime concern.[6]

2

and civil servants who participated in these conferences did not in their declarations go far beyond what they could have seriously intended. For what they promised was little less than the United States of Europe: the step between a complete Economic and Monetary Union (as described in the Werner Report) to a European Federal State would be both small and inevitable.

What then is the reason of this verbal euphory of the Summit conferences and its sharp contrast to ministerial meetings? It can hardly be the result of political romanticism or compulsively good diplomat's manners. There is probably a compound of political calculation, political convention, and political belief, of varying proportions and with various motives, dominated by rules which are different from those of a meeting at ministerial level. Be that as it may, it has certainly not supported confidence in summit conferences as a powerful and effective factor of integration.

The reluctance as regards a real emancipation of the Community from the Member States is not confined to governments and national bureaucracies. It is, if anything, sometimes stronger with the people. While a close co-operation and a flexible approximation of rules and policies is generally desired and, therefore, politically backed, any far-reaching centralization in Brussels is often strongly resented and rejected. The goal of Europe as a world power arouses little enthusiasm. There is no 'European nationalism' and hardly anyone seriously wants it. Enthusiastic Europeans refer to *the* European People but the Treaties speak of the 'peoples' of Europe, and the peoples of Europe behave as separate nations.

In fact, 'bigness' does not seem to exercise now the fascination it used to radiate in the fifties and early sixties. As economic growth, indispensable though it obviously is, is no longer everywhere regarded as the supreme goal which justifies all sorts of sacrifices, political growth, i.e. the creation of a super power, is considered even less to be a necessarily desirable objective. Preference for small co-operating units sometimes reflects a nostalgic provincialism but it can also be based on more human values than an attitude thoroughly orientated towards growth and expansion. It is also unrealistic to ignore the far-reaching disparities between the political standards and political stability of the different Member States, which do not encourage mutual political trust and confidence. On the other hand, the 'four freedoms' of the Common Market are certainly an achievement; reason speaks for their accomplishment. Industry and commerce are promoted but also checked by the EEC; the rules of free competition with their significance for the consumer are sometimes more consistently and efficiently protected by the Commission and the European Court than by the national governments for whom big business, both national and multinational, sometimes proves too strong. (The problem of checking trade union power remains still unsolved.) Monetary instability, the oil crisis, and defence problems have demonstrated repeatedly in the recent past how necessary it is for the Europeans to close their ranks.

xii

the Member States are still a far more important factor in the life of the Community than the Community in the life of its Member States.

This development was not and is not always inevitable, and certainly not accidental. The structural weakness of the Community, the uncooperativeness of some Member States, or both and, in the last analysis, a weak 'integration drive', or the lack of a strong uniting force ('federator') have thus confined integration to merely administrative arrangements, and kept the influence of the Community on the Member States at a low level. That this is so is shown rather clearly by the three fruitless medium-term economic programmes of 1967, 1969 and 1971.[5]

It is perhaps not surprising but nevertheless unedifying that it is not what obviously needs integration (like transport, science, or energy policy) but what is backed by vested and organized interests (like agriculture) which achieves integration. That this is sometimes done (and even more often seems to be done) at the expense of the consumer, does not add to the popularity of the Community—the more so as the consumer in the Community, owing to the lack of an effective European-wide organization and political representation, is even more helpless than at national level.

Not least for these reasons, uniting Europe cannot be and is no longer considered as a self-evident goal and an inevitable course of history. In other words: the meaning and aim of European integration is not regarded any longer as a question of belief which can only be answered with an unconditional yes or no, but it is questioned and examined and quite often answered in a varying, conditional way. European integration is no longer understood to be an end in itself. Each step of it must be worth its price (albeit in a broad view), and this must be established in a factual, not emotional way. It is not enough to justify measures and policies as promoting European integration, but public opinion must also be satisfied that a European integration demanding such measures or policies is still worth pursuing.

Over and above this: public opinion must be continually persuaded that European integration is a rewarding goal. Re-winning public opinion is a basic problem of the European Community—in the long run a problem of decisive importance.

Not considering European integration as inevitable also means rejecting any kind of 'automatism' in European integration. Automatism can neither be relied upon nor, indeed, be accepted as a substitute for political decision. Moreover, it remains a fact, which cannot be altered simply by protest and indignation, that everything of consequence depends in the last analysis on the political will of the Member States. Any doubts about this truism should have been dispersed the latest by developments related to the intended economic and monetary union which, despite the triumphant *communiqués* of the Hague and Paris Summits of 1969 and 1972 and a number of council decisions, have hitherto produced few results. Moreover, it remains open to discussion whether the experienced politicians

The basic problems of the European Community are thus of constitutional character: who has or should have which power and who does or should control it? This is perhaps a rather brutal way of talking of European integration but such questions cannot be solved by dressing them up in a way which either belittles the Community or considers integration as the natural and inevitable course of European history. In fact, the Community is already a compelling reality deciding on increasingly important matters, and also, which is easily overlooked, influencing them even by its unwillingness or inability to tackle them in time and adequately. Talleyrand's definition of non-intervention (that it means about the same as intervention) applies to the Community already and might increasingly apply to it in the future. The suggestion now seems rather extraordinary that there is no need for any control of the Community's power because the Community has no power.[4] Power in Brussels is, unlike state power, limited to certain aims and means defined by the Treaties; it certainly does not need to be more sinister or arrogant than in the capitals of the Member States, and is often far less secretive. But it is (not only in the eyes of the public) more remote, less comprehensible, and hardly accessible to the control of the national oppositions.

There is also a widespread disillusionment about methods and achievements of the Community. Nothing is (or was!) more 'integrated' than the Common Agriculture Policy and nothing more unpopular. In almost every other respect integration seems to fall short of the expectations of the public and to leave it with the feeling that there is much and expensive ado in Brussels and yet another Marathon session of the Council in order to achieve or to avert some too levelling or too protectionist Community policy. Of course, this is a *simplification terrible* of what happens in Brussels but, as far as public opinion was concerned, monetary anarchy, 'trotting' inflation and soaring prices were in the last years much more noticeable than any integration. Even the much celebrated though recently challenged Customs Union has only been achieved to an extent which hardly touches any sensitive areas of national sovereignty. As customs control still exists at the frontier, harbours and the airports, and prices greatly differ from country to country within the EEC, the public hears much but sees little of the Customs Union.

The idea that the Common Market is a rich man's club with not too many social concerns and sensitivities is rather more widespread than is good for the Community and the cause of European integration. The recent emphasis on social and regional policy has yet to lead to concrete and substantial results before it can change this image. It is true that the Community has gone a long way towards achieving freedom of movement for workers but it has done, and probably could do, little to avert or mitigate the immense social problems of the foreign workers in Germany or in France. That Italy's basic political, social and economic instability remains unchanged and even becomes worse, demonstrates *inter alia* that

INTRODUCTION

The most basic problem of the European Community[1]* is doubtless whether it is to progress or even survive as an integrated and integrating Community, or whether it is going to recede further towards a simple free trade area.

This uncertainty about the Community's future has been generally realized comparatively recently. In the 1950s and 1960s there was a widespread belief that the European Treaties incorporated a machinery which would automatically transform the economic community into a political confederation or even a federal state. Experienced politicians shared this belief till very recently.[2] In the years immediately after the foundation of the EEC leading scholars argued that, unlike the nineteenth century, modern European integration was not a problem of a common constitution but one of a common administration.[3]

In other words, it was thought that European integration could and would gradually and inescapably be achieved through the Community administration. For that reason the 'federalists' agreed reluctantly but confidently to play down the political character of the EEC and emphasize its more technical-economic features in order to soften the 'nationalists'' misgivings. The solution of the 'hot' constitutional problems would be eventually reached almost unnoticeably, as a result of the structural change brought about step by step by the day-to-day administration of the Community.

The development has, however, clearly shown that there is no way of avoiding the basic constitutional questions of power and its control.

* Notes are to be found at the end of the chapter to which they refer.

ix

VWD—*Nachrichten aus den Europäischen Gemeinschaften. Hrsg. VWD—Vereinigte Wirtschaftsdienste GmbH* (News of the European Communities)

ZaöR (V)—*Zeitschrift für ausländisches öffentliches Recht und Völkerrecht* (periodical)

ZgesStW—*Zeitschrift für die gesamte Staatswissenschaft* (periodical)

ZZ—*Zeitschrift für Zölle und Verbrauchersteuern* (periodical)

ZHR—*Zeitschrift für das gesamte Handelsrecht und Wirtschaftsrecht* (periodical)

ZParl—*Zeitschrift für Parlamentsfragen* (periodical)

ZPol—*Zeitschrift für Politik* (periodical)

ZRP—*Zeitschrift für Rechtspolitik* (periodical)

DJT—*Deutscher Juristentag* (Papers of the German Lawyers' Association)

DöV—*Die öffentliche Verwaltung* (periodical)

Dok KOM—*Dokumente der Kommission* (German edition of the Documents of the Commission of the European Communities)

DVBL—*Deutsches Verwaltungsblatt*

EA—*Europa Archiv* (periodical)

EA/D—Europa Archiv/Dokumente (Supplement)

EC—European Court of Justice

EEC—European Economic Communities

ECSC—European Coal and Steel Community

EP—Europäisches Parlament (European Parliament)

EuR—*Europarecht* (periodical)

Euratom—European Community for Atomic Energy

GG—*Grundgesetz für die Bundesrepublik Deutschland* (Constitution of the Federal Republic of Germany)

ICLQ—*The International and Comparative Law Quarterly*

Integration—*Integration* (European Studies Review)

JböR—*Jahrbuch des öffentlichen Rechts der Gegenwart* (periodical)

JCMSt—*Journal of Common Market Studies*

JJb.—*Juristen-Jarbuch* (periodical)

JO—*Journal Officiel des Communautés Européennes* (French edition)

Journ Dr Int—*Journal du Droit International*

JR—*Juristische Rundschau* (periodical)

JuS—*Juristische Schulung* (periodical)

JZ—*Juristenzeitung* (periodical)

NJW—*Neue Juristische Wochenschrift* (periodical)

OJ—*Official Journal of the European Communities* (English edition)

ÖstZöffR—*Österreichische Zeitschrift für öffentliches Recht* (periodical)

PVS—*Politische Vierteljahresschrift* (periodical)

Rec. Dalloz—*Recueil Dalloz Sirey*

Rev. MC—*Revue du Marché Commun*

SEW—*Sociaal-economische wetgewing* (periodical)

Staat—*Der Staat—Zeitschrift für Staatslehre, öffentliches Recht und Verfassungsgeschichte* (periodical)

VerwRspr—*Verwaltungsrechtsprechung in Deutschland* (Entscheidungssammlung) (Law Reports)

VVDStRL—*Veröffentlichung der Vereinigung der Deutschen Staatsrechtslehrer* (papers of the Association of German Constitutional Lawyers)

ABBREVIATIONS

AdG=Abl.EG—*Amtsblatt der Europäischen Gemeinschaften* (German edition of the Official Journal of the European Communities)

AJIL—*American Journal of International Law*

AöR—*Archiv des öffentlichen Rechts* (periodical)

ArchVR—*Archiv des Völkerrechts* (periodical)

Auss Pol—*Aussenpolitik* (periodical)

AWD—*Aussenwirtschaftsdienst des Betriebsberaters* (periodical)

BGBL—*Bundesgesetzblatt* (German Law Gazette)

BGHZ—*Entscheidungen des Bundesgerichtshofes in Zivilsachen* (Reports of the German Federal Court for Civil and Criminal Cases)

BRatsD (rucks.)—*Bundesratsdrucksache* (Papers of the German Upper Chamber)

BT-D(rucks.)—*Bundestagsdrucksache* (German parliamentary papers)

Bull EG—*Bulletin der Europäischen Gemeinschaften* (German edition of the Bulletin of the European Communities)

BVerfGE—*Entscheidungen des Bundesverfassungsgerichts* (Reports of the German Federal Constitutional Court)

BVerwGE—*Entscheidungen des Bundesverwaltungsgerichts* (Reports of the German Federal Administrative Court)

CIJ Recueil—*Recueil des Décisions du Cour International de Justice*

CMLR—*Common Market Law Reports*

CML Rev—*Common Market Law Review*

CONTENTS

In all probability, it is largely this lack of historical research that explains the gap in the theoretical literature about methods of integration. Actually, only *one* method of integration has been extensively set out and considered from a theoretical point of view—this is supra-national functionalism as practised in the European Communities.[7] Interest in research on this has naturally been strengthened by the successes of the Coal and Steel Community and the EEC. Probably the fact that the institutions and civil servants of the Community are easily accessible to researchers in the social sciences has played a part in this; the wealth of data is stimulating the growth of theory.

Yet on the other hand, the European movement is still awaiting its historians; historical research on the creation of the Council of Europe and on the work of the *ad hoc* Assembly is lacking, just as it is on the ECSC or on the creation and development of the EEC and Euratom. No wonder, then, that there is also a dearth of systematic praxeological studies in which the individual concepts are presented and discussed with all their pros and cons.

Since there are no preliminary studies, the following paper has had to resort in the first instance to printed sources. This material is distinctly sparse for the particularly important initial period 1945–49—not least because of the paper shortage at the time. Not until the passionate and excellent debates of the advisory Assembly of the Council of Europe and the sessions of the *ad hoc* Assembly, which exist verbatim, is it possible to make a more precise investigation of the currents of opinion and arguments. The great era of discussions on methods of integration comes to an end with the final collapse of these early initiatives in the early fifties; such discussions shift back to small circles of leading groups—as had already been the case in 1947 and 1948—for whose deliberations no detailed minutes are available. From the middle 50s onwards, the pronouncements of the politicians on the subject become increasingly vague—evidently a result of the fact that all constitutional initiatives of federation had failed, while the hour of EEC functionalism, as effective as it was dull, was yet to come, a method whose exponents promised the painless birth of the United States of Europe, even if only after a somewhat prolonged pregnancy. Nevertheless, the study of the considerations and techniques of operation of the political pragmatists can provide a mass of insights, provided one does not expect them to be systematic.

There are hardly any critical discussions dealing with the integration process as a whole and able to stand as adequate end-means analyses— not even among political writers.[8] There are exceptions: a politician like Walter Hallstein is one,[9] Paul Henri Spaak is another, similarly Altiero Spinelli.[10] But, all things considered, the process of European integration over the past twenty-five years has been characterized by a remarkable lack of any systematic and generally accepted theory on the part of the leading figures involved. Understandably enough, any scientific discussion

3

of method limits itself to examining functionalism; and, on the whole, what Herbert Lüthy concluded very early on about the reality of European politics also applies to the theoretical basis for European integration:

> That was . . . the fate of all European enterprises: that they were never able to come to fruition, but were always either stifled while still growing by a hasty new approach in some completely different direction using different methods, or else they were squeezed onto the periphery, so that 'Europe' finished up looking like a chaotic building-site, where the early stages of half-erected and abandoned scaffolding stand in complete disorder on all sides . . .[11]

The remarks which follow are designed to outline the drafts which formed the basis for the ground-plan of these ruins and half-completed structures and to show where the advantages and weaknesses of the working drawings lie.

2. The Problem: The Voluntary Union of Democratic States

The methodology of political federation is concerned with how autonomous states can be united with each other in such a fashion that the change takes place in a manner which can be calculated and controlled. The central problems of this kind of theory were formulated as early as Machiavelli, who, like few other theoreticians, thought about *change* as a basic fact of politics. In his *Il principe*, he stated:

> And it ought to be remembered that there is nothing more difficult to take in hand, more perilous to conduct, or more uncertain in its success, than to take the lead in the introduction of a new order of things. Because the innovator has for enemies all those who have done well under the old conditions, and lukewarm defenders in those who may do well under the new. This coolness arises partly . . . from the incredulity of men, who do not readily believe in new things until they have had a long experience of them.[12]

What was stated here in respect of individual innovators applies equally in respect of innovatory movements, which seek to create a new state out of already existing ones. Citizens and politicians of an existing state generally set little store by exchanging conditions which, uncomfortable or even disadvantageous though they may be, are nevertheless familiar, for an uncertain future in a new state. To have to transfer little by little to a new state one's growing loyalty to the old one would entail some uncomfortable reorganization of those cosy preconceived notions so dear to every citizen's heart. A more or less well practised and reciprocally

4

arranged system of expectations and outputs would have to be completely re-structured. Neatly established structures and power positions would be turned upside down. If polls show time and again that in important western European states there is an impressive majority in favour of the continuance of political integration—and this majority is also in the leading political and social groups!—one cannot help asking whether these citizens and politicians are actually aware of the revolutionary nature of their wishes. More probably, this positive attitude to the United States of Europe belongs in the category of those political daydreams, which are soon forgotten when practical problems rear their heads. Otherwise the European federation would already have taken firmer shape. There is certainly more than a grain of truth in a caustic remark by David Mitrany, whose enthusiasm for international co-operation is exceeded only by his aversion to a Federal State of Europe: 'European federalism has been a blend of myth and some very mixed sentiments.' [13] Yet, whatever the reasons for reacting positively to the idea while at the same time remaining cautious when it comes to practice, the fact remains that an attempt to persuade countries with differing political systems and social structures to form a voluntary federation represents one of the most difficult tasks, calling for considerable political strategy and tactics—above all, because the *foederandi* are at one and the same time sovereign states and democracies.

The willingness of individual governments to federate varies in intensity at different times—but federation can only come about if *all parties* agree to it without any constraint. Even the co-ordination of measures for federation between autonomous governments presupposes a favourable conjunction and a large measure of expertise in foreign affairs on the part of the Cabinets which take the initiative. Moreover, the interests of the individual states prompt each of them to obtain the best possible conditions of federation for their own subjects. Nights of abnegation like that of 14 August 1789, on the part of the *Etats Généraux*, are as rare in a society of States as they are in home affairs.

And the fact that the western European States are democracies—which they rightly consider an advantage—only complicates any attempt at federation still further. Those leading groups which agree on definite plans for federation have to assure themselves of parliamentary majorities, and in some cases they must even obtain the backing of the majority of the electorate in order to get their projects accepted. They have to win over the public opinion and especially the organized groups in their society, and all this in harmony with the other governments that are prepared to federate.

Thus it is not by chance that successful federations that have come about voluntarily between constitutional states belong to the extreme rarities of modern and recent times. The overwhelming majority of democratic federations have not come about by free consensus—like the Netherlands, the USA or Switzerland—but have been created under the guiding hand of

5

colonial governments.[14] It is not easy to say whether the unified state of Italy and the German Empire are to be regarded more as voluntary federations or as the results of politics of dynamic hegemony. At any rate, the creation of federations by pressure on the part of some hegemonical state is more frequent than is the formation of a union on the basis of the co-ordinated co-operation of independent states.

Of course, in the case of the proposed European federation, a process of federation along hegemonic lines would be a contradiction in terms: here it was, after all, the intention of the federalists that an '*aequm foedus*' (Grotius) of democratic states be created. No one has pointed this out more clearly than General de Gaulle, in his great attack on the EEC Commission, in which he sarcastically criticized the 'unrealistic project' ('*ce projet contraire à toute réalité*') of a European Federation, where the different countries, 'lacking a federator of the stamp aspired to, though of course in different ways, by Caesar and his successors, Charlemagne, Otto, Charles V, Napoleon and Hitler in the west, and by Stalin in the east—would be governed by a technocratic, countryless and irresponsible areopagus.'[15] European Federation by hegemony and federation at the expense of democracy: both, in fact, would be a price that no Western European state would be prepared to pay.

But are there any other methods? Methods which make possible a voluntary, democratic and rationally controllable federation process? A process actually culminating in the goal which European federalists are striving to achieve from the most varied of motives: a European Federal State, not merely the close co-operation of independent states.

3. Basic Concepts: Federation, Political Integration, Federator

The discussion of the past decade in politics and scholarship was often likely to blur the issue that the goal was a federal state. Thus, no less a person than Walter Hallstein considered it right and proper in an important speech to describe the alternatives 'federation' or 'confederation', 'national sovereignty' or 'European unity' as '*faux problèmes*'.[16] This made it easy for David Mitrany to point to the contradictory nature of hypotheses,[17] which are due to the practical attempts to create irrevocable European realities behind the backs of the European Cabinets. For, in actual fact, Hallstein has time and again proclaimed the founding of a federal state (of a 'complete federation'—*Vollföderation*) as the ultimate aim.[18]

If, in what follows, the methods of European integration are discussed exclusively with the aim of a federal state in view, this is in no way to ignore the fact that the same methods may be claimed for *other* functions—for the settlement of intergovernmental disputes, for the simple co-ordination of economic policy, for better communication between national bureaucracies. In his contributions to the theory of integration, Ernst Haas has convincingly shown that international organizations flourish best (and hence encourage processes of political integration) when they satisfy numerous different needs of different parties *simultaneously*. Looked at from this aspect it can even be useful, if individual groups strive to realize incompatible aims via the same organization. Naturally, this conclusion ought not to be exaggerated. In fact, despite all the quirks of the prevailing attitude which is active in international organizations, it must be shown whether or not they correspond to specific aims, providing these have been sufficiently precisely set out.

Of course, it can sometimes appear politically expedient to blur the distinction between the two concepts confederation (*Staatenbund*) and federation (*Bundestaat*). But to obliterate contours in this way prevents any careful end-means analysis and is one of the main reasons for the present, so unsatisfactory state of methodology. For this reason, the classical distinctions between confederation and federation will be maintained in what follows.

It is recognized that the minimal criterion for a federation however structured, or for a confederation, is its character as a legal subject in international law, and this must entail a corresponding extensive, far-reaching loss of international legal capacity of the member states themselves.[19]. As a condition of this, what were formerly external relations between the partners of the federation now become internal. Looked at from outside the federation is one unit of action; with regard to internal politics, it has—if a disintegration is to be avoided—to display features which Ernst Haas has defined as 'a condition in which specific groups and individuals show more loyalty to their central political institutions than to any other political authority, in a specific period of time and in a defineable geographic space'.[20] Political integration, as understood in the remarks following, thus has as its purpose the founding of a new state. John Galtung sums up this interpretation of integration most succinctly: 'Integration is the process whereby two or more actors form a new actor. When the process is completed the actors are said to be integrated'.[21]

Even though the following discussion of methods of integration is in terms of a clearly defined complex of aims (federation, federal state), it does not ignore the fact that political integration represents a process.[22] Social Science research dealing with the last century has led to an increased awareness of this. A process of integration mostly begins long before the founding of a federation, and is anything but complete by the time the central political institutions have been created.[23] Over and above this, the research work of the neo-functionalist school has brought into the picture the economic and social processes of integration which run parallel to the political one and whose significance must equally not be ignored when the main focus of attention moves to the shaping of central political institutions and power centres.

7

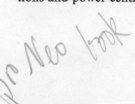

Nevertheless, it would be wrong if, out of sheer enthusiasm at discovering that political integration is a process, one were to mistake the decisive threshold which is crossed when a central state is founded. This step does not only mean a qualitative change in the conditions of foreign politics, but in most of the cases known to us, it has also activated the integration of the societies scheduled to grow together to an extent which those researchers who devote their special attention to the smooth transitions of international integration are all too apt to understate.

To talk of the establishment of central institutions sounds very static. In fact, it is not the institutions that make up the decisive factor, but the activities of a central government, of a federal parliament and of a federal judiciary. These form power centres which counteract the centrifugal forces of the federal states and probably they alone are in a position to amalgamate the heterogeneous societies with each other.

In Max Huber's compendium on sociological elements of international law, *Soziologische Grundlagen des Völkerrechts*, which appeared in 1912, there is a chapter worth noting with the heading: 'Integration of the Society of States' (*'Integration der Staatengesellschaft'*). Huber remarks there:

> As long as it is only government interests and government institutions that are considered to have any bearing on the development of international law, any tendency to lay emphasis on international commitments, let alone organizations, which are not of merely economic character but are related to politics, will be extremely small. *Radical innovations* can only come about by *outside* forces pressing governments, and the interest groups within society which directly influence them, to move in that direction.[24]

These are in outline the essential problems confronting any methodology of European integration:

1. How can states which are linked to each other by being very closely interdependent, yet which, at the same time, have an autonomous political decision-making process be encouraged to form a federation?

2. Can one rely for this on the co-operation of the various governments, or are non-governmental forces and institutions essential?

3. If yes, what form must they take?

All experience of the politics of European integration has, in fact, shown that it will not work without the forces and institutions 'from outside'. On the other hand, even the most enthusiastic of the European federalists has had to recognize that there is no way of bypassing the individual governments. The central problem for any method of integration lies in interlocking the external forces with the work of the governments in such a way that radical reorganization is possible.

What Huber loosely terms 'political forces' are, among other things, political parties, associations both political and politically relevant, the press and mass media, bureaucracies, autonomous corporations, and important individuals. More or less organized co-operation on the part of these groups ought to induce reluctant governments to join a federation.

True, experience shows that there can be no exclusive adherence to any single method if political integration is to progress. Despite this, however, the practicians and theoreticians of European integration have hitherto been inclined to rely on specific combinations of forces that are in favour of integration. This kind of combination of forces which initiates, co-ordinates and provides the impetus for processes of political integration, will be referred to in what follows as a federator—to develop a term used by de Gaulle.[25] Theorems and strategical/tactical considerations referring to this, we shall call *federator concepts*.

Looked at formally, political integration of two and more states can be initiated, developed and completed by various federators:

(*a*) by an especially powerful or otherwise particularly well-placed state which makes itself the head of the federation. There are two conceivable variants of this: the relevant state adopts the leading role and this is recognized as legitimate by the other *foederandi*, or else a hegemonic power brings the federation about by force.

(*b*) by a state which furthers the federation *without* joining it (external federator).

(*c*) by political and social groups which co-operate at an inter-state level (European movements).

(*d*) by groups which base themselves on international or supranational bodies and institutions which have been set up with the agreement of the states concerned (international and supranational federators).

In history, several or all of these factors are found combined though they differ in importance. Nevertheless, it is still admissible to examine the peculiarities of the individual concepts, provided only that their connexion with other factors is not overlooked.

4. Federators in the Process of European Integration

1. Leading Powers as Federators

The general view on European federation is that it is conceivable only as a union of equals. Thus hegemonic federators are unacceptable. On the other hand, it is quite conceivable that *one* state can function as a federator in its capacity as legitimate leading power. In the years immediately following the Second World War, Great Britain had some chance of being accepted as a federator—even though not as a hegemonic power. In fact, this role then fell to France, which tried to do justice to it until the middle sixties.

But the leading role is just not the same thing as a hegemonic position. The other western European states were jealous and successfully

9

endeavoured to block French hegemonic aspirations; the failure of the political union suggested by de Gaulle provides the classic example of this. Quite apart from this, not all the initiatives came from the French Government by any means. For example, no small credit for the setting up of the EEC is due to the skilful leadership of a few politicians from the Benelux Countries. As Germany and Italy grew out of their depressed position in the fifties, a federator concept based on a leading state became less and less acceptable. The stubborn resistance of the Netherlands to de Gaulle's European plan proves that the smaller countries, for their part, are not prepared to agree to a federator concept where *one* State is a dominant power, either.

States are, of course, not individuals, but complex action units governed by political forces. Any federator concept would have to suggest conditions which make it possible for those political groups *inside* the federator state that welcome federation both to direct government policy towards their ends and, at the same time, to win that legitimacy *outside* it, without which a federation having *a single* state as nucleus is inconceivable.

In the case of western Europe, it is also unacceptable, if not inconceivable, that a state should bring about a federation and yet remain outside it. To be sure, theoreticians of federalism are all too prone to overlook the fact that the federations in Africa and Asia have come about through the influence of external federators—as parting gifts from the departing Colonial powers. And finally, European integration did have a potential external federator until the mid sixties—the United States of America.

The American contribution may have been described several times already, but it has not yet been systematically evaluated. Its significance cannot be overestimated.[26] Yet even at the peak of its political and economic influence—between 1947 and 1958—the United States was not in a position to push through certain integration projects against the will of the European states. It did not succeed in making the OEEC (Organization for European Economic Co-operation) a federator instrument, nor was Washington able to overcome the French opposition to the EDC (European Defence Community).

For many reasons, the American readiness to play the part of external federator for Europe decreased during the sixties. The economic competition of the EEC played its part in this, as did the attempts to reach agreement with the Soviet Union and the latest signs of regional world politics.

So a State that is prepared to set up a federation, or an external world power, can play a role as federators only with considerable tact and self-restraint. Any excess pressure and dynamism would be unacceptable to the other partners, and this would only be counterproductive. The lack of success of American pressure during the EDC debates in Paris has clearly shown this. But that means that in western Europe it is at most in a subsidiary capacity that States come into question as federators. The pressure 'from outside' which Max Huber mentions must be expected mainly from other centres of power. All varieties of the European movements recognize this.

2. The Federating Potential of the European Movements[27]

Ever since a federator concept of this kind was first propagated by Count Coudenhove-Kalergi in the period between the two world wars, considerable experience has been gained on this basis. The chances of success and the weaknesses of this concept can be judged more or less objectively.

The basic idea is as such temptingly simple. The European movements unite all those persons and groups who recognize in the idea of federation the great panacea for the ills and difficulties of the European states. In the opinion of the federalists, all the major problems confronting the states of Europe in the twentieth century could be solved by the creation of a federal State: it would guarantee peace between Member States, provide security *vis-à-vis* the Soviet Union, give renewed importance to the European position in world affairs, solve the German problem in a way equally acceptable to the Germans and their neighbours, and create a large economic area which would provide mass prosperity and social progress *within* itself and which would be capable of competing with the United States in *foreign* markets. According to this concept, all Europeans who have seen the light must co-operate in a supranational movement. That movement is to rid the individual nations of their particularistic prejudices by concentrated propaganda, it is to plan and carry out practical initiatives for federation, and above all, to bring governments round to the right way of thinking by persuasion and pressure.

Difficulties arise as soon as it is a question of the methods and modalities of political integration. And, indeed, in the first instance it was the dissension over programme and methods which knocked the vitality out of the European movements. These critical questions in respect of the programme for integration are just as controversial and complicated today as they were immediately after the Second World War: ought the federation to take place in one great leap (formation of a Constituent Assembly, working-out and acceptance of a constitution, formation of a Government)—or 'by instalments'? And, if one relies on gradualism from the very start: where and how ought one to begin (with the basic industries, with the communications network, with defence)? And with what partners (with or without Eastern Europe, with or without England)? How will the interests of the individual States be guaranteed in the transition period, without jeopardizing the goal of federal union? How are the foreign relations of the federation to be conceived (relations with the United States, the Soviet Union, Asia and Africa)? And what must be the nature of the *internal* system (more or less centralist, socialist, liberal or corporate)?

It is quite natural that the answers given to these basic questions should vary considerably even among the most convinced federalists. To this one must add the problem of how feasible it is to carry out the programmes in the individual states, in order to make the circle of participants as wide as possible. Does it not make sense to bear in mind that individual key states are prepared only for a cautious policy of progress by small steps? If the answer is yes, then progress will inevitably be at a snail's pace. On the contrary, should one back the concept of a nucleus of federation between those states that are willing to federate? In this case the rate of integration can be forced.

These questions of political programming and methodology have cropped up at every stage along the road to Calvary up which the European Movement has been toiling since the Second World War. They caused— inevitably, one must add—the splitting up of the Movement into 'Federal- ists' and 'Unionists', into advocates of a new Federation including only the countries of the former Carolingian empire or of an alliance including the British and Scandinavians, into Liberals and Socialists, into technocrats and populists, into anti-communists and proponents of a mediating line in the Cold War. Incidentally, it was only natural for personal rivalries and national ressentiments to give added piquancy to these differences of approach. Even in the individual nations it was again and again absolutely impossible to co-ordinate all the divergent efforts in one organization. And this was only too obviously doomed to failure at the European level. No loosely-structured national organizations and compromise resolutions reached after tough bargaining[28] could disguise the fact that the so-called European Movement did not constitute a powerful driving force for European union but resembled rather a mechanism of many small cogs spinning both with and against each other.

But the federator concept of a supranational European movement does not only suffer from a multiplicity of programmes. Over and above this, it is dependent on parties, parliaments and governments to take up its proposals and put them into effect. It is these alone who have the oligopoly of political organization and decision. The movements as such are con- demned to operate by lobbying.

The protagonists of the European federation have attempted to bypass this political impotence of theirs by the most varied methods. Two funda- mentally different approaches emerge from the great variety of activities. On the one hand, the movements could try to put their ideas into political practice by winning leading politicians and representatives of the most influential parties and interest groups for their programmes and could place themselves under their leadership. The other way consisted in widening the scope of some independent political party which did not have to make use of the leading groups in national politics but which these groups had rather to serve. In this instance, co-operation or competition with the political establishment of the individual nation States were the alternatives.

The committee of public figures, run on national or international lines, is the typical form of organization found in the co-operation approach. Over and against this, bound up with the competition-concept, we find the

12

notion of a European *Popular Movement* or *European Party*. Roughly speaking, the national councils and congress boards of the Pan-European Union,[29] the United Europe Movement and the European Movement corresponded to the first, co-operative, kind of approach. On the other hand, the *Union Européenne des Fédéralistes* (UEF) which had developed from the European resistance movements supported the concept of a popular movement of 'militants' organized from the grass roots level. The theory of this kind of approach has been developed first and foremost by Altiero Spinelli who played a leading role in the fragmentation of the populist *Congrès du Peuple Européen* (CPE). The experience gained shows that the committee of public figures is the only method with a reasonable chance of success. The concept of a popular movement has not hitherto got beyond the stage of a likeable sectarian group.

To be sure, those who were concentrating primarily on the realistic aim of activating supranational groups of politicians were equally concerned to deck out their activities with the brilliant trappings of a popular movement. But it is, on the whole, to the leading classes rather than to the broad mass of the population that the committees of public figures address their activities. Their public relations work is mainly concerned with achieving or cultivating a positive basic attitude towards the idea of federation, to woo support for specific unification projects, to support concrete government initiatives and to ward off adverse tendencies (for example, de Gaulle's European initiatives). Efforts to put political parties under popular pressure are quite alien to the federator concept of the supranational committee of public figures.

Certainly, it is no mean feat that the Councils of the European Movements have been able to set up something like a 'background ideology of a non-antagonistic nature' (Schelsky) via the co-operating representatives of parties and interest groups. A European Federation is not going to grow out of efforts directed to the public in the first instance. Progress was achieved only by such initiatives which were aiming at co-operation between the highest political and social functional elites. Essentially, two types of approach have led to a certain amount of progress: international co-operation of parliamentarians and the methods of the Action Committee.

3. A Parliamentarian Movement as a Federator

Parliamentarians already had a decisive role to play as early as the Pan-European Movement of the inter-war period. And after the Second World War, it was once again Count Coudenhove-Kalergi, who went in this direction with the founding of the European Parliamentary Union. In his memoirs he outlines the basic conception that lay at the bottom of this variant of the committee of public figures:

Everywhere parliaments are mediators between people and government. The governments are dependent on them, just as they in turn depend

13

upon the voters. Thus, an alliance of parliamentarians with the unification of Europe as its aim would be the quickest means of causing the Governments to effect the United States of Europe.[30]

Winston Churchill and Duncan Sandys also chose parliamentarians in the first instance for the United Europe Committee. The *Conseil Français pour l'Europe Unie* was constructed on similar lines.

But, of course, there was more than mere methodological calculation behind the notion of employing as a federator a group of parliamentarians co-operating at international level. The few published protocols of the Hague Congress of 1948 show that, at that time, the French parliamentarians were especially keen to combine this federator concept with the principle of popular sovereignty.[31] It is not clear to what extent any part was played in those deliberations by the notion of a rift between the governments as the guardians of national sovereignty and the peace-hungry masses, a rift that would have to be bridged by the people's representatives.[32] But the decisive factor was the conviction that the responsibility for uniting Europe ought to be borne first and foremost by persons with a mandate from the voters.

It was consistent with the logic of their approach that the concept of a parliamentarian movement quickly developed into the concrete demand for a European Constituent Assembly. It is indeed possible to regard a group of influential parliamentarians operating internationally and independent of party loyalties as one of the most important federators—although only if it can manage to form a Constituent Assembly relatively quickly, or at least a supranational institution, whose political terms of reference are sufficiently vaguely drawn up for it to get on with the task of working out a constitution and preparing for European elections. If it is not the aim to form a Constituent Assembly, then, while international co-operation by parliamentarians might indeed be valuable and prepare the ground for later integration initiatives, no further-reaching stimulus is to be expected from a body of this type.

On two occasions such a Constituent Assembly was to have opened up the *via regia* to a European Constitutional State. The first attempt failed with the founding of the Council of Europe, the second ran aground in 1952/3, together with the over-hasty plan of setting up the European Political Community. The failure of these all-or-nothing methods forced federalists to subscribe henceforth to a pragmatic gradualism and to leave aside the concept of the Parliamentarian Movement. In the course of this there developed a new and uncommonly effective type of committee of public figures—Jean Monnet's 'Action Committee'.

4. Jean Monnet's Approach: An Action Committee with Corporate Representation
The Action Committee is a prime example of the committee of public

14

figures, and fairly precise details of the way in which it works are available.[33] It developed from Jean Monnet's own rich and varied network of personal contacts, and it unites leading politicians and union leaders[34] in a committee which operates internationally. Monnet's invitation to the founder meeting established the aim of the committee which was unanimously agreed by the members: the founding of the United States of Europe.[35] The members were invited as representatives of their organizations and they expressly endorsed the notion of corporate representation in the founding resolution of 18 January 1956: 'The Committee shall guarantee the concerted action of those organizations numbered among its members, in order to arrive at the United States of Europe by concrete and gradual steps.' [36]

All observers agree that the support of this committee was of decisive importance for a series of successful federation initiatives—first and foremost for the success of the Rome Treaties, but also for the merging of the Communities.

The practicability and success of this body are due to a number of factors:

1. The personal prestige of Jean Monnet was of great importance since it enabled him to bring together top politicians and trade unionists.

2. The Committee was founded at a time when the ideological orientation of Western European party politics was beginning to give way to an increasingly pragmatic basic attitude. Without this—as it was to prove, provisional—'end of the ideological age' (Daniel Bell) such agreement about integration initiatives dealing with practical problems and pragmatic considerations would have been barely conceivable.

3. The consensus procedure adopted in the Committee[37] helps to avoid voting and hence unproductive outvoting of minorities. Unanimous resolutions were made possible by thorough preparation of the sessions by a small staff, by the persuasiveness and patience of Jean Monnet and by his expertise in conjunction with the consciousness of the members that they constitute an exclusive group.

4. The fact that these functional elites have bound themselves to concrete projects for integration secures them a high measure of support at the national level. This effectiveness is attained by consistently accepting the principle of corporate representation. Jean Monnet and his staff provide the indispensable contact with the leading functionaries and civil servants of the Communities.

5. The fact that the Committee Members (except for the Chairman) are elected to public offices prevents the not easily refuted accusation that the Committee is striving to set up a federal state having an authoritarian political structure.

Within the framework of the gradualistic method of integration, the Action Committee is the most ideal federator anyone could think of. Hitherto—considering the depressing experiences of the early fifties—it has rightly been wary of starting any initiatives on the Constitution. Monnet swears by the method of gradualism. But, even if the constellation were favourable for constitutional initiatives, then any initiative would probably carry furthest if it were supported by this or some similar body.

Of course, even a committee of this kind is doomed to failure if its initiatives come up against governments where the political powers that be are not prepared to co-operate. Naturally, Monnet has avoided the mistake made by the Council of Europe and has not brought in any representatives who are against the formation of a European State *in principle*. This ensured a consensus on fundamental issues, but the price was the absence of the Gaullists and, at the beginning, of the British and the representatives of other EFTA states as well. So it comes about that the Committee's strong support for British entry into the EEC left the Gaullists completely unmoved and fizzled out ineffectually. The capability of this ingenious Committee for bringing about integration stands and falls with the will to integrate of the politicians in the relevant States.

5. *Concepts of a European Popular Movement*

The concept of a European Popular Movement as a federating force is as old as that of federation via political leaders. Count Coudenhove-Kalergi himself, a virtuoso in establishing committees of leading figures, was at some pains to anoint his elitist methods of federation with the democratic charisma of a popular movement. But above all, the European Resistance Groups, from which the UEF arose, were seriously resolved to build up the United States of Europe *from the rank and file*. These groups, dedicated as they were to the traditions of the personalist movement,[38] of a popular socialism,[39] of proudhonism,[40] or of a Christian conservative philosophy, were endeavouring to achieve not only a revolutionary transformation of the 'anarchistic' international order, but also radical social reform. The emphasis that was laid on mobilizing the rank and file corresponded exactly to this socio-political reformist tendency. Moreover, the resistance groups would have been in a position to bring in their 'militants'. Denis de Rougemont maintains that in 1947 the UEF comprised twenty eight movements with over 100,000 registered members.[41]

The distrust of political parties was extremely marked at times. Many people regarded them as the most effective instruments of national egoism.[42] Yet it was not clear at the start whether some movement competing with the established political parties ought to be attempted or whether it was better to 'establish a league with the object of providing every democratic and progressive party with an international political programme.'[43] De Rougement tells of plans to send delegates from the representatives of all *forces créatrices* to a European States General. Many people believed that representatives of the industrial, agricultural and co-operative associations, of the local councils, parliaments, youth movements and churches might be able to present *'Cahiers de revendication'*

16

after the fashion of the *Etats Généraux* of 1789, and might change into a Constituent Assembly in the course of the talks. The leaders of this assembly were to form the nucleus of a future European Government.[44]

Of course, examined closely, the leading groups of the UEF also work on the principle of committees of public figures, and when it came to taking the oath, they joined together with the other European Movements—with some reservation, may be, but in full recognition of their own weakness.[45] Like it or not, the UEF, too, had to count on permeating the established political forces with its ideology. This effort failed. When the concept of union by means of committees of public figures was clearly seen to be a dead end, this appeared to prove right those radical federalists who had demanded the creation of a Popular Movement from the very start. So, at the end of the fifties, Spinelli and others of like mind tried to have a European People's Congress elected in a number of European constituencies. This congress was supposed to establish itself as a Constituent Assembly and even go so far as revolution if the occasion arose. Naturally, this attempt merely goes to show the fruitlessness of an approach which is attuned to the idea of one European people, whereas the European peoples continue to consider themselves nations.[46] The idea of the resistance movements in the first hours of liberation not to reassemble their old inefficient national machinery of government, but to create a federation with a replaced inner structure, just could not be resuscitated in the fifties and sixties. Moreover, the anarchist-federalist group, the 'Federalist Autonomy', split off from the *Mouvement Fédéraliste Européen* (MFE), which was aiming at co-operation between international leadership and local groups at the grass roots level, and thus brought this federator concept still further into disrepute as a sectarian movement run by Italians and Frenchmen who had lost their sense of reality through too much reading of Proudhon.

6. The Prospects for European Parties and European Party Congresses

For the sake of completeness, let us also consider the federator concept of a European Party. The notion of raising a European Popular Movement as a federator had led to absurd results at the end of the fifties by the experiment with the MFE's 'People's Congress Movement'. If one wanted to retain the idea of an organization that was in competition with the established parties while renouncing the revolutionary phraseology and at the same time not sacrificing party democracy as such, there remained only the European Party as a way out. At the beginning of the sixties, parties with the label 'European Federalist Party' were founded in Austria, the Netherlands and the Federal Republic of Germany and these parties recruit their supporters from the ranks of the European Movement.[47]

Links between the failure of the European Political Union and the experiment with European Parties cannot be excluded. At some stage even the warmest federalists had to realize that decisive impulses could no

17

longer radiate from a cross-party movement. But the insufficiency of government initiatives, too, could no longer be overlooked; for the existing parties seemed unwilling to or incapable of coping with the forces of inertia. Surely, in this situation was not the only remaining way out to found a party and to try to get it into power?

However, the political successes of the European Party up to date make it doubtful whether much can be expected of this concept.[48] Nevertheless, this approach makes it justifiable to consider in exactly what kind of circumstances the expectations placed in a European Party might possibly be fulfilled.

It is probable that any attempts to set up European parties from scratch with a few idealistic groups will yield little in future either, whereas this method might be more successful if a European party were to arise from a split in one of the larger established parties. But can one really see this happening in the foreseeable future? There is nothing to suggest that it will, and nothing illustrates more clearly the second-class status of European political discussions in all the continental European parties. Nevertheless, such developments are not to be excluded absolutely.

Of course, to express the thought—as is done in the European Parties from time to time—that a federation could be created only when European Parties had gained parliamentary majorities in all the States, is tantamount to an admission of the Utopian character of one's own aims. The probability of any party oriented primarily towards foreign policy gaining a majority in a state is slight. The privileged position of home policy, so characteristic of modern democracies, would require any European party to offer an attractive programme of domestic policy, and in particular a first-class leadership in conjunction with the indispensable cachet of political representatives of the most varied interest groups.

And if by any chance such a party were to succeed, this would mean, in the first instance, that it has integrated itself particularly well in the pluralistic society of the relevant state.

Of course, examples of parties which were skilful enough to combine a strong assimilative power on the domestic front with a pronouncedly pro-federation foreign policy, are not entirely lacking. The heyday of Christian democratic European policy in the years 1950–53 was possible because de Gasperi's Christian Democrats in Italy, the *Mouvement républicain populaire* (MRP) in France and Adenauer's *Christliche Demokratische Union* (CDU) in the Federal Republic of Germany all had success with it for a short time. Nevertheless, the weakening of the will to federate among the parties mentioned only goes to show how swiftly the opposite tendencies grow when the party concerned is forced to create a broad political consensus.

But the real crux of the concept of a European Party lies though in the fact that European Parties would actually have to exert a decisive influence in all the States that might possibly join the federation. Favourable

18

constellations like this are barely conceivable, and, what is more, the greater the success a federalist party has at home, the greater the difficulties in the way of reaching agreement with its European sister parties who have been equally successful in integrating themselves into the political systems of *their* states! Even if the special interests of all the important groups were satisfied, serious conflicts, with respect to the inner structure of a federation or, in particular, concerning the circle of participants, might still arise even between parties that were in favour of such federation in principle. And the controversies about the external relations of the federation would probably also have a slowing down effect time and time again.

Now, in this context people always point to the success of the American 'Federalists' in founding the United States of America. But how simply the field of international politics was structured in those days, when the American states were sorting themselves out, compared with the fifties and sixties of this century!

At any event, it would be wrong to conclude that the federator concept of a European Party is totally ineffective. The most important function of this kind of party might lie in injecting a kind of 'europolitical' extremism into the national party systems. In certain circumstances, even small extremist parties or extra-parliamentary groups are in a position to exert considerable influence on the course of large parties. This depends on the 'marginal vote' as well as on the affinity of the political extremes to certain currents of opinion *inside* parties of which the majority of members are not extremist. It depends also on the state of parliamentary majorities at the time. This, of course, does not affect the difficulties in the way of international co-operation between elements supporting federation.

Present-day European Federalist Party (EFP) groups subscribe to the realistic principle that the parties in the individual states should be organized independently whilst at the same time they should try to co-ordinate their policies in a federalist congress. The possibilities of this kind of co-operation have already been tried out during collaboration of federalistically-inclined sister parties which got under way especially in the early post-war years.

Collaboration between the great socialist parties turned out to be least productive.[49] In the decisive years, the domination of the Labour Party and of the Scandinavian Socialist parties killed off all attempts to develop impulses for federation from the regular contact between the party-leaders. During the early fifties it was primarily disagreement about the Army of Europe which prevented the Socialist Internationale that had been revived in 1951 from developing into a source of initiatives and a centre of co-operation in European politics.

In those years the socialist federalists were compelled to organize themselves outside the leading parties: in the *Mouvement Socialiste pour les Etats-Unis d'Europe* (MSEUE).[50] This movement relied in the beginning on activists from the extreme left-wing groups in the European Socialist

19

movements—and above all on the Independent Labour Party. With the joining of the British Labour Party, and after the French Socialists had allowed their members the option of joining individually, an ideological change of course took place under the leadership of André Philip and Paul Henri Spaak. In this connexion, the Advisory Assembly of the Council of Europe proved especially valuable as a platform for the co-operation of Socialist federalists. However, the opposition of the German Social Democratic Party (SPD) and the Labour Party could not be overcome. At no time during the period at which it was effective did the MSEUE correspond to the ideal conception of a socialist European Internationale operating supranationally.

The Christian Democrats were blessed with more favourable circumstances. While it is true that we know relatively little about the early contacts in and about the *Nouvelles Equipes Internationales* (NEI), the general view holds that this supranational Christian-Democratic European Movement was of considerable importance in the incubation period of integration politics.[51] Like the MSEUE, the NEI was the result of initiatives by leading individuals. The period at which it had most effect on European politics falls in the years 1947–1949 when the links between the Christian parties of Western Europe were having to be reforged.[52]

The function of these party groupings within the European movement must be seen to lie in the first instance in bringing about an active process of communication between sister parties. The NEI became progressively less interesting as numerous other platforms for political contact began to compete with it—the Advisory Assembly of the Council of Europe, the European Parliament, the Assembly of NATO Parliamentarians, the Interparliamentary Union, etc. The same also applied to European initiatives in the narrower sense for which the Advisory Assembly of the Council of Europe, the Cabinets or the cross-party action groups proved more suitable.

The ideological climate of the late fifties and early sixties weakened the integration potential of the Christian Democrat parties, too. Just like the socialists, they fell prey to those forces which were clamouring to reject ideology. As the cohesive force of the Christian Democrat idea weakened, there was a growing sense of identification with interest groups within the individual countries. In the same way, the affinity with other parties within each state was growing more and more marked, for one had to compete with these parties to win the floating voters and also rule in coalition with them. To be sure, all this opened up a vast field of inter-party collaboration precisely on European questions both within a national and an international framework, but as against this, the importance of inter-state collaboration between sister parties on the same ideological course declined. An international Action Committee is to this extent much more appropriate to the post-ideological phase of Western European party politics than the federator concept of an ideologically homogeneous

European Party. To this must be added the fact that the activity of the pro-federalist European Christian Democrats was particularly adversely affected by the weakening of the MRP—that meant the breakdown of the sister party in one of the key states. General de Gaulle took over the position of the MRP, and, while it is true that he continued the French initiative function in European politics, he did so without having a federation as his aim.

One may venture to predict that this basically attractive concept of international collaboration between sister parties will continue to presuppose a primarily ideological agreement in future, too. If this is lacking, then action groups without party or national affiliation, where there is collaboration between representatives of pluralistically structured and pragmatically operating democratic centre parties, are quite clearly superior to it.

So the concept of a federation with the aid of sister parties that share the same ideological course has no chance—at least, not in the near future. Its intrinsic value is problematical in any case, because international collaboration with the emphasis on ideology has as corollary a simultaneous dissensus on the domestic front with regard to basic socio-political issues. This is nowhere better illustrated than in the conflicts between CDU and SPD in Germany in the early fifties. But it is questionable whether a party dispute that has been transposed onto the international level would really bring about the fundamental socio-political consensus between democratic parties so vital to the success of any federation.[53] One can, of course, conceive of a federation coming about against the declared intention of some powerful party, which is nationalistic but at the same time democratic, but the prospects for the internal peace of the federation would be grim indeed, if, in addition to disputes about the federation's policy, basic socio-political differences had to be thrashed out as well. The integration of anti-democratic communist forces into a federation—which would in any case be one of the pressing tasks—would be difficult enough by itself!

7. Institutionalized Federators

The activity of European Movements, Action Committees or Parties is indispensable. It can create a favourable climate for concrete integration projects and support government initiatives. But it is not enough on its own. Committees of public figures and popular movements can only initiate developments, agitate and lobby, they are not in a position to negotiate responsibly nor to take decisions. The parties and governments of the individual state are not compelled to take up any of the movements' demands and suggestions. Moreover, it turns out that any concrete initiative is capable of realization only if compromises are worked out which do justice to the divergent views and interests of the individual states and the interest groups within them. But the highest political officials, who have a political mandate from the electorate, rightly insist that this is their natural prerogative.

Sooner or later, experience has taught most of the convinced federalists that the bold leap from the European Movement to the ready-made Federal State can be made only in dreams. In the real world, there is no way past the states: political integration can progress only if they show willingness to develop forms of *institutionalized federation*.[54] Of course, such forms constitute anything but a federation, yet they are designed to lead to it. The expectation is that common organizations and institutions might function as institutionalized federators producing powerful impulses.

If federator institutions are to meet this expectation, they must satisfy various specifications.

1. Legality: Governments and parliamentary unions will only enter into institutionalized procedures which are approved by them.

2. Legitimacy: Even if supranational institutions were set up with the approval of the relevant parliaments, it is still utterly indispensable that their activities—even if they remain within the framework of the statutory provisions governing them—should always be approved by the governments as well. General de Gaulle's criticisms of the activities of the EEC Commission showed how necessary it is for the partners of an alliance to consider the present working of the integration institution as legitimate.

3. Autonomy: In dialectical opposition to the legitimacy requirement stands a further desideratum: this calls for autonomy of the institutionalized federators. The political forces which operate within the framework of international institutions and negotiating bodies must enjoy a certain freedom of action if any impulses for integration are to be expected from them. This latitude must be sufficient to permit them their own initiatives for federation, yet it must not be allowed to undermine the basis of legitimacy of the federator institution.

4. Potential for transformation: One of the most important methodological problems affecting political integration consists in attuning strategies for federation that have been conceived on an international basis to the decision-making processes and balance of power in the individual states. There are two prerequisites for this: firstly, an institution that will organize supranational stratagems for federation and deploy them tactically, and secondly, a channel of communication between this institution and the decision-making bodies of each individual state. International institutions or negotiating bodies will only work as federator institutions if pro-federation forces can succeed in establishing themselves there, and these forces in their turn will only achieve success if they are powerful enough and at the same time flexible enough to incorporate into their own initiatives for federation the divergent impulses that emanate from individual states or from the broader international field. A major presupposition for the advance of any federation process is probably that the

22

international integrating bodies should keep permanently in touch with the centres of decision-making within each state.

Protagonists of European federation have sometimes thought fit to brand governments as the major enemies of integration. This attitude was strikingly expressed in Paul Henri Spaak's demand that 'the peoples must get their governments on the run'. But the political integration of Western Europe has actually been brought a whole stage further by a series of rounds of intergovernment talks, which led to the conclusion of treaties. But it must be said that the government efforts were more intensive the stronger the pressure 'from outside'.

But the setting up of shared institutions is only the start. And there is a difference from, say, the conclusion of military alliances of the classical type because, in this case, the pattern of relations has not taken on its definitive shape by the time the process of ratification is complete. Integration is, then, to use the pregnant formulation of Walter Hallstein 'not something that exists already but a process of development (*création continué*)'.[55]

In essence, three kinds of integration institution have been tried out or suggested:

(1) the regular conference of governments;
(2) the European Parliament; and
(3) the European Communities.

All these methods are designed to further the process of integration within the *framework* of methods of procedure which have already been institutionalized and accepted in International Law. But before we go into these in detail, we must still consider what methods are likely to favour the conclusion of these types of treaty. Do any kinds of federator play a significant role in this?

If a highly simplified and selective treatment in the matter of the European movements was indispensable, then this is even more necessary in respect of the following discussion of the suggestions and experiments with intergovernmental and supranational federators.

8. *Federator Elements in Negotiations on Integration*

Negotiations about integration are international 'negotiations about innovation' (F.Ch.Iklé). As such they manifest a typical rhythm. The first stage can be termed the *incubation phase*. A government lets itself be convinced of the advantages of some plan for integration. Usually the stimulus to do this comes from the most varied quarters. In Briand's initiative, for example, we have the consolidation of suggestions of the Pan-European Movement. Bidault's and Spaak's invitations to start talks about the formation of a Council of Europe were prompted by the European Movements, and in particular by the federalist parliamentarians. The Schuman Plan derived from the impulse of a high-ranking civil servant—the *commissaire général au plan* Jean Monnet. The merging of the Communities corresponded to a suggestion of the EEC Commission and the Monnet Committee. *Which* government is won over for a particular project, and how strongly it identifies itself with that project, is of paramount importance at this early stage.

Once one or several governments have been won over for some concrete integration project, there follows as a rule the second phase: *preparation for a conference*. This phase is characterized by activity at ambassadorial level, by visits of foreign ministers or special envoys and mostly also by the exchange of diplomatic notes. Either an international conference results from this phase, or else the initiative is buried. Briand's European Plan[56] was only the first in a long line of integration projects that went the way of all flesh before things even reached the conference stage. And it is precisely this case of the Briand Plan which also illustrates that, during this phase of more or less discreet negotiation just about everything depends on heads of government, foreign ministers and secretaries of state. Their decisions are taken with a view to the national interest and opportunism in home affairs.

Influences from outside the government may be important, but in point of fact, in this phase, the fate of a project rests largely in the hands of the governments.

If an integration project succeeds in passing through this phase too, there follows as phase three the *inaugural conference*, where heads of government or ministers take it up. If things go well, this leads to the creation of a commission of experts and also to a resolution on the guidelines for the project's operation.

The data on a series of integration projects show that the procedural modalities agreed at this stage are of decisive importance for the progress of the negotiations. Certainly, those governments that are genuinely interested in the success of a venture will follow the generally accepted diplomatic practice of entrusting only such civil servants with the negotiations of whom it can be expected that they will identify themselves with the project's goal. The success of the talks on the ECSC, for example, depended to a large extent on the leader of the French delegation who, at the same time, was appointed to head the commission of experts—on Jean Monnet in fact.[57] It has proved particularly effective to have, as head of the government delegations entrusted with the task of working out the treaty, some 'leading political figure' [58] of considerable prestige who is a tried and tested negotiator and a dynamic politician with an unambiguously federalist outlook.

In the view of many observers, the EEC Treaty would never have been concluded without these procedural precautions. In those days it was Paul Henri Spaak who steered the talks safely through all the rocks. It is true that conferences of delegates operate in the service of and according to instructions from their governments, but if leading figures with considerable personality direct the work, these commissions of experts can assume the

24

function of effective federators. Personalities like Spaak and Monnet not only hammered out compromises between the delegations, they also knew how to mobilize political support for projects and how to cope with the opposition.

The *ad hoc* Assembly forms the special case of a body which worked in the service of and according to the directives of a conference of ministers. It was entrusted with the working out of the Statute of a European Political Community (EPC) in accordance with Paragraph 38 of the European Defence Community (EDC) Treaty. The directives assured the Assembly a certain measure of autonomy, and as a body it had considerable potential for change because of its composition (fifty per cent members of the ECSC parliament and fifty per cent parliamentarians co-opted by this parliament from the national parliaments). It proved—under the leadership of Paul Henri Spaak—equal to the task of bringing about a fundamental constitutional agreement between the pro-federalist parliamentarians of the community of the Six. But it must be admitted that these parliamentarians did not manage to carry their parliaments at home along with them. The EPC went down with the EDC in the French *Assemblée Nationale*. But the method as such was not discredited by this.

If some day the Western European governments should actually agree to draw up a federal constitution, an essential presupposition for successful ratification of that constitution would probably be that it be worked out by an *ad hoc* assembly of influential parliamentarians. It is probable that the leading politicians in the individual states would be more in sympathy with a constitutional convention of this type in which they might participate or which they might at least control, than with the idea of a constituent assembly elected by popular vote.

Whether further conferences prove necessary before an integration treaty is signed, or whether the foreign ministers—as was possible in the case of the EEC Treaty—simply appropriate the outline produced by the negotiating delegation without any major cuts, depends on the circumstances. The paradigmatic case of the EEC/Euroatom Treaties shows that it is advantageous if the leader of the negotiators of the commission of experts keeps his mandate until the Treaty is concluded. On the other hand, there is no more certain method of sinking a project than setting aside the group of persons who have been responsible for working out the treaty-draft. This was the course taken by the Council of Ministers of the ECSC when it took the preparation of statutes out of the hands of the *ad hoc* Assembly on 8 August 1953 and entrusted all further work on the project to government representatives.[59] The courtesy with which this handful of representatives 'consulted' the *ad hoc* Assembly disguised only with difficulty the fact that the initiative had been robbed of its driving force and was now being honoured only with a first-class funeral.

This short survey shows how indispensable the good will of all governments is, if talks on integration are to succeed. But this goodwill must be

25

furthered by initiators and leaders of negotiations who are intellectually and if possible also politically independent, otherwise it is all too easy for initiatives to come to grief in the well-oiled treadmills of day to day conference diplomacy.

9. Ineffective but Popular: 'the Concert of Europe'

The notion of political integration by means of an intergovernmental conference was first put forward in the twentieth century by Count Coudenhove-Kalergi. His plan for setting up the United States of Europe consisted of the following phases:

(1) a propaganda campaign to win over as many leading and if possible influential pan-Europeans as possible; (2) the establishment of a Pan-European Union; (3) the convening of a Pan-European Conference; (4) the formation of a European group within the League of Nations according to Article XXI of the Statutes of the League of Nations; (5) the setting up of a pan-European political organization which would hold periodic conferences; (6) the signing of an obligatory system of arbitration, of an alliance and of a guarantee pact between the European states. Some safeguard for minorities would be introduced in connexion with the abolition of strategic frontiers; (7) the re-introduction of pan-European free trade. Pan-European territory would be developed into one uniform economic region; and (8) 'The culmination of the Pan-Europe Movement is to be reached some day when the European Confederation will turn into a Pan-European Federal State by means of the introduction of one pan-European constitution.' [60]

The Briand plan of 1 May 1930 largely took over this concept. It provided for an obligation on the part of the signatory governments 'to enter into regular contact with each other at periodic or special meetings, in order to examine collectively such issues as may in the first instance affect the interests of the community of European peoples.' [61] At the heart of this cautious proposal, which might have allowed development in the most diverse directions, there lay the conviction that institutionalized co-operation between governments would create 'links of solidarity' and lead via agreements on individual issues to a more intensive form of collaboration.

This approach has often been suggested since, with the imaginative addition of elements which might speed up the process of integration. The conference of governments as a federator element seems to have played just as big a role in Churchill's view, which he first developed in a speech broadcast on 21 March 1943,[62] as it did in General de Gaulle's. The concept was partially realized in the construction of the Council of Europe. It was discussed time and again in the fifties, had some real chance of succeeding with the talks on a European Political Union in the early sixties,[63] and is at present—after the departure of General de Gaulle—once more being conjured up from the depths of the diplomatic archives like some thoroughly dusty spectre, every bit as pallid as before.

The basic philosophy of this approach is very well expressed in a plan of Antoine Pinay's in this connexion:

Creating the Council would be to give concrete political shape to the European idea in a most striking fashion. With the progress of its practical work, the Council would gradually come to be accountable to public opinion for the Community interests of the European states. In this way, the instrument for a slow and lasting effort to bring about European unification would have been created . . . The federalists, logically enough, ought to see in this the first step along the path to European unification . . . Those who support national sovereignty ought to see in it the practical means of bringing about European co-operation while at the same time preserving national sovereignty. The way in which the international situation and public opinion develop will make the choice between the two directions and will result in the confederation remaining as such and [sic!] in its progressing gradually towards a federal state.[64]

The ambivalence of this approach is indeed glaring. The method of institutionalized co-operation through regular government conferences constitutes a minimal compromise between those forces which wish to leave the nation state behind them and the others which are reluctant or utterly unwilling to come out from under its shell. Regular government talks in no way prejudge the issue. They do not limit freedom of action from the very start, but merely make it subservient to the gentle laws of group dynamics. Within the framework of this institution a tightly-knit or freer collaboration is just as possible as a consolidation or loosening of the association itself.[65]

The method corresponds to that pragmatic caution in which most pro-federalist politicians discern the better part of valour. Since it is uncertain whether the future belongs to the existing states or to a European union of whatever kind, it seems only prudent to plan a two-lane policy for federation—so that it can lead to 'full federation' (Hallstein) but at the same time does not for the time being compromise the national interests of the existing states. What the convinced federalists see as a first step on the way to a federal state, which may lead on to others, appears in the eyes of the guardians of national sovereignty to be a kind of final stage. Statesmen like General de Gaulle or Winston Churchill, who clearly recognized the interdependence of modern foreign policy, saw in organized intergovernmental *co-operation*, albeit carefully directed by autonomous governments, the real alternative to the anarchy of rivalry between nation states. The fundamental contradiction between this concept of co-operation and the plans of the federalists has been clearly recognized in the discussions of the European Movement, and above all, in the great debates on basic principles

27

between federalists and unionists in the Advisory Assembly of the Council of Europe.

For sceptics and the guardians of national sovereignty, organized co-operation between governments does not constitute a method for the long-term removal of national autonomy. They argue that such co-operation is not intended to bring about a political merging of the states, but, on the contrary, to allow them to retain ultimate authority over their internal and external affairs despite the inescapable restrictions on freedom of action. The snapping nation state is not to have its teeth drawn—as the most convinced federalists would wish; it is quite sufficient if it is restrained by the long leash of functionalist co-operation, which is held in the firm grip of cautious governments.

It is not only nationalists of the traditional stamp that give preference to the co-operative approach. The theoreticians[66] and practicians[67] of a global functionalism also consider the co-operative nexus to be by far the most useful and, in the long run, the sole desirable method of collaboration. In this regard, it is immaterial whether they lay greater emphasis on the politico-economic, the security or the cultural function.

The theoreticians of international functionalism justify their approach by arguing that a state has to co-operate with different partners, according to the nature of its various interests. So the Federal Republic, say, would have to recognize that its security interests were best served within the functionalist framework of NATO, its currency policy within the Ten, its programme for aid to developing countries with the OECD, etc. A flexible attitude towards different reference groups, which vary according to the problem involved, has the effect that 'it is not one geographically conditioned community with unlimited powers that would be desirable, but rather various geographically unlimited groups with a different membership and with only limited powers'.[68]

In our context, this basic problem affecting the goal of integration is not important, but only the question as to whether any considerable federation effect might possibly result from the institution of regular summit conferences. Such expectations as can be linked to them by the federalist camp are largely summarized in the Pinay plan we have already mentioned: The public gets used to the close co-operation of a group of governments; in the states concerned there is a heightened awareness of the problems of neighbouring countries (and understanding is one of the major presuppositions for living together happily in future!); growing understanding leads to an increased trust; in the end, the attempt to solve common problems together and in the same way automatically leads to an assimilation of the economic and social structures in the individual states; in this way the proper climate for a further development of the institutionalized integration up to the threshold of a federal union is gradually created, psychologically as well as from the material situation. Consistently enough, various suggestions for the European Political Union also contained the provision that the agreements should be revised after three years in accordance with the needs of further integration.[69]

But in the face of these optimistic expectations it is necessary to assert numerous reservations which rest on experience with institutionalized government co-operation:

1. Governments can (and must!) pursue their own special interests as individual states, both internally and externally, and these interests will be only partially congruent with those of the treaty partners. It is all too natural for governments to try to use the union to strengthen their political position at home and abroad, but such attempts often lead just as naturally to conflicts with the partners, from whom sacrifices in the interest of the community are being expected. The probable occurrence of these conflicts makes it seem that there is just as much likelihood of a worsening of relations in a system of government summit conferences as there is of an improvement. All the more so if especially sanguine expectations of harmony have been pinned on the co-operation.

2. The relationship between larger and smaller partners will turn out to be particularly problematical in this. It is not uncommon for the larger partners to engage in prestige politics—as is demonstrated by the example of France under de Gaulle or of Egypt in the Arab League—which is designed to profit their own state, but which has to draw to a large extent for its effect on the support of the state's partners in the regional alliances. The situation becomes even more critical when a leading power inside the union would also like, or is compelled to adjust its policies in conjunction with great powers outside and calls upon the aid of its partners. Statesmen of General de Gaulle's type who not only recognize in states the least impartial and least disinterested creations in existence,[70] but also act accordingly, will therefore use just this institution of permanent summit conferences as a means of bolstering up their power politics and prestige, and so will discredit the whole idea of federation. Inclinations like these are naturally not limited only to the former French president.

3. But even if, under favourable conditions, a fruitful co-operation has developed between the governments, the consensus can be withdrawn by changes in a country's home affairs and also by outside political events. At a press conference held on 5 September 1960, de Gaulle, with his unfailing nose for the weaknesses of supranational Communities made the following statement: 'As long as nothing serious happens, they work without many complications. But as soon as some dramatic event occurs or there is a major problem to solve, one realizes that this or that "High Authority" has no authority over the various groups within the nations, and that it is only the states who do have such power.' [71] The argument is a good one, but it can be applied with still more justification to the concept of the institutionalized summit conferences that de Gaulle himself favoured.

4. As soon as the collaboration shows signs of extending to important areas and of intensifying, it will be absolutely indispensable to entrust the

29

carrying out and supervision of resolutions to specialist authorities. This will then raise a number of questions concerning the status of such bureaucracies—to whom do they belong, who leads them, what legal rules govern their operation and how can national legal systems and economies be modified in any controllable way in the light of community decisions? The supranational concept of the European Communities contains these kinds of bureaucratic apparatus and the judiciary to go with them.

It is difficult to see how a summit conference with no European bureaucratic machine and, in the last analysis, with no judiciary either, might hope to bring about any practical progress in integration. But if such a conference really intends to serve the communities and to further them, then it is again baffling why the co-operation, which was the whole aim of the summit conference, should not be built into the smooth-running machinery of the Communities. Even the idea, first launched by Paul Henri Spaak, of a dialectical collaboration between regular summit conferences and a commission of political administrators of the Community interests could at the most only introduce a somewhat more dynamic element into co-operation—comparable, say, to the role of the Secretary General in NATO, which Spaak was probably thinking of. But an executive cannot be conjured up out of a hat just like that. There are good grounds for fearing that even three prominent politicians, who would have to relinquish their power at home in this undertaking—as Spaak suggested—would achieve little more in this than international co-operation along the hackneyed lines of the Western European Union.[72]

5. Against the concept of a summit conference is also the fact that only the representatives of parliamentary majorities are represented there. Depending on the particular situation in each individual state, it would not be inconceivable that important parties might be kept out of European politics for a long time to come. In the same way, the interest groups would be able to come into contact with the process of integration only indirectly —via whatever government they had at the time. This would be not to utilize one of the most productive federator elements—the institutional orientation of interest groups towards central supranational bureaucracies.[73]

6. Above all, these methods would not be able to solve the main problem of any policy of federation: to establish an overlapping political sphere of influence, which takes in parties, interest groups and public opinion, and leads them out of the province of national centres of decision-making. As long as the bestowal of political positions and government services continues to be decided within the individual states, there is no chance of a weakening of those institutions and socio-political structures, which keep the existing states alive. It is true that provision is often made for embarking on further steps for integration when the plans for establishing summit conferences are drawn up, but this is simply a device for putting off the decision on matters of principle until later.

30

One may state, by way of summing up, that institutional integration via summit conferences may, in favourable circumstances, improve the climate for integration in respect of ministers, high-ranking civil servants, and in public, and it may bring about some approximation of policies. Dynamic impulses can hardly be expected from this concept. German and French politicians, who have surely had enough experience of the conference mechanism in the Franco-German Treaty ought actually to shy away from foisting these ineffectual procedures on a wider company, if they are sincerely concerned about making genuine progress towards federation and not merely about other aims. If the latter were to be the case, such conferences may indeed make very good sense, but one ought not to trick out this kind of venture designed to advance purely national interests with the halo of a federalist purpose.

A statement made in 1950 in the debates of the Advisory Assembly of the Council of Europe by the French parliamentarian Jaquet will probably also apply to future experiments with summit conferences; in his opinion, talks at government level were as old as society itself, and were consequently of dubious effectiveness, 'for society is already pretty old, and a United Europe has still not been created'.[74] Jaquet thought at the time that any progress would be conceivable only if one were to tackle the working-out of a European constitution without more ado.

10. The Possibilities and Limitations of a European Parliament

The idea of making a supranational assembly the nucleus of crystallization for the forces of federation developed logically enough from the European parliamentarian movement. Various methods of putting this idea into practice have been tried in the past, without this particular federator concept having proved very effective up to now.

In the beginning, the demand was for a European Constituent Assembly —it occurred in 1947 in the Union of European Parliamentarians and in the European Union of Federalists. At the Hague Congress these impulses were consolidated into an outline-resolution, which was presented by such distinguished figures as the former French Prime Minister Paul Ramadier and Edouard Bonnefous, the President of the Foreign Committee of the Assemblée Nationale. To be sure, the congress rejected any immediate popular election of deputies to a 'European Assembly', and so took the democratic bloom off the concept. Still, the delegates demanded the convening of a parliamentary assembly to which the individual parliaments would send representatives. Among other things, it would have had in its jurisdiction the power to prepare a constitution, as may be inferred from one rather euphuistic formulation.

In the deliberations of the Executive Committee of the European Movement which took place on 23 November 1948, the demand was still further cut down. Point 3 of the memorandum reads: 'In order to avoid any misunderstanding, it is desirable that the Assembly should receive a

31

designation and tasks which clearly express that it is not a federal parliament and not even a constituent assembly or preliminary assembly, and that it possesses no law-giving or constituent powers.' [75] And the governments cut back the concept of a constituent assembly yet more radically by introducing a council of ministers. The regulations of the Council of Europe of 5 May 1949 were so drawn up as to put a stop to any temptations of the Assembly to usurp any powers.

Nevertheless, after the meeting of the Advisory Assembly, a *new* variant of the concept of bringing about European integration by a supranational assembly of parliamentarians quickly developed. For the parliamentary body was attempting in many directions to shrug off the yoke of the regulations and to win at least some of the competence of a genuine parliament. Whereas the concept of a constituent assembly orientated itself after the historical pattern of the Philadelphia Convention,[76] the method of enlarging the parliament's terms of reference *gradually*, through its operation, could take as a model the British House of Commons and the *Etats Généraux* of 1789. This policy was not even completely hopeless. In the first sessions the Council of Ministers was confronted by a large number of prominent and confident parliamentarians. Moreover, the international political situation at the time made many things seem possible. All individual sallies by the Assembly were directed to the same ends:

(1) an attack on the requirement of ministerial approval for the agenda and against government influence on the election of delegates;

(2) the demand for the setting up of a 'European Authority' with limited functions but with real powers[77] by means of which the Council of Ministers would have become the nucleus of a Federal Council and the Advisory Assembly a kind of Federal Parliament, whose jurisdiction might have been extended bit by bit through unanimous resolutions of the ministers;[78]

(3) finally, when this concept of a 'political authority' proved equally impossible to put into effect, there was a demand that the specialized, supranational authorities of the same type as the High Authority of the ECSC be placed under the Council of Europe, in order thereby to turn the Council into a supranational decision-making body.

But all these attempts at a gradualistic groping towards the status of a true supranational parliament failed to attain their objective. Generally speaking, that the Advisory Assembly has made a valuable contribution to the 'transformation of Europe from a multitude of individual states jealously guarding their independence into a community of nations', while difficult to assess in detail, must surely be beyond dispute. The Assembly was a clearing-house for the politics of union; at times it was also a base for operation and co-ordination for the federalist parliamentarians; and it was certainly a great forum for debate and experimentation, where European parliamentarians drew on their experience to discuss realizable plans for federation and to let these flow into many and varied draft statutes. Certainly one will have to pay positive tribute to the significance

32

of the body as a supranational parliamentary pressure-group, but this parliamentary assembly did not develop into a dynamic federator. It was condemned to degenerate into a pleasant and not entirely useless sub-culture, but one that was totally ineffective as a federator. De Gaulle's remark about the parliamentary assembly 'which, I am told, is wasting away on the periphery of events where it has been abandoned' [79] is malicious but accurate.

The method of gradually extending powers is always being suggested for the parliamentary assemblies of the Six as well, and the constitutional and political opposition is in part identical to that against which the Advisory Assembly has been chafing itself.

Must one therefore write off as ineffective the concept of a European Parliament which might act as a dynamic federator to force states into union? Any such conclusion would be over-hasty.

The reasons for the failure of experiments hitherto are fairly easy to ascertain. These reasons lie less in the limited powers entrusted by the treaties—although this is said to be the case time and again.[80] The biggest handicap for the Council of Europe lay in the fact that the circle of member states was too large from the very outset. The indispensable compromises which had to be arrived at with the pro-union Britons and Scandinavians only sapped the vitality of the Assembly. And when it became apparent in 1950 and 1951 that only the governments who were later to make up the Community of the Six were open to concrete attempts at integration, the Advisory Assembly was no longer in a position to be linked institutionally with the European Communities—because its composition had been definitively fixed. The somewhat artificial personal attachment to the Common Assembly of the ECSC did not manage to give the Council of Europe the kiss of life.

The Council of Europe's unsuitable composition was probably a major reason why governments were disinclined to approve far-reaching powers for it. By 1951 at the latest it was clear beyond all doubt that, while the British government was pleased to go along with initiatives for a European union, it had no intention of participating itself. The gradualistic concept of the 'political authority' was ingenious, but its weakness was that it presupposed in all participating governments the readiness, at least in principle, to get involved in a process of integration which would have been furthered by a dialectical interplay between Parliamentary Assembly and Council of Ministers.

The question poses itself as to why, in that case, neither the Common Assembly of the ECSC nor the European Parliament managed to get such a dynamic process of federation off the ground. Here we find the negative effects of the specialization of functions. The Advisory Assembly can concern itself with 'high politics', but it receives no concrete functions at this level because the numbers of participants are much too large. The cream of the European politicians soon became aware of this and kept

33

away. No further powerful impulses for federation can now be expected from the members of Parliament who are at present working in Strasbourg. As against that, the Community Treaties do assign concrete tasks to the parliamentarians, but they are too specialized for the leading groups from the national parliaments at Strasbourg to have considered them a rewarding field of operations.[81] It was still possible to talk with complete justification of a 'European Parliamentarian elite' with respect to the Advisory Assembly at the beginning of the fifties, or the *ad hoc* Assembly of 1953, whereas, in the European Parliament, we find primarily European specialists who are only of average importance in their national parties. And it happens from time to time that some of these politicians do not even belong to a national parliament any more!

These examples of European parliamentary assemblies with relatively slight federation potential rightly raise the question as to whether a European Parliament could ever play the part of a federator. The answer to this will not be a simple yes or no, but must keep different factors in mind.

(*1*) The dynamic effect of a federator can only be expected if many leading federalist politicians from the individual states co-operate with one another. This pre-supposes, however, that a European Parliament is *attractive* for the real elite from among the members of the individual parliaments; but such will only be the case either if it possesses far-reaching powers, or if the parliamentarians have good grounds for believing that a decision-making body of the highest importance might shortly develop out of the supranational assembly. In fact, when the Advisory Assembly met in spring 1949, there was considerable indication that something could come of this body; so it was not difficult to get together a large number of prominent parliamentarians at Strasbourg.

The international political scene, against the backdrop of which the Assembly met in the *Allée de la Robertsau* promised dramatic developments. Everyone was still very much affected by the Prague Revolution, by the Berlin Blockade with its threat of war and by the powerful American initiative for a united Europe. In the middle of 1950, the feeling of security that had been slowly spreading in the latter half of 1949 was shaken once again by the Korean War. Moreover, the formation of a European Parliament answered the genuine need felt by Western European parliamentarians to resume international contacts that the War had interrupted. To this was added the inner threat to democracy in France and Italy. Then, if at any time, conditions for a European Constituent Assembly were more favourable than ever before or since.

If some future attempt at federation with a parliamentary assembly is to be successful, the international political conditions would probably have to be at the very least no less favourable than they were in those days. Only in a situation as open-ended as that would leading politicians of the individual states be prepared to invest power and prestige in a European Parliament. It is in the nature of parliamentarians that they pursue many

34

goals and that they have, in the first instance, to have regard for a complex field of political forces within the national framework. As long as no new interesting positions of power with a secure base of operation are appearing on the horizon at the supranational level, they tend to shrink from disregarding the obligations of the national systems of which they are members. But since the interests of the European peoples are still centred on the particular nation state, even federalist parliamentarians are prone to trim their federation policy discreetly to suit the situation at home. Winston Churchill's European policy provided a typical example, which went just as far as his own interest in a comeback in Great Britain permitted. Churchill used the European Movement like a virtuoso in order to strengthen his political position at home by spectacular performances on the European stage. This was only natural. If top politicians cannot count on their political position in home affairs being strengthened—or at least not weakened—by a decisively pro-federation line, no impulses for federation of any consequence can be expected from them.

Admittedly, European activities are a splendid means for second- and third-rate politicians to gain some prominence for themselves in their own home parliaments or to escape from a depressing situation within their national party or union. However, experience shows that any impulses that fail to attract the interest of the front bench—that is to say of the party leaders or members of government—are doomed to failure.

A modern federator concept ought to start by understanding 'representative government' in the widest sense. The distinction between parliament and government which people were so fond of making in the European Movement in the forties was expressing a view of the parliamentary system which was not adequate even at the time. A way of looking at things that understands governments as watchdogs of national sovereignty and popular representatives as potential partisans supporting European interests not only overlooks the fact that the real division runs between a ruling majority and an opposition. It also fails to realize that government and parliament are only parts of an inter-connected constitutional decision-making process, which must be considered as a whole.

(2) This raises a further central problem of the parliamentary federator concept. Even if a European Parliament numbers the most brilliant brains among its delegates, this alone is not enough. The federation process would only make any headway if there were a genuine Executive as the counterpart of the parliament. One will have to admit that David Mitrany is right to criticize the fact that, while many federalists appeared concerned to give the European Parliament real powers, few bothered about what the Executive should look like.[82]

Naturally, in a gradual process of integration, the Executive too would start off by having only limited powers at its disposal. But in the initial phase of its existence, its ability to function is probably more important as such than the extent of its powers. Alexander Hamilton, who thought

35

about this specific problem in *Federalist Papers*, has said all that needs to be said on the topic:

> Energy in the Executive is a leading character in the definition of good government . . . The ingredients which constitute energy in the Executive are, first, unity; secondly, duration; thirdly, an adequate provision for its support; fourthly, competent power.[83]

This demand is incompatible with the highly popular institution of a Council of Ministers and national governments. Even within the framework of each individual state, a united Executive is a great rarity, thanks to departmental egoism and the demands of coalition government. Such difficulties will only be compounded in a supranational body of ministers each of whom has his own instructions. Each government is bound to reflect, in the first instance, such currents of opinion as have established themselves in the autonomous political decision-making process of its state. And this Council of Ministers that is divided among itself would be confronted by a Parliament which, like all parliamentary assemblies, would probably not be conspicuous by the homogeneity of its views! The notion of a unanimously pro-federalist parliament which will bring a recalcitrant government back onto the straight and narrow path of federalism, is more than far-fetched. Once one had deducted from a European Parliament the common aim of all parliamentarians, namely, to win more competence and a greater prestige, there would be little common ground left that might offset the equally divided Executive.

The best brains of the Advisory Assembly of the Council of Europe were very well aware of the direction in which the solution is to be found. The draft statute of the *ad hoc* Assembly for the European Political Community drawn up on 10 March 1953, indicates which combination of governmental institutions would probably give most hope of success: the trilogy of Parliament, Council of national Ministers and European Executive Council, from which a two-chamber system along American or Swiss lines might develop in the course of time! On the other hand, however much this may be true, it is quite clear that by it the decisive step in the direction of a constitutional federation would have been taken. A decision-making process with this structure would not be reached via the gradualism of a federator-concept linked to a parliament. Such a structure presupposes the intention to work out and ratify a federal treaty or some analogous treaty. Even the most inventive gradualistic federator concept involving a European Parliament would be doomed to failure *without* the dialectic of Executive and Parliament.

(*3*) But the demand for an efficient Executive implies at the same time the need for a European Bureaucracy, without which no modern government would be able to cope with the requirements of a social state and economic planning. Only central bureaucracies acting in conjunction with political decision-making bodies which also have the necessary funds at their disposal, are in a position to move the many groups which wish to be nurtured and supported by the state to re-orientate themselves towards the new political centre of gravity.

Recent research on integration has made clear just how false the idea of governments being obsessed by sovereignty (once so dear to federalists) really is. It was Ernst B. Haas above all who directed attention to the social dimension of political integration in his epoch-making study *The Uniting of Europe*.

Ministers, parliamentarians and state bureaucracies do not, of course, operate in a vacuum. The more open they are for impulses from society, the more promptly must they seek to satisfy its short-term or imaginary wishes. A method of integration which was only prepared to back the leading parliamentary groups, without paying any heed to these overall social considerations, would soon be finished. Today, it is not the governments which are the major obstacle on the road to federation, but the nationally organized societies! *One* task—and it is by no means the least important—is the re-orientation of the politicians' whole outlook which is at present orientated along national lines. A European Parliament and an Executive might meet this need. But connected with this there ought to be the re-orientation of the social interests as well, and this would be unlikely without a central government controlling central bureaucracies, and without the central institutions having far-reaching legislative and budgetary powers.

So the chances of a gradualistic development that might be furthered by a European Parliament are slim indeed. Either the indispensable political central institutions will actually be created, in which case it will become apparent that the Parliament can only play second fiddle to the Executives which are propped up by the Administration. Or else the creation of an Executive is omitted, in which event the parliamentary federator will also prove to be an impracticable method.

Historic moments, like those in 1949/50 and 1953 in which the most prominent parliamentarians are prepared to make a parliamentary assembly the driving force of union, are rare, and if attempts to make it commit itself to the aim of federation were actually to succeed, the breakthrough to a constitutional State of Europe would probably not be too long in coming. Delays cause even pro-federalist delegates to turn back to where the basis of their power lies and where they have real powers at their disposal—that is, back to the national parliaments.

11. The Concepts of Supranational Functionalism
Associated with the methods of integration discussed up to now has been the notion that political integration must be advanced, in the first instance, by the organized activity of groups operating at a supranational level. These are primarily voluntary federator concepts. This also applies—

despite all assertions of an apparent 'automatism'—equally of those methods which are being tried out with the European Communities. 'Our success is a question of will-power . . .' as Walter Hallstein never tires of repeating.[84] But in the European Communities, the goodwill of statesmen and civil servants alike is helped along a bit both by anonymous factual pressures and by institutional mechanisms. The combination of the two is supposed to make that gradual progress towards federation possible, which neither conferences of governments nor a European Parliament have as yet managed to bring about. Gradualism and the judicious use of material pressures—these two approaches were combined in the much-quoted sentence of Robert Schuman's from a government statement of 9 May 1950: 'Europe will not be created at a stroke, nor as a comprehensive and complete structure: it will be created by concrete achievements producing at the outset a solidarity that is real.' [85] A few years later in another context, Robert Schuman characterized the key notion underlying his project for integration in a thoroughly convincing manner, even if its theoretical bases was a trifle crude:

> Would it not have been more logical to have attempted to create an organized Europe with regard to politics first?. . . For the practical politician there exists another rule, namely that one should and must begin with what promises the most chance of success and the quickest results. If we had begun with the question: 'to federate or not to federate', we would have let ourselves in for limitless discussion, but as it is we have given these talks a firm basis by the creation of the ECSC and have thus already reached a preliminary stage (of federation).[86]

Schuman counted on an 'inner dynamism', but without explaining in more detail exactly in what this consisted.[87] In this he found in Chancellor Adenauer a kindred spirit who, like himself, swore by pragmatism and placed his trust in the inherent automatism of development. Looking back on the EDC talks, Adenauer wrote, 'By this Treaty, a *rapprochement* of the participating states in questions of foreign and economic policy was to be created *automatically, as it were*, which, together with the Schuman Plan and other projects that were at the stage of being discussed, was intended to lead on very soon to a European Federation or Confederation.' [88]

Adenauer, Schuman and those of like mind had decided at the beginning of the fifties on a method of federation for which it was of cardinal importance to obtain parliamentary majorities in order to conclude complicated treaties for the integration of particular sectors. But which factors should, according to the view of these leading politicians and their advisors like Walter Hallstein or Jean Monnet, effect the *progress* of gradual partial integration? One only comes across vaguely formulated expectations, but looks in vain for even a half-developed theory.

High hopes were placed in the improvement of the psychological climate.

In reversal of the dictum about the evil deed which must inevitably breed further evil, people hoped for the stimulating positive effect of the success-ful good deeds that result from a common solution of problems where mutual interests are respected. The formula 'change through *rapproche-ment*' which was a catchword for sometime in the Ostpolitik of the sixties also pervaded the politics of integration of the fifties as a maxim for policy. At that time the question How was much less important than the fact of co-operation as such. And so, at the beginning of the fifties, not a year went by without some minister hatching out new plans in the applica-tion of which all conceivable areas were to become a field for experi-mentation in the solution of community problems within the framework of Western Europe: the coal and steel industry, transport, agriculture and energy, technology and defence.

With the expectation of a psychological chain reaction there were com-bined barely thought-out notions of interdependence. The integration in the Coal and Steel area was supposed to radiate out into other sectors of the economy (an expectation which was never fulfilled). The integration of defence was also supposed to affect all the other functions of 'high politics'. And when this ambitious plan failed, many people hoped for a 'spill-over' from the horizontal economic integration into the preserves of classical foreign policy.

In the years when the ECSC and the EDC were embarked upon, the concept 'functionalism' became established as a label for these methods of partial integration. It is worth while examining the connection of this concept with the European idea somewhat more closely.

The term crops up in connection with the European union as early as the first discussions on basic principles held in the two first sessions of the Advisory Assembly and it was actually meant as an opposing concept to the Constituent Assembly concept of the federalists. While the latter were anxious to place the working out of a constitution at the head of the co-operation, a number of Labour MPs, supported by the Scandinavians, were arguing for a functional approach. The MP, Maurice Edelman, for example, expressed the following view: 'There is, first of all, the *consti-tutional* approach, and then there is the approach which occupies itself with extending and multiplying the working arrangement between the states of Europe. That has been called the *functional role*.' [89] It is not difficult to see in this approach which found so much favour, particularly with Labour parliamentarians, a version of David Mitrany's functional integration theory. His writings had strongly influenced the English dis-cussion at the time. Throughout his life this theorist of pragmatic inter-national co-operation had been more than sceptical of all federalistic attempts at integration. Such attempts represent a dangerous aberration so far as he is concerned, which he warns against sometimes passionately, always decisively.

In his view, international collaboration must do justice to the functional

39

contexts—'binding together . . . those interests which are common, where they are common, and to the extent . . . they are common'.[90] According to him, internal and external politics are concerned primarily with satisfying needs and solving problems. The manifold and varied nature of such needs and problems forbids any one-sided commitment to particular partners on the part of a state—say, to some group of states that is characterized by geographical proximity or ideological affinity. 'Once we accept the idea of the functional organization of government, those instances will become self-evident in which the regional or global extension of the service and of the attendant power would be claimed by the obvious needs of the case.' [91]

While Mitrany's concept of international co-operation can also serve as a justification of the national standpoint, his intention is actually quite the reverse. He is attempting to overcome the characteristic tendency of modern power politics to think in categories of autonomous national actors, by giving priority to society, its 'welfare needs' and manifold functions. He believes that it is precisely when the needs of society are taken seriously that an organization to cope with international problems is necessary and that this reduces the importance of the state's role. However, in view of the forces of inertia and the power of modern states, a functional organization of world society is only possible if functional integration makes a start in those function contexts in which the needs to be satisfied are primarily of a pre-political nature or have only a peripheral political character. Among such may be numbered, for example, communications, the health service, the fight against crime, the provision of raw materials, etc.

Mitrany feels that functional co-operation ought to be arranged in the first instance by specialist international organizations, whose structure ought to be flexible enough to suit whatever task confronts them and to fit in with the needs of the moment.[92] This linking of societies by specialist organizations is what he calls international integration. In the process he develops a theory containing a series of stages, and this in turn rests on the conviction that the national functions are amenable to being split up into the more technical kind directed to dynamic social welfare on the one hand, and into the more 'political' kind on the other.

1. *Within the same* group of functions probably there would have to be co-ordination either simply for technical purposes or for wider functional ends, and this would be the first stage toward a wider integration. . . .

2. The next degree or stage might be, if found desirable, the co-ordination of *several groups* of functional agencies . . .

3. The co-ordination of such working functional agencies with any *international planning* agencies would present a third stage . . .

4. Beyond this, there remains the habitual assumption . . . that

international action must have some overall *political authority* above it. . . .[93]

It is logically consistent with this approach when Mitrany considers 'conspicuous and partial transfers of authority to an international organ' both possible and desirable, and he employs in this connection an attractive metaphor: 'Specific functional arrangements . . . would not steal the crown of sovereignty, while they would promise something for the purse of necessity.' [94]

Mitrany's highly regarded work *A Working Peace System* appeared in 1943. In the fourth edition of 1946 he devoted particular attention to the problem of the gradual transfer of sovereignty to new authorities, at first with reference to home policy:

> Sovereignty cannot . . . be transferred effectively through a formula, only through a function. By entrusting an authority with a certain task, carrying with it command over the requisite powers and means, a slice of sovereignty is transferred from the old authority to the new; and the accumulation of such partial transfers in time brings about a translation of the true seat of authority. If that had been the considered process in the domestic sphere, is it not still more relevant in the international sphere, where even the elements of unity have to be built up laboriously by this very process of patient change?[95]

This extensive account of the thought of this highly influential theorist of functionalism should have made clear who at least the English members of the Advisory Assembly have to thank for a good deal of their integration theory. Concepts and basic notions intrinsic to this theory crop up everywhere in the debates: the concept of functional partial integration, the institution of 'functional agencies' operating over state boundaries, the hope for a co-ordination of several 'agencies', and also—indirectly—the idea that functional integration requires some umbrella of 'political authority' over it, and finally, the notion of a partial transfer of sovereignty to international authorities 'by this very process of patient change.'

But it was not only the British Unionists in the Advisory Assembly who were committed to Mitrany. There is considerable indication that the supranational variant of functionalism took his concept as a starting point, as well. The supposition that Jean Monnet—who was well acquainted with Anglo Saxon attitudes—knew Mitrany's theories intimately and put them into practice on a grand scale is not to be rejected out of hand. Monnet's reputation would not be diminished in any way if biographical research were actually to succeed in showing that the Schuman plan as put forward by Monnet was an attempt to try out Mitrany's concepts in a practical application.

Mitrany would indeed by a very reluctant father to such a project! For his idea of a partial functional integration that would in principle transcend the individual states was designed to accomplish anything—excepting only a regional federation, a new state! One will have to ask oneself in any case whether Jean Monnet was really thinking primarily of a European federation when he conceived the Schuman plan. This exemplary project of partial integration was intended—true to Mitrany's reasoning—to solve concrete needs with the aid of a supranational High Authority. Not a thought about a parliamentary assembly, a court of justice or even a council of ministers![96] The Schuman plan set out to provide a solution for the controls on the Ruhr which would take account of the French security interests while at the same time not proving a hindrance to future relations with the Federal Republic whose swift post-war recovery was already becoming apparent. To mark the end of Franco-German antagonism, it seemed appropriate to make a new start which was both an effective symbol and of some practical significance. And Monnet's ambitious projects for industrialization meant that France's increased energy requirement also called for some far reaching planning which would cross over state boundaries.

One can only speculate whether the famous interpolation into the Government statement of 9 May 1950 which designated the ECSC as 'the first stage of European federation' represented perhaps only the European frills on what was really a project in line with Mitrany's view—added by Jean Monnet in deference to the 'European' Schuman, or perhaps added by Schuman himself, and added not least with an eye to Washington and Bonn.[97] In actual fact it was only the decision to combine the two heterogeneous elements—federalism and functionalism—which constituted the real originality of the Schuman plan. Certainly, it would be to distort the facts if one set out to see all the expectations that were bound up with the functionalist method in the Europe of the early fifties merely as offshoots of Mitrany's theories. After all, he was only describing and analysing phenomena that could already be seen in the nineteenth century and which became especially evident after the First World War. It was precisely in the post-war period that interesting models like the UNRRA, OEEC and the Ruhr Statute were created, whose connection with the European idea was in the air at the time. Besides, a historical evaluation of the origins of supranational functionalism would have to do more justice to the contribution of the British MP Ronald W. G. Mackay in the Advisory Assembly.

In any case, a few months after Robert Schuman launched the plan which bears his name, a large part of the federalists in the Council of Europe had been won over to the functionalist method enriched with a federalist purpose, although it was and remained totally unproven whether the hopes placed in functional gradualism were more than groundless speculation.

As we have already mentioned, the functional method was thoroughly suited—even in Mitrany's eyes as he saw it at the time—to lead the integration process up to even higher levels. In his view, willingness to intensify relations must inevitably result in the first instance from the educational process which successful supranational co-operation would initiate in the minds of the public and, more important, in those of the functionaries and civil servants involved. The notions as to how this process might affect the decisions of 'high politics' were fairly vague. Anyway, they had no proper place in a theoretical approach which was geared to avoiding regional integration. What is more, everything speaks for the supposition that the ECSC would not have differed very radically from international organizations like the OEEC, ILO, etc., if matters had rested with the creation of the High Authority, which was the only institution for which Monnet had originally made provision. The decisive factor was the enriching of the concept in the course of negotiations by the addition of all those many institutional arrangements which together brought about for the first time an interlocking of the authorities and the decision-making processes in the individual states.

Exactly how this came about is still far from completely clear.[98] Different material and political reasons combined to affect developments:

(*1*) If the High Authority was to be provided with powers of its own, the problem of control assumed cardinal importance. The establishment of the Council of Ministers was a direct result of this material constraint. On the other hand, so far as the Common Assembly is concerned, it is not quite clear whether this institution was designed in the first instance in order to satisfy superficially, at least, the demands for some 'parliamentary control',[99] or whether any further aims were bound up with it right from the start. The setting up of a judiciary, too, was a compelling material need.

(*2*) By these institutions the originally purely functional concept was enriched by the addition of elements whose analogy to those of a federal state was glaringly obvious. Certainly: the High Authority, the Common Assemblies, the Special Council of Ministers and the Court of Justice differed considerably from the familiar models found in federal constitutions, but with some imagination—and this was not lacking among the European federalists at Strasbourg[100]—one could recognize in them the four classical institutions of the federation: Executive, Parliament, Federative Institution and Judiciary.

So two things had happened to Mitrany's functional concept at the beginning of the fifties. It had been combined with a regionalistic purpose which was originally alien to it and had at the same time become highly politicized. For the insertion of the Parliamentary Assembly and especially of the Council of Ministers signified nothing less. It is true that the ECSC was anything but a federation in embryo, but it did give the federalists a model which they were prompted to transfer to other sectors and which at the same time suggested the possibility of further development into a federation.

According to the vague notions of those years, 'United Europe' was to be characterized in some initial phase by the integration of various key sectors. In the fullness of time, it would then prove to be indispensable and at the same time possible to provide the whole structure of integrated and not yet integrated areas with a 'political umbrella' in the form of federal institutions.[101] The details of how this should come about remained open, and finally according to this concept as well, everything finished up by depending yet again on the decisions of governments and parliamentarians.

The experiment with vertical partial integration was, to be sure, only repeated once—in the case of the Euratom Treaty. And, as with the ECSC, the hoped for spill-over effect did not live up to expectation, so that the later fusion of the Communities commended itself as the most elegant way of getting shot of this hardly convincing concept.

The two other projects for supranational communities—the EDC and the EEC—departed still further from Mitrany's functional starting point. The para-federal techniques for decision-making were stressed much more in these cases. Instead of functional integration by international institutions with the states remaining intact, there arose at the hands of the federalists (who were by now speculating in functionalist terms) supranational decision-making processes and bodies, which were linked as closely as possible with the national governments. This supranational functionalism constitutes the most effective federator concept of all those that have been tried out in practice hitherto.

The federal component was most clearly expressed in the EDC Treaty. This Treaty has also moved furthest away from the original idea of partial integration. Article 38 saw the Assembly as the nucleus of a Constituent Assembly and regarded the collaboration of Council and Assembly as a method of bringing about dynamic institutional further development.[102] The draft statutes of the *ad hoc* Assembly show where the federalists wanted this development to lead. The original functional basis which intended exclusively the integration of 'welfare' functions was thus equally discarded. Not only did this correspond to the federal aims of the signatories, but it was also dictated by the nature of the matters to which that Treaty related. Defence policy, as a central component of 'high politics', is not amenable to being isolated as a sector. The EDC would have had to have been further developed into a federation, or else it would not have been in a position to fulfil its proper functions.

This double speculation, so characteristic of the EDC has also found a place in the EEC Treaty:

(*1*) the inherent laws of the matters to which the Treaty related were to show sooner or later that it would be absurd to integrate some sectors but not others.

(*2*) built-in institutional mechanisms were to ensure that all decisions taken to overcome this absurdity had to bring about an intensification of the integration and a spill-over into other sectors.

44

Whereas one had expected the institutional dynamics of the dialectic between the Assembly and the Council—the effectiveness of this institution has never been tried out!—the new federation project was tuned to the dialogue between the Commission and the Council of Ministers.[103] The Commission is an independent political body, whose task consists in working for the interests of the *whole* Community. The Council of Ministers, on the contrary, before it comes to a decision, expresses and defends national interests.[104] This built-in dynamic is supported by numerous other institutional arrangements, like the provisions for the various phases, the rules governing majority decisions and the important regulations concerning Community law. Similarly significant is the fact that the Treaty, just like the political system of the ECSC before it, initiates socio-political processes: the national bureaucracies are impregnated with a supranational spirit,[105] the interest groups within the individual states become orientated towards supranational central bureaucracies and an embryonic European Parliament begins to operate.[106] When the EEC with its interwoven supranational and national powers and decision-making processes first proved itself practicable, the right method of integration seemed to have been found. Even sceptics like Altiero Spinelli became converted to the concept of the Communities. The task seemed to consist in strengthening more and more that '*solidarité de fait*' on which Robert Schuman had placed his hopes, and in increasingly emphasizing the embryonic federal structures.

This concept is not attuned to the operation of *one* integration factor. It combines a whole bundle of federators whose federation potential forces the most diverse interest groups, governments, parliaments, firms and associations into a supranational approach to solving problems.

It is above all Ernst B. Haas who has drawn attention to the fact that it would be most superficial to see in the growth of the Communities merely the result of the pressures of economic development. Such speculation does indeed play a substantial part. Eliminating a sector from the collective economy by politico-administrative decisions creates an artificial imbalance, because it stands 'in inner contradiction to the interdependence of all economic contexts'.[107] But the 'material logic'[108] of economic interdependence forces the creation of a new equilibrium. It is now of decisive importance that the solution is sought in *strengthened* supranational integration. After all, a theoretical way out of the difficulty might be to reverse the supranationalism that had led to the imbalance in the first place. This method will only have any prospect of succeeding if all the participants learn to look for a solution of the difficulties in a strengthening of the supranational organization, in an intentional spill-over of integration.[109] As a result of the Treaties, of group interaction and of economy related constraints, the political practice has developed of solving the tensions produced through partial integration not by agreeing on the lowest common denominator but rather by extending integration, since this offered the possibility of compensating. Haas has called this method

45

'upgrading the common interests',[110] that is, overcoming differences by proceeding to a higher level of integration in hopes of finding a solution there.

However, it is anything but certain that the leading interest groups will go along with this educational process. During the most successful years of the EEC, the illusion spread here and there that one could unite Europe behind the backs of the peoples, thanks to the cunning device of the functional idea. However, the successes of this method depend upon various political components as well as on sociological considerations relevant to organizations. It is of paramount importance that the functionaries and high civil servants of the Community are indoctrinated with the ideology of federation. This will come about if a certain continuity and independence of the supranational staffs is secured. For experience shows that bureaucracies, and especially international ones, usually tend to identify with the ideology of their organization and to attribute a high degree of priority to strengthening that organization.

At the same time, the leading bodies of the Communities must also be in a position to develop initiatives of their own, and to exert influence through flexible negotiations. In the same way, the closest possible connection with national decision-making processes is indispensable. Only given these presuppositions can governments be persuaded that the problems bound up with mutual functional co-operation can best be solved by strengthening supranational organization.[111] This is not out of the question, as the history of the EEC has shown, if a fairly long and undisturbed period of development is possible, if obvious advantages result from it for both the member States and the interest groups, if a pragmatic basic attitude generally predominates, and if there is, within the States, a willingness to give a relatively free hand to the high functional elites, on whose collaboration the process of integration rests.

The method does not exactly appeal to those who are inclined to seek edification in basic democratic notions, as Ernst Haas explains: 'And the technical decisions always incorporated in the major choices must be made by technocrats'.[112] Provided these preconditions are met, 'integration will be accomplished almost automatically'—at least, according to theory. However, the plain fact is that the success of this method hinges on all political powers of any consequence seeing the basic prerequisite for progress in integration as a continual strengthening of supranational organization.

The architects of this method—in the first instance Paul Henri Spaak—were occasionally prone, 'out of some kind of historical fatalism',[113] to nourish pious hopes that the further integration progressed, the more easily differences would be overcome. All the disadvantages of other methods seemed in this case to have vanished as if by magic. It appeared that one could save oneself the trouble of a direct confrontation with opposition on the part of individual governments or, indeed, from society

46

attuned as it was to the *status quo*. Those who are inwardly opposed—but without placing any large obstacles in the way of the 'salame tactics' employed by functional integration—must at some stage in the proceedings capitulate willy-nilly in the face of the *'solidarité de fait'*, once the much-invoked 'point of no return' has been reached.[114] It was not until 1964 that the series of crises which was beginning to afflict the Community led to a critical reappraisal of this concept among the federalists as well. The discussion which resulted from the practical experience gained has since shed light on a string of weaknesses of this approach.

Progress depended in large measure on the fact that the Commission, as the 'planning, promoting and mediating body',[115] received support from all the governments. At the times 'eurocrats' in Brussels may well have considered themselves to be the nucleus of a Western European Government. But in the meantime it has become clear that their role hitherto is much more adequately summed up if they are understood as a particularly powerful species of international functionary. The task of such diplomats and experts generally consists in serving not the national interests of *one* particular state, but rather in promoting those supranational aims which the individual governments expect to be furthered by the organization. The political influence of international functionaries—one might mention the UN General Secretary or the General Secretary of NATO, for instance—can be immense. In initiatives, modifications and attempts at mediation, they mostly occupy a key position between the states involved, but their power stands and falls with the readiness of the governments to make use of the relevant organization and to look after their national interests with its help. Top international functionaries can entice, persuade, get together coalitions behind the scenes to support their projects and pave the way for solutions—but they lack the power to put their projects into practice. The international functionary is all-powerful, so long as the governments leave him freedom to act, but he shrinks to a pygmy, once any conflict arises. His situation becomes particularly precarious when a majority of governments participating in the work of an organization clashes with a minority or with a single state about methods and aims. The Commission learned this by bitter experience when its great initiative of 1965 was shattered by General de Gaulle.

The more prominent politicians the members of the Commission are, the greater is their disillusionment. No-one recognized the institutional weaknesses of the Commission more clearly than General de Gaulle:

These institutions have their technical uses, but they have no authority and, consequently, no political effectiveness, nor can they have any. As long as nothing serious happens, they function without many complications. But, as soon as some dramatic event occurs or there is a major problem to solve, one realizes that this or that 'High Authority' has no authority over the various groups within the nations, and that it is only the States who do have such authority . . .[116]

The spill-over within the framework of the Communities, precisely because it is partially successful, sets off a process which has been aptly called the 'spill-back effect'.[117] As early as the beginning of the sixties, Stanley Hoffmann predicted this kind of development. If all sides can see profit for themselves, if interests can be quantified and if only an insignificant part of a State's resources is involved, the assent for a supranational solution of problems can be attained. Even if the functioned areas being considered for supranational integration do comprise a considerable fraction of the national income, and if influential group interests are involved, the method of 'upgrading the common interest' is probably still acceptable. This for the simple reason that, when it comes down to it, this method does not differ significantly from 'fifty-fifty compromises'. But it is quite a different matter when it is a question of national functions in the domain of 'high politics', from which prestige, status, security and freedom of action depend. Here the rival pursuit of national interests between states really comes into its own. It is no longer possible to weigh up gains and losses objectively. A method which consists in finely adjusting the balance between the conflicting interests is over-taxed here. Looked at like this, the thesis may be advanced that the opposition against a 'full federation', far from diminishing as the integration process consolidates itself, actually becomes stronger.[118] To this must be added the fact that the attempt to develop the Free Trade Area still further and to make it into an Economic Community affects all the sensitive sectors of home policy: social policy, monetary policy, the economic system, taxation, government subsidies, short-term economic policy, and investment policy. Many observers hold the view that after a customs union has been set up the disequilibrium on the one or other side will have to be compensated for. Either the half-finished Common Market will be further expanded—this is probably barely possible without its becoming a state—or else regression to a mere customs union is inevitable.[119]

The progression to political federation, however, would be in the first instance an act of volition and as such only attainable with considerable effort. On the other hand, the already established foundations of an economic union would begin to crumble more or less automatically if they are not quickly built up into a political federation. The breaking up of the common agricultural market in the train of the monetary reforms of 1969 illustrates this inevitability. It is a logical consequence of the fact that the monetary policy of the Six could not be integrated, and the difficulties in the way of integrating it merely show that domestic economic policy and social policy continue to remain the preserves of national governments, despite all efforts within the EEC framework.

A glance at the political history of states would have suppressed any over-hasty hopes of a 'point of no return'. A considerable number of federal states, some of which existed for decades on end and displayed a high degree of economic integration, have actually disintegrated—one need only mention the United States during the War of Secession, the Habsburg Dual Monarchy or, more recently, Nigeria. If even fully developed federations are not safe from disintegration, then it appears still less likely that a process of integration between autonomous states must proceed according to the laws of some historical determinant, which ought to lead the 'unfinished federation' (Hallstein) to its completion.

In view of the uncertainty as to whether a federation is desirable and even possible, governments understandably show a tendency to avoid or to loosen any restriction of their domestic and foreign policy by community powers.

The crisis of supranational functionalism is, however, also attributable in large measure to unclarified conceptions as to what its aims really are. Now, as ever, functionalism represents the compromise formula on which the proponents of a European federal state and the defenders of national privilege have agreed—each side in the hope that the wiles of history would prove it right. In the process, the federalists had presented their demand for a federal union as the only alternative to the downfall of European democracy, culture and prosperity. But the development of the past fifteen years seems to have shown that economic achievement, security abroad and the guaranteeing of peace together—in other words, all the great goals of Western European foreign and domestic policy—are also attainable in a loose association of autonomous states and do not need a federal union. One is probably even justified in stating that it was precisely the success of the functional method which has contributed to keeping the European nation states alive—a counterproductive by-product of partial integration which the federalists had not anticipated.

To be sure, most people recognized that the Western European states are no longer adequate for the needs of the large-scale economy and defence policy of to-day. But in a world fraught with uncertainty, what is familiar still seems safest: and that is, of course, the existing states. In this respect, most people prefer to hold to Lichtenberg's 'incremental' maxim: 'Don't tear down a slightly inconvenient building straight away, thereby giving yourself even more discomfort. Make *small* improvements instead.' [120]

Have events not proven the functional theoreticians like Mitrany and the functional practicians like Churchill, Macmillan and de Gaulle right? This question is asked by many one-time federalists. So it is hardly surprising that the proponents of federalism today produce a major argument that is better attuned to the present global political situation: they point to the danger that the fragmented European states will be subjugated to the hegemony of the two world powers. [121]

What federation will cost in terms of home politics is also becoming

49

clearer, since the governments have fumbled their way via a customs union into the experiment with an economic union. A few years ago, Theodor Eschenburg described how difficult the administrative, social and domestic problems would be that would have to be solved in the event of a re-unification of Germany. It also holds good for the politics of European federation that not a few people support it so decisively 'either because they consider it unlikely that it will ever be achieved or because they do not appreciate the problems involved, whether through refusing to see them, or because they lack practical imagination.' [122] It is high time that the costs of revolutionizing European domestic policy were calculated in a similar detached fashion, costs which might be incurred if a single pan-European party system needed to be set up, if waves of strikes in France, Italy or West Germany were to have a direct effect on all the other nations and if a European federal state—provided with an unwelcome dowry of Com-munist voters by France and Italy—were to have to define its foreign policy. Would a federation really strengthen Western Europe to the extent that this is generally expected, or would one not have to fear that internal tensions would absorb all the external political energies, so that the final result was even worse chaos? At any event, the internal political risks are becoming more apparent the closer the states come together. And since the status quo, with today's Western European system of states is not intolerable, whereas the costs and advantages of a federation are uncertain, all governments are shying away from commitments that are not easily reversible. For years the question of the entry of Britain and the other applicants was a convenient excuse to perpetuate the methods of supra-national functionalism which ought to permit one to take a bath without getting wet.

Besides, the active attempts—especially of the European left wing—to bring about a *détente* between East and West are equally likely to prevent the setting up of a Western European federation. There is an honourable tradition among liberals and socialists of mistrusting regional exclusive-ness at the expense of universal understanding and collaboration, and this was revived during the period of *détente* from 1963–1968, and both the USA and the Soviet Union were quick to foster it.

But two other factors impede the effectiveness of the European Com-munities, and these are closely connected with each other. The concept requires that those participating, both governments and societies, are interested in the first case in satisfying their economic needs as best they can. It further presupposes that the decisions of the government repre-sentatives and supranational civil servants will be accepted by the popula-tion. As soon as political leaders or the influential parties start putting immaterial values like national prestige, national independence, etc., at the top of the list of priorities, supranational functionalism and its so characteristic combination of give and take with consolidation of the integration process will be made more difficult, or—as the constitutional crisis of the Community in the summer of 1965 showed—will be made impossible. There is nothing new in that. The protagonists of the European Movement have always known that national basic attitudes and the power politics of individual states were incompatible with their aims. The Commission has been acquainted with these kinds of idiosyncrasy of the French President for a long time. But it ventured on the controversy in the hope that the General would get himself caught in the snare of the neofunctionalist strategy of 'upgrading the common interest'. As a *quid pro quo* in order to obtain the regulation of prices in the farming sector desired by France, he was supposed to accept that the Commission should have its own finances and that the European Parliament should have a say in financing agriculture, thus authorizing an important step in the direction of federation. De Gaulle decided against this deal and thereby demonstrated what Haas with impressive self-criticism has rightly stressed, namely that the glow of non-utilitarian convictions is stronger than the slow fuel of economic expectations.[123]

Whereas in the course of the sixties the integration concept of the European Communities ran aground in the first instance on the nationalistic ideology of the French President (which, moreover, provided an excellent shield for the reluctance of other EEC partners to a speedy furtherance of integration), nowadays, another kind of irrationalism is threatening to impede the functional unification process. With the 'New Left' movement, influences are coming to bear on Western European politics which are already making themselves felt indirectly, and which will probably also have a direct effect on integration policy in the foreseeable future.

Supranational functionalism presupposes the pragmatic, utilitarian approach which was and still is typical for the democratic centre parties of Western Europe. But it also postulates that the resolutions of the highest governmental and technocratic functional elites will be accepted by the population. The rediscovered totalitarian ideologies, heterogeneous though their origins and aims may be, deny that a cautious maximizing of interests has any justification and affirm, for their part, the priority of absolute immaterial values. In this regard, whether the politics of the new movement are fired by radical-democratic participation ideology, by anarchistic utopias or by the class struggle slogans of the neo-marxists plays only a minor role. At any event, the legitimacy of the present leading groups is being contested, but so is their administrative and political practice, which has up to now supported the process of integration. There is simply no common ground between this new movement, with its totalitarian impulses or its longing for small community participation on the one hand, and the decision-making practice which has developed in the European Communities on the other.

It is true that there is every indication that the influences of the discontented groups which have become noticeable of recent years will peter out in the constraints of industrial society, just as did the essentially related anarchist and fascist movements of the first half of this century, which drew their vitality from similar frustrations and sentimentalism. The question is only what price will have to be paid until the lesson has been learned once again that no-one is able to sin against the spirit of a bureaucratized industrial society and go unpunished. Some part of this price might consist in a considerable setback for European integration. The full effects of the new ideological syndrome have probably yet to show themselves. So there is considerable indication that radical criticism of the legitimacy of functional supranationalism could play a not unimportant role in European politics in the future. Whether these critical cultural stimuli can be successfully harnessed to the cause of federalism by giving the Communities the desirable parliamentary system, remains to be seen. At any event, in future one will have to reckon not only with the old familiar irrationalism of the nationalists, but equally with that of the radical democrats and communists of Western Europe, who reject any bureaucracy and planning.

This new peril for liberal democracy, rational politics and effective economic activity is already having a direct influence on integration. Home affairs is increasingly absorbing the attention and energy of the political leading groups. Eruptions like the French May Revolution endanger economic stability, force governments to act autonomously and so jeopardize indirectly the successes already obtained in the extension of the Common Market.

It is in any case only to be expected that the Western European states will be affected in varying degrees by the internal upheavals connected with the new movement. Neither governments which are especially plagued by internal unrest, nor those which have remained more or less unscathed are likely to show a superabundance of willingness to enter into a federation with other states. Periods in which existing political and social orders are being called into question are ill-suited for the creation of a new federation.[124] A constellation like that which obtained in America after Shay's Rebellion in 1787 is hardly likely to appear again under conditions of mass democracy.

Thus, the federator concept of the European Communities, like all those discussed up to now, is probably not capable on its own of leading to a federation, either. It is true that it does create the indispensable economic and administrative pre-requisites for federation. It helps the governments and their civil servants to get practice in the art of solving problems supranationally. But a smooth transition to a federation via many individual stages of pragmatic co-operation is not on the cards. Granted, there would be much in favour of letting federal institutions grow out of the Community ones and in favour of making use of the central bureaucracy set up in Brussels. Walter Hallstein recently outlined how an extension like this ought to proceed: further development of the Commission into a

European *Executive* with unitary function, investiture through a European Parliament, eventual introduction of departmental responsibility; the gradual transformation of the Council of Ministers into a Federal Chamber by the consistent introduction of the majority decision principle and by making vetos more difficult; adding to the weight of the European *Parliament* by direct election, expansion of parliamentary control over the Commission and the Council of Ministers; extension of the Judiciary.[125] But, however plausible this is, the mere recognition of a suitable institutional line of approach does nothing to answer what is the really central issue in our considerations, which Professor Erhard, the former German Chancellor, in a happy moment once formulated as follows: 'Though one might well talk about giving up national responsibilities in favour of a United Europe, the big question would be how one might bring the governments and parliaments of all six countries to take the plunge.' [126]

Clearly, trust in the '*solidarité de fait*' is not enough. Most depends in the case of supranational functionalism too on the readiness to integrate of the leading political groups in the individual states.

5. Summary

The discussion of the various concepts has clearly indicated that the central problem lies in the organized co-operation of the leading groups in the individual member states. But it has also made it plain that, so far as the concepts developed hitherto are concerned, we are still living in hopes of finding the 'philosopher's stone'. Each of the methods named has its advantages and its particular weaknesses. Each can be redeployed in the future or developed further. So one can continue to expect much from the activities of a supranationally operating body of the 'Action Committee' type. In the same way, it ought to be possible to steer individual political parties onto an integration course in order to give the process of integration a new impetus. This, admittedly, only if the pro-federation elements within the individual parties develop more consciously organized forms of co-operation than they have up to now. Why should not the federalists in the once so enthusiastically pro-federation CDU—but equally inside other parties—form themselves into a special organization within the party, like the local politicians, the small employers or women? Carl Joachim Friedrich pointed out more than ten years ago now that there are still unexplored possibilities in this direction.[127] Modernized groups of federalists inside the parties might co-operate at the MP level and in inter-party working-groups with other national parties or else with foreign party organizations. In this way, a resuscitation of the federalist international party congress would be conceivable. Probably a special role would accrue to the delegates of the European Parliament in the process. Of course, even the best organization and the most attractive method are of no avail if there is no agreement about aims. But uniformity of aims cannot be expected in any party in view of the relatively numerous alternatives to the politics of European integration. Even if unanimity over the basic issue of European politics—Co-operation or Federation—were attainable (and it is not), agreement would hardly be forthcoming on such questions as the circle of members of any union, the relationship of those members to the USA, to the Soviet Union and, indeed, also to other European states in the Russian sphere of power. This plurality of opinions and interests is in turn the best guarantee for the *status quo* of European national states, somewhat improved by arrangements serving the purpose of functional co-operation.

That, last but not least, the federator potential of the Communities was to be strengthened makes good sense. Hallstein's demand that only politicians of ministerial status or better still, members of government, should be suggested for posts in the Commission can be sure of the approval of all well-meaning people.[128] Though, of course, members of the Commission of high political rank will only be found if there is some assurance that the Council of Ministers understands the Commission as an initiating and executive political body, not merely as a panel of international functionaries in a subservient position. Among other things, this will depend to a large extent on whether the principle of majority decisions is successfully and rigorously applied to the Council. If this were so, the Commission's status would be automatically strengthened.

The results of these considerations can be summarized in four theses:

(1) All the subtle and gradualistic approaches in the world cannot alter the circumstance that a federation becomes an established fact *only* when a central government is ruling. Under the conditions of a free democracy this means: an Executive that is answerable to a popularly elected parliament as well as to some federal institution, and equipped with legal capacity in foreign relations. Even if integration processes on many levels have preceded it, the formation of a state still implies straightforward qualitative innovation, which presupposes a conscious and irrevocable political decision on the part of all *foederandi*.

(2) Gradualistic methods of integration can pave the way for a decision to federate. They create the administrative and economic pre-conditions without which any newly formed federation would inevitably break up. But their thrust cannot carry the states over the threshold of forming a federation. While it has proved advantageous for the start of the Communities that many politicians lulled themselves in functionalist illusions, these illusions have been threatening to bypass the central problem for some time.

(3) All experience teaches that the decision to change the quality of international relations must be borne by small political elites operating supranationally. Europe is only able to be federated 'from above', if at all. And this would require an inconceivably favourable constellation.

(4) A consensus between the political elites of the member states would

54

probably disintegrate very rapidly if it were not given permanence by the setting up without delay of a central government. The closed shells of national political systems can only be prized open using the instrument of a government. Only when central political ministries with far-reaching powers have been set up, will that orientation of the leading political groups to the institutions of the federation take place without which a partial weakening of the power of the member states in favour of the federation is unthinkable. In that event alone will all groups who expect state aid orientate themselves towards the new unit, and only then will that restructuring of the party systems also take place, without which any more ambitious political federation would be inconceivable.

So the democratic legitimacy of a European government is not merely a constitutional requirement on principle. It would be a highly practical consideration at the same time. Only if a new state had a democratic structure from the very beginning, that is to say, if it had an active reciprocal effect on all forces of society, could the dissenting forces of the previously nationally structured society be outmanoeuvred. Only in this way would the founding of the state 'from above' receive legitimacy from the population.

Thus, the present situation of the movement for European unity is paradoxical and anything but straightforward. In order to reach its goal— political federation—it would have, to some extent, to have already reached it. That extremely powerful political gravitational field which might neutralize the centrifugal tendencies of the national systems of government could only build up round some supranational federator. But conversely, this federator comes about only if the centrifugal forces of the existing member states have already been counteracted. Thus we have a vicious circle from which, as yet, there is no visible way out. The European Movement which started with such high-flying expectations today somewhat resembles the man stuck in a quagmire who attempts to pull himself out by his own forelock. But that is only possible in cock and bull stories.

Only if one becomes aware of the requirements we have just been discussing does one realize how far away we still are from the United States of Europe. To this extent methodological analysis must inevitably bring all those people back to earth with a bump who would like to see in a European Federation the fulfilment of all their dreams. But in the realm of politics dreams mostly only come true if followed by sober thoughts in the grim light of day about how to put those dreams into practice.

Notes

Hans-Peter Schwarz is Professor of Political Science at the University of Cologne. The essay was originally published in: Demokratisches System und politische Praxis der Bundesrepublik, Festschrift für Theodor Eschenburg (1972, *R. Piper & Co. Verlag, Munich) pp. 377–445. Translated by C. J. Wells.*

1. *Political Community and the North Atlantic Area: International Organization in the Light of Historical Experience,* Princeton 1968; see also Karl W. Deutsch and William Foltz (eds.), *Nation-Building,* New York 1963.

2. Seymour Martin Lipset, *The First New Nation,* New York 1963.

3. A critical review of research is given by Roger D. Hansen, 'Regional Integration. Reflections on a Decade of Theoretical Efforts', in *World Politics* XXI (1969), pp. 242–271. Many of the most important contributions on the subject can be found in the collection *International Political Communities: An Anthology,* New York 1966.

4. 'L'Europe des Savants. Die europäische Integration und die Sozialwissenschaften', in *Integration* I (1968), p. 12.

5. One exception is Walter Lipgens who conceives of the European Movement as being at one and the same time a national and an international movement—as is indeed necessary, cf. 'Europa-Föderationspläne der Widerstandsbewegungen 1940–1945. Eine Dokumentation' (*Schriftenreihe des Forschungsinstituts der Deutschen Gesellschaft für Auswärtige Politik,* vol. 26), Munich 1968.

6. After all, some of the most important theoretical contributions from the German-speaking area derive from lawyers. In this connection, not only the widely scattered studies of Walter Hallstein spring to mind, but also studies like Hartwig Bülck, 'Föderalismus als internationales Ordnungsprinzip', in VVDStRL 21 (1964), pp. 1–60; 'Raum und Zeit im Europarecht', in *Archiv des Völkerrechts* 12 (1964/65), pp. 399–425; Josef H. Kaiser, 'Modi der Integration. Ökonomische Elemente und juristische Relevanz', in *Probleme des Europäischen Rechts* (hereafter referred to as the *Hallstein Festschrift*), Frankfurt 1966, pp. 266–274; and Hans-Peter Ipsen, *Fusionsverfassung Europäische Gemeinschaften,* Bad Homburg/Berlin/Zürich 1969. Just as significant are the contributions of lawyers to the study of contemporary history, cf. particularly the study by Hermann Mosler, 'Die Entstehung des Modells supranationaler und gewaltenteilender Staatenverbindungen in den Verhandlungen über den Schumann-Plan', in *Hallstein-Festschrift,* pp. 355–358, or Carl Friedrich Ophüls' study: 'Zur ideengeschichtlichen Herkunft der Gemeinschaftsverfassung', *ibid.* pp. 387–413.

7. Cf. the works of Ernst B. Haas, Leon Lindberg, and Dusan Sidjanski cited below. Descriptive and problem-orientated studies dealing with the Institutions and policy of the Communities are not lacking either.

8. Books like Walter Kuby's *Provokation Europa* (Cologne/Berlin 1965) are rare. Systematic discussion of method is not especially the rule in the European Movement, either; still, there are exceptions, like the self-presentation of various approaches in one number of the *Bulletin du Centre européen de la culture* (vol. 6, May 1958), 'Méthodes et mouvements pour unir l'Europe', with contributions by François Fontaine, Henri Brugmans, Altiero Spinelli and Denis de Rougemont.

9. Hallstein's integration theory appears in numerous speeches and papers, only some of which have been edited. For the work which has appeared, see the *Hallstein Festschrift.* However, this does not contain some important mimeographed speeches, nor the post-1965 statements which are equally important for the understanding of his thought. See also the recent work: *Der unvollendete Bundesstaat. Europäische Erfahrungen und Erkenntnisse,* Düsseldorf/Vienna 1969.

10. Cf. Spinelli's essays in Lipgens, *loc. cit.* (fn. 5), pp. 36–60; 'Das Wachstum

der Europa-Bewegung seit dem 2. Weltkrieg', in C. Grove Haines (ed.), *Europäische Integration*, Göttingen 1958, pp. 35–59; *Manifest der europäischen Föderalisten*, Frankfurt 1958; 'Ein europäisches Europa—Föderation oder Konföderation', in Gilbert Ziebura (ed.), *Nationale Souveränität oder übernationale Integration?*, Berlin 1966; *The Eurocrats. Conflict and Crisis in the European Community*, Baltimore 1966.

11. Herbert Lüthy, *Frankreichs Uhren gehen anders*, Zürich/Stuttgart/Vienna 1954, p. 285.

12. Niccolò Machiavelli, *The Prince,* trs. by W. K. Mariott, London (J. M. Dent) 1958, ch. VI, pp. 29–30.

13. 'The Prospect of Integration', in *Journal of Common Market Studies* 4 (1965/66), p. 135.

14. This applies to all Commonwealth federations, and here the intentions of the 'external elites' (Etzioni) might be brought into connexion with those of the leading groups in the Colonies and Dominions. To this extent the study of these federation processes is extremely instructive with regard to the methodology of European integration as well. (On the more recent federations, see R. L. Watts, *New Federations. Experiments in the Commonwealth*, London 1966. A bibliography on the older Commonwealth federations is provided by K. C. Wheare, *Federal Government*, 4th ed., 1963 (1946).

15. Press conference of 9 September 1965, quoted from Charles de Gaulle, *Discours et Messages*, vol. 4: 'Pour l'effort, Août 1962–Décembre 1965', Paris 1970, p. 379.

16. 'A few of our Phony Problems', 14*th Sir Daniel Stevenson Memorial Lecture*, 4 December 1964, Chatham House, London (hectograph: 13733/X/64/D).

17. David Mitrany, *The Prospect of Integration, loc. cit.* (fn. 13), p. 130 *et seq.*

18. Before the Royal Institute of International Affairs in London on 4 December 1964, for example (*Europa-Archiv* [referred to as EA in what follows] 20, 1965, D 176); and similarly on 20 January 1968 in Rome, before the Federal Council of the European Movement EA/D 23 (1968), 152.

19. The Imperial Constitution (*Reichsverfassung*) of 1871 showed that, from the constitutional point of view at least, a construction was conceivable and practicable which granted both the federation and the member states the responsibility for foreign affairs. Admittedly, the capacity of the individual member states was restricted by the political supremacy of Prussia. This kind of preponderance on the part of *one* state would be impossible in a Western European federation. Consequently, this competing capacity would probably be impracticable without the federation having any competence; the power in external affairs would have to be transferred to the federation with some measure of exclusiveness, if the latter were not to be condemned to be ineffectual from the very outset. Besides, in the technical literature dealing with European integration, and in the political debates as well, there reigns a partly intentional confusion regarding the concept 'federation'. The term 'federation' has as a rule been used by the federalists as a concept which contrasts with the regulated co-operation of interdependent but autonomous states. It will also be employed in this sense in the following analysis.

20. *The Uniting of Europe: Political, Social and Economic Forces 1950–1957,* Stanford, 2nd ed., 1968 (1958), p. 5.

21. 'A Structural Theory of Integration', in *Journal of Peace Research* 5 (1968), p. 377.

22. Thus C. J. Friedrich talks of the 'federalizing process' ('International Federalism in Theory and Practice', in Elmer Plischke (ed.), *Systems of Integrating the International Community,* Princeton 1964).

23. Since Karl W. Deutsch and his school, as well as Ernst B. Haas, presented their analyses of integration in terms of a process, this approach has largely become established in the American research, cf. Amitai Etzioni, *Political Unification. A Comparative Study of Leaders and Forces,* New York 1965; Leo N. Lindberg, 'The European Community as a Political System: Notes toward the Construction of a Model', in *Journal of Common Market Studies,* 5 (1966), pp. 344–387; Josef S. Nye, 'Comparative Regional Integration: Concept and Measurement', in *International Organization,* 22 (1968), pp. 355–380.

24. Quoted from *Gesellschaft und Humanität. Gesammelte Aufsätze,* Zürich 1948, p. 130. The italics stem from the author.

25. Thus, for example, at a press conference held on 15 May 1962, he rejected the notion of a federation of the Six with the remark: 'Mais cette entité-là est impossible à découvrir faute d'un fédérateur qui ait aujourd'hui en Europe la force, l'adresse et le crédit suffisants' (quoted from Charles de Gaulle, *Discours et Messages,* vol. 3, 'Avec le Renouveau, Mai 1958–Juillet 1962', Paris 1970, p. 408). Also note the quotation in Footnote 15.

26. Cf. Max Beloff, *The United States and the Unity of Europe,* Washington 1963, and Ernst H. van der Beugel, *From Marshall Aid to Atlantic Partnership,* Amsterdam/London/New York 1966.

27. No comprehensive historical account yet exists; Walter Lipgens' documentation of the European plans in the Resistance Movement is valuable (cf. fn. 5); he has also announced a presentation of the European Movement in the years 1945–50. The broad outlines can be found in Achille Albonetti, 'Vorgeschichte der Vereinigten Staaten von Europa' (*Schriftenreihe zum Handbuch für europäische Wirtschaft,* vol. 22), Baden-Baden/Bonn 1961; Altiero Spinelli, *The Eurocrats, loc. cit.* (fn. 8), and Henri Brugmans, *L'idée européenne* 1918–1966, Bruges (2nd ed.) 1966 (1965=Cahiers de Bruges, N.S. 12). *The Bulletin du Centre européen de la culture,* ed. by Denis de Rougement, no. 6 (1958), pp. 43–82, provides a good survey of the organizations down to 1958. The objectives in the years 1950–53 have left their mark in the debates of the Advisory Assembly of the Council of Europe and of the *ad hoc* Assembly; a comprehensive examination of the approaches of these years is equally lacking at the present time. A particularly attractive undertaking would be the systematic comparison of the European Movements with analogous movements for unification in the nineteenth century, say the *Società Nazionale* or the *Deutscher Nationalverein.* The latest developments in the European Movements can be gleaned from Karl-Heinz Koppe, 'Der Stand der programmatischen Diskussion in den europäischen Verbänden', in EA, 19 (1964), pp. 569–580.

28. Cf. Denis de Rougemont's account of the Congress Movement which is positively saturated with personal opinions: 'The Campaign of the European Congresses', in *Government and Opposition,* 2 (1966–67), pp. 329–349.

29. The Honorary Presidium of the First European Congress of the Pan-European Union in Vienna in October 1926 was composed of Eduard Benesch, Josef Caillaux, Paul Löbe, Francesco Nitti, Nicolas Politis and Ignaz Seipel.

The Presidents of the European Movement founded in October 1948 were Winston Churchill, Léon Blum, Paul Henri Spaak and Alcide de Gasperi.

30. *Eine Idee erobert Europa. Meine Lebenserinnerungen,* Vienna/Munich/Basel, 1958 p. 278.

31. A summary is found in *Europa Unites. The Story of the Campaign for European Unity*, including a full Report of the Congress of Europe, held at The Hague, May 1948, London 1949, p. 23 *et seq.*

32. Per Fischer suspects this to be the case: 'Europarat und parlamentarische Aussenpolitik' (*Forschungsinstitut der deutschen Gesellschaft für Auswärtige Politik*, vol. 16), Munich 1962, p. 22, in which connexion he draws attention to earlier discussion on the Statutes of the League of Nations and in the Inter-parliamentary Union (p. 17 *et seq.*). The idea played a particularly important role among the populist UEF groups.

33. The best accounts are given by Walter Yondorf, 'Monnet and the Action Committee: The Formative Period of the European Communities', in *International Organization*, 19 (1965), pp. 885–912, and Richard Mayne, 'The Role of Jean Monnet', in *Government and Opposition*, 2 (1966–67), pp. 349–371. In addition, the background information given by Merry and Serge Bromberger, *Les coulisses de l'Europe*, Paris 1968.—On the whole Monnet's own remarks about his approach are not especially productive (most informative: 'Europe—why and how', *Addresses and Papers given at the Cotton Board Conference*, Manchester 1957). Alf Dieter Dobbertin is about to present a historico-analytical study of Monnet's contributions to the theory and practice of European integration, as a Hamburg dissertation.

34. In May 1960, the Committee was composed of, among others, Léopold Collard, President of the Belgian Socialist Party; Guy Mollet, President of the SFIO; Erich Ollenhauer, First Chairman of the SPD; Herbert Wehner, Vice-Chairman of the SPD; Giuseppe Saragat, General Secretary of the Italian Social Democrats; J. A. Burger, President of the Dutch Workers' Party; Théo Lefèvre, President of the Belgian Christian Socialist Party; Charles Bosson, Chairman of the MRP Parliamentarian Group; Kurt Georg Kiesinger, Prime Minister of Baden-Württemberg; Heinrich Krone, Chairman of the CDU/CSU Parliamentary Group; Aldo Moro, Secretary of the Italian Christian Democrats; J. A. H. J. S. Bruins-Slot, Dutch Anti-Revolutionary Party; Maurice Faure; Antoine Pinay; René Pleven; Giovanni Malagodi, General Secretary of the Italian Liberals; Ugo La Malfa; Willi Richter, Chairman of the German Trade Union Association (DGB); Ludwig Rosenberg; Otto Brenner, Chairman of the German Metal Workers' Union (IG Metall); and Heinrich Gutermuth, Chairman of the German Miners' Union (IG Bergbau) (quoted from Yondorf, *loc. cit.* above, fn. 33, pp. 891–893).

35. Letter of 14 October 1955, quoted from Heinrich von Siegler, *Europäische politische Einigung. Dokumentation von Vorschlägen und Stellungnahmen 1949–1968,* p. 86.

36. Siegler, *ibid.*, p. 86 *et seq.*

37. This is described in Mayne, *op. cit.* (fn. 33), p. 369 *et seq.*

38. Denis de Rougemont, Alexandre Marc and Robert Aron came from the circle around Emanuel Mounier's *Esprit* and around the periodical *Ordre Nouveau*; Eugen Kogon and Walter Dirks in Germany and Henri Brugmans in

Belgium feel themselves in sympathy with the social reformist movement for the restoration of the Christian Democrats.

39. Represented above all in the 'Movimento Federalista Europeo' by Altiero Spinelli and Ernesto Rossi.

40. The main exponent of integral federalism was André Voisin.

41. *The Campaign of the Congresses, loc. cit.* (fn. 28), p. 338.

42. Cf. the Open Letter of the Italian Federalist Movement for Europe (MFE) to the French Committee for European Federation (CFFE): 'The Parties today are necessarily national. The experience of the Socialists and the Communists demonstrates this, since they have several times tried, during the course of their history, to found an international party, but have always, of necessity, fallen back onto the level of national parties.' (Quoted from Lipgens, *Europa-Föderationspläne . . ., loc. cit.*, fn. 5, p. 91.)

43. Thus the Manifesto of the MFE, *ibid.*

44. De Rougemont, *loc. cit.* (fn. 28), p. 336.

45. Cf. *ibid.*, pp. 337–347.

46. The splitting up of the UEF can best be followed in the periodical *Der Föderalist*, Mitteilungen für europäische Föderalisten, nos. 1–3, Frankfurt 1957–59. In addition, the writings of Spinelli, particularly the collection of articles *L'Europa non cade dal Cielo*, Bologna 1959. Cf. also Brugmans, *L'idée européenne, loc. cit.* (fn. 27), pp. 175–180, Koppe, *Die Reaktivierung der europäischen Bewegung*, and 'Der Stand der programmatischen Diskussion in den europäischen Verbänden . . .' in EA, 13 (1962), pp. 473–476 and 15 (1964), pp. 569–580 respectively.

47. Wilhelm Hermes, the first President of the German Europa-Union, was toying with this idea as early as 1948 and it provoked reactions of sheer horror from his Committee, who were all dedicated to keeping aloof from party politics. The Austrian foundation in 1961 was the work of Otto Molden, who had founded the Europäisches Forum in Alpbach after the war. The German EFP went back to a palace revolution in the Bremen youth organization of the Europa-Union. France also possesses a European Party with a strong right-wing bias, under the leadership of Jean Thiriart.

48. In the State Government elections for Lower Saxony in 1967, the EFP gained 2,101 votes. In the Presidential elections held in 1963, the Austrian EFP managed to win about 4% of the votes cast for its candidate, the retired general Dr. Josef Kimmel, but dropped back again to 1% in the following regional elections. (Cf. *Archiv der Gegenwart* (1963), 10546 D; (1964), 11191 B and 11500 A.)

49. See *Encyclopaedia Britannica*, Vol. 12, Chicago/London/Toronto 1959, p. 512.

50. On the MSEUE cf. *Méthodes et mouvements . . ., loc. cit.* (fn. 8), p. 53 *et seq.*; and also Brugmans, *L'idée européenne . . ., loc. cit.* (fn. 27), p. 104.

51. Cf. *Méthodes et mouvements . . ., loc. cit.* (fn. 8), p. 51 *et seq.* Admittedly, the federalist orientation does not emerge clearly from the Statutes, according to which the NEI has the goal of 'making possible regular contacts between the groups and leading political figures of the various nations whose basic philosophy is that of Christian democracy, in order to study the national and international situations in the light of these principles, to exchange experiences and programmes and to seek international harmony within the framework of democracy and also of political and social stability.' (Quoted from Werner Allmeyer,

Christliche Demokratie in Europa und Latein-Amerika. Geschichte, Strukturen, Programme, Bonn 1964, p. 212 *et seq.*)

52. On the significance of the NEI for the early period of West German foreign policy, see Arnulf Baring, *Aussenpolitik in Adenauers Kanzlerdemokratie,* Munich 1969, p. 32 *et seq.*

53. Against this it may be argued that, for example, the founding of the United States took place at a time marked by the most violent internal political antagonisms, and that this foundation was forced through by the federalists in the avowed intention of furthering their own socio-economic interests. (Since Beard this has been pointed out repeatedly, especially recently by Douglas Adair, 'The Federalist Papers', in *William and Mary Quarterly,* 22 (1965), pp. 131–139, and J. R. Pole, *Political Representation and the Origins of the American Republic,* New York 1966, *passim.*).

54. The concept is here used in the same way as it is by Hans-R. Krämer, 'Formen und Methoden der internationalen wirtschaftlichen Integration', Kiel 1969 (*Kieler Studien. Forschungsberichte des Instituts für Weltwritschaft an der Universität Kiel, 95*), p. 22: 'Institutionelle Integration'.

55. 'Die institutionellen Probleme des Beitritts von Grossbritannien zur Europäischen Gemeinschaft', ed. Walter Hallstein, Bonn 1969 (*Zum Dialog. Schriftenreihe des Wirtschaftsrats der CDU, no. 20*), p. 22.

56. The best account of these talks to date is given by Walter Lipgens, *Europäische Einigungsidee 1929–30,* and Briand's 'Europaplan im Urteil der deutschen Akten', in *Historische Zeitschrift* 20t, (1966), pp. 46–89 and pp. 316–363.

57. Cf. William Diebold, *The Schuman Plan,* New York 1959, pp. 60–77, as well as Mosler, *loc. cit.* (fn. 6), p. 364.

58. A formulation from the final communiqué of the Conference of Messina dated 3 June 1955.

59. The text of the communiqué appears in *Europa. Dokumente zur Frage der europäischen Elnlgung,* vol. 2, Bonn 1962, p. 982 *et seq.*

60. 'Kampf um Paneuropa', from the first number of *Paneuropa,* Vlenna-Leipzig 1925, p. 27 *et seq.*

61. *Europa. Dokumente . . ., loc. cit.* (fn. 59), vol. 1, p. 33.

62. The text is given in Lipgens, *Europa-Föderationspläne . . ., loc. cit.* (fn. 5), pp. 474–477.

63. On this, see Susanne J. Bodenheimer, *Political Union: A Microcosm of European Politics 1960–1966,* Leyden 1967.

64. Quoted from Konrad Adenauer, *Erinnerungen 1955–1959,* Stuttgart 1967, p. 26.

65. On this see Hans-R. Krämer, *loc. cit.* (fn. 54), pp. 22–28.

66. The federal European Plans have variously been criticized by the functionalist school, particularly by David Mitrany, 'The Prospect of Integration: Federal or Functional', in *Journal of Common Market Studies,* 4 (1965–66), pp. 119–149: 'It no longer makes sense politically or economically, and certainly not historically' (p. 124).

67. Bundeskanzler Erhard, for example (strongly influenced by Wilhelm Röpke), understood political integration primarily in terms of *organized* governmental co-operation. Beside the free trade motive, the idea of the 'Atlantic Community' played a decisive role in his thinking, as it did in Röpke's.

61

68. Norbert Kohlhase, 'Die europäische Gemeinschaft vor der Gefahr der Desintegration', in EA, 24 (1969), p. 266.

69. Cf. 'Entwürfe für einen Vertrag über die Gründung einer Union der europäischen Völker', in EA/D, 19 (1964), p. 483, 488.

70. *Mémoires de guerre. Le salut, 1944–1946*, Paris 1961, p. 234.

71. Quoted from Charles de Gaulle, *loc. cit*, vol. 3 (fn. 25), p. 245.

72. Radio interview of the Belgian Foreign Minister Paul Henri Spaak, 10 September 1964, in EA/D, 19 (1964), p. 495.

73. The literature on the problem of the supranational restructuring of the interest groups is extensive, cf., in addition to the well-known work by Fritz Fischer, *Die institutionalisierte Vertretung der Verbände in der Europäischen Wirtschaftsgemeinschaft*, Hamburg 1965, also Jean Meynaud and Dusan Sidjanski, *L'Europe des Affaires: role et structure des groupes*, Paris 1967.

74. *Council of Europe. Consultative Assembly. Official Report of Debates*, III, 12 Session, p. 365.

75. *Europa. Dokumente* . . . , *loc. cit.* (fn. 59), vol. 1, p. 165.

76. Thus Spinelli and Rossi, for example, protagonists of the Constituent Assembly idea, have been strongly influenced by their study of the 'Federalist' during their imprisonment. (Cf. Lipgens, *Europa-Föderationspläne* . . . , *loc. cit.*, fn. 5, p. 36).

77. Thus the text of the Mackay Resolution which had been agreed between the 'Federalists' and the 'Unionists' on 23 November 1950 (quoted from *Europa. Dokumente* . . . , *loc. cit.*, fn. 59, vol. 1, p. 397).

78. The decisive passage of the Mackay Resolution in this regard reads: 'No kind of executive powers for legislation shall be accorded to the Council of Europe in advance. The Council shall from time to time as appropriate acquire these powers in connexion with its various aims and functions. These powers would be granted to it individually for each particular matter by special laws, when these bills have been passed by the Assembly and the Committee of Ministers.' (*Europa. Dokumente* . . . , *loc. cit.*, fn. 59, vol. 1, p. 398).

79. Press conference of 15 May 1962. Quoted from Charles de Gaulle, *loc. cit.* (fn. 25), vol. 3, p. 408.

80. Thus Per Fischer, *loc. cit.* (fn. 32), p. 93.

81. Taking, for example, membership of the central committees of both party and parliamentary group as an indication of political importance in the state of origin, we see that out of 137 members of the European Parliament in 1966 only twenty-five occupied such an influential position. On the other hand, former Ministers and Secretaries of State are strongly represented with forty-three delegates. This shows, together with the equally remarkable continuity (seventy delegates have belonged to the European Parliament since 1959!), that an assembly of European parliamentary notables has here emerged whose dynamism —should they ever wish to develop any—can be absorbed quite nicely by the national parliaments. On this, see the Hamburg dissertation by Peter Reichel, *Die europäischen Abgeordneten des deutschen Bundestages* (1973).

82. David Mitrany, *The Prospect of Integration, loc. cit.* (fn. 13), p. 132.

83. *The Federalist*, LXX.

84. Before the Federal Council of the European Movement on 20 January 1968 in Rome, quoted from EA/D, 23 (1968), p. 154. Hallstein also held this view

before the crisis period of 1965–1969, cf. his *United Europe. Challenge and Opportunity*, Cambridge (Mass.) 1962, esp. p. 58 *et seq.*

85. *Année Politique* 1950, p. 306.

86. 'Die politischen Aspekte', in *Die Integration des europäischen Westens* (Veröffentlichungen der Handelshochschule St. Gallen, Series B, Part 11), Zürich St. Gallen 1954, p. 77.

87. *Origines et élaboration du Plan Schuman*, Bruges 1953 (Cahiers de Bruges, No. 3), p. 270.

88. *Erinnerungen 1945–1953*, Stuttgart 1965, p. 545; author's italics. Cf. also: *Erinnerungen 1955–1959*, Bonn 1967, p. 30.

89. *Council of Europe. Consultative Assembly Report*, Strasbourg 1949, p. 180. On the hitherto neglected history of the concepts of integration, cf. C. C. Walton, 'The Fate of Neo-Federalism in Western Europe', in *The Western Political Quarterly*, 5 (1952), pp. 366–390. Illuminating for the state of the discussion in 1951 is D. U. Stikker, 'The Functional Approach to European Integration', in *Foreign Affairs*, 29 (1951), pp. 436–444.

90. *A Working Peace System*, London 1943, p. 32. Mitrany's theories are presented and discussed by Ernst B. Haas, *Beyond the Nation State*, Stanford 1964, pp. 1–25 and *passim*; Inis L. Claude, *Swords into Plowshares. The Problems and Progress of International Organization*, New York (4th ed.) 1964 (1956), pp. 344–367, and James Patrick Sewell, *Functionalism and World Politics. A Study Based on Nations' Programs Financing Economic Development*, Princeton 1966, pp. 3–72.

91. *The Progress of International Government*, London 1933, p. 128.

92. *A Working Peace System*, *loc. cit.* (fn. 90), p. 34.

93. *Ibid.*, pp. 35–37.

94. *Ibid.*, p. 29. At this point, our interpretation of Mitrany is particularly indebted to the study by Sewell, *loc. cit.*, (fn. 90).

95. Mitrany, Introduction to the 4th ed. of *A Working Peace System*, London 1964, p. 9.

96. Thus Hermann Mosler, *loc. cit.* (fn. 6), p. 360: 'So, if one disregards the only imperfectly hinted at legal control, the carrying out of the plan lay solely with the High Authority . . .'

97. On the history of the Schuman Plan cf. Pierre Gerbert, 'La genèse du plan Schuman. Des origines à la déclaration du 9 mai 1950', in *Revue Française de Science Politique*, 6 (1956), p. 525 *et seq.*, and Hermann Mosler, *loc. cit.* (fn. 6), pp. 355–386. Merry and Serge Bromberger, *loc. cit.* (fn. 33), pp. 116–131, report interesting background anecdotes, the authenticity of which is admittedly unverifiable. They state on p. 124 that all the drafts of the Memorandum of 9 May 1950 have been destroyed. That the High Authority in the Schuman Plan was originally conceived of in purely functional terms is also stated by Pierre Uri: 'The Schuman Plan had no intention of providing the prototype for integration brought about by the successive integration of sectors' ('Economics and politics of the Common Market', in J. P. Miller (ed.), *Competition, Cartels, and their Regulation*, Amsterdam 1962, p. 378).

98. Most informative in this respect is the article by Mosler which has often been referred to above; also various studies by C. F. Ophüls, particularly *Zur ideengeschichtlichen Herkunft . . ., loc. cit.* (fn. 6), pp. 387–413.

99. The notion of some kind of parliamentary control was also suggested to

63

Monnet by the British government. After the failure of the Franco-British negotiations on the Schuman Plan, Prime Minister Attlee commented in the House of Commons: 'We on this side are not prepared to accept the principle that the most vital economic forces of this country should be handed over to an authority that is utterly undemocratic and is responsible to nobody.' (Quoted from Mosler, *loc. cit.*, fn. 6, p. 369).

100. The initiatives in the Council of Europe ran parallel to the talks on the ECSC. They aimed firstly to create a 'political authority' but later directed their attention to the more modest goal of specialist authorities under the control of a Council of Ministers and a supranational Assembly. (Cf. 'Empfehlung zur Bildung von europäischen Sonderbehörden', in *Europa. Dokumente . . ., loc. cit.*, fn. 59, vol. 1, p. 497 *et seq.*)

101. Other metaphors were: 'political hat' (Karlheinz Neunreither, 'Die politische Union', in *Europäische Gegenwart. Schriften zur Europapolitik*, vol. 2, Cologne/Opladen 1965, p. 7), or 'political head', which would be set on the economic body of the EEC (Altiero Spinelli, *Ein europäisches Europa—Föderation oder Konföderation? loc. cit.*, fn. 8, p. 56).

102. A similarly built-in federator mechanism had been suggested during the ECSC negotiations from the German side, and had been rejected. (Mosler, *loc. cit.*, fn. 6, p. 378.)

103. Hallstein sees the Commission as the 'planning, propulsive and mediating body in the decision-making process' (*Die institutionellen Probleme . . ., loc. cit.*, fn. 55, p. 14). The latest literature is treated by Robert Knöpfle, 'Organisation und Arbeitsweise der Gemeinsamen Kommission der Europäischen Gemeinschaften', in *Europarecht*, 3 (1968), pp. 30–62.

104. John Lambert, 'Decision-making in the Community: the Commission-Council-Dialogue', in *Government and Opposition*, 2 (1966/67), pp. 391–396.

105. Particularly informative on this is Altiero Spinelli, *The Eurocrats, loc. cit.* (fn. 8), pp. 71–99.

106. On the political potential of the European Parliament, cf. Karl-Heinz Neunreither, 'Das parlamentarische Element im Entscheidungsprozess der Europäischen Gemeinschaften', in EA, 21 (1966), pp. 811–812. Generally on the European Parliament, see Henri Manzanarès, *Le parlement européen*, Paris 1964.

107. *Das zweckmässigste Verfahren zur wirtschaftlichen Integrierung Europas*, ed. by CEPES, Frankfurt, no date, p. 17.

108. Hallstein, 'Die echten Probleme der europäischen Integration' (*Kieler Vorträge*, N.F. 37), Kiel 1965, p. 18.

109. Cf. on this Ernst Haas, *loc. cit.* (fn. 90), pp. 79–81.

110. 'International Integration. The European and the Universal Process', in *International Organization*, 15 (1961), p. 368.

111. Ernst. B. Haas. 'The Uniting of Europe and the Uniting of Latin America', in *Journal of Common Market Studies*, 5 (1966/67), pp. 315 et seq.

111a. Cf. Haas, *loc. cit.* (fn. 90), pp. 51–125. The beginnings of this federation strategy have already been sketched out by Jean Monnet, when he describes the effect of supranational institutions as follows: 'Elles accumulent l'expérience collective et, de cette expérience et de cette sagesse, les hommes soumis aux mêmes règles verront non pas leur nature changer, mais leur comportement graduellement se transformer' (*Les Etats-Unis d'Europe ont commencé*, Paris 1955, p. 44).

112. Ernst B. Haas, *loc. cit.* (fn. 111), p. 330.

113. 'Chancen einer konstruktiven Ostpolitik', in *Wege nach Gesamteuropa*, 14. Ord. Kongress der Europa-Union Deutschlands (*Schriftenreihe der Europa-Union Deutschland*, part 17), Bonn, no date, p. 16.

114. Cf. the considered statements of Fritz Hellwig, 'Die politische Tragweite der europäischen Wirtschaftsintegration' (*Kieler Vorträge*, N.F. 45), Kiel 1966.

115. Hallstein, *Die institutionellen Probleme . . ., loc. cit.* (fn. 55), p. 114.

116. Press conference of 5 September 1960, quoted from Charles de Gaulle, *loc. cit.*, (fn. 25), vol. 3, p. 245.

117. Cf. Klaus F. Bauer, 'Spill-over oder spill-back', in EA, 21 (1966), pp. 519–526.

118. 'Discord in Community: The North Atlantic Area as a Partial International System', in Francis O. Wilcox—H. Field Haviland, *The Atlantic Community*, New York/London 1963, p. 13.

119. This view is taken particularly by Andreas Sattler in the study: *Das Prinzip der 'funktionellen Integration' und die Einigung Europas. Die Übertragung von Hoheitsrechten und ihre Konsequenzen, untersucht am Beispiel der Europäischen Gemeinschaften*, Göttingen 1967, pp. 215–224.

120. Quoted from Georg Christoph Lichtenberg, *Aphorismen*, ed. by Max Rychner, Zürich 1958, p. 588.

121. This argument has cropped up in the thinking of the European Movement time and again, ever since Count Coudenhove-Kalergi first expressed it in the programmatic publication *Pan-Europa* in 1923.

122. Theodor Eschenburg, 'Die DDR respektieren', in Theo Sommer (ed.), *Denken an Deutschland. Zum Problem der Wiedervereinigung-Ansichten und Einsichten*, Hamburg 1966, p. 162.

123. *Die Einigung Europas, loc. cit.* (fn. 111), p. 328; also the Preface to the new edition of the work *The Uniting of Europe* (see fn. 20).

124. Bundeskanzler Kiesinger, for example, has expressed this consideration in a highly regarded after dinner speech on the occasion of the state visit of the French Prime Minister (*Neue Zürcher Zeitung*, 12 September 1969).

125. *Die institutionellen Probleme . . ., loc. cit.* (fn. 55), pp. 8–22. An extensive discussion of the Community's chances of developing in the direction of a European Federal State is given by Sattler, *loc. cit.* (fn. 120), pp. 165–214.

126. *Open Letter of the Presidium of the European Union to Bundeskanzler Erhard* of 17 September 1964, in EA, 19 (1964), p. 498.

127. 'Der Weg zur europäischen Föderation', in *Der Föderalist*, part 6 (1957), p. 7.

128. Speech made on 20 January 1968, EA/D, 23 (1968), p. 153.

Ulrich Scheuner

CONSTITUTIONAL PROBLEMS OF THE DEVELOPMENT OF THE EUROPEAN COMMUNITY

I. From Ambitious Aims to Crisis

From the beginning, the European Community has been dynamic in character. The treaties which founded it did not consolidate an existing situation nor an historic achievement, such as is more or less the case in the constitutions of states. They were, on the contrary, orientated towards achieving far-reaching objectives, which could only become concrete in the work of the Community and to which the institutional structure and the mode of work of the Community's institutions had first to conform. These aims, however, formed merely a transitional stage and, once this was achieved, further perspectives emerged. In the case of the Coal and Steel Community, it was clear from the beginning that the abolition of customs duties could not be restricted to a portion of the market and would aim at being extended and applied to the whole exchange of goods. This is what occurred in the Treaties of Rome of 25 March 1957. The establishment, envisaged by them, of a common market for all goods has been basically achieved—with some factual gaps—at the end of 1969. But since the later sixties a new stage in the development of European economic unity came to be initiated, going beyond the customs union, in the direction of a closer economic concentration of the Member States. A mere customs union is insufficient to bring about a completely free movement of persons, goods and services. Therefore the wider concept of an economic and monetary union demanding an active co-ordination of national economic policies and a laying down of monetary barriers was now envisaged.

66

On 13 October 1970, a Working Party addressed its report, known as the Werner Report,[1] to Council and Commission in which it outlined the fundamental lines of an economic and monetary union. The Council and the Representatives of the Member States, on 22 March 1971, accepted the main lines of this report and fixed the beginning of its implementation at 1 January 1972. In the same period, the idea of a closer political co-operation of the Member States, first proposed by the Davignon Committee in 1970, led to meetings of the foreign ministers at regular intervals and found the approbation of the Paris Summit of October 1972. A third event opened up new possibilities for the Community: the entry of Great Britain and two other nations enlarged the Community and seemed to promise wider possibilities.

The beginning of the realization of the economic and monetary union should have marked a new epoch in the evolution of the EEC. The aims of the union, the elaboration of a common economic and cyclical policy, and the establishment of an irreversible convertibility of the currencies were clearly set out. However, the last years have not fulfilled the sanguine hopes entertained. The period in which the customs union came to be completed was one of economic growth and relative stability of the world economy. Since the middle of the sixties, however, the world monetary system showed signs of serious strain. In 1969 France had to devalue the Franc, whereas the Federal Republic of Germany was forced to revalue the Deutschmark.[2] This was just the beginning of a deeper crisis in the international monetary system which received a further severe blow when the USA government renounced the gold standard for the dollar. Inflationary difficulties in all European countries as well as in the USA provoked a return to national solutions of economic questions in several Member States of the EEC. The outcome was that not only did the economic and monetary union fail to make any progress, but even the former achievements of the Common Market became endangered by a slow erosion through ever-changing currency levels. Within the European Community the decision process slowed down more and more. The latent crisis came to the open in October 1973, when the Arab-Israeli war and the ensuing partial oil boycott of the Arab States made it clear that the members of the Community were unable to unite on a common reaction to this danger but sought their own national advantage by isolated action. There is now no doubt that the Community is passing through a critical period which could even endanger its former results.

Ultimate responsibility for the critical situation lies in the first line with the attitude of the Member States, their national egotism and lack of real co-operation. At the same time, there is a strong feeling that also the institutional framework of the EEC has not proved adequate to the situation. Time and again proposals of the Commission have not been accepted or not even been deliberated by the Council of Ministers. The suggested enlargement of the powers of community on the other side, has focused attention on the weak part played by the European Parliament and the consequential lack of democratic legitimacy. A deeper sense of the necessity of a better and more efficient organization of the Community has arisen. It is strengthened by an evaluation of the new policies on which the EEC is embarking in striving for a closer economic co-operation, a regional policy and a European energy programme securing greater independence from outside resources. Do the present treaty provisions form a basis for these new developments, do the existing institutions correspond to the future needs? These are urgent questions. We will try to discuss them in the following pages. First we will turn to the consequences which are involved in the pursuit of an economic and monetary union, a regional policy and a new scheme for common action on energy resources. That leads to the following questions:

(*a*) What will the attainment of these goals mean? What powers are thereby transferred to the Community?

(*b*) Will it be necessary to give the Community new powers by treaty or are the terms of the present treaty sufficient for the execution of the intended policies?

(*c*) What will be the structural consequences of the new aims for the institutions of the Community? Can their efficiency be strengthened? Is it advisable, especially in view of the increased powers, to underline the democratic elements within the Community?

II. The Introduction of New Policies and the Member States

In its present state the Common Market is a Customs Union, in which basically the freedom of movement of persons, goods, capital and services is guaranteed, but which, over and beyond this, shows the beginning of a co-ordinated economic and cyclical policy. Within the framework of the existing order, the Commission had introduced a co-ordination of the economic policy of Member States and, proceeding from Article 92 of the EEC Treaty, had developed a programme for a positive regional policy.[3] But the Treaty still left the economic and monetary policy basically to national governments. The Rome Treaty does indeed refer 'conjunctural' (cyclical) policy, as a matter of common interest, to the decision of the Community (Article 103), but recognizes the decision on the rate of exchange as a reservation of national jurisdiction (Article 107). This last point has been widely practised in the last years.

The economic and monetary union extends, in its final phase at any rate, beyond the initial stages of a mere co-ordination of the different national economies through the issuing of orientation data and recommendations,[4] and opens the way for a far-reaching and, if necessary, binding control of the central economic areas by the Community. As its goal it envisages an integrated market, the functioning of which can proceed freely without

68

distortion through national differences in currency parity or economic and financial policy and in which essential decisions rest with the Community. The changes which are envisaged comprise the following:

(*a*) A full and irreversible convertibility of currencies is set up in which it is irrelevant whether or not national money tokens are retained. The control of this uniform monetary union demands a central banking system with a corresponding system of intervention and credit policy. It remains an open question meanwhile, whether one envisages this banking system as more centrally or federally structured and whether it can itself take independent decisions or depends as regards the fundamentals of its powers upon decisions of the Community institutions.[5]

(*b*) The Community influences the common economic policy and economic trends, especially through budgetary and fiscal policy. It lays down as binding basic data for the elaboration of national budgets (scope, relationship or budgetary expenditure on investment, consumption, etc.) and tries to harmonize fiscal policy. Beyond this the Community may set up data for a medium-term economic policy as well as for counter-cyclical measures.

(*c*) In addition, a regional policy is developed including some elements of a financial equalization of burdens throughout the Member States.[6]

In order to achieve these goals important powers of the Member States must be transferred to the Community. These can no longer manipulate their currency as a means of adjustment for any imbalance caused by their interior economic or social policy. Further, the states have not only to organize their budgets upon a common scheme, but adapt them to common data set up by the Community. If a national economic crisis occurs the Member States will have to take their measures according to co-ordinated guidelines which take into reckoning the situation of the other states.

For Member States this implies a relinquishing of essential parts of their national powers. The focal point of national politics today is economic and social policy. Prosperity, standard of living, and growth are regarded as the barometers of development. On these elements depends the success of a government and its political survival. The European peoples still look to their national governments, when they think of their socio-economic state of health. This is all the more true in a time of crisis.

The extent of the proposed change can be assessed if one considers that it was only by the Finance Reform of 8 June 1967 that the Federal Republic of Germany equipped itself with the legal means for a global economic policy and cyclical control. The obligation to maintain a stable economic balance, expressed in Article 109 (2 and 4) of the Federal Constitution imposes upon the Federal Republic the task of devising a systematic cyclical policy.[7] Any renunciation of these faculties would strike at a fundamental part of national sovereignty. One can wonder whether it could come about as rapidly as the Werner Plan envisages and whether the desire of some Member States to preserve their own independence will not draw a line at a point where the common policy of the Community will still leave a wide field open for national decision.[8] Moreover, the experience of the Federal Republic with the instruments of economic and cyclical steering devised in its financial reform of 1967 has not in all points been encouraging and the same may be true of other countries which have tried to develop a coherent cyclical policy.

Only one area remains free of future control of the Community. The fixation of wages remains entirely in the hands of employers and employees according to the Werner Report (p. 20). Here only a consultation of interested parties, organizations of employers and trade unions, is envisaged. This reflects the actual situation in the Member States which similarly leave crucial elements of their economic planning to the decisions of the two sides of industry. Anyone who reflects upon the towering position of the trade unions in modern European democracies will recognize the difficulty of coping with this problem on an international level.[9]

The regional policy destined to raise the income and standard of life in the poorer regions of the Community, will demand considerable sacrifices from some of the Member States.[10]

At the Paris Summit of October 1972, the heads of states and governments proclaimed it their aim to develop the relationship between the Member States into a European Union by the end of the seventies.[11] Does that mean an alteration of the structure of the Community into a sort of federal unity? It would be too soon to seek an answer to this question now. But there is no doubt that the realization of the economic and monetary union as well as the pursuit of the other goals, would lead to a considerable enlargement of the powers of the Community. How will this influence the status of the Member States?

Through the application of Article 235 of the Treaty and through the jurisprudence of the European Court a certain expansion of the powers of the Community has taken place. I need only refer to the well-known ERTA judgment on the right of the Community to represent their members *vis-à-vis* foreign nations in economic negotiations.[12] Also, the Paris Summit of 1972 underlined the necessity to make the widest possible use of Article 235.[13] But there seem to me to be limits here. Within the Community, the idea of implied powers can certainly be applied.[14] But can the Treaty of Rome or the whole legal basis of the Community simply be re-interpreted into a Constitution under which powers can be derived from the system as a whole?[15] Even if one does not stress the nature of the Treaty as an international agreement and recognizes an evolutionary force working within the Community, one will still have to insist on explicit legal bases for structural changes in its situation *vis-à-vis* the individual states. It is true that the Community's situation cannot simply be compared with that of other functional international organizations. But as far as one of the most important of these is concerned, i.e. the United Nations, the British judge at the International Court of Justice, Sir Gerald Fitzmaurice, recently in a

70

dissenting vote rejected emphatically, from a legal point of view, any extension of functions of its institutions by an interpretation of the Charter.[16] I do not therefore consider it possible that the mere extension of community jurisdiction brought about by the realization of the economic and monetary union can in itself be interpreted as a change in status of the Member States, as a transition to confederal or even federal forms. After all, the members of the EEC still indubitably wish to remain internationally independent states and be recognized as such within the international sphere. Probably the Member States will eventually pose more stringently the question of what powers remain at their disposal and they will perhaps try to reach agreement on the distribution of competences between the Community and its members.

I am conscious—and to this extent I agree with Ipsen[17]—that these problems cannot be dealt with by a simple adoption of the institutions of a federal or confederal model. But however one wishes to describe the Community legally—and I refrain from a definition—it is a union of independent states. A fundamental alteration of this status cannot take place in the guise of a gradual, so to speak imperceptible, evolution, as a result following from a growing economic interdependence. I find myself unconvinced by this previously much propagated view. What is needed here, if fundamental changes take place, is a clear and explicit decision. This will not be needed for the development of closer co-operation in foreign relations on the basis of the Davignon Report of 20 July 1970. That will not exceed normal forms of international understanding between independent states. But the new economic policies may pose other questions. The extension of the Community's powers in the crucial sphere of national economic independence, brought about by alterations in the Treaty could possibly involve a change in the constitutional status of the Member States. As far as the law of the Federal Republic of Germany is concerned, the question may be asked at this point whether the authorization of Article 24 of the Federal Constitution would support a step which would in fact put responsibility for the economic and social policy in the hands of a supranational authority.[18]

III. The New Policies and the Powers of the Community

Let us now turn to the question whether the wide powers envisaged for the Community can be ascribed to it on the basis of the existing treaty or whether amendments are necessary. The question also has to be answered how far a model of an economic and monetary union can be carried out within the powers of the different Community institutions as they exist at present. In this respect it should first be made clear that the joint control envisaged in the economic and monetary union is throughout concerned with areas in which a start has already been made towards co-operation and control. I will now list the main areas briefly:

(a) Monetary Policy

The necessity for co-ordinating monetary policy was recognized at an early date[19] and in 1964 a Monetary Committee with advisory status and a Committee of Central Bank Presidents was set up with the consent of the European Parliament.[20] It was, too, decided at this time that alterations in rates of exchange by the Member States—which are reserved to them under Article 107 (2) of the EEC Treaty—should only take place after previous consultation.[21] For credit and interest rate policy, however, no progress has been achieved beyond a non-binding determination of data. The basis for a co-ordination in monetary matters can be derived quite easily from Article 107 (1) of the EEC Treaty. For credit policy the Community could rely on the powers contained in Article 67 for setting up a free capital market, as well as drawing on Article 70 which authorizes the co-ordination of foreign exchange policy, also by means of directives. These provisions provide in particular the basis for measures of a binding character, which abolish the disparities and discriminations in the movement of capital. Since, however, Article 107 (2) explicitly leaves the responsibility for the change rates to the individual states, it cannot be regarded as a sufficient basis for setting up binding provisions in this field. This is particularly true of the establishment of a Central Bank System, since Article 107 provides no basis for such an institution. For the establishment of a monetary union, therefore, the EEC Treaty does not offer an adequate legal basis.[22]

(b) Economic Policy

In this area, in which a Committee for medium-term economic policy was set up in 1964,[23] the Community has so far embarked on co-ordination by producing three programmes for medium-term economic orientation (1967, 1969, 1971),[24] which fix orientation data of indicative character, especially on the subject of the evolution of prices and growth. A policy of co-ordination can be founded upon the provisions of Article 105 whereas decisions taken for financial assistance to Member States are regarded by the Council as coming under the special norm of Article 108.[25] Article 105, however, does not provide a basis for the setting up of binding data on economic development[26] which anyhow would scarcely be practicable if they should serve beyond a short-term period.

(c) Cyclical Policy

In this field the Treaty grants the Community institutions—in Article 103 (2 and 3)—the power to make binding regulations. It could, therefore, in a crisis for example, issue directives for a short-term economic policy.[27] Drawing the line between short-term and general economic policy is not helped by the unclear definitions of Article 104 of the Treaty and should be

72

done according to general principles: short-term measures of economic policy are to be regarded as 'conjunctural' or cyclical policy, placed under Article 103, whereas the long-term overall economic policy must be brought under Articles 104–109 which do not offer the same powers to the Community.[28]

(d) Budgetary Policy

In this sphere, not specially considered in the Treaty, the Community has already shown considerable activity. The importance of co-ordination on this point was early recognized and by 1964 the Council had set up a Committee for budgetary policy.[29] Consultations take place. But the economic and monetary union will here have to achieve the introduction of basic data both for the scope and for the interior structure of the budgets of the single states. A legal basis for these measures has yet to be created. For the progressive harmonization of indirect taxes, however, Article 99 gives the Council adequate decision powers.

(e) Regional Policy

Until the late sixties the regional policy of the Community was mainly orientated towards the approbation of national programmes according to Articles 92–94 of the EEC Treaty. Since then, and with the enlargement of the Community by the entry of the new members, a new and wider conception has been elaborated, which found the approvement of the representatives of the governments of Member States in a resolution of 20 October 1971.[30] The regional policy is now destined to bring about, using as a basis Article 92, a massive assistance to those areas of the Member States which stay behind the average level of income and industrial activity within the Community. Following the resolution of the Paris summit of 1972, a Regional Fund has been established in 1973.[31] No decision has yet been reached as to the volume of financial contributions for this Fund. Nevertheless, one can expect that this domain will acquire greater importance in the future. Assistance to the backward areas is an essential contribution towards a closer economic co-operation.

To sum up the conclusions of this survey, some of the wider aims of the Community, especially in the field of cyclical and regional policy, can be reached by making use of the existing dispositions of the EEC Treaty. For other purposes, especially in the sphere of monetary, economic and budgetary policies, new powers for the Community will have to be provided. As the Werner Report itself recognized (pp. 13, 14), alterations in the Articles 103, 105 and 107 will become necessary if the Community is to be empowered to issue binding directives for a common economic and monetary policy. Action of the Community in the forms of consultation and recommendation which have been applied for a long time will not be sufficient to bring about the deeper changes demanded by such a common policy.[32] Amendments to the Rome Treaty, however, have always proved to be attainable only by a slow and difficult process. It is therefore understandable that there is a search for legal solutions within the general provisions of the Rome Treaty so that formal alterations of the Treaty could be avoided. We shall now examine briefly these legal possibilities, which could be found in making use of Articles 100, 145 and 235 of the Treaty.

(a) The view has been put forward that Article 100 gives the Community institutions the power of enacting regulations for reasons of legal harmonization in economic spheres, even where these would otherwise be outside its jurisdiction. In principle this is correct, but this view does not take into account the meaning and scope of Article 100. It serves to harmonize national laws wherever the realization of the Treaty's aims comes up against differences in such national laws—even in spheres outside these aims of the Treaty. But as far as economic policy is concerned, it is not a difference in legal rules which has to be overcome but one of politico-economic outlook which causes the disagreements. Article 100 allows the abolition of barriers against achieving the intended aims of the Community, but not the determination of the aims themselves.[33]

(b) Nor can any basis for an extension of powers be found in Article 145. It is true that it gives the Council a part to play in decisions about economic policy and its co-ordination, but it affords no independent allocation of powers, which could for instance extend the powers of the Community in a general way. The importance of Article 145 lies in its division of functions between the institutions of the Community, not in its determining the powers of the Community itself in relation to the Member States.[34]

(c) Among the Treaty provisions which make an extension of the powers of the Community possible the most important is Article 235. In cases where activities are deployed within the framework of the general aims of the Common Market, it permits the supplementation of such powers which are lacking but which are essential for the realization of these overall aims. Such powers, which are not specifically provided in the Treaty, but are required for the execution of its general aims, may be supplied by a resolution of the Council on a proposal by the Commission and after consultation with the European Parliament. To this extent Article 235 permits within the limits provided by the aims of the Treaty a completion of the Treaty system of powers by particular procedure. In doing so it does not provide the basis for a general extension of powers as they are allocated by the Treaty, establishes no 'Kompetenz-Kompetenz'; but it authorizes the limited supplementation of the Treaty. On the other hand, Article 235 does not contain, as is occasionally suggested, an authorization of the use of 'implied powers'. The application of this concept may be founded on other, general conclusions. Article 235 does not relate to individual allocations of powers which might be extended by interpretation; it envisages the case where such powers are not contained in the Treaty.[35] Article 235 also makes possible the enactment of substantive provisions alongside that of procedural regulations. But in the latter case, too, there are limits of applicability. The general aims of the Community within which Article 235 can be applied comprise those aims named in the Treaty itself. Along with Article 3 of the Treaty in which those aims are described in more precise form, Article 2 must also be included, although it should be noted that it contains very general definitions of aims, which cannot be simply translated into rules authorizing actions and powers.[36] Article 235 can never provide the basis for going beyond those tasks laid down by the Treaty. In the interpretation of Article 235, too, the prevailing view tends rather towards a cautious assessment of its scope.[37] The same is true of its practical application, which has restricted itself till now to supplementary clauses in more restricted spheres.[38] Article 235 seems only to be applicable where the aims formulated in the Treaty are clearly indicated as being tasks and fields of action. It affords no basis for any widening of the aims of the Treaty or of the powers of the Community into new spheres not covered by the general principles formulated at the beginning of the EEC Treaty. Therefore I do not think that Article 235 can offer an adequate basis for the authorization of activities for whole areas (e.g. economic policy) if these areas are not covered by the general terms of the first articles of the EEC Treaty.[39]

In view of the long procedure required for formal alterations of the Treaty and the difficulty of achieving the necessary agreement for them from all Member States, a marked tendency can be observed to use Article 235 to its utmost limits. That corresponds to the recommendation made by the Paris Summit of October 1972 which explicitly demanded that the possibilities of Article 235 should be fully exploited.[40]

IV. Reforms in the Institutional Structure of the Community

The last years have seen an extensive debate on the effectiveness of the existing institutional framework of the Community. This debate was initiated not only in view of the future development of new policies of the Community which will demand a high degree of efficiency from the organs of the European Association, it was also provoked by the shortcomings visible in the action of the Community organs. If the Commission has continued to work out new programmes and new measures for the implementation of the aims of the Community, the readiness of the Council to discuss these proposals and to pass the necessary enactments has been weakened during recent years. A further impetus for a new examination of the distribution of powers among the organs of the Community comes from the demands of the European Parliament that its participation in the decision-making process should be strengthened. The discussion has not led to general agreement on the future shape of the organization but it has produced valuable analysis of the problems involved.

First, the former preoccupation with federal or confederal structures has now receded into the background. The process of a long and voluntary integration of a number of European states by freely entered agreement takes a different course from the establishment of federal units depending sometimes on particular sweeping historical events. On the other side, it should not be overlooked that in the Community, too, the taking over of central functions of social control results in repercussions and problems which may be similar to those of a national unification in federal form. It will nonetheless be useful to recall the particular features which the structure of the Community possesses in contrast with the organization of a state.

(a) The pattern of decisions to be taken at Brussels does not completely correspond to the pattern on which a state functions. The Community is chiefly geared to action through issuing general rules or through non-binding co-operation, beside which individual decisions play only a limited role. But the acts of the Community are not to be compared simply with legislative acts. In many cases they represent rather measures (*Massnahmen*), that means directives for the economic decisions of the Governments, adjustments to changing economic circumstances, establishment of data for economic decision-making. It would therefore be incorrect to work here simply with the traditional pattern of separation of powers.[41] A better starting point would be the proportionate participation of the different institutions in the decision-making process which varies according to the type and structure of these institutions. It is increasingly recognized today, as regards national decision-making, too, that precisely such decisions as economic planning, fixing budgetary priorities and short-term economic measures do not sufficiently involve parliamentary action if this is confined to formal legislation or subsequent control and that therefore 'preventive control', that is participation in preliminary decisions, is becoming essential.[42]

(b) The Community forms an organization which has to combine two levels of decisions, the Community level and the national one. This cannot be without effect on the structure of the institutions. They must on the one side serve Community interests and common orientation but on the other side they must express the variety of the Members and their agreement by means of special procedures. The present structure takes this situation into account: on the one hand, the Commission embodies and activates the common European element; on the other hand, the Council of Ministers reflects in its composition and in its voting rules the combined decision-making which is taking place among the Members. Any development will have to retain this basic structure for the immediately foreseeable future.

In the last decade, the Council of Ministers has taken the leading role in the Community. The hope, embodied in the constitution of the Community, that the common spirit of unity would become the decisive element, has not been realized. The Community has stayed at the level of an organization, in which actual agreement must perpetually renew itself. The Council of Ministers, therefore, created as a common organ of the Members,[43] approaches today more the character of a ministerial conference. It is the place where the Member States must meet in order to reach decision. This function of the Council means that its procedure is less important: whether more in the manner of pre-established unanimity or majority decision, or in the form of negotiations orientated towards a necessary agreement. The application of the majority principle within this framework may therefore not necessarily seem to be a problem of the first magnitude. As long as a certain degree of integration is not attained, the stronger members at any rate can evade any pressure from the majority in points essential to them. Although one may regret the Luxembourg protocol of 19 January 1966, factually instituting the unanimity rule, as affairs stand at present, it is not unrealistic. One should, however, demand that the Council be ready to follow another rule in all such matters as do not touch important questions.[44]

(c) An important question remains: Is there a sufficient democratic basis for the decisions of the Community? Upon closer examination the legitimacy of the decisions still rests substantially on the representation of the Member States in the Council and so on the democratic structure on national level.

In practice the Parliament, too, as it is today, does not play a purely European or Community role. As a result of its being composed of members from national Parliaments it is based indirectly on national representation. It is true that the Parliament has, in its votes, always expressed the common European interest. But it lacks still the background of a transnational party organization and of strong interest groups on the European level. One could attribute to the Commission—in a metaphorical sense—a sort of functional European legitimacy,[45] which admittedly is no real substitute for a true democratic legitimacy. In general, European legitimacy coming from the entire population of the Common Market area is still only weakly developed, since there is still no unified European consciousness. The European Community therefore will need for a long time yet the legitimacy coming from the single Member States. The idea that the Council should cease to play the leading role and develop into a second chamber seems to me to be not justified. Such a change could only come about if truly federal structures would result.

In the discussion on the improvement of the institutions of the Community two demands were strongly expressed: The call for a strengthening of the power of decision-making of the main organs, springing from a critical assessment of the relations between Commission and Council; and second, the need for a better democratic legitimacy of the whole activity of the European bureaucracy. In recent years, the Council has adopted some small improvements in its procedure. But the main attention has been fixed on the enlargement of the powers of the European Parliament. When

77

an amendment to the Treaty regarding certain budgetary provisions was accepted by the Member States on 22 April 1970, creating independent financial resources of the Community, the Commission undertook to submit proposals for a strengthening of the budgetary powers of the European Parliament. In preparing its suggestions, the Commission instituted in July 1971 a Working Party with the mandate to study the whole range of questions connected with the extension of the powers of the Parliament. The group, under the chairmanship of the French Professor Georges Vedel, laid its report before the Commission on 25 March 1972. The report discusses critically the situation within the Community and recommends a gradual extension of the budgetary and legislative powers of Parliament, closer co-operation between Parliament and Commission, and adds some proposals on the improvement of the decision-making process and on the composition of the Parliament. It dwells explicitly on the legal means by which some of the intended reforms could be transferred into practice by agreement between the organs of the Community without alteration of the Treaty itself.[46]

Sharing the usual fate of such reports, the Vedel Report has not had any immediate effect. Its proposals have been debated in the European Parliament on 5 July 1972, and later proposals have drawn upon its ideas. The discussion is still going on. The Parliament has repeatedly passed resolutions on the strengthening of its legislative and budgetary powers,[47] and the Commission has laid before the Council proposals for an enlargement of the budgetary powers of the Parliament.[48] I will return to these developments when discussing the future position of the individual organs of the Community. But it is not intended here to go into details or to put forward precise suggestions or a model for the future institutional structure.[49]

First, I may make some preliminary observations on the difference between the structure of the Community and the constitutional organization of a national government.

National constitutions and their principles, especially the system of parliamentary government (responsible government) seem to me not to offer suitable models for the future development of the European Community. Here are some reasons for this opinion.

The European work at Brussels rests on a constant creation of a consensus between independent states and governments. The main task is to provide a general agreement. Therefore, the agonizing form of changing party governments, familiar to parliamentary regimes, would be unsuitable for this purpose. At the present stage of development a European administration cannot take on a party character, but must stand on the common interest of all concerned, on their common consensus. This makes me incline to the view that the possibility, which is often put forward, of giving the European Parliament the power to pass a vote of censure to the Council of Ministers, does not assess the situation correctly. Even the

78

power, given by Article 144 of the EEC Treaty, to pass such a vote against the Commission is somewhat artificial.[50]

One has also to look carefully into what lies behind the concepts of responsibility and control. In so far as they mean information and co-operation, in so far as Parliament is more deeply involved in decisions and its point of view heard and considered, then responsibility describes a justified demand. As far as control is concerned, it will have to be closely examined whether this is an appropriate concept as regards, for instance, medium-term planning or the budget. Here any subsequent control would come for the most part too late and would not open up any effective possibility of influence. What could be of help here, as has already been indicated, is some kind of 'preventive control', a participation in the basic decision-making at an earlier stage. This need not necessarily take place at a plenary session of Parliament; it could also be done by committees. In the framework of the Community, the Parliament is not the sole body with legislative faculties. It can, therefore, in matters of legislation, aspire to a role of participation in the form of co-decision.

Finally the idea of a division of powers is not one which seems to me to be simply transferable by adopting the national division between executive and legislative. I have already pointed out that the nature of the decisions taken here is structured differently from those within domestic politics. In addition, there is in the European institutions a division of power implicit in the working together of European and national elements, which also operates in the institutional structure of the main organs. To sum up, it must be stressed that models which consider European development in the sense of a European government stemming from the Commission with the counterweight in the form of the European Parliament leave out of consideration the changes which have already taken place since the beginning of the sixties in the functions and in the influence of the organs of the Community. For the span of time with which we are in practical terms concerned, the central decision-making power of the 'federal' element embodied in the Council of Ministers will remain indispensable and decisive.

If we turn now to a discussion of the future position which should be ascribed to the main organs of the Community in the development of the next period, emphasis should be laid on a greater efficiency of the decision-making process. The necessity to reach common decisions based on a recognition of a common interest should be strengthened. A change to forms of international negotiation, to a style practised in organizations of a looser coherence, the tendency to find agreement on the point of least resistance, will not form an adequate basis for the creative processes demanded by the tasks of the Community and will endanger its future. It is essential to retain a strong element of common interest, of readiness and capacity to set a priority for the common interest even if sometimes the balance between the national give and take is not secured. The question

79

whether the vote in the Council is taken by majority vote or by unanimity, seems to me, I repeat, not to be of primary importance.

The great European function and the political role of the Commission have to be underlined. Even if the Commission cannot be regarded as the basis for a future European government, but rather as a central administrative authority for the Community, its role must be considered as fundamental. On it devolve two decisive functions:

(a) It has to a great extent the initiative for future developments, as is provided in the Treaty of Rome by concentrating the initiative for new measures substantially in the hands of the Commission. It must remain the dynamic, progressive institution which derives its 'functional legitimacy' from its European mandate.

(b) The Commission has not only to make the day-to-day decisions, it is also responsible as a political institution for the cohesion of the Communities. It can suggest and bring about compromises, it must remain the driving force of the Community, the factor which can promote the higher interests of the whole union beyond the particular national interests. The position of the Commission ought not to shrink down to the limited functions of a general secretariat of the Council.

This position of the Commission should not be impaired by new institutional developments within the Community which create new separate organs of co-operation. It would not be a healthy outcome if a situation of rival bureaucracies grew up through the creation of a second bureaucratic machinery attached to the Council of Ministers. New Committees and institutions should in principle be attached to the Commission. It should be added that there are often substantial advantages inherent in an extension of the committee system, also because it offers interested parties an opportunity to participate.

The Commission can only remain equal to its tasks if it continues as an organ with a genuine political destination. This depends also on the personal capacities and weight it can assemble. In order to underline the importance of securing for the Commission the nomination of personalities of political status, the Vedel Report has suggested that the choice of the members of this body, which must remain in the hands of the single Member States and their agreement, should undergo approval by the Parliament through a procedure of investiture.[51]

As regards the Council of Ministers, its strong position as expression of the agreement achieved in the consensus of Member States will be indispensable throughout the next period. One should not, however, fail to recognize that the legitimacy obtained through the Council of Ministers which can only be one that has national support, does not adequately correspond to democratic requirements. But each individual national government remains responsible to its own Parliament, even if in most countries of the Community the control of the national legislature over European affairs is not too strongly developed. In a structure consisting of independent states, this second national-chain of legitimacy, to a certain extent a federal one, is of great importance, though it may give place one day in the more distant future to a real European legitimacy based upon institutions of a European character. As the Council remains the main source of decision in the Community, it will be useful to strengthen in a limited way the direct contacts between the Council and Parliament. This has been done already in recent years by the elaboration of practical devices. The Council has declared itself ready to explain any considerable deviation from the lines Parliament has indicated in the course of the legislative procedure. It is also ready to report from time to time to the Parliament and discuss matters. There is, however, a limit to these procedures which also affects the answers given to questions from Parliament. The representative of the Council must speak for the whole Council and his statements rest on previous agreement in the Council. That sets limits to the representation of the Council before Parliament.

An urgent necessity is the better organization of the deliberations within the Council in order to facilitate agreement and overcome the stagnation which has occurred in the last years on many fields of common activity because the Council could not find time and opportunity to deliberate on many proposals of the Commission. Various proposals of a merely technical nature have been prepared,[52] but the real problem lies in the readiness of the governments not to insist in every detail on a pursuit of national interest.

In the last years, a new method of co-operation among the Members of the Community has opened up with their co-operation in the domain of foreign policy. Following the suggestions made in the Davignon Report of 27 October 1970, the foreign ministers of the single states meet at regular intervals and seek to elaborate a common attitude towards international events, even, as in the Copenhagen Conference of December 1973 to define a common 'European Identity'.[53] One should not overestimate this development. In the autumn of 1973, no understanding was possible against the threat of the Arab Oil boycott. But there is no doubt that closer economic co-operation presupposes also a common basis in foreign policy.[54] Up to now, political co-operation, according to the conceptions of some Member States, remains separate from the other institutions of the Community. One can doubt whether this situation will serve its purpose in the long run.

During the last years the debate on institutional reform of the Community laid its main emphasis on the position of the European Parliament.[55] With the widening of the powers of the Community, the need for a stronger democratic legitimacy of its decisions and its whole machinery became more seriously understood.[56] The first step towards a strengthening of the powers of Parliament, especially in the budgetary field, was made at the time of the Luxembourg Treaty of 22 April 1970 which amended the EEC Treaty, introducing from 1975 on a financial system for the Community based on own resources. The new dispositions gave Parliament wider powers for the period up till 1975 and more so after that time. But still they were very limited powers. Parliament obtained a free decision only for those expenses that did not necessarily result from the Treaty or from acts adopted in accordance with it (Article 203 (8)). They amount to no more than 3—4% of the whole budget. There was also no agreement whether, even after 1975, Parliament should have the right to reject the whole budget in toto. Unlike Parliament the Commission and the Council did not accede to this opinion.[57] The Paris Summit of 1972 restated the intention of the other organs of the Community to provide for larger participation of Parliament.

In the legislative field, the Vedel Report developed the idea that Parliament, which now is normally only consulted on specified matters, should acquire a right of co-decision (with the Council) for a limited area of important acts, such as ratification of international treaties, application of Article 235 or enactments of great financial consequences.[58] Parliament, in its resolution of 5 July 1972, demanded similar powers and even went as far as to demand participation in all legislative acts of the Community. In this domain, however, no great change has occurred. The Commission proposes no more than a second consultation of Parliament if after its first deliberation considerable changes in the draft have occurred in the ensuing procedure.[59]

The main enlargement of parliamentary powers is foreseen in the budgetary sphere. The proposals of the Commission of 10 October 1973[60] recognizes the Parliament's power of global (not partial) rejection of the budget. If Parliament rejects the draft budget, a procedure of conciliation between it and the Council will have to be instituted. This change would have to be achieved by a further amendment to the Treaty. The Council, in its meeting of 5 June 1974, has now acceded to these alterations. The Parliament will also acquire powers for the subsequent control of the execution of the budget.[61]

These new powers will not drastically alter the role of Parliament, but they reveal a tendency to lay more emphasis than formerly on the legitimacy resulting from parliamentary approbation. In the past, the European Parliament has always proved a firm advocate of the European interest. This is remarkable if one considers its composition of members of national Parliaments who derive their democratic legitimacy from a national election to a national body. Until the disposition of Article 138 (3) of the EEC Treaty, providing for direct election for the members of the European Parliament through the peoples of the Member States, is transformed into binding Community law, the composition of Parliament raises some problems. The dual function of the members of the European Parliament, sitting at the same time in their national assemblies, which is intended as an active link between the European problems and the institutions of national representation unfortunately fulfils this role only incompletely. The

European delegates, who are often absent, sometimes for a considerable time, from their domestic parliaments, are not influential enough when at home. It also occasionally happens that the national Parliaments do not take sufficient notice of the decisions taken at European level. The connection between those two levels, therefore, is not sufficiently safeguarded.[62] The problem is not easy to solve, but recently some useful suggestions have been made (European delegates as additional members of national Parliaments, perhaps with limited vote, composition of the European Parliament by other persons than members of national Parliaments, or combinations of these methods).[63]

The opinion is widely held that the introduction of direct elections to the European Parliament, as foreseen in Article 138 of the EEC Treaty, would result in a much stronger position of the Assembly. One may entertain some doubts whether these hopes could be so easily fulfilled. There are as yet no genuine European parties and many interest groups still see their main task in acting on the national scene. It is doubtful whether deputies who are not at the same time representatives in the national Parliament would exercise great influence at home, and whether important personalities could be found for this function. There is also the danger that independent European elections—not connected in time with national elections—would not attract a big enough electoral poll to be truly representative. Nevertheless, the call for direct elections finds considerable backing, and it might even be possible that national Parliaments act for themselves in altering the form of election of their national members.[64]

In conclusion, I would like to underline once more that the real problems of the Community in its present crisis do not lie with the institutional problems alone. What is needed in order to overcome the present actual stagnation is a sober realism, laying aside a somewhat euphoric outlook which for a long time has been regarded as a guarantee of progress, the restoration of a real solidarity between the members, and the limitation of a narrow national viewpoint and a firm resolution to stick to the fundamental principles of the Treaty. If it is possible to set in motion a 'relance' of the European spirit, institutional changes in the directions indicated here could assist the much needed return of the Community to more vigorous action.

Notes

Ulrich Scheuner is Emeritus Professor of Public Law at the University of Bonn. The essay was originally published in (1971) Integration, *European Studies Review, edited by the Commission of the European Communities, Brussels, pp. 145–161. It was revised by the author in May 1974. Translated by R. H. Ockenden.*

1. The basic resolution on the economic and monetary union was taken at the conference of heads of State and governments in The Hague on 1–2 December

1969 (No. 8 of the Communiqué cf. *The Times* of 3 December 1969, p. 5). Its more precise form was the subject of the report of the Werner Committee appointed by the Council which after consultation with the Council on 8–9 June 1970 published its report on 13 October 1970. (Special Supplement to the *Bulletin* 11/1970 of the European Communities). The Council and the representatives of the government of the Member States voiced their opinion on it favourably in a decision of 22 March 1971 (*Journal Officiel* C 28, 27 March 1971, p. 1 *et seq.*). See Beate Kohler and Gert Schlaeger, *Wirtschafts- und Währungsunion für Europa*, 2nd ed. (Bonn 1971); K. D. Ehlermann, 'Entscheidungen des Rates zur Einleitung der Wirtschafts- und Währungsunion', (1972) *Europarecht*, p. 16 *et seq.*

2. The devaluation of the French franc on 10 August 1969 amounted to 11·11%, the revaluation of the Deutschmark on 27 October 1969 made a 9·29% difference. On the duty of previous consultation Chr. Tomuschat, 'Die Aufwertung der Deutschen Mark', in *Beiträge zum ausl. öffentlichen Recht und Völkerrecht*, vol. 55 (1970), p. 15 *et seq.*

3. See the suggestions worked out by the Commission in: *Third General Report on the Activities of the* EEC, 1969, para. 1, III, para. 2.

4. For the present situation as regards co-ordination see Everling, *Die Koodinierung der Wirtschaftspolitik in der Europäischen Wirtschaftsgemeinschaft als Rechtsproblem* (1964), p. 19 *et seq.* and Hans von der Groeben, *Die Europäische Wirtschaftsgemeinschaft als Motor der gesellschaftlichen und politischen Integration* (1970), p. 17 *et seq.*; Andreas Sattler, *Die Europäischen Gemeinschaften an der Schwelle zur Wirtschafts- und Währungsunion* (Tübingen 1972), p. 95 *et seq.* An example of a medium term programme which provides data and orientation is the Third Programme agreed by the Council on 9 February 1971 for medium term economic policy (J.O. 1 March 1971, p. 1 *et seq.*).

5. For the very different legal position of the Central Banks of the Member States, see the publication of the Monetary Committee: *Die währungspolitischen Instrumentarien in den Mitgliedstaaten der europäischen Wirtschaftsgemeinschaft* (1962). On the independence of the Federal Bank in the Federal Republic and its connection with the economic policy of the government see Dirk Uhlenbruck, *Die verfassungsmässige Unabhängigkeit der Deutschen Bundesbank und ihre Grenzen* (Munich 1968); Heiko Faber, *Wirtschaftsplanung und Bundesbankautonomie* (Baden-Baden 1969). For the development of the powers of the Community necessary to achieve the aims of the economic and monetary union see Report of the Commission to the Council of 19 April 1973, KOM (73) 570—D final.

6. For the conception of regional policy, see *General Report* 1969, Chapter IV, para. 6, and *General Report* 1970, Chapter II, Part I, para. 2.

7. Cp. here Badura, *Wirtschaftsverfassung und Wirtschaftsverwaltung* (1971), p. 55 *et seq.*; Reiner Schmidt, *Wirtschaftspolitik und Verfassung* (Baden-Baden 1971), p. 180 *et seq.*; Klaus Stern/Paul Münch/Karl Heinrich Hansmeyer, *Gesetz zur Förderung der Stabilität und des Wachstums der Wirtschaft* (2nd edn. 1973).

8. On the other side, a mere co-ordination of economic policies will not be sufficient to secure an effective common cyclical guidance. There must be a real transfer of decision-making powers. See Hans von der Groeben/Ernst Joachim Mestmäcker, *Ziel und Methode der europäischen Integration* (1972), p. 98.

9. Cf. Ludwig Rosenberg, 'Die Verantwortung der Gewerkschaften in einer zukünftigen Währungs- und Wirtschaftsunion, in (1972) *Europa-Archiv*, p. 305 *et seq.*

10. Cf. Hugh M. Begg and J. Alan Stewart, 'Die Regionalpolitik der Europäischen Gemeinschaften, in (1973) *Europa-Archiv*, p. 489 *et seq.*; Second Report of the Committee for Regional Policy to the European Parliament, Doc. 228/73 of 13 November 1973.

11. Communiqué of the Conference at Paris of 19 and 20 October 1972, para. 16 (*The Times* of 10 October 1972, p. 4).

12. (1971) 10, *Common Market Law Report*, p. 335, with a commentary by Sasse (1971) 6 *Europarecht*, p. 208 *et seq.*; see Werbke (1971) *Neue Juristische Wochenschrift*, p. 2103 *et seq.*, and the debates in the European Parliament of 5 July 1972 (J.O. 1972, No. 152).

13. Communiqué, para. 15.

14. On the relevance of this concept to the EEC, see Nicolaysen, 'Zur Theorie von den implied powers in den Gemeinschaften', (1966) *Europarecht*, p. 129 *et seq.*; H. P. Ipsen, *Europäisches Gemeinschaftsrecht* (Tübingen 1972), p. 436 *et seq.*; P. J. G. Kapteyn/P. Verloren van Themaat, *Introduction to the Law of the European Communities* (1973), p. 73.

15. To a limited extent in this sense Nicolaysen, *ibid.*, p. 140 *et seq.*

16. International Court of Justice, Advisory Opinion of 21 June 1971: *Legal Consequences for States of the Continued Presence of South Africa in Namibia* (*South West Africa*), *notwithstanding Security Council Resolution 276 (1970)*, Diss. Opinion of Sir Gerald Fitzmaurice, p. 208 *et seq.* Sir Gerald ascribes to the Assembly certain implied powers, but he considers any actual 'extension of functions' to be inadmissible.

17. H. P. Ipsen, *Verfassungsperspektiven der Europäischen Gemeinschaften* (Berlin 1970), p. 10; *idem, Europ. Gemeinschaftsrecht*, p. 189.

18. This problem is also broached by Everling in *Die Entwicklung der Europäischen Gemeinschaft zur Wirtschafts- und Währungsunion* (1971) *Neue Juristische Wochenschrift*, p. 1486.

19. Cf. Report of the Economic and Finance Committee of the European Parliament (Ph. C. M. van Campen), Doc. 17/1962/63 of 7 April 1962, p. 15, and the resolution of the Parliament of 7 October 1964 (J.O., p. 2664).

20. See the report of the Economic and Finance Committee of the Parliament (Francis Vals), Doc. 103/1963/64 of 10 January 1964, as well as the resolution of the Council of 8 May 1964 (J.O., p. 1207).

21. See the declaration of the Permanent Representatives of the Governments of Member States of 8 May 1964 (J.O., p. 1226). On the question of powers which led to the decision of the Permanent Representatives, see Everling, *Koordinierung*, p. 27; H. P. Ipsen, *Gemeinschaftsrecht*, p. 800 *et seq.*

22. See to the lack of adequate powers, Kapteyn/Verloren van Themaat, *ibid.*, p. 282; Ipsen, *Gemeinschaftsrecht*, p. 808.

23. Cf. Resolution of the Council of 15 April 1964 (J.O., p. 1031).

24. First Programme for a medium-term economic policy, 11 April 1967, J.O. No. 79, 25 April 1967; Second Programme of 12 May 1969 (J.O. L 29, 30 May 1969); Third Programme of 9 February 1971 (J.O. L 49, 1 March 1971). See K. D. Ehlermann (1972) 7 *Europarecht*, p. 16 *et seq.*

25. The Council interpreted Article 108 as forming a special provision for

credit or financial assistance and excluding Article 103 (2), on which the Commission had founded its proposal. It rejected implicitly this wide interpretation of Article 103 (2). See Ehlermann (1972) 7 *Europarecht*, p. 19 *et seq.*; Kapteyn/Verloren van Themaat, *ibid.*, p. 289.

26. Similarly Waelbroeck, *Droit des Communautés Européennes* (*Les Novelles*) (Brussels 1969), No. 2260; Ipsen, *Gemeinschaftsrecht*, p. 783. Economic programmes of a non-binding character can be based upon Article 105, EEC Treaty (Ipsen, *ibid.*, p. 786 *et seq.*).

27. Cf. Waelbroeck, *Les Novelles*, Nos. 2270 and 2271; Everling, *Koordination*, p. 23 *et seq.*; Fuss, *Mitteilungen der Gesellschaft der Freunde der Universität Mannheim* (1969), vol. 1, offprint, p. 5; Ipsen, *Gemeinschaftsrecht*, p. 788 *et seq.*

28. Similarly Waelbroeck, *Les Novelles*, No. 2264. On Article 103(2) see now: Eur. Court of Justice Case 5/73, Rec. 1973 p. 1107 *et seq.*

29. Resolution of 8 May 1964, J.O. No. 77, 21 May 1964.

30. Resolution of the representatives of the governments of Member States of 20 October 1971 (J.O. C 111). See Kapteyn/Verloren van Themaat, *ibid.*, p. 247.

31. Communiqué of the Paris Summit of 1972, para. 5. Report of the Commission of 4 May 1973, Doc. KOM (73) 530 final, and the report of the European Parliament, Doc. 120/73.

32. Cf. on the disappointing effects of the beginnings of the economic and monetary union, General Report 1070, Chapter II, Part I, para. 2; Interim Report on the gradual realization of the economic and monetary union of 5 November 1970, Doc. 148/70 of the European Parliament, p. 9.

33. Similarly Berthold Goldman, *Les Novelles*, Nos. 2212, 2217. See also H. P. Ipsen, *Gemeinschaftsrecht*, p. 687 *et seq.*

34. See Everling, *Koordinierung*, p. 21; Fuss, *ibid.*, p. 6; Kapteyn/Verloren van Themaat, *ibid.*, p. 278 *et seq.*

35. Cf. on the nature and scope of Article 235, Hans Peter Gericke, *Rechtsetzungsbefugnisse nach Article 235 EWG Vertrag* (Hamburg 1970), p. 74 *et seq.*; H. P. Ipsen, *Gemeinschaftsrecht*, p. 433 *et seq.*; Kapteyn/Verloren van Themaat, *ibid.*, p. 72 *et seq.*

36. A general summary of the aims described in Article 2 in view of their application in the context of Article 235 is given by Gericke, *ibid.*, p. 22 *et seq.* There is, however, no possibility of deriving new spheres of action from the vague declarations of Article 2 where these were explicitly left by Article 3 to the jurisdiction of the Member States. Similarly Oppermann, (1971) 6 *Europarecht*, p. 133.

37. A cautious interpretation is offered also by Everling, *Koordinierung*, p. 22; Nicolaysen, *ibid.*, p. 133, who rejects new objectives introduced via Article 235; equally Roger Pinto, *Les Novelles*, No. 1711, who dismisses any extension of powers vis-à-vis Member States; Kipp, 'Verhandlungen der 11. Tagung der Deutschen Gesellschaft für Völkerrecht', *Berichte der Gesellschaft Heft* 10 (1971), p. 233; Jaenicke (*ibid.*, p. 219) is rather more open, also H. P. Ipsen, *Gemeinschaftsrecht*, p. 433 *et seq.* See further for a moderate interpretation, G. Graf Henckel von Donnersmarck, *Planimmanente Krisensteuerung in der Europäischen Wirtschaftsgemeinschaft* (1971), p. 21 *et seq.*, and Zuleeg, (1974) 99 *Archiv des öffentlichen Rechts*, p. 152 *et seq.*

38. On the subject of the practical application see Gericke, *ibid.*, p. 94 *et seq.* Article 235 has won a new importance through the declaration of the Heads of State and Governments at Paris on 20 October 1972. It seems to be the intention

of the organs of the EEC to base the necessary steps as far as possible on the existing powers of the Treaty. In this sense also the report of the Commission to the Council of 19 April 1973 (point IV A) Doc. KOM (73) 570—D final.

39. Similarly see Oppermann, *ibid.*, p. 133 *et seq.*

40. See to these questions also Ehlermann, (1971) *Integration*, p. 166.

41. See in the same sense Much in 'Staat und Wirtschaft im nationalen und internationalen Recht', *Schriftenreihe der Hochschule Speyer*, Vol. 22 (1964), p. 156; similarly H. P. Ipsen, *Fusionsverfassung europäischer Gemeinschaften* (1969), pp. 28, 30.

42. On the problem of an early participation of Parliament on the decision-making process, see Bäumlin, 'Schweizer Jusristenverein', 1966, *Heft* 3, p. 244 *et seq.*; my own interpretation in 'Das Grundgesetz in der Entwicklung zweier Jahrzehnte' (1970) 95 *Archiv des öffentlichen Rechts*, pp. 378/379; W. Kewenig, *Staatsrechtliche Probleme parlamentarischer Mitregierung am Beispiel der Arbeit der Bundestagsausschüsse* (Hamburg 1970), p. 23 *et seq.*

43. For further details see Walter Hallstein, *Die Europäische Gemeinschaft* (Düsseldorf 1973), p. 62 *et seq.*

44. This opinion is not shared by a strong group which regards the application of the majority principle as indispensable for any progress in the Community. See Hallstein, *ibid.*, p. 66, who justifies it with the view of a future role of the Council as second Chamber; Apel, 'Europa am Scheideweg', (1974) *Europa-Archiv*, p. 100.

45. On this 'legitimacy by procedure' see Ipsen, *Gemeinschaftsrecht*, pp. 163/164.

46. 'Report of the Working Party examining the problem of the enlargement of the powers of the European Parliament', *Bulletin of the European Communities* Supplement 4/72. For a critical evaluation see E. W. Fuss, 'Positionsstärkung des Europäischen Parlaments' (1972) 7 *Europarecht*, p. 358 *et seq.*; J. A. Frowein, 'Zur institutionellen Fortentwicklung der Europäischen Gemeinschaften' (1972) *Europa Archiv*, p. 623 *et seq.* (both papers are also published in this volume, p. 143 *et seq.* and p. 127 *et seq.*).

47. See resolutions of 5 July 1972, J.O. C 82, 21 July 1972; 5 July 1973, J.O. C 62, 31 July 1973.

48. Report of 5 October 1973, Doc. 1848/73. Document on Strengthening of the Budgetary Powers of the Parliament, COM (73) 1000 final of 10 October 1973.

49. For a discussion of the institutional structure and suggestions about its future see Karlheinz Neunreither, 'Bemerkungen zum gegenwärtigen Zeitbild des Europäischen Parlaments' (1971) *Zeitschrift für Parlamentsfragen*, p. 321 *et seq.*; Maurice Lagrange, 'L'Europe institutionelle. Réflexions d'un témoin', offprint from No. 144 (June 1971) *Revue du Marché Commun*; Chr. Sasse, 'Die Zukunft der Verfassung der Europäischen Gemeinschaft' in (1972) *Europa-Archiv*, p. 87 *et seq.*; Ipsen, *Gemeinschaftsrecht*, p. 1026 *et seq.*

50. In November 1972, M. Spénale, chairman of the Finance Committee of the Parliament, brought a motion of censure to the Parliament (Doc. 214/72). Its aim was to censure the Commission for not having laid before Parliament in time proposals for the extension of the budgetary powers of Parliament. In the debate on 11 December 1972, M. Mansholt, President of the Commission, succeeded in explaining the delay involved, and on 12 December M. Spénale withdrew his motion (J.O. Annexe, No. 156, December 1972). Later, Parliament reached the

conclusion that a motion of censure should not be brought by a single member. Altering Article 21 of its Standing Orders, Parliament decided that such motion would require in future the support of a parliamentary party or of a tenth of the members actually serving in Parliament (session of 11 December 1973, J.O. Annexe No. 166, December 1973). On this occasion, Sir Derek Walker-Smith spoke of the vote of censure as a 'brutum fulmen' (J.O. Annexe No. 166, p. 73).

51. 'Vedel Report', English version, Chapter IV, section 7, p. 58. This suggestion has met with approval in the literature and has found acceptance even in papers of the Commission. Cf. SEC (72) 1597 final of 25 May 1972. Sometimes it has also been suggested that the President of the Commission should be given a more prominent role. See Frowein, *ibid.*, p. 624 (and in this volume, p. 128). See further Karlheinz Neunreither, 'Transformation of a political role: Reconsidering the case of the Commission of the European Communities' (1971/72) 10 *Journal of Common Market Studies*, p. 233 *et seq.*

52. See 'Vedel Report', Chapter VII, section 4, p. 77 *et seq.*; Frowein, *ibid.*, p. 624 *et seq.* (and in this volume, p. 128).

53. The political cooperation was underlined at the Paris Summit of October 1972. Its limited effect is critically recorded by Hallstein, *ibid.*, p. 336 *et seq.*

54. See Everling, 'Europäisches Gemeinschaftsrecht' (1974) 13 *Der Staat* p. 81.

55. On the weak position of the Parliament among the institutions of the Community and the serious limitations on its participation in decisions see Alexander Schaub, *Die Anhörung des Europäischen Parlaments im Rechtsetzungsverfahren der EWG* (Berlin 1971); Andreas Sattler, *ibid.*, p. 150 *et seq.*

56. Indeed, in the first session of the European Parliament, in which the British delegates participated (16 January 1973), Mr. Peter Kirk insisted on the need for strengthening the powers of the democratic institution of the Community (J.O. 1973 Annexe No. 157).

57. See Ehlermann, (1973) *Europa-Archiv*, p. 826 *et seq.*; Kapteyn/Verloren van Themaat, *ibid.*, p. 123 *et seq.*

58. 'Vedel Report', Chapter IV, section 2, p. 37 *et seq.*

59. In its proposal of 10 October 1973 the Commission went a step further and admitted in cases where important financial consequences would result from an enactment, that instead of a second consultation Parliament should be able to ask for a conciliation procedure between itself and the Council. Doc. COM (73) 1000 final Part V, and cf. Ehlermann, *ibid.*, p. 827.

60. COM (73) 1000 final.

61. See Ehlermann, *ibid.*, p. 829 *et seq.*

62. On the problems of the composition of the European Parliament and of the institution of direct elections to the Parliament see Neunreither, 'Bemerkungen zum gegenwärtigen Leitbild des Europäischen Parlaments' (1971)[2] *Zeitschrift für Parlamentsfragen*, p. 321 *et seq.*; the article of the author, 'Bestandsaufnahme und Prognose zur Fortentwicklung des Europäischen Parlaments', *ibid.*, vol. 3 (1972), p. 496 *et seq.*

63. Such suggestions were amply discussed in the Symposium organized by the European Parliament at Luxembourg on 2 and 3 May 1974.

64. The Bundestag has repeatedly had such proposals laid before it by the political parties. See the latest of them in a bill laid before Parliament by the Socialist and Liberal parliamentary parties on 5 December 1973 (Bundestag, 7th electoral Period Drucks. No. 7/1352).

Christoph Sasse

THE COMMISSION AND THE COUNCIL

*Functional Partners
or Constitutional Rivals?*

1

Even those of us who, beyond the expectations of Professor Ipsen, in
whose honour this article appears, have read more than merely the chapter
'Constitutional Perspectives' in his *Summa iuris europaei*,[1] will be particularly intrigued by the new perspectives opened up there. This may explain
the direction taken by this short contribution, since the institutional perspectives in Professor Ipsen's work on European law have long enjoyed
a position every bit the equal of his assessment of the legal issues themselves.[2] This lies in the nature of the material. Hardly anywhere is the
legal view of the forms of political association so marked by 'dynamism'
and progress, or so vulnerable to the maelstrom of time[3] as in studies on
European law.

2

Unfortunately it must be added that for some years now it has no longer
been possible to explain this need for perspective in terms of a wave of
juridical enthusiasm sweeping the imagination along with it. We have to
look rather to a growing feeling that the development of the Community is
tending to run counter to all expectations. One hardly need stress that this
also applies to its institutional framework, and in particular to the duo
'Commission—Council' which are the focus of attention in the discussion
here.

In this context it is irrelevant whether a part is played by secret hopes
of European constitutional policies out-manoeuvring the rigidity of
national political systems. At any event it seems clear that the zeal for

European reform remains undaunted in theory[4] and in—above all, parliamentary—practice.[5] This cannot be adequately explained as mere wishful thinking on the part of federalists—especially the German.

The depths and scope of the discussion on reform have their origin rather in the array of—seemingly surmountable—discrepancies, some inherent in the founding treaties, others only becoming apparent during their application.

I. The Antinomies of the Integration Concepts

3

The Community Treaties, particularly the Treaty of Rome, employ numerous federal instruments to realize their aims.[6] These include self-executing legislation as well as the establishment of an independent Commission as a planning and inceptive institution, the Council of government delegates with majority consensus and a comprehensive legality control. It may be recalled that these elements played a decisive role in the heated discussion which continued into the mid-sixties on the so-called precedence of Community law over national law.[7] The federal thesis of overlapping laws, requiring unrestricted effect within their own realm, or at any event, autonomy, is also taken up as a basis for the resolution of the conflict in Ipsen's study[8]; this may well have had a decisive influence on the course of the juristical discussion of the issue.

The same line is adopted in the official communiqués of the EEC Commission on the same subject[9] and in the important verdicts of the Court of Justice of the European Communities on 15 July 1964,[10] of the Italian Constitutional Court on 27 December 1965 and 27 December 1973,[11] and of the Federal Constitutional Court on 18 October 1967, [12] and 9 June 1971.[13] The interpretation of the effectiveness, of the '*effet utile*', which is by no means an innovation, although it creates the impression of a 'functional' approach, has in this context more the task of a public relations emballage.

4

But the Treaties themselves already show divergences from this federal technique. Directives and decisions to be passed to the Member States are given far wider scope than, for instance, comparable forms of legislation set down in the German constitutions in the Weimar and present Federal Republic.[14]

The independent Community institutions lack the right of initiative in situations of considerable significance.[15] The Commission's power to implement normative acts of the Council is subject to the latter's discretion.[16]

Important sectors whose key function was apparent from the onset have been taken out of the hands of the federal instruments—areas like economic

90

and monetary policy[17] and social policy[18]—or else they have, if at all, been only vaguely or partially allotted to the Communities—such as energy policy, research (technological) policy, and regional policy.

The imbalance between the Institutions in the Treaty also deviates from the requirements of a federation, if this implies the premises for the creation of a new viable political unit, within its jurisdiction.[19] The burgeoning of the federative institution 'Council' in both legislation and administration conflicts with such an aim just as much as the constitutional weakness of the Commission and the Parliament do. The Treaties only provide the latter with the role of an embryo nurturing democratic ideals, not that of an institution participating in decision-making, a complete contrast for instance to the German 'Customs Parliament' (*Zollparlament*) set up almost a century earlier,[20] empowered through direct mandate and serving as a genuine second chamber.

The vigour with which Bismarck established this institution in the face of considerable opposition from the South German States,[21] notably from Bavaria and Württemberg, can hardly be adequately explained by Prussia's aspirations of economic hegemony. The more important motive was the supposition—quickly borne out in practice—that the unitarian forces within the Customs Parliament would gain ground and thereby radically improve the decision-making capacity of the Customs Union (*Zollverein*) as a whole.

II. Elements in Comparing the Efficiency of the two Concepts

5

Fifteen years of application—the ECSC system can safely be disregarded as a series of experiments that was discontinued as early as 1957—have sharpened the contours of the typological ambivalence anticipated in the Treaties. The provisional result need not be gone into again here.[22] It permits a string of hypotheses.

6

The successes gained in establishing the Community are not independent of the available procedures for decision-making. Relatively speaking, it has been the creation of the Customs Union which has given rise to least friction, for it was provided with an outline structure in the Treaty and required only the peripheral support of acts of the Community Institutions. It has occasioned no crises. Of course its early establishment on 1 July 1968 may have been facilitated by the continued availability to the Member States of common[23] and autonomous[24] regulating mechanisms for inter-Union trade.

7

The abolition of discrimination, particularly concerning the liberalization of establishment and the right to supply services, can be said to have been successful in as far as no radical or re-structural intervention in national law was necessary. So it is not surprising that controls could be lifted on numerous technical trades,[25] whereas this has not yet been possible for the professions. An equally clear illustration is the relaxing of restrictive regulations on re-insurance and retrocession,[26] compared with the great difficulties in liberalizing forms of underwriting subject to public control.[26 bis]

Similar criteria apply to the free movement of capital (Articles 67 *et seq.*, EEC Treaty). This justifies the assumption that, within the framework of the Community constitution, we may expect federal decision-making procedures to bring about a satisfactory degree of assimilation only where the muscle of vested interests is not felt and which are only loosely subject to administrative regulation of the market structure.

8

It requires greater integration pressure to offset established systems with their vested interests than can normally be produced through the application of instruments available in the Treaty. This explains why the agricultural policy, but not the transport policy,[27] developed into an immense inverted pyramid, balancing on a few provisions in the Treaty. But anyone who would find the cause of this in a singular constellation of national interests alone would, again, only be getting at half of the truth. Without the Commission's active support, and without its tireless and imaginative deployment of the whole arsenal of decision-making devices of Community law, there would be no common agricultural policy, leaving aside the question of its service or disservice to the Community or individual Member States. Moreover, it is clear that the degree of integration in agricultural policy would be far less without the federal instruments provided under Articles 40 and 43. The government most immediately concerned is obviously aware of this connection. Apart from the unique case of Hallstein's 'crisis proposals' of 31 March 1965[28] this government, against its wont, has hardly ever criticized the Commission's stance in the agricultural sector, nor the Commission's—admittedly moderate—use of its powers, and it has come to terms with Community mechanisms such as the so-called Management Committee Procedure in this sector, whereas the extension of such procedures to other Treaty matters has always met with bitter opposition.[29]

9

The counterproof of the opinion discussed hitherto also leads to a fairly clear conclusion: where no provision is made for federal procedures in the Treaties, no concerted Community actions worth naming have as yet developed. The Commission's recommendations pursuant to Article 37 (6) EEC Treaty regarding the adjustment of commercial State monopolies were largely disregarded.[30] Of the conventions provided for in Article 220 only two were concluded, both in 1968. Since then one has finally come into effect on 1 February 1973.[31] Co-operation on medium-term economic policy, which emerged from the Council's resolution of 15 April 1964[32] has brought only very disappointing results.[32a]

Not even an optimist could pretend that any of the three programmes drawn up on medium-term economic policy[33] have had any relevant influence on the economic actions taken by the six governments. The co-operation between the committees concerned with short term economic policy[34] and budgeting[35] was just as unproductive—if one is seeking a greater degree of cohesion between the various national policies.

Over and above this, the lack of any decision-making mechanism laid down in the Treaties has a noticeably detrimental effect on the development of common, or at least co-ordinated policies in the areas of research and technology, industry, energy, and regional policy.

10

While it would certainly be a gross simplification to see in the uneven distribution of federal procedures more than one of the various elements determining progress or stagnation, it would, on the other hand, be too naïve to deny the import of this circumstance or to see in it merely the expression of differing degrees of an *a priori* willingness to integrate. This willingness to integrate was and is no greater in the agricultural than in the scientific and technological sector, no more strongly developed in the foreign trade sector than in relation to a common energy supply. The view that the powers of the Community Institutions gain greater acceptance as a result of the norming of aims and functions[36] is unable to explain these differing degrees of success satisfactorily. With some exaggeration, one might say: The common agricultural policy exists despite the most far-reaching popular dissatisfaction with its results; there is as yet no prospect of a common research or energy policy despite the largely positive reaction of the self-same public. It may well be that a whole complex of causes is behind this, as we have already stated, but one of them at least is also the differing extent of the availability of federal decision-making procedures.

III. Keeping Options Open as a Task

11

The continuing flexibility of the integration process, with respect to its final result,[37] is as apparent in the clashing procedures of the day to day pursuit of integration, already indicated, as in the contradictory ultimate aims. Indeed, one can say that these ultimate aims of a participating elite and of relevant groupings permeate—although with rather more negative than positive contours—Community routine as ever-present antagonisms, constantly seeking to polarize its timetable and actions around symbolic rather than real issues.

12

Thus it is that one will have to take a long, hard look at history before coming up with another decision-making body where arguments about procedure have such pride of place as they occupy in the European Community. Such things—mocked even by the press on occasion—as the question as to whether the Commission should be permitted to sign the Accession Treaty on 22 January 1972—which it played an essential part in formulating[38]—are merely the pin-sized tip of a depressingly large iceberg. Its nether regions extend from the ceremonial to be observed when heads of mission are accredited, the dispute about the publication of proposals made by the Commission before they have been passed, and the proper allocation of new committees under the Council's or the Commission's responsibility,[39] right down to the technical details of numerous sessions of committees and subcommittees, in which the Commission's role in implementing Community law—for instance relating to such important items as the power to determine the foodstuff analysis methods—is just as bitterly and doggedly fought for, as is the legal basis (Article 43 or 100) of the harmonization of the legislation on agriculture—by the way, a German speciality, for a change—or the 'form' for active and passive participation in a mixed Community delegation at some international negotiations or other, which are usually unproductive anyway. It would be a delightful historiographical task to chronicle the long years of this trench warfare of procedural experts in all its scurrility and with all its absurdities for the amazed scrutiny of a posterity who would have expected to find the enterprise being governed by the laws of reason and efficiency.

13

But it is not this latter viewpoint, nor the details of the squabble about Community procedures which are of interest here. It is rather the fact that the flexibility of the future of integration, its virtual spread between federation and 'special relationships', demands unremitting effort. This is taking place on all fronts, not only in the procedural skirmishes just mentioned, but also in the jostling for political influence in the capitals and before the public. In this connection, Vice-President Mansholt's controversial 'zero-growth' initiative[40] with its attendant publicity, particularly in France,[41] was certainly one of the most effective tactical moves to demonstrate to the informed public, in a counterattack as it were, the political value of an independent Commission, and to hit the governments in one of their vulnerable spots, namely their inability to introduce painful innovations.

14

The flexibility of the integration process is embodied in an arduous attempt to keep options open. One need only cast a sidelong glance at the Euratom Commission in the last years before the merger of the Executives (1 July 1967) to find confirmation for this statement. Here all was petrified apart from the ever deeper entanglement in governmental methods of procedure, the inadequacy of which led partly to the lethal consequence. That the EC-Commission has been incapable of undertaking any countermeasures only proves the untenability of the position.[42]

15

If our hypothesis holds good that the decision-making capacity of the Community is decisively influenced by the application of federal enactment mechanisms provided for in the Treaty, then much depends on maintaining these methods of procedure and if possible developing them further. From this aspect, the Commission's defensive behaviour—which the European Court of Justice has often supported[43], thereby carrying out the spirit of the Treaties in exemplary fashion, while others have misunderstood it as ivory-tower, prestige-hungry dogmatism[44]—takes on a deeper political significance. At the same time, attention focuses on the question of how the contradictory relationship between the mechanisms for federal decision-making and those for international consultation is going to develop in the foreseeable future. Will the former withstand erosion or perhaps even emerge strengthened and enlarged from the present criticisms? Or will they gradually crumble away and, strangled by new procedures, dwindle to a fossilized reminiscence?

IV. Partnership or Rivalry?

16

The question of procedures is at the same time a question of the Institutions to which they are attributed or which are identified with them. What are the forces which will have a formative effect on the relationship of the Council to the Commission in the coming years?

17

It would be too good to be true if this relationship were to develop in such a way that the two Institutions converged in a harmonious manner and complemented each other by dividing up the work-load.[45] Clearly, it is unproductive to look at the interrelationship of the two Institutions only from the point of view of the confrontation as to which of them represents the nucleus of a future European government, because it in fact remains highly uncertain whether the integration process will in any relevant future enter a stage in which this question will require an answer. So here, too, it is a matter of holding on to the principle of flexibility in the ultimate constitutional structure. But that also means rejecting such constraints as the late French President—who was renowned for his pragmatism—from time to time attempted to impose when he declared that any Government of Europe could only ever emerge from the Council.[46]

18

Unproductive as it is to extract criteria for the analysis of the present situation from such long-range hypotheses alone, it can in fact appear all the more tempting simply to combine the two rivals and to ascribe the leadership of the Community to one double Institution[47] which, in fruitful application of the principle of dialectic, conceives solutions in its planning head (Commission) while the executive arm (Council) decides on them. The problem with this model is, of course, drawing up such a sound definition of the scope and competence of the two part institutions, that the intended concord could gain ground. For planning does not take place only in the bosom of the Commission but also—mostly to the accompaniment of more publicity—on the part of the governments of the Member States, who for that very reason do not simply subordinate themselves to the expert knowledge of the Commission. When the Commission does succeed in pushing through some reform—which happens rarely enough[48] —this is more likely to result from tactical components (choice of the right moment, profiting from some particular constellation of interests) than from its proposals being carried by virtue of conviction. Generally speaking, the proposals which met another fate[49] were not lacking in such conviction either. To this must be added that the Commission's successes must be credited to some of its top men of the highest political calibre, and such men will become increasingly difficult to find if this Institution develops into simply a panel of experts in the employ of the governments.

19

The conception of a double Institution 'Council and Commission' implies in reality a significant shift of emphasis. Whereas the role of the Commission was formerly characterized by the political prestige of the task of leadership originally intended for it, a prestige to which parliament and public opinion continue to contribute, the transformation of the competitive relationship of the two Institutions into a team of government conference and planning committee already sets the seal on one of the possible lines of development. Even if, in the event, the Commission were still a valuable negotiating partner, because it alone would be in a position to formulate a supranational Community view, it must be realized that its unitarian political responsibility would be exhausted.

20

The rivalry between the two Institutions leading the Community also comes under the category 'flexibility' in the present integration process.

The European common interest,[50] the Commission has been at pains to seek out, has derived no small profit from it. This common interest would be served least of all by any premature judgement on the Commission's political future, since this would of necessity affect the application of Community procedures and hence the chain of decision-making.

V. Future Opportunities: 'Deepening' the Community and Economic and Monetary Union

21

It is of course quite apparent that the federalistic decision-making process under the auspices of the Commission will in any event be put to severe test in the near future. Judging from the late President Pompidou's remarks on the status of the new committees[51] there is scant hope of directing the accumulated 'spill-over' in the sectors of industrial structure, research and development, regional policy, and environment into the network established by the Treaty of Rome.[52] Alone the creation of official Commission participation in programme-planning and instrument utilization, as recently proposed by the same in relation to the distribution of development contracts based on Article 235,[53] would be considered a success in this context.

22

But it is just as conceivable that the Committees of top-ranking national civil servants[54] here provided for with their far-reaching competence especially in finance should force the Commission into a peripheral role. Such a development is even relatively probable, although it would run directly counter to the idea of globalizing the politico-economic decision-making processes under the control of a European Institution.

23

The Commission's chances of any real collaboration and those for the formation of some federal decision-making procedure are, if anything, even less favourable in that sector which it has become customary to designate as 'the gradual realization of economic and monetary union'.[55] The approaches in this direction so far, namely the three decisions of the Council of 22 March 1971,[56] have been characterized by an extremely meagre content as far as compulsory provisions are concerned,[57] in strange contrast with the verbose proclamation of aims in the non-binding resolution of 9 February—22 March 1971.[58]

Tri-annual examination of the economic situation; increasing the scope and volume of consultation in the Monetary Committee and the Committee of Central Bank Presidents; mid-term credits, narrowly restricted in extent,[59] reduced to insignificance by the politico-economic conditions

97

attached[60] and moreover made up of voluntary contributions[61]—all these are just as far removed from any procedural integration of economic and monetary policy as is the creation of the 'Co-ordination Group', a special body of high-ranking national officials to act as a Co-ordinator for short-term economic policy under the Council.[62] So far its results are not en-couraging. As far as economic policy is concerned this is unlikely to change in the immediate future—a fact attributable to the Community Institution system's lack of legitimation[63] and the reluctance of the part-ners to put forward a united front in this central area offering such fruitful opportunities for national governmental publicity.

24

So, in the context of these observations, the misgiving gains impetus that the harmonization of the economic policies of the Member States—regardless of its results[64]—will weaken the autonomy potential of the Community. Instead of 'deepening'—as we know the Economic and Monetary Union was embarked upon under the second motto of the French triptych '*achèvement, approfondissement, élargissement*'—it might be more appropriate to speak of a 'levelling off'.

25

The efforts to achieve progress towards monetary union have taken a somewhat different course, at least for the time being. A means of co-operation independent of other sectors has grown up since the central banks' agreement on a system of short-term intervention.[65] It found its clearest expression in the narrowing of the Community exchange-margins to ±2·25% in the Basle Agreement of 24 April 1972[66] and in the establish-ment of the European Monetary Co-operation Fund through the Council regulation of 3 April 1973.[67] If in the near future this fund were to administer a part of the reserves of the Member States as provided for in the com-muniqué to the Paris Summit (Par. 2)—the Commission's proposals in 1973 to entrust the fund with an initial 20% of national monetary reserves (reduced later to 10%) has however not found the approval of the Council —and was to be in possession of instruments to mould monetary policy, a kind of European monetary federalism could quietly crystallize, isolated from ideological confrontation and only loosely aligned to the Com-munity. As the need for consensus hardly arises here, in fact technocratic control is even expected, this particular method of integration ought only to reach its limits where continuing divergencies in the various national economies cause economic and social tensions which can no longer be absorbed by a system of monetary co-operation alone. This diagnosis proves itself in the decision taken by France—under the threat of a deple-tion of national reserves in the face of continuing trade deficits—to leave the 'snake' for an initial six months, beginning 18 January 1974. It remains to be seen how long the 'ailing earthworm' thus remaining can withstand the pressures threatening to erupt from such divergences in foreign political, monetary, and employment spheres. Nonetheless, for the jurist interested in the aspects of integration these seeds sown towards a consolidation of monetary co-operation remain a worthy effort for further progress of the decision-making technique in this particular domain without prejudicing the principle of flexibility in the further course of integration.

VI. Political Co-operation

26

The labile equilibrium of the antagonistic structure of decision-making as laid down in the Treaties is threatened from yet another quarter. We are talking about the European Political Co-operation (EPC) initiated in the so-called Luxembourg Report of 27 October 1970 and further developed by the Copenhagen Report of 23 July 1973.[68] Nothing need be added to the highly competent accounts of EPC which already exist.[69]

27

While EPC itself is a consequence and, at any event, an important corollary of Community integration, it cannot, on the other hand, be denied that as the political octopus flourishes and reaches out its tentacles to embrace all sectors,[70] a state of affairs might arise which could only be described as a restoration of earlier complexity. Certainly as a result of its deficiency in foreign policy, the Community has been unable in many matters relevant to external affairs—one need mention only farm prices, Mediterranean associations, and trade with East Block countries—to adjust its operations to the whole spectrum of politically significant situations. It is, however, just as certain that decisions have often been made possible precisely because of this. If in the case of agricultural policy the whole burden of considerations affecting world trade and development had been under consideration right from the outset, there would still be no Common Agricultural Market to-day—with all that would imply for the rest of the Community.

28

So the filling in of all political gaps in the integration chessboard can easily result in manoeuvrability diminishing rather than increasing. Whereas the Community has recently—in trade policy towards the USA, for example —been not infrequently able to derive advantages from its political indolence, this will probably change in direct ratio to the integration process's increasing sensitivity to foreign policy transactions. This will apply particularly if one supposes that EPC will not lead to the establishment of a European political power centre in the foreseeable future, but will limit itself instead to more or less successful efforts at harmonization.[71]

29

Numerous facts speak for this hypothesis. The EPC method is suitable for formulating a limited consensus but not for the development of any autonomous unit capable of independent action and reaction to stimulus. Diverging attitudes have hitherto prevented the extension of EPC into certain sensitive areas such as security and transatlantic relations, which could not be excluded from any attempt at a genuinely joint foreign policy. But the most important obstacle in the way of political integration lies in its military costs: For the Western European states the interim retention of their advantageous 'parasite role' depends firstly on their ability to act individually in foreign policy and secondly on their collective capacity remaining correspondingly negligible.[72] As opposed to this, the attraction of political association, in so far as the latter is to transcend the level of reflection found in soap-box oratory, tends to be slight and appears to be dwindling still further in the train of East-West *détente*.[73] Not even the wish to counter the multinational companies with a political parallel will—however justified it is—lend wings to political unity at the moment. So a political union worthy of the name lies in the remote future.

30

The danger of unsettling pulsations emanating from the EPC and disturbing the function of Community procedure must be considered against this background. If Mediterranean questions, the possible co-operation with state-controlled trading-partners, or external monetary policy are raised within the framework of EPC, these and their possible results cannot fail to influence the programming and timing of corresponding Community initiatives. Negative experiences gained through EPC, as well as inhibiting effects produced by foreign political considerations, threaten to penetrate through to the Community's delicately balanced decision-making process.

31

One misunderstanding must be cleared up immediately, however: With or without EPC, the Community's 'need of politics' is considerable, bearing in mind its high-pitched aim of economic and monetary union. To believe that economic integration might still make substantial progress as some kind of functional process under expert control is an illusion. The limits of this technocratic method have already been reached in most sectors, especially the central ones. How does the optimal satisfaction of needs by the Community (is it really so optimal?[74]) engender so much loyalty that the existential importance of such issues as taxation, value of money, and full employment is no longer felt as having to be dealt with within the framework of the *national* political system?

So it is not a question of denying the Community decision-making process any element of the 'political'—which is admittedly complex and encumbered by the need to obtain democratic legitimation—but the

100

question is merely of *how* this element can be so attributed to the integration process, that its flexibility and productivity suffer as little as possible. Looked at in this way, EPC—if it is to flourish—is still a not completely satisfying construction.[75]

VII. Consequences

32

The federal machinery for decision-making incorporated into the Treaty of Rome and with it the basic openness of integration, even in the direction of an autonomous political union, are threatened with retreat into the background. Verbal aggression on the one hand, a lukewarm rejoinder on the other, and everybody's need to take a 'concrete' line are contributing to the promotion of the 'Davignon formula'. The fashionable cloak of pragmatism which is draped round it should not deceive anyone as to its insignificance for integration—i.e. its sluggish innovation and the instability of its results.[76]

33

If the opinion stated above holds good, that the goals attained so far were conditioned *inter alia* by the use of the machinery of federal procedures, other consequences become apparent: Any attempt to encroach on the mechanisms for federal decision-making, even if only *de facto*, as a by-product of *'approfondissement'*, *'élargissement'*, or Pan-European disciplining, is fundamentally incompatible with the Treaty of Rome—its normative nature remaining unimpeached—as well as with the unanimously confirmed role of the Community as the 'original nucleus' of nascent European unity.[77]

If at present, as it appears, no 'strengthening' of the unitarian Community Institutions[78] is possible, it would be logical if the Commission in its very specific function as watch-dog were to find a more general support from *these* governments whose political equality in European questions is essentially connected with the constitutional structure of the Community.[79]

34

In Community practice, this end would be served if the status of the Commission could be raised in terms of its members and international consideration. This could be achieved at small political cost. Also, the principle of majority voting ought not—*horribile dictu*!—to become completely obsolete, especially since it will not be as easy in the future as it has been in the past[80] for the government particularly averse to this procedure to prevent its use in every application by abstaining. It is hardly to be expected that this government will find much of a following among the new members—except on vital issues[81]—for its systematic boycotting.

35

Among the open possibilities one must also include attempts to subject the complementary actions in industrial, research and technological, regional, and environmental policy to the discipline of the Community. It is beyond dispute that Article 235 EEC Treaty does permit a multi-stage elaboration of provisions[82] necessary for this purpose. If this attempt is not made, not only will the result be a negative prognosis for the success of the new activities mentioned, but increased tensions will arise within the Community system, which will work towards the dismantling of the 'classical' procedures. This applies in still greater measure to the pursuit of the common economic policy once this stage has been reached. If things stop short—contrary to the clear conceptions of the Werner Committee[83]— at attempts at co-ordination using the Commission purely in an advisory capacity, this will have severe repercussions on its role in implementing the Treaty itself. One can get some indication of this by observing the reluctance of the merged Commission to rid itself of the obsolete duties of the High Authority—laid down in the ECSC Treaty.[84]

36

Anyone who is concerned to preserve the Community's character as—if one may venture to repeat this ugly word from so prominent a circle—'original nucleus' with regard to the future form of Europe cannot simply pass over the confused relationship between the Community and EPC without a thought. The first Luxembourg Report is remarkably terse on the point:

> Comment is required of the Commission insofar as the work of the Ministers has any effects on the activities of the European Communities.[85]

This can have various interpretations: from the inclusion of the Commission as early as in the preliminary work of the Political Committee on relevant issues (the optimal solution), down to the opportunity of comment in writing on acts which the Ministers after private preparation have already provisionally passed (the minimal solution). Actual practice, which seems to be establishing itself somewhere in the bottom third of this scale[86] is not yet considered as definite by many governments, especially as far as the prospect of setting up a special secretariat for EPC is concerned. What possible solutions are there?

37

Since it is difficult to decide in problems of foreign policy which issues will affect the Communities and which will not, the President of the Commission, who should enjoy the confidence of all governments, ought to participate regularly in the ministerial consultations. It might safely be left to his tact to stay away from sittings on certain points like, for example, the recognition of Bangladesh.

The alliances at the Political Committee and its sub-committees level must, if possible, lead to an osmosis of Community procedure and EPC, if one takes into account the objections mentioned above under VI.[87] Only in this way can an imbalance of political authority between the two be prevented in the long term, and the EPC be co-ordinated into the highly differentiated and correspondingly sensitive decision-making system of the Community with the least disturbance. This could be attained if the Commission were represented in the Political Committee by one of its highest civil servants,[88] and conversely, the Chairman of the Political Committee were given direct access to the President of the Commission and possibly the right to speak directly before the Commission. Corresponding measures must also apply to the sub-committees of the Political Committee insofar as they are concerned with Community affairs.[89] The embryonic personal contact which is present here would have to be extended and a reciprocal relationship of the PC sub-committees to the Council groups with the same responsibilities created.

38

The alliances indicated could be effected most effortlessly under two hypothetical conditions—though not dependent upon either. If a political secretariat is set up in Brussels, this is a clear preliminary decision in favour of an institutional approximation towards the Community. If this secretariat is further connected with that of the Council or if the EPC comes within the sphere of European Secretaries of State who would have their headquarters in Brussels, the interaction we have described will result almost of necessity. However, since both these hypotheses are fraught with numerous uncertainties, the less controversial goal of simply linking EPC and Community ought to be given priority.

VIII. Conclusions

39

The foregoing plea for the retention of the federal features in the Community's constitution may strike many as the typical blind faith in salvation of a credulous constitutionalist. It is nothing but the expression of the idea, tempered by experience, that the machinery for decision-making constitutes an independent, decisive if not a lone integration factor. The transformation of Community procedures into notoriously inefficient forms of co-operation thus also entails a truncation of the content of the objectives as these are laid down, as valid as ever, in the Treaty of Rome. The same achievements in integration that are being enticed out of government bureaucracies with the aid of Community procedure—even if arduously and recalcitrantly—require under other methodological conditions an incomparably higher degree of developed social integration. In this is seen immediately the inadequacy of formulaic recipes like 'form follows function'[90] or vice versa. The reality of Western European Community-making long ago left the rudimentary stage in which issues call out for the diffuse transnational solution and produce the forms and groupings appropriate to them more or less automatically. To place one's hopes in this kind of automatic process when the Community is confronted by new tasks is thus either a naïve childish trust or else a resolute dismantling of the Treaty.

The openness of the final goal of integration multiplies the possible political choices in the future. The jurist's modest contribution on this topic is to draw attention to the task of preserving this constitutional flexibility in the face of daily strife with conflicting systems of organization.

Notes

Christoph Sasse is Professor of Public Law and European Community Law at the University of Hamburg. The essay was originally published in (1972), 7 Europarecht, pp. 341–357 (Verlag C. H. Beck, Munich). It was revised by the author in June 1974. Translated by C. J. Wells.

1. Ipsen, *Europäisches Gemeinschaftsrecht*, 1972, Section 54, p. 975 *et seq.*
2. *Der deutsche Jurist und das europäische Gemeinschaftsrecht, Verhandlungen des 45. Deutschen Juristentages*, vol. II L, 1964; *Fusionsverfassung Europäische Gemeinschaften* (1969); *Verfassungsperspektiven der Europäischen Gemeinschaften* (1970).
3. On this, see Ipsen, *'Constitutional Perspectives of the European Communities'*, in this volume, p. 217 *et seq.*
4. Cf. the imposing volume of secondary literature used by Ipsen in the chapter mentioned above.
5. Cf. *inter alia* Rainer Barzel's *Vier-Stufen-Plan für die politische Union Europas*, (1971) 16 EA p. D 384 *et seq.*; the Resolution of the 8th Congress of the Social Democratic Parties of the European Community (28–30 June 1971); (1971), 16 EA p. D 386 *et seq.*; the programme for action of the CDU/CSU Parliamentary Group outlined in a statement to the press of 18 January 1972; the official publication of the Proceedings on the First Colloquium of the European Parliament on the topic: 'The position of European Unification and the Role of the Parliaments', Strasbourg, 15 and 16 March 1972; the report of the Member of Parliament Prof. Furler on the extension of the powers of the European Parliament, made on behalf of the Political Committee of the European Parliament, Doc. No. PE 28.266; the Resolution of the CD Parliamentary Group of the European Parliament 'on the constitutional and institutional further development of the European Community', Doc. GT/519/72 of 4 April 1972; see also the so-called Vedel Report of 25 March 1972 and the suggestions of the Commission regarding the 3rd item on the agenda of the summit conference based on that Report.

6. This statement on community formation has nothing to do with whether the Community is a full, partial or prefederation. This is not the question here. The word 'federal' is used here instead of 'supranational' as found in Schwarz, 'Federating Europe—but how?' in this volume, p. 1 *et seq.* at p. 37, or in Etzioni, *Political Unification,* 1965, *passim* (e.g. p. 301).

7. Cf. especially the work of Ophüls, whose influence on the formulation of the Treaty is notorious (see Hallstein, *Festschrift Ophüls,* 1965, p. 1, in particular: (1951) NJW p. 289; (1961) ZHR p. 136; (1963) NJW p. 1697; (1963) b. p. 137.

8. *Das Verhältnis des Rechts der europäischen Gemeinschaften zum nationalen Recht,* Beiheft 1965 to the periodical ZHR, p. 29.

9. See particularly the speech of the then EEC Commission's President, Walter Hallstein, delivered before the European Parliament on 18 June 1964.

10. Case 6/64 *Costa v. Enel,* 1964, p. 425. For a detailed discussion cf. Sasse, 'The Common Market: Between International and Municipal Law', in (1966) *Yale Law Review,* p. 695 *et seq.*

11. Case 98, *Acciaierie San Michele v. ECSC, Foro Italiano* (1964) I, col. 460; (1967) 6 CMLR p. 160; (1966) EuR p. 146 and Note *Glaesner;* sentenza no. 183/Anno 1973.

12. BVerfGE vol. 22, p. 293.

13. BVerfGE vol. 31, p. 145.

14. *Grundsatzgesetzgebung* and *Rahmengesetzgebung,* Article 11 of the Weimar Constitution and Article 75 of the present Federal Constitution (*Grundgesetz*).

15. E.g. Articles 28, 111, 113, of the EEC Treaty.

16. Article 155 (4) of the EEC Treaty.

17. Articles 104, 105 and 107 (1) of the EEC Treaty.

18. Article 117 *et seq.* of the EEC Treaty.

19. Cf. H.-P. Schwarz, *op. cit.* (fn. 6), in this volume p. 7, with additional literature.

20. Treaty of 8 July 1867, BGBl. 1, p. 81 *et seq.*

21. See E. R. Huber, *Deutsche Verfassungsgeschichte* (2nd ed.), vol. III, 1969, p. 632 *et seq.*

22. Cf. in this respect Klaus Meyer, 'Die Integration und ihre Institutionen', in *Aussenpolitik* No. 22, 1971, p. 646 *et seq.*; Sasse, 'Die Zukunft der Verfassung der Europäischen Gemeinschaft', (1972) 32 EA, p. 87 *et seq.,* and in *Kölner Schriften zum Europarecht* (KSE), vol. 22, 1973.

23. Protective measures pursuant to Articles 115 and 226 of the EEC Treaty.

24. Turnover tax and purchase duty.

25. For example, the production of provisions and fine foods, beverages, iron- and metal goods, leather goods, shoes and clothing etc., cf. Sattler, 'Die Entwicklung der Europäischen Gemeinschaften von ihrer Gründung bis zum Ende der EWG-Übergangszeit', (1970) JöR NF p. 4 *et seq.* (at p. 12 *et seq.*).

26. Sattler, *ibid.,* p. 14.

26 bis. Cf. Directive of 24 July 1973, *Official Journal of the European Communities,* (O.J.) No. L 228/20.

27. The same applies to the fact that a third multiannual Euratom research programme (Article 7, Euratom Treaty) could only be adopted on 5 February 1973, i.e. more than five years after the end of the last five-year programme. This is due, among other reasons, to the fact that no government has had more than a marginal interest in the achievements of Euratom's research since the French

re-orientation of their reactor policy in 1969. In a political constellation like this, any treaty machinery for decision-making must simply remain idle.

28. Doc. COM (65) 150. Document 27, *Sessions of European Parl.*, 1965–66.

29. See the article by Ehlermann, (1971) EuR pp. 250 *et seq.*, at pp. 253–259.

30. Cf. the survey given by Deringer, 'Die staatlichen Handelsmonopole nach Ablauf der Übergangszeit, Zur Auslegung und Anwendung des Art. 37 EWGV', (1971) EuR pp. 193 *et seq.*

31. For details, see Ipsen, *Europ. Gemeinschaftsrecht*, p. 696–7 and Seventh General Report on the Activities of the E.C., 1974, p. 144 *et seq.*

32. *Official Journal of the European Communities* (O.J.) 1964, p. 103.

32 bis. In this connection one may cite the Werner Report as a key witness: p. 8 of the printed version (Special Supplement to the Bulletin No. 11, 1970).

33. The programmes of 11 April 1967, O.J. p. 1513; of 12 May 1969, O.J. p. 1; of 9 February 1971, O.J. L 49, p. 1.

34. Council Decision of 9 March 1960, O.J. p. 764. The competence available to the Council under Article 103 (2 and 3) was not used to influence the short term economic policy directly.

35. Council Decision of 8 May 1964, O.J. p. 1205.

36. Ipsen, *Fusionsverfassung*, p. 62; *loc. cit.* (fn. 3).

37. Ipsen, *Europ. Gemeinschaftsrecht*, p. 995–996, 1054–1055 (and in this volume p. 183 *et seq.* at p. 196 and 242).

38. See K. O. Nass, *Englands Aufbruch nach Europa*, 1971, p. 57–65.

39. The squabble about the Committees for Industrial Policy, Science and Development, Regional Policy and the Environment, which went on for years, was considered important enough by the French President for him to make a statement in person on the topic. In his press conference of 21 January 1971 he declared that such auxiliary institutions were both necessary and useful, insofar as they were subordinated to the Council (*Le Monde*, 23 January 1971, p. 2 *et seq.*).

40. Letter to President Malfatti of 9 February 1972, *Le Monde*, 6 April 1972, p. 2.

41. See, e.g., the reply given by Vice-President Barre on 9 June 1972—*Communauté Européenne—Informations*, No. 29, 1972, p. 3 = 30 *jours d'Europe* No. 168–69, p. 21 *et seq.*; also the rejoinder by M. Marchais, *Le Monde*, 6 April 1972, p. 2; good summary in L. Reboul, La Lettre Mansholt, Réactions et Commentaires 1972; further, the ORTF broadcast, *A armes égales*, Mansholt *versus* Gaston Roux on 18 May 1972; see also the report in the *Nouvel Observateur* on the open discussion between Mansholt, Marcuse, Edmond Maire and others, No. 27, p. 41 *et seq.*, and the comment by P. Chatenet, *Le Monde*, 12 September 1972, p. 21.

42. Little has been changed, either, by the Memorandum with which the Commission recommended to the Council in the middle of June 1972 a total re-structuring of nuclear research and its incorporation into an all-embracing Community policy for Research and Development (Résumé in *Communauté Européenne—Informations*, No. 29 1972, pp. 6–7), apart from a very modest pluriannual Euratom research programme. The attempt to 'upgrade the common interest' has come to grief because of the terrain lost up to date on the procedural front, and because of the particularly bitter resistance of the national bureaucracies in that sector for which there are various reasons.

43. Recently, for example, in the European Road Transport Agreement Case, No. 22/70, (1971) 10 CMLR 33 and in the Supply Agency Case, Rs. 7/71.

44. In this direction, for instance, Wieland Europa (Ralf Dahrendorf), *Die Zeit*, 9 July and 16 July 1971.

45. As considered possible by, e.g., K. Meyer (Deputy Secretary General of the Commission) in a very interesting contribution ('Die Integration und ihre Institutionen', (1971) 11 *Aussenpolitik*, p. 646 *et seq.*).

46. Press conference of 21 January 1971, cf. fn. 39.

47. Meyer, *loc. cit.* (fn. 45) pp. 654–655.

48. The only more recent examples are the Directives for the Reform of the Agrarian Structure decided on 17 April 1972 (O.J. No. L 96, p. 1 *et seq.*), a watered down concoction from the famous 'Mansholt Plan' of December 1968.

49. Starting with the gradual transference to the Community of customs duties and levies and the extension of the budgetary powers of the Parliament (proposals made on 31 March 1965), and going via the constant warnings against excessively high agricultural prices (especially for milk, sugar and soft wheat) down to the numerous proposals for a new pluriannual research programme for Euratom which were made during 1968–71.

50. Ipsen, *Europ. Gemeinschaftsrecht, loc. cit.*, fn. 3, in this volume p. 228.

51. Press conference 21 January 1971 *vid. sup.* fn. 39.

52. According to the final communiqué of the summit conference in Paris (19 and 20 October 1972, cf. *The Times* of 23 October 1972, p. 4) the nine governments agreed to consider implementing Article 235 of the EEC Treaty for these matters. But hardly anything of this has as yet been felt in the every-day life of the Community.

53. Doc. COM (72) 710, 18 July 1972.

54. For instance, the Commission's Memorandum on Science and Development Policy issued in mid June 1972 (*Communauté Européenne—Informations* No. 29, pp. 6–7) provides, in addition to a body of experts, for a '*Comité de consultation et de concertation*' of top civil servants, where the national research programmes and expenditure are to be compared and where the initiatives of the Commission are to be prepared and examined.

55. Council Resolutions of 9 February, 22 March 1971 (O.J. No. C 28, p. 1) and 21 March 1972 (O.J. No. C 38, p. 3).

56. (1) The strenghthening of the co-ordination of the short-term economic policy of the Member States; (2) the strengthening of the co-operation between the Central Banks; (3) the introduction of some mechanism for medium-term financial assistance; all in O.J. 1971, No. C 73 12 *et seq.*

57. See the careful analysis by Ehlermann, 'Die Entscheidungen des Rates zur Einleitung der ersten Stufe der Wirtschafts- und Währungsunion, (1972) EuR pp. 17 *et seq.*

58. Cf. the Resolution first referred to in fn. 55 above: 'The Economic and Monetary Union signifies that the most important politico-economic decisions shall be reached at the Community level, and that, in consequence, the requisite powers shall be transferred(!) to the Community level.'

59. Two thousand million UA (Units of Account).

60. Article 3 (1) of the 3rd Resolution, O.J. 1971, No. L 73/15.

61. Article 4 (1).

62. 'For the purpose that the Member States shall continuously inform each other of their short-term economic and financial policy and shall co-ordinate

this policy within the framework of the politico-economic guide-lines established by the Council . . .' Resolution of 21 March 1972, O.J. No. C 38, p. 3.

63. See the author's remarks quoted under fn. 22 above.

64. In the light of everything which can be said concerning this from the methodological angle, these results will probably be very modest, cf. Etzioni, *op. cit.* (fn. 6), p. 300 *et seq.*; Schwarz, *op. cit.* (fn. 6) in this volume, p. 26 *et seq.*

65. Agreement concluded on 6 February 1970.

66. It is based on No. III of the Council decision of 21 March 1972, see above, fn. 62.

67. Regulation E.C. No. 907/73 O.J. 1973 No. L 89/2.

68. (1970) 22 EA p. D 520.

69. Niels Hansen, 'Politische Zusammenarbeit in Westeuropa', (1971) 13 EA p. 456 *et seq.*; Berndt von Staden, 'Politische Zusammenarbeit der EG-Staaten', (1972) *Aussenpolitik*, p. 200 *et seq.* Herr von Staden has for a long time been German member of the so-called Davignon-Committee.

70. Part II, Section IV, of the first Luxembourg Report reads: 'The Governments shall consult jointly on all important questions of foreign policy. The Member States may propose any question whatsoever for political consultation.'

71. Which it is probably very euphemistic to term 'direct integration of the Foreign Ministries' (von Staden, *op. cit.*, fn. 69, p. 209) via mixed working groups and the like.

72. See on this aspect the remarkable study by H. Mendershausen, 'Western European Power: Mirage and Realities', Southern California Arms Control and Foreign Policy Seminar, Los Angeles 1972, p. 31 *et seq.*

73. Gerda Zellentin, *Intersystemare Beziehungen in Europa*, 1970, p. 181 *et seq.*

74. See Karl W. Deutsch, (1966) *Politische Vierteljahresschrift*, p. 330 *et seq.*, Heinrich Schneider, (1969) *Integration*, p. 23 *et seq.*

75. Similarly: von Staden, *op. cit.* (fn. 69), pp. 207–209.

76. Cf. for example: Etzioni, *op. cit.* (fn. 6), p. 300 *et seq.*; Schwarz, *op. cit.* (fn. 6) in this volume, p. 26 *et seq.*

77. Hague Communiqué of 2 December 1969 No. 4, (1970) EA p. D 42 *et seq.*; 'Luxembourg Report', Part I, (1970) EA p. D 520.

78. Cf. the references to the state of the discussion, fn. 5 above.

79. One may assume that the Conference on Security and Cooperation in Europe (CSCE) will once more focus attention on this interrelationship which seems to have been forgotten in many places.

80. Cf. Meyer, *op. cit.* (fn. 45), pp. 648–649. In the Community of Six the French delegation was able to avoid a majority vote against any other member except Luxembourg by simple abstention. This possibility does not exist in the Community of Nine.

81. See the Prime Minister's statement before the House of Commons on 24 May 1971, (1971) EA p. D 277.

82. Cf. most recently: von Donnersmarck, 'Planimmanente Krisensteuerung in der Europäischen Wirtschaftsgemeinschaft', *Planungsstudien*, No. 8 1971, p. 63 *et seq.*

83. Documents of the sessions of the EP 1970–71, No. 147, p. 5.

84. With regard to price control pursuant to Article 60, to the drawing up of programmes and laying down of general objectives according to Article 46, to

the control of investments according to Article 54, and to the close cooperation with the Consultative Committee, as provided for in Article 19.

85. Part II, ch. V, *loc. cit.* This practice is maintained by the Copenhagen communiqué, para. 12.

86. *Ad hoc* participation of the President of the Commission for individual items on the agenda in the consultations at ministerial level, participation of a high-ranking official of the Commission in an *ad hoc* sub-committee of the Political Committee for the preparation of the commercial side of the CSCE, no participation in the sessions of the Political Committee and its regular sub-committees. It must be noted, however, that the Commission was being represented at the Copenhagen meeting of Foreign Ministers on 22–23 July 1973. A few high-ranking officials of the Commission invited to participate in the 'basket No. 2' negotiations of CSCE figure as members of the Presidency's delegation.

87. Evidently taking the same line: von Staden, *op. cit.* (fn. 69), p. 209.

88. For example, the Secretary General or his deputy.

89. E.g. Mediterranean policy, Cooperation and Commercial policy in the CSCE.

90. On the theories of Mitrany which apply at most to administrative unions, see G. Zellentin, *op. cit.* (fn. 73), p. 181 *et seq.* (187, 88).

Manfred Zuleeg

THE PARLIAMENTARY
SYSTEM AND THE
EUROPEAN COMMUNITIES

I

At a conference of the German Academy of Judges (*Deutsche Richter-akademie*) in Trier at the beginning of 1970, Hans-Heinrich Rupp described the European Communities as 'rule without rulers' and spoke of the 'exercise of sovereignty without a democratic sovereign'.[1] Referring to the lack of democratic legitimacy and the ostensibly inadequate guarantees of constitutional rights, he defended the Financial Court in Neustadt which had denied the constitutionality of the law endorsing the EEC Treaty.[2] Carl Friedrich Ophüls justifiably pointed out that the Court's reservations concerning the rule of law in the European Communities are easier to overcome than the objections which spring from the democratic principle.[3] For the 'democratic deficit of the Communities'[4] is something that is frequently deplored.

Many critics advance the therapy at the same time as the complaint: the rights of the European Parliament must be strengthened.[5] The 'democratization of the communities' is by and large understood in the sense of having a parliamentary system on the pattern of West European parliamentary democracies.[6] In face of the attacks on parliamentarism which are flaring up violently again today, this is a remarkable demand.[7] To be sure, at a colloquium in Liége on the merger of the European Communities in April 1966, the general desire became clear to escape from national forms of organization.[8] The basic trend was, however, to create wider powers for the European Parliament.[9]

Only occasionally are voices to be heard among the experts, which view

110

a strengthened European Parliament with scepticism.[10] Hans Peter Ipsen regards the efforts towards finding parliamentary 'forms of consensus' legitimate, only so long as they are not superseded by new and better forms. He sees in the factual constraints of planning, in the—as he calls it— 'scientifically organized decision-making process' an approach towards an alternative. In comparison with a parliamentary system, he clearly regards the present structures of supranational powers as more appropriate.[11]

The latest development has shown that it is not *idée* to give thought to the strengthening of the rights of the European Parliament. Even if the budgetary powers granted to it are in fact rudimentary, they nonetheless indicate the direction in which matters are being steered. With the expansion of the EEC into the economic and monetary union[13] the handing over of further powers will certainly be an issue.[13] The progress towards European integration is therefore closely bound up with the applicability of the parliamentary system to the European Communities. The objections that might be put forward, based on experience with national state models and on specifically European conditions, have as yet received little attention. The ability of Parliament to overthrow the government is not in fact the only point of interest, although it is regarded as the characteristic feature of the system.[14] What is needed (in order to reflect the political objectives) is a comprehensive discussion of the role of Parliament, that is the role which this institution is commonly intended to play in the West European democracies. Almost as a by-product, so to speak, arguments can be drawn for such a discussion, which bear on the dispute over the constitutionality of the Community Treaties from the viewpoint of the German constitution.

II

In order to judge the usefulness of political systems, political experts propose criteria such as transparency, participation and efficiency.[15] The democratic ideas of transparency and participation find expression in the functions of national parliaments. But also the functions of solving problems, in particular settling conflicts by arbitration, and introducing innovations has to be taken into account.[16] The efficiency with which these functions can be fulfilled decides the question whether the *status quo* of the Communities should be replaced by a parliamentary system.[17]

Which functions are at issue here? One well-known textbook on German constitutional law puts first and foremost, probably not without reason, the legislative function.[18] At present in the Communities, the assembly composed of parliamentarians from the Member States, which calls itself the European Parliament, only takes part in this activity in an advisory capacity. The authoritative decision-making bodies are the Commission,

111

with its right of proposal and the Council, as the institution which does actually pass resolutions.

The European Parliament has no influence over the appointment of these bodies. It was however, this electoral function which Bagehot considered of paramount importance,[19] and rightly so when the extent of governmental powers within the national States is taken into account. In the Europe of the Six only the French Parliament shares the fate of the European one, in that it has no influence on the appointment of the head of the executive.[20]

Nonetheless both Parliaments have a certain function of control: the French Parliament has the power of overthrowing the Prime Minister,[21] the European Parliament can dismiss the Commission from office with a majority of two-thirds of the votes cast, representing the majority of its members.[22] The governments of the Member States can, however, appoint the same people again immediately afterwards. The institution, which takes the fundamental decisions, that is the Council, is by no means dependent on Parliament, and in this respect can be compared to the President of the French Republic. Further powers of control—oral and written questions[23] as well as the debate on the annual general report[24]—are directed also against the Commission. The influence of Parliament on the Council is similarly small.[25]

This has a negative effect on another function, which might be called the articulating function. It includes the expression of criticism and complaints against the executive; therefore in the national sphere this is first and foremost the task of the opposition. Legally this function is not denied to the European Parliament, but it cannot demand the presence either of the Commission or of the Council.[26] The powerlessness of Parliament influences the effectiveness of its criticism. There is, moreover, no definite opposition.

Petitions are one way in which the opinions of ordinary people are articulated at state level. In Article 48 of its standing orders the European Parliament has itself created a legal basis for this. The articulation of opinions does not, however, work only in one direction from the people through Parliament to the apparatus of government, but the other way round too. Bagehot has described this as the teaching function.[27] Today it might be more accurate to speak of a propaganda function, since the government majority is, and must be, concerned to make government policy transparent and intelligible to people. Both Commission and Council often use the European Parliament as a forum for presenting their opinions. A typical example was the 'German professoral dispute' between Walter Hallstein, the former President of the Commission, and the then German Minister for Economics, Ludwig Erhard, on the necessity of planning.[28] However, the extent of the information made available in these cases does not approach that which is usual in national parliaments.

The function of integration—in Rudolf Smend's sense of communicating

112

a feeling of unity to the people—is almost totally lacking from the European Parliament. No elections take place. Genuine decisions are taken elsewhere. The activity of Parliament reaches, at most, the minds of the school-children and students, who are driven in coaches to Strasbourg in order to improve their political education.

Bagehot regarded the financial function, not as something separate, but as supplementary to the control function. But even in his day and age he could scarcely praise thrift as a virtue of Parliament,[29] so that the approval of expenditures does not have to be seen chiefly from the viewpoint of any curtailment of power *vis-à-vis* the executive. According to the Communities' new financial constitution, limits have at any rate been set to any spendthrift action on the part of the assembly. Even in the final phase it has no control over the amounts budgeted by law. The European Parliament has the last word only as regards the small 'free' part of the budget.[30]

As the German word for budget ('*Haushaltsplan*') suggests, the financial function is closely linked with the planning function. Planning has already largely slipped out of the control of the national parliaments, and there can be even less question of there being a planning function in the case of the European Parliament.[31] Nonetheless, this aspect ought not to be neglected at the present time when the idea of planning is enjoying a renaissance.

Finally it should not be ignored that in general national constitutions recognize no clear separation between '*pouvoir constituant*' and '*pouvoir constitué*': as a rule the national parliament takes part in amending the constitution. It is true that the so-called 'small amendment' of the ECSC Treaty requires the approval of three-quarters of the voters and two-thirds of the members of the assembly, but this procedure has not attained great importance as regards widening the powers of the Community. The Treaties of Rome dispensed with the assent of the assembly for establishing wider Community powers. In the proceedings according to Article 235 of the EEC Treaty or Article 203 of the Euratom Treaty, the assembly is only to be consulted. The Member States have proved themselves 'masters of the treaties'; so they have the final word on the constitution of the Communities.[32] The European Parliament possesses a constituent function only to a dwindling extent.

III

Strengthening the European Parliament in all or, at any rate, some of the functions mentioned above, presupposes that it is in a position to fulfil these functions. The majority of functions demand that decisions be taken on the basis of national consideration in conjunction with other Community institutions. The language problem is scarcely an obstacle, given the state of modern translation techniques. The seat of the Parliament in

Strasbourg and not in Brussels, on the other hand, considerably complicates co-operation with the institutions resident there. Further difficulties
are provided by the bulk of work expected from European Parliamentarians who are already over-burdened in their national Parliaments. In
addition to that they have to make the often lengthy journeys to Strasbourg. There is certainly agreement that any European Parliament with
considerably more rights would have to be directly elected, so that the
same people would no longer be representatives at both national and
European parliaments. Nonetheless, an enormous quantity of work will
fall on the European representatives and the possibilities for relieving this
burden ought to be considered.

The recent criticism of the parliamentary system sweeps aside this
problem as merely an outlet for a 'hectic activity', which conceals Parliament's loss of power.[33] As far as Carl Schmitt's *leitmotiv*[34] is simply
resumed, namely that Parliament as a place for the rational exchange of
ideas had its spiritual home in the nineteenth century and with the disappearance of the conditions for its existence, in particular the antagonism
between a rising middle class and the monarch, there disappeared too the
justification for its existence,[35] I need probe no further into its criticism.
Others have already demonstrated adequately that political institutions
can prove to be meaningful under changed conditions. Leibholz has shown
that it is the political parties in particular that have made possible the
change in the significance of parliaments and thus provided justification
for their continued existence.[36]

At present one cannot, however, speak of workable parties at the
European level. The fractions in the European Parliament are composed of
fairly heterogeneous elements, one national group (the Gaullists) has
splintered off, the group solidarity of the rest has not yet really been put to
the test. The British Labour Party does not even participate in the work
of the Assembly. The danger is that national interest will triumph over
party alliances after the transference of decision-making powers. It lies
nevertheless at the heart of European integration, that national thinking
must be overcome.[37] The European Communities came up against national
egoism right from the beginning. The risk arising from confrontation can
be mitigated by proceeding gradually, as happened when the Common
Market itself was established. In the beginning there would be very few,
then later on gradually more and more parliamentary powers which could
be transferred to the then directly elected body. In this way there is a
prospect that the present groupings would gradually become accustomed
to concerted action and develop into genuine European parties.[38]

Contemporary criticism of parliamentary system does not stop at
historical reminiscences. It is not necessary at the present stage of the
discussion to go into the alternative models of presidential constitution,
soviet democracy or one-party rule. But it is worth examining the reasons
which have led to the rejection of the parliamentary system. To put it in

114

its briefest form, the critics accuse the system either of being unable to attain workable majorities and consequently being extremely unstable,[39] or of promoting specific interests inequitably and thus in the long run also losing support among ordinary people.[40]

Nonetheless instability is not the inevitable price that a country has to pay for a democratic institution like Parliament. The development in Great Britain, in the Federal Republic of Germany, and in the French Fifth Republic shows this. Certain precautions are indeed necessary, such as an appropriate electoral law or a minimum number of votes all over the country as a prerequisite for a party's representation in Parliament. The introduction of the British first-past-the-post system in Europe would certainly give large sections of the population the feeling that they were not properly represented, which would again present yet another threat to stability. A barrier clause of five per cent, such as is operative in the Federal Republic, could be adopted without any great danger into the election process of the European Parliament. By this means many of the nationally orientated splinter groups could be eliminated.

There is still no proven means of preventing bias in the stressing of interests. It is certainly possible in a pluralistic society to balance out a whole series of opposing interests by means of organizations, which are oppositely geared—for instance those of the employers and the workers— even if the balances are variously distributed. The Communities have even gathered the various pressure groups into one Economic and Social Committee and canalized the influence they exert, without granting the institution any deciding powers.[41] There are, however, a number of groups who do not know how to organize themselves effectively; one has only to think of old people, children, women. Even subjects of general interests such as education or pollution can suffer, because they cannot find strong organized advocates. The deciding factor here is that this disadvantage of parliamentary democracy cannot be eliminated by transferring power from Parliament to executive institutions. This is shown clearly by the way in which consumer interests are neglected in the common agricultural market, which is tailored exclusively to the interests of the producers.[42] It owes its existence to the influence of the Commission and a Council consisting of government representatives. If it is a question of their losing power in favour of Parliament, the criticism of parliamentary system has no real substance.[43]

IV

1

It is usual today, among adherents as well as opponents of the parliamentary system, to talk about Parliament's loss of power. Either this loss is regretted or else regarded as a symptom of the perverted nature of the system. Concentration is invariably focused first and foremost on the legislative function. Bagehot was already aware that such large assemblies were quite unsuitable for continuous and expert legislative work. In more than a hundred intervening years the efficiency of parliamentary legislation has not substantially improved, in fact the contrary is truer. There is a good deal of evidence for this: for example, the many often far-reaching delegations to the executive, the small number of bills introduced by private Members, the obstruction of important legislation, the 'whipping through' of some government bills, the French Parliament's loss of power under the constitution of the Fifth Republic and much more besides. The executive has built up an advantage in expertise *vis-à-vis* Parliament in the form of the ministerial bureaucracy. It is in a better position than the sluggishly moving Parliament to achieve rapid legislation. There has certainly been no lack of attempts to increase the efficiency of parliamentary legislation,[44] but the advantage of the executive will not be evened out by the intensification of committee work, hearings, assistants for members of Parliaments, a Research Service as the one at the disposal of the German Federal Parliament or the speedy procedure as in the Netherlands, however important these improvements may be where other functions of Parliament are concerned. If it is to fulfil its legislative function fully, these attempts are no more than makeshift. By simply affirming prefabricated drafts, on the other hand, the system incurs the suspicion of disguising the true power relationships. Should a crumbling system of this kind be transferred to the Communities?

What is in addition needed in the Communities is an exhausting and complicated procedure to reduce the conflicting national interests to a common denominator. If the small group of the Council of Ministers find this compromise very difficult, Parliament, which could not negotiate 'a package deal' behind really closed doors, would find it almost impossible. Would it not then be better simply to leave the existing situation as it stands?

The key-words in any answer to this question are provided in fact by a severe critic of the parliamentary system: Agnoli points to the well-known aspects of control and public opinion.[45] He seems himself to have a poor estimation of their importance, however both aspects contribute to the democratic idea of participation, without at the same time completely incapacitating the system's ability to solve its problems. Parliament's inclusion in the legislative process fulfils at the moment more the function of controlling the executive through the people's representatives under the scrutiny of an alert public opinion than the function of legislative work of its own.[46] The degree of control sometimes seems very slight only because the government has to endeavour to adjust its bills to the expectations of the majority.

The European Parliament too could exercise this sort of controlling function. In this case, however, the correct conclusions should be drawn from the functional change of national parliaments and the European Parliament should not be declared the legislative organ at Community level; in this way the new constitution would not be provided with a misleading label right from the beginning. It is enough to grant Parliament the right of participation, for which there is a ready-made example in the German Upper Chamber (*Bundesrat*). But the community institution, which would check but not decide, would not be an institution composed of representatives from the executives of the Member States (as in Germany), but the European Parliament.[47] This pattern would have the advantage that the members of the Council could continue to balance out national interests in non-public sessions. They would, however, have to take into account the reaction of the parliamentary majority in order not to come to grief with their package as a whole. A good interim solution would be for the Parliament to have a suspensory veto which is relatively easy to outmanoeuvre. Later it would have to be strengthened into a requirement of parliamentary consent.[48] Before a bill would be finally rejected a mediation committee on the German model would have to go into the matter thoroughly.[49] No significant reform can be expected from any right of the European Parliament to introduce Bills,[50] given the role which such an assembly has in the prevailing political conditions; the Commission should retain or even extend its right of proposal.[51]

2

For the electoral functioning of the European Parliament to be complete, a European government would be necessary. But at the moment it would present a real danger to the existence of the Communities if Council and Commission were replaced by an executive elected by the Parliament. They are too greatly dependent on the loyalty of the Member States for this to be successful. As soon as the individual governments no longer have a voice in the fate of the Communities at an influential level, they feel their national interest has no further protection.[52] The situation which immediately springs to mind is one in which a European majority would not correspond politically to the majority in power in one of the Member States. Therefore the institution of a Council of representatives from Member States is a vital condition of the Communities' existence and consequently Parliament can have no influence on its composition.

It is at any rate worth considering whether one or several representatives of Parliament with either voting or consultative rights could not be delegated to the Council, as Sereni has suggested.[53] Participation in the passing of resolutions does not, however, promise an enormous gain for democratic control. Parliament cannot know how its representative voted behind closed doors and consequently cannot hold him to account, if he had, for instance, put his national viewpoint before the mandate given him by Parliament. Participation in an advisory capacity could lead to Parliament's viewpoint having influence at a juncture at which decisions had not

117

yet been finalized. A prerequisite here would, however, be the assembly's right of participating in legislation.

Parliament could only exercise its electoral function *vis-à-vis* the Commission, which has proved to be the guardian of the Community interest.[54] Its election by Parliament would be of great importance, if Parliament also had the right of participating in legislation. In exercising its right of proposal, the Commission would carry the far greater influence warranted by its connection with national representatives. It could anticipate the prevailing wishes of the European Parliament which would lead it at the end of the procedure to exercise its right of suspensory veto or to give its consent. The participation could be institutionalized if the Commission would request representatives from Parliament to join the numerous groups of experts and committees, which advise the Commission, at the stage of working out proposals. It would perhaps be even more effective, if Parliament's own special committees were concerned with the matter at this stage.

In this way the Commission would to some extent be the instrument of Parliament. The decline of power from members of Parliament, which is much deplored, could be remedied to a certain extent at the European level. Parliament could make use of the help of a huge bureaucratic apparatus, counterbalanced by the Council with the ministerial bureaucracies of the Member States at its back. This 'balance of bureaucracies' would possibly lead to a more effective functioning of Parliament than in the national state models.

3

The dependency of the Commission on Parliament would consequently have to be emphasized by extending the control function. The parliamentary majority at present required before the Commission can be forced to resign is too difficult to attain. If it were possible to defeat the Commission with a smaller majority, then admittedly the danger of instability would be increased. Whether the so-called 'constructive vote of lack of confidence' after the German pattern (i.e. vote of lack of confidence combined with the election of a new Prime Minister by Parliament) is in the position of obviating this danger effectively, is something about which there is still considerable disagreement in Germany. Its introduction in multinational parliaments ought, nonetheless, to be more of a stabilizing factor than in the national sphere, since agreement on successors can be more difficult.

In any case, the parliamentary defeat of national governments is only of significance in exceptional circumstances, in which government and parliamentary majority are no longer working in agreement. Thus it is the Opposition[55] which bears real responsibility for the control function in Parliament, if one leaves out of account the legislative process. The possibility of a defeat at the next election forces the government majority to show consideration for the wishes of the electors. It is still not clear whether a powerful opposition can come about in Europe which can work towards

118

democratic changes of power. Stronger rights for Parliament contribute in all probability to a polarization of the parties in the European Parliament. In the hands of a watchful Opposition the already operative practice of parliamentary questions could prove a useful weapon.

4

The articulating function of Parliament cannot be separated from the control exercised by the Opposition. Only if the latter has the opportunity of expressing its alternative suggestions, can it demonstrate the desirability of a change of power; the proper place for the elucidation of these alternatives is Parliament. This particular mechanism could be transferred to the European level without further ado. One advantage of this system would be the right of a minority in Parliament to demand the presence of representatives of the Commission or the Council or both.

If the ordinary citizen is to be more aware of his powers of participation, the right of petition would have to be transplanted from the standing orders into the Community treaties. The debates in the European Parliament and the general statements of Commission and Council should be easily available to the public. The high costs of translation and distribution should not be accepted as a barrier.

5

Whether the European Parliament fulfils its function of integration depends very largely on the style which develops after the enlargement of its deciding powers. While in the national spheres there is still a good deal to be done, there is no patent recipe for any improvement at the European level. Any strengthening of the rights of Parliament would have the advantage, in comparison with the present system, that real decisions would be worked out in an institution meeting publicly.

This would in addition have an integrative effect[56] on direct elections to the European Parliament.[57] As long as Parliament, however, possesses no deciding powers, it is to be feared that direct elections would founder into the exact opposite. The voters would feel themselves actors in a farce, perhaps not the first time, but certainly on subsequent occasions. If the members of Parliament were to feel emboldened by the direct elections to allocate themselves powers without international treaties and in this way impose themselves as a European constituent Assembly[58] the failure would be almost unavoidable. National governments and the courts as guardians of the constitution will scarcely be inclined to accept any usurpation of powers by the European Parliament. At best there will be a muddle, at worst the Communities will break up under this forced step.

6

If Parliament has complete control over the financial resources of the Communities, pressure from interest groups sets in. It is true that this

119

could have some integrative effect, but biased advancement of individual interests is frequently to be observed where the allocation of monies is concerned, especially in an economic community. First and foremost there springs to mind the abuse of subsidies, which are frequently given without sufficient check that they achieve their purpose. Nor should the disintegrative effect on those discriminated against be overlooked. Thus the idea of transferring the financial function completely to the European Parliament is something that needs to be questioned.

Possibly it would be more meaningful if in financial matters the Council and European Parliament continued to co-operate, since the representatives of the Member States might be more inclined to dam the flood of expenditure; nevertheless no final judgement can be made without practical experience of the new financial reforms.

7

There is still very little pressure felt in the European Communities from the 'inherent pressures of planning'. The products of Community decision-making process cannot disguise their compromise character and are in fact anything but the result of a 'scientifically organized decision-making process'. In the long run, however, even the supranational power of sovereignty will not be able to escape the planners. It cannot be expected that the European Parliament will retain a planning function, when the national parliaments themselves take scarcely any part in it. A prerequisite for any planning is, however, to establish basic aims and the necessary tools for realizing them. Parliament could certainly participate in deciding these[59] and the data for further planning would be put before the bureaucrats. A good starting-point would be the orientation programmes which are prescribed in many areas of the Community activity. Just as in the case of legislation so in planning, the European Parliament would be a kind of a control body, which is already tuned in to public opinion at an early stage.

8

Any enlargement of the constitution-making function of the European Parliament beyond the so-called 'small amendment' of Article 95 (3, 4), ECSC Treaty will doubtless come up against the fear of the complete transformation of the *'pouvoir constitué'* into a constituent assembly. At least it would be possible to model the procedure of the Treaties of Rome for broadening the powers after the 'small amendment'.[60] At the same time it would be possible to formulate the rather vague Article 235, EEC Treaty and Article 203, Euratom Treaty in a more precise way. In the two more recent Communities there was a need for supplementary powers more frequently than in the European Coal and Steel Community. The collaboration of members of Parliament could be the first step towards a loosening-up of

120

the cumbersome procedure for amending the founding treaties, although it will doubtless only be realized in the distant future.

V

It should be borne in mind during the discussion on the constitutionality of the Community treaties, that as far as nearly all the functions reserved for the national parliaments are concerned, any strengthening of the powers of the European Parliament promises greater efficiency. It would nonetheless be a mistake to transfer the parliamentary system developed in the national states to the Communities without restrictions and modifications. This rejection of structural congruence started emerging at the conference of German constitutional lawyers held in Kiel in 1964.[61] Structures practised in national states could even, under certain circumstances, lead to the collapse of the Communities. The commitment to a united Europe in the preamble to the German Constitution[62] and the principle of 'open government' [63] expressed in Article 24 (1) of the German Constitution provide the basis for choosing suitable forms for supranational co-operation. Even in those cases where an approximation to the parliamentary system might be appropriate or even desirable, it can founder in face of the opposition of the partner states. The advantages and disadvantages have still not been conclusively discussed, and in spite of all the considerations which have been taken into account, any enlargement of the powers of the European Parliament would nonetheless involve taking a political risk.

The Constitutional Court of the German Federal Republic is consequently well-advised to observe the prudent restraint which it showed towards those responsible for taking the political decision in the Saar Case.[64] As long as democracy in the Federal Republic is not obviously threatened, the preamble and Article 24 (1) of the German Constitution make good the 'democratic deficit' of the Communities. The Constitution does not put the principles of democracy above the readiness for integration, but gives both equal weight. The political leadership of the German Federal Republic is, however, bound to reconcile these principles as far as possible. The more powers the Communities have, the more urgent will the demand for their 'democratization' become. The Federal Constitutional Court has the task of guarding against any disregarding the extreme limits.

Conclusions

1. A parliamentary system with the same character as that in the national states cannot be transferred to the European Community without reservations and modifications.

2. This transference presupposes a European Parliament capable of functioning, which has its seat in Brussels and is supported by European parties capable of action.

3. European parties can come into being through the gradual transference of powers to the Parliament. To eliminate splinter groups there would need to be a 'barrier clause'.

4. Any complete taking-over of the legislative function would be detrimental to European integration and not very efficient. Parliament should preferably be given a right of participation, such as is enjoyed by the German Upper Chamber.

5. Parliament should be able to appoint the Commission and dismiss it with a 'constructive' vote of lack of confidence; but this does not hold good for the Council.

6. To include a delegation of parliamentary representatives in the committees concerned with working on proposals and to introduce early participation by parliamentary committees would increase the influence of Parliament.

7. It should be made possible for the opposition in the European Parliament to exercise control over the ruling majority and to put forward alternative proposals.

8. The right of petition should be firmly embodied in the Community Treaties.

9. Direct elections to the European Parliament are not advisable until such time as the Parliament possesses genuine deciding powers.

10. If sole power and responsibility over financial matters were the prerogative of the European Parliament, this could have a negative effect on European integration.

11. Parliament should participate in planning by establishing basic data in orientation programmes.

12. Any enlargement of the constitution-making powers of the European Parliament comes up against political obstacles and is therefore to be considered as a long-term policy. Initially all that is possible is participation in policy aimed at establishing supplementary powers in accordance with the Treaties of Rome.

13. The principle of openness towards integration which is expressed in the German constitution provides the constitutional basis for the Federal Republic's membership of supranational Communities with a certain degree of 'democratic deficit'.

14. The political leadership of the Federal Republic of Germany is bound to work towards a harmonization of the demands of democracy with the principle of openness towards integration.

Notes

Manfred Zuleeg is Associated Professor of Public Law and European Community Law at the University of Bonn. The essay was originally published in Europarecht *7 (1972) pp. 1–15 (Verlag C. H. Beck, Munich). It was revised by the author in May 1974. Translated by R. M. Ockenden.*

1. 'Die Grundrechte und das Europäische Gemeinschaftsrecht', NJW 1970, p. 353 *et seq.*, p. 354.
2. Decision of 14 November 1963, AWD 1964, p. 26; dismissed by the decision of BVerfG on 5 July 1967, BVerfGE vol. 22, p. 134 *et seq.*, p. 146.
3. 'Deutsches Zustimmungsgesetz zum EWG-Vertrag teilweise verfassungs-widrig?' AWD 1964, p. 65 *et seq.*, p. 68.
4. For example Beate Kohler, 'Direkte Wahlen zum Europäischen Parlament, Grundlagen und Probleme der gegenwärtigen Initiativen', EA 26 (1971), p. 727.
5. See in particular Hallstein, *Der unvollendete Bundesstaat*, 1969, p. 251. Naturally most of the representatives in the European Parliament share this view (see, e.g., the interview with the President of the Parliament, Walter Behrendt, in *Europäische Gemeinschaft*, Issue 5/1971, p. 28 *et seq.*).
6. Cf. for instance Sattler, *Das Prinzip der 'funktionellen Integration' und die Einigung Europas*, 1967, p. 221.
7. Critical of this attitude: Neunreither, 'Bemerkungen zum gegenwärtigen Leitbild des Europäischen Parlaments', Zeitschrift für Parlamentsfragen 2 (1971), p. 321; Warnecke, *Integration*, 1971, p. 1 *et seq.*, p. 18.
8. Particularly emphatic is: Duvieusart, 'L'Avenir de la Démocratie Euro-péene', in *La Fusion des Communautés Européennes au lendemain des Accords de Luxembourg,* Colloque organisé à Liège, 27–29 April 1966, 1967 p. 145 *et seq.*, p. 148.
9. See Duvieusart, *ibid.*, p. 154; in addition, Fernand Dehousse, *Allocution de clôture, ibid.*, p. 219 *et seq.*, p. 223.
10. The objections on the political side were voiced in particular by the French President Pompidou at his Press Conference on 21 January 1971 (EA/D 26, 1971, p. 131). For him the only point to be emphasized was 'that on the day on which a real European government comes into being, there must also be a real European Parliament' (*loc. cit.*, p. 133). Pompidou's suggestions are analysed by Berger, 'Vor der Wiedergeburt Europas à la Wiener Kongress? Die Europa-Vorschläge Staatspräsident Pompidous', EA 26 (1971), p. 665.
11. Ipsen, *Verfassungsperspektiven der Europäischen Gemeinschaften, Schriften-reihe der Jur. Gesellschaft,* Berlin 1970, Issue 37, p. 20 *et seq.*
12. See the decision of the Council and of the Representatives of the Member States of 9 February 1971 on the gradual implementation of the economic and monetary union, EA/D 26 (1971), p. 139.
13. See Everling, 'Die Entwicklung der Europäischen Gemeinschaft zur Wirtschafts- und Währungsunion', NJW 1971, p. 1481; Gert Meier, 'Die Weiter-entwicklung des Gemeinsamen Marktes zur Wirtschafts- und Währungsunion— Aufgabe des Integrationsprinzips?', AWD 1971, p. 497 as well as the papers by Scheuner and Ehlermann on 'Verfassungsprobleme der Wirtschafts- und Wäh-rungsunion' at the colloquium of the Arbeitskreis Europäische Integration Inc. in Bonn–Bad Godesberg on 26 November 1971, in *Integration*, 1971, p. 145 *et*

seq. and p. 162 *et seq.* The new developments are analysed by Leonard Gleske, *Stand- u. Zukunftsperspektiven der Wirtschafts- und Währungsunion,* Europarecht, (1974) p. 6 *et seq.*

14. See Herzog, 'Parlamentarisches System', in *Evangelisches Staatslexikon,* edited by Kunst and others, 1966, column 1479.

15. Steffani, 'Parlamentarische Demokratie—Zur Problematik von Effizienz, Transparenz und Partizipation', in *Parlamentarismus ohne Transparenz,* edited by Steffani, 1971, p. 17 *et seq.,* p. 20.

16. Steffani, *ibid.,* pp. 17, 19 *et seq.* and 29.

17. This disregards the criticism of Narr-Naschold, *Theorie der Demokratie,* 1971, pp. 29–30 and 154 *et seq.,* of the application of the concept of efficiency, since according to my starting-point it cannot be a question of 'having to carry out other than "modernizing" changes' (p. 30), the legitimacy of which ought equally to be compared with the processes of 'articulation, information, participation and control' (p. 18). (Apparently, the authors think of a change of the capitalistic system.)

19. Ekkehart Stein, *Lehrbuch des Staatsrechts,* 2nd ed., 1971, p. 51.

19. Bagehot, *The English Constitution,* 1961, ch. V, p. 117.

20. Articles 7 and 8 of the Constitution of the Fifth Republic.

21. Article 50 of the Constitution.

22. Article 24, section 3, subs. 1 ECSC Treaty; Article 144, section 2, subs. 1 EEC Treaty; Article 114, section 2, subs. 1 Euratom Treaty.

23. Article 23 (3) ECSC Treaty, Article 140 (3) EEC Treaty, Article 110 (3) Euratom Treaty.

24. Article 24 (1) ECSC Treaty, Article 143 EEC Treaty, Article 113 Euratom Treaty.

25. Cf. Neunreither, 'Le rôle du Parlement européen', in *La décision dans les Communautés européennes,* 1969, p. 109 *et seq.,* p. 119.

26. Both institutions have the right to be consulted by Parliament (Article 23, section 2, subs. 2 and section 4 ECSC Treaty; 140, section 2 and 4 EEC Treaty; 110, section 2 and 4 Euratom Treaty).

27. *Op. cit.,* (fn. 19), p. 117.

28. Verhandlungen des Europäischen Parlaments 1962–3, session on 20 November 1962, pp. 58 and 74.

29. *Op. cit.,* (fn. 19), p. 120.

30. On the financial constitution see Junker, 'Das neue Haushaltsrecht der Europäischen Gemeinschaften', JZ 1971, p. 48; Kohlhase, 'Probleme einer künftigen Finanzverfassung der Europäischen Gemeinschaften', EA 25 (1970), p. 857.

31. Cf. Molitor, 'Die mittelfristige Wirtschaftspolitik in der Europäischen Wirtschaftsgemeinschaft', in *Planung* IV, edited by Joseph H. Kaiser, 1970, p. 129 *et seq.,* p. 139.

32. Carstens, 'Die kleine Revision des Vertrages über die Europäischen Gemeinschaft für Kohle und Stahl', ZaöRV 21 (1961), p. 1 *et seq.,* p. 6 *et seq.;* on the applicability of the concept of the Constitution, see Pescatore, 'La Cour en tant que juridiction fédérale et constitutionelle', in *Zehn Jahre Rechtsprechung des Gerichthofes der Europäischen Gemeinschaften, Kölner Schriften zum Europarecht,* vol. 1, 1965, p. 520 *et seq.,* p. 521.

33. Blank-Hirsch, 'Kritische Bemerkungen zur Parlamentarismusdiskussion in der deutschen Politikwissenschaft', in *Probleme der Demokratie heute,* Con-

ference of the German Association for Political Science in Berlin (Autumn 1969), 1971, p. 156 *et seq.*, p. 160.

34. Very clearly in *Die geistesgeschichtliche Lage des heutigen Parlamentarismus,* 3rd ed. 1961, p. 11 *et seq.*

35. See especially Agnoli, 'Thesen zur Transformation der Demokratie und zur ausserparlamentarischen Opposition', in *Neue Kritik,* 1968, p. 24.

36. E.g. in *Strukturprobleme der modernen Demokratie,* 3rd ed. 1967, pp. 71 *et seq.* and 90 *et seq.*

37. See Maunz in *Maunz-Dürig-Herzog, Kommentar zum Grundgesetz,* 3rd ed. 1970, comment No. 7 to Article 24.

38. This is also predicted by Van Oudenhove, *The Political Parties in the European Parliament, The First Ten Years.* (September 1952–September 1962), 1965, p. 239.

39. In the post-war period the lack was most noticeable in France and led to the fall of the Fourth Republic (see Ziebura, *Die V. Republik, Frankreichs neues Regierungssystem,* 1960, p. 14). The critics were mainly in the de Gaulle camp (survey in Ziebura, *ibid.,* p. 19 *et seq.*); the constitution of the Fifth Republic is marked by this.

40. Especially Offe, 'Politische Herrschaft und Klassenstrukturen. Zur Analyse spätkapitalistischer Gesellschaftssysteme', in *Politikwissenschaft. Eine Einführung in ihre Probleme,* ed. by Kress and Senghaas, 1969, p. 155 (1968 *et seq.,* 185 and 188). A similar but considerably more biased work is Hirsch, *Zur politischen Ökonomie des politischen Systems, ibid.,* p. 190 *et seq.,* p. 208.

41. Stressed positively by Jean-Maurice Dehousse, in the discussion on the colloquium in Liége, quoted in fn. 8, p. 159; a critical reaction: Melchior, *ibid.,* p. 177.

42. See the informative study by Leitolf, *Das Einwirken der Wirtschaftsverbände auf die Agrarmarktorganisation der EWG,* 1971.

43. In agreement is Bracher, 'Gegenwart und Zukunft der parlamentarischen Demokratie in Europa', in *Parlamentarismus,* ed. by Kluxen, 1967, p. 70 *et seq.,* p. 85.

44. See Hereth, *Die Reform des Deutschen Bundestags, Analysen,* ed. by Bilstein, vol. 9, 1971, with numerous proofs; and from a legal viewpoint, Partsch, 'Parlament und Regierung im modernen Staat', VVDStRL 16 (1958), p. 74 *et seq.,* p. 85.

45. 'Die Transformation der Demokratie', in the work of the same name by Agnoli and Brückner, p. 7 *et seq.,* p. 57.

46. Cf. Loewenberg, *Parlamentarismus im politischen System der Bundesrepublik Deutschland,* 1969, p. 446 *et seq.*

47. Similarly Everling, *loc. cit.* (fn. 13), p. 1486.

48. Hallstein, *op. cit.* (fn. 5), p. 70, reaches similar ideas in spite of a very different starting-point. Gert Meier *loc. cit.* (fn. 13), p. 501, goes even further in this direction.

49. With reference to the establishment of such an institution in the context of the Communities, see Glaesner, *Perspectives d'avenir des organes exécutifs (Conseil et Commission) des Communautés Européennes,* Colloquium in Liège, quoted in fn. 8, p. 51 *et seq.,* p. 58.

50. See Hallstein, *op. cit.,* fn. 5, p. 70.

51. Glaesner, *op. cit.* (fn. 49), p. 57.

52. Well argued by Kuby, *Provokation Europa*, 1965, especially on p. 302.

53. *L'avenir de la Démocratie Européenne,* Colloquium in Liège, quoted in fn. 8, p. 127 *et seq.*, p. 142.

54. Dealt with in more detail by Cartou, *Perspectives d'avenir des organes exécutifs* (*Conseil et Commission*) *des Communautés Européennes*, Colloquium in Liége, quoted in fn. 8, p. 23 (33 *et seq.*), as well as Glaesner, quoted in fn. 49.

55. From the many statements in support of this view, see Gehrig, *Parlament-Regierung-Opposition*, 1969, p. 94 *et seq.* with further references.

56. Reports on the efforts made for this mode of election are documented in *Für allgemeine direkte Wahlen zum Europäischen Parlament*, ed. by the Political Committee of the European Parliament, September 1969.

57. In agreement is Kohler, *loc. cit.* (fn. 4), p. 733.

58. Such a plan is being earnestly discussed. See the Colloquium in Liège, quoted in fn. 8, p. 143; thus, *Fernand Dehousse*: '. . . Ici c'est clair, il faut élire d'abord et, pour les pouvoirs, on verra après'. *Sereni*: 'Les parlementaires s'en empareront d'ailleurs eux-mêmes.' *Dehousse*: 'Je suis en effet convaincu que les parlementaires prendront eux-mêmes ces pouvoirs. Ensuite viendront les règles, qui transformeront en droit ces conquêtes de fait.' Neunreither, *Zeitschrift für Parlamentsfragen, loc. cit.* (fn. 7), p. 325, also considers it possible that the European Parliament could turn itself into a European constituant, at any rate only after the concession of real legislative powers.

59. See also Ipsen (fn. 11), p. 21.

60. It would be possible nevertheless to refuse the involvement of the Court of Justice of the European Communities in the political decision-making process.

61. Known as 'Kiel Wave' (cf. Heinz Wagner, 'Bericht zur Staatsrechtslehrertagung 1964', AöR 89 (1964), p. 476); see the reports of J. H. Kaiser and P. Badura as well as the discussion on the first subject of the conference 'Bewahrung und Veränderung demokratischer und rechtsstaatlicher Verfassungsstrukturen in den internationalen Gemeinschaften', VVDStRL vol. 23 (1966), p. 1 *et seq.*

62. Clauder, 'Die Grundlegung des Gemeinschaftsrechts in der deutschen Verfassung, in *Einführung in die Rechtsfragen der europäischen Integration*, ed. by the Gustav Stresemann-Institut e.V. 1969, p. 21 *et seq.* On p. 24, he infers the 'constitutional mandate' for European integration.

63. Klaus Vogel, 'Die Verfassungsentscheidung des Grundgesetzes für eine internationale Zusammenarbeit'. *Recht und Staat series* No. 292/293, 1964, p. 42.

64. Judgment of 4 May 1955, BVerfGE vol. 4, p. 157 *et seq.*, p. 178; confirmed by the decision of 20 December 1960, BVerfGE vol. 12, p. 45 *et seq.*, pp. 51/52.

Jochen Abr. Frowein

THE FURTHER INSTITUTIONAL DEVELOPMENT OF THE EUROPEAN COMMUNITIES

Is the decision of 9 February/22 March 1971[1] of the Council of the European Communities on the gradual implementation of the economic and monetary union anything more than a compromise on formulae? What kind of economic and monetary union is envisaged by the Community institutions and Member States, old and new? There is already some talk of a 'flexible' economic and monetary union, '*une union économique et monétaire souple*'. This would have to be envisaged as the development of the co-ordination in the sphere of monetary and economic policy, which could function as long as the disparities in the development of the individual states did not exceed a certain degree and which put pressure on these states to take action of their own when a crisis develops.

More important than the question of which is the greater danger, inflation or stagnation, which is clearly adjudged differently on different sides of the Rhine, should be the problem of how to establish institutions, which can decide on priorities in a way acceptable to the parties concerned. Co-ordinating bodies—even if set at the level of parliamentary secretaries —will not be able to achieve this. This holds good too for the Davignon consultations, although they should not be underestimated. In the field of traditional foreign policy no more integration can be achieved for quite a long time. But with such methods an economic and monetary union worthy of the name can neither be initiated nor maintained.

In the long run anyway effective institutions can not be achieved without a certain autonomy, without an orientation towards a common interest, which does not merely represent the common denominator, established in negotiations, of the interests of all the Member States. To keep open the

127

opportunity for their formation or strengthening is a vital concern for European politics of our time. A full and complete reorganization of the institutions is not possible, nor would it be in any way desirable. It is a question of a continued development for which the ways must be kept open.

Strengthening the Role of the President of the Commission

The Commission of the European Communities is still in general relatively favourably judged. Nonetheless voices in favour of reform are increasingly heard. It has been under consideration whether the Commission should be given more political weight through a parliamentary investiture. Since the states cannot in the foreseeable future be ready to hand over the decision about the composition of the Commission it is, however, debatable whether a reform of this kind would really have the desired successful outcome. Such an investiture would probably be more formal in character and would remain just as ineffective as the present power of the Parliament to overthrow the entire Commission.

It seems more meaningful to increase the standing of the position of the President by involving him in the selection of the members of the Commission and also providing for a parliamentary assent. In this way a still tolerable degree of his influence might be brought to bear on the selection of members and the problem of the Commission's coherence from the President's point of view could be brought into play at an early stage. It should be recognized as an important aim to strengthen this coherence. It is true clear limits are set to the achievement of this aim by the fact that a Commission composed into a political bias is unacceptable for the Member States and so excludes the most important form of coherence, such as exists within the governments of states. This should not, however, prevent the possibility of exploring and exploiting to the full the setting up of a factual programme, on which the Commission agrees and which would achieve a certain coherence. Parliament can make an important contribution here, if it judges the Commission and its members more than hitherto according to this programme.

A More Concise Working Style for the Council of Ministers

The institution of the Council of Ministers will keep its central role for a long time to come. The only room for scope would seem to lie in alterations to its mode of work. Nonetheless there is still some hope that in an enlarged Council majority decisions would no longer remain completely excluded. It should be possible for the Luxembourg compromise of January 1966, which has been essentially confirmed and thus consolidated by Great

128

Britain, only in fact to be invoked, as its terms imply, when issues are at stake which concern the vital interests of one of the Member States. Certainly only the Member State in question can decide when this is the case, but it should not be taken for granted that this is so for every decision. The Council would also have to find a way to deal with proposals of the Commission within certain time and in accordance with a definite programme. Some type of system of second reading would have to be created here, which could at any rate alleviate the effect of the fortuitousness operating up till now in the time taken to deal with proposals.

A politically strong Commission could attempt to exercise pressure on the Council through a sort of emergency legislation procedure. It could, for example, describe a specific proposal as essential for its programme and demand that the Council take action within a certain period. If there were no action or a refusal, a debate in Parliament on the Commission's motion would be possible. Also the Commission could consider formally informing the heads of state and government in the Member States about the situation and thus indicating the necessity of a political decision at the highest level. More than a political pressure on the governments of Member States could not be exerted even in this way. Resignation would at any rate remain an option for the Commission, if it saw no other solution.

It is sometimes suggested that the President of the Council should be given a special position and be appointed from outside or, at least, be disengaged from his role as a national representative which would mean that the presiding Foreign Minister of a Member State would be sitting opposite another minister from his own country. Quite apart from the practical difficulties of this suggestion, one ought not to underestimate the salutary position of constraint on the Member State in the chair, which obliges it to act in the Community interest.

Priority for Strengthening the Powers of Parliament

There is widespread agreement that the Communities suffer from a democratic deficit. This might have been acceptable as long as it was principally a question of achieving objectives clearly laid down in the Treaty and thus based on democratic legitimacy. However, the necessity for a stronger democratic legitimacy of Community decisions became abundantly clear, once the development of policies not laid down within the Treaty were tackled. Within the framework of an economic and monetary union the problem would culminate.

Democratic legitimacy of the decision-making process is not only valuable in itself, but at the same time forms a prerequisite for the acceptability of the results and so is the only real guarantee of an effective decision-making system. This becomes quite clear when one considers the present trends in the British House of Commons, which could lead to a

129

far closer commitment of the British Member of the Council than under the German or Dutch report and control procedure. A parliament with the tradition and the self-confidence of the House of Commons will be far more awkward for the Communities than the parliaments of the present members, of whom only the two already mentioned have made serious efforts to exercise any control over the conduct of their own Minister in the Council.

Once the necessity for a stronger democratic legitimacy is accepted, the question arises how this can be achieved. In this respect the demands for strengthening the powers of the European Parliament are in a way completely opposed to demands for its direct election and this can put obstacles in the way of any progress. No new powers for a parliament that is not directly elected, but also no direct election for a parliament without powers—these are the objections sometimes put forward.

But are direct elections desirable without the infrastructure, 'intermediary powers', and political parties which alone make them meaningful? The danger might lie more in carrying out elections throughout Europe too early, of witnessing a largely fictitious electoral campaign without any real possibility of decision for the voters, of risking a very small electoral poll and thus discrediting the important means of integration, which direct elections at the right time could create. In this case the damage might outweigh any gain. Elections should be the last stage of development. Before this the Parliament must be made more attractive to politicians of standing and the co-operation between parties promoted, so that European electoral decisions appear possible.

These critical observations do not apply to direct elections to the European Parliament where they are combined with national elections, as they have been repeatedly suggested and indeed have a real chance in Great Britain. They could create a higher degree of legitimacy for European parliamentarians without running the dangers outlined above.

If direct elections are excluded as a short-term possibility for strengthening the legitimacy of the European Parliament, there remains the increasing of its powers. This could give the Parliament a more important place in the institutional system of the community. Since after all this Parliament consists today too of parliamentarians elected within the Member States and thus possessing a clear legitimacy, considerable importance might well be attached to the strengthening of its powers. It is only in the Parliament that the opposition parties in the European states have a chance to speak at all, since they are not represented in the Council of Ministers. But, above all, parliamentary debate makes it possible for consensus to be achieved in public opinion and thus also democratic legitimacy.

How can the powers of the European Parliament be enlarged? First of all, the powers already in existence can be taken more seriously in practice than has been the case up till now. There is nothing to prevent the Council and the Commission from according considerable weight to the vote of the

European Parliament in the event of a hearing. To be sure, there should be no question of any compromise agreed upon among national governments before the taking of this vote. Nor is there anything to stop the institutions of the community giving due respect to Parliament's having a broad right of control, to be accountable to it, and to share responsibility with it in important decisions.

Opportunity for a greater participation of the Parliament exists especially in the field of community legislation, in the case of regulations, directives and decisions addressed to the States, in so far as they have a normative character, that is, alter state law or make such an alteration compulsory. Nonetheless such participation cannot possibly take place in the case of every act of this kind.

The Recommendation of the Vedel Group

The Treaty names individually the cases in which Parliament must be consulted. The same system should be applied to parliamentary participation above the level of consultation. Here it seems on the one hand unnecessary to schedule all cases, in which up till now consultation has been prescribed, automatically for more participation, nor should other cases necessarily be excluded. The most important criterion in coming to a decision will have to be whether the treaty is here so precise that a real political decision is no longer necessary.

Bearing this criterion in mind, the Vedel group[2] confirmed the necessity for the agreement of Parliament in a whole range of cases, which can be gathered into different groups. Firstly the agreement of the Parliament seemed essential for those decisions which determine the constitutional development of the community, that is for actual revision of the treaty, the application of Article 235 of the EEC Treaty and the comparable provisions of the other treaties, and the decision on the admission of new members according to Article 237 (1) of the EEC Treaty. Furthermore, an agreement of the Parliament was considered necessary, where common policies have to be worked out, which are not laid down in precise terms in the treaty. This is true of common agricultural policy, transport policy, short-term economic policy and common commercial policy. To this were added the rulings of Articles 84, 87, 126 and 128. To the extent that the treaty only provides for a co-ordination of policies, there seems to be no possibility of Parliament's intervention.

It should be emphasized from the start that the Vedel group naturally did not think in terms of Parliament's participation in all acts coming within the scope of these policies. Just as in agricultural policy, however, it should be possible to distinguish at times between fundamental provisions and their implementation. While the Parliament would have to have power of co-decision in respect of fundamental questions and therefore

131

also of genuinely political problems, some delegation of the executive power, whether based on the treaty itself or on the Main regulations, seems both possible and necessary.

In addition to common policies the Vedel group regarded the area of harmonization of laws as one in which the participation of Parliament is necessary. Here a problem arises which has frequently been illustrated: national law has to be altered on the basis of directives not approved by Parliament, and so the national parliaments here frequently have the function of simply recasting into national laws legal norms that are already formulated down to the last detail. Here there would seem to be urgent need for change, which would lead to a clear democratic legitimacy of directives regarding the approximation of laws. The British Parliament in particular would react adversely if confronted with this type of directives. Finally, some participation of Parliament seems necessary in the conclusion of commercial treaties in accordance with the constitutional traditions of the Member States, because they belong to the framing of the commercial policy of the Community.

The Participation of Parliament in Legislation

If some such methods of greater participation of Parliament in legislation are decided upon, there is then the question of what form it would take. There is general agreement that the Parliament cannot take over the Council's position, but that it is simply a question of its approving the Council's resolutions. The procedure suggested by the Vedel group looks as follows: the Commission's proposals go to both Council and Parliament, Parliament gives its opinion, then the Council takes its decision, and Parliament either grants or refuses its consent. The involvement of the Parliament at an early stage gives it the opportunity to make clear, for which solutions majorities can be found. This can be taken into account by the Council when it takes its decisions, and the Commission can react to this by modifying its proposal.

Should Council and Parliament not be able to reach agreement, then the Vedel group suggests that the Commission should take on the role of inter-mediary. The Vedel group pronounced itself explicitly against the setting-up of a mediation committee between Council and Parliament. What was clearly decisive here was the fact that the creation of a mediation committee alongside the Council would inevitably produce difficult problems. The real deciding reason was, however, the wish to maintain the role of the Commission in the decision-making process.

If the Commission is not to be the institution, through which efforts at mediation are made and which would then in general endorse them by modifying its proposals, a not inconsiderable danger exists for the balance between institutions concerned with the Community interest and those more nationally orientated. There is no reason to assume that the Parliament will always tend towards a solution favourable to the Community. The danger exists rather that with any increase in its powers it will be to a certain extent renationalized and its attitudes towards questions which touch on matters of vital national interest will not be any different from those of the Council. For this reason it seems necessary to bring the Commission into play here as a corrective to purely national solutions and to hand over the mediatory role to it. For the same reasons it would seem not to be right to give Parliament a formal right of initiative. Naturally, it can recommend to the attention of the other institutions, by means of a resolution, legislative proposals, which it has worked out—indeed, this has already happened. On the other hand to entrust Parliament with a formal right of initiative would deprive the Commission of one of its most important functions. Here, too, it is not unthinkable that Council and Parliament might in certain circumstances more easily agree on solutions which did not lie in the interest of the Community. For this reason it should be agreed that only the Commission can set the decision-making process formally in motion with its proposals.

Budget-framing and Programming in the Community

Besides legislation there is the question of Parliament's participation in decisions about the budget as well as the programmes which will probably become even more important in the future. As far as the budget is concerned, a start has already been made and it is consistent with the suggestions made here to give Parliament a full right of participation in budgetary decision-making. The importance of this should of course not be over-rated. In the foreseeable future, the Community budget will scarcely have any real importance of its own, but will be a consequence of Community legislation.

What is of greater importance is the question of the involvement of Parliament in the approval of programmes about the Community's activity. This is an aspect of a constitutional question under discussion in many countries at the moment: parliamentary participation in planning and programming. As far as the non-binding phase is concerned, Parliament can participate by exercising its controlling rights of debate and resolution. Both Commission and Council must have an interest in provoking debates in Parliament on the subject of further development, if they need Parliament's consent for the realization of their proposals. To this extent any formal extension of Parliament's powers in this sector seems unnecessary. This is supported by the fact that precisely in this area Parliament has already succeeded in making its voice heard at the right time. The full weight of this voice and thus the willingness to take notice

133

of it will arise at the point, at which individual decisions can no longer be taken without the Parliament's consent.

If it is decided that Parliament should participate in fundamental law-making, then the treaties must be amended. To be sure, a rearrangement of powers by agreement between the institutions is not allowed. This means that any arrangement of this kind does not effect a formal shift of powers but also that it is in itself inadmissible. Insofar, the formula 'constitutional conventions' which stems from a system without clear allocation of powers is, at least, open to misunderstanding. However, every constitutional lawyer knows that rules about co-operation of institutions in exercising their powers leave considerable scope for shaping their interaction. Making use of the scope offered is not only legitimate but, provided that the constitution is rightly understood, even enjoined. The treaty, rightly understood, does not wish Parliament to be just formally consulted, but wants the results of this consultation to be given due consideration by the other institutions. Such consideration can have a wide application if the importance of Parliament is given its proper value and can under normal circumstances lead to the adoption of Parliament's viewpoint. Equally, where no consultation is formally prescribed today Parliament's participation and the consideration of its opinion could become the rule on the basis of Parliament's right of control.

In this context it seems of considerable importance that the Vedel group —despite a few initial hesitations of some of its members—emphasized unanimously that any change of practice, precisely with respect to the participation of Parliament, could be of considerable significance and should be tackled immediately.

European Parliament and National Parliaments

In its report the Vedel group touched on an institutional problem which was not explicitly indicated in its terms of reference. This is the question of the relationship between the European Parliament and the national parliaments. If our aim is to achieve democratic legitimacy of the community process, then in the long run this relationship will be of more decisive importance than all other institutional reforms.

The situation at the moment is hampered by the fact that the European Parliament leads a largely isolated individual existence. It has almost ceased to attract influential parliamentarians from the national parliaments, because these latter are not content with mere consultative functions. Because of the increasingly longer sessions of the European Parliament, younger members, who have gained expertise in that Parliament, have insufficient opportunity to influence the working of their national parliament on European matters, since they frequently cannot be there at the right time.

It is likely that an enlargement of the powers of the European Parliament will automatically bring with it changes in this situation, since any mandate becomes more attractive as it gains in importance. Experience up till now seems to indicate, however, that special efforts are necessary. Meanwhile, the European Parliament should not claim so ambitiously the position of a parliament enjoying all honours and independence or even, possibly, the position of a 'supranational' parliament superior to the national parliaments. Rather it should aim at being a centre of European parliamentary activity based on the member parliaments. The European Parliament should consist of the committees for European affairs from the national parliaments and thus be the centre for their contact and co-ordination.

Only if European integration is based on the national parliaments in this way, is there any hope of an economic and monetary union finding the substructure without which it will not be able to develop. If this more far going participation of the national parliaments in the process of integration is lacking, the danger will increase, that national parliaments will exert undue influence through the control of the ministers in the Council. This can lead to great difficulties if it happens in an unco-ordinated fashion.

It is up to the European Parliament and the national parliaments to reflect on the opportunities available here. Common sessions of committees of the European Parliament and of the national parliaments could offer a good opportunity to extend the circle of those in the national committees who have a real knowledge of European problems. Another method could be the participation of members of the Commission and the European Parliament in debates in the national parliaments.

Reservations about Ministers for Europe

As far as the repeated recommendation of ministers for Europe and an institutionalization of the summit meetings is concerned, a certain sober reserve is to the point. Ministers for Europe would at best provide an intermediate stage between the Permanent Representatives and the Council of foreign ministers or economic and finance ministers. The danger of additional frictions arising is, however, not small. Also the almost inevitable consequence of the permanent presence of ministers for Europe in Brussels would be a weakening of the role of the Commission. If the institutions which do not work only on the basis of co-ordination are to be given open chances it should not be overlooked that the system of Ministers for Europe conceals not inconsiderable dangers.

This is similarly true of the idea of institutionalizing the summit conference. However useful such conferences can be at a given time in order to give a new impetus and lend spectacular expression to some political agreement already reached, held periodically, they could easily have a crippling effect on the other Community institutions, which would then, like the Member States, have a shining excuse for postponing their decisions.

The Political Secretariat

In conclusion, there is one principle which is particularly worth emphasizing again: unity of the institutional system of the Community which has been achieved by the merger of the different institutions. This unity ought not to be endangered by the creation of more and more new institutions for certain spheres. A particular problem arises here from the plans for a political secretariat, which is to be prepared by the Davignon consultations of foreign ministers and political executives in the foreign departments. The institution has already been decided upon and is in itself to be welcomed. It is obvious that the Community institutions have neither the competence nor the expertise in all the different spheres of traditional foreign policy. Nonetheless, the importance of the question for the Community institutions can scarcely be overestimated. Economic foreign policy has for a long time been both the basis and the consequence of foreign policy. For that reason no conflict should be allowed to develop between the system of co-ordinating foreign policy and the Community.

This means that the only possible place for the political secretariat is in Brussels. Some participation of the Community institutions in the consultation mechanism must be firmly established. It would be appropriate for the President of the Commission to be present at the consultations between foreign ministers and his chief of cabinet at those of the political executives. This should be raised to a general rule, so that there could be an end to the undignified dispute over what are the individual points on the agenda, on which the Community should be represented. How will Europe convince the rest of the world of the necessity of taking the Community seriously and accepting it as a partner, if it cannot itself even reach agreement about its participation simply in foreign policy consultation, let alone decision-making?

Postscript: The Paris Communique and the Accession

On 1 January 1973 the European Community underwent the most important change since its inception. The enlargement which resulted from the accession of further members is far from being simply a quantitative extension of the Common Market. On Britain's entry, a country without which European history is unthinkable, but which had outgrown the purely European dimension, the Community finally acquires the weight, which gives Europe the chance, as it is put in the Paris Communiqué, 'to make its voice heard in world affairs, and to make an original contribution commensurate with its human, intellectual and material resources. It must affirm its own views in international relations as befits its mission to be open to the world and for progress, peace and co-operation'.[3]

Great Britain's entry coincides, apparently accidentally, with a phase in which an East–West decrease in tension is being consciously pursued. The most obvious expression of this is to be seen in the Conference on Security and Co-operation in Europe, the impetus for which had been given by the smoothing of the relationship between the Federal Republic of Germany and its most important Eastern neighbours, including the German Democratic Republic. This development will lead to a recession in the importance of military alliances, at the very least in their own self-esteem, which can already be clearly perceived today. In this way the European Community will necessarily become very much stronger as a factor of international politics. If it was able up till now—as in the case of the USA in the nineteenth century under the protection of the Royal Navy—to concentrate its activity on internal development and devote itself primarily to the economy under the NATO umbrella, while leaving high politics and defence to others, then a recession in NATO's importance will place the European Community, here too, more emphatically at the centre. Great Britain's frequent raising of defence questions points clearly in this direction. The statement in the Paris Communiqué that relations between the Member States should undergo a total change into a European Union before 1980, includes the West European Union, although here some opposition, notably from Denmark, is to be expected.[4] Co-operation in foreign policy must be intensified, as the heads of state or government have emphasized, and carried beyond the point envisaged by the Davignon consultations.[5]

There are many indications that European policy will be put to a hard test. The Conference on Security and Co-operation in Europe is clearly conceived by the USSR as a disruptive factor for the European Community and it is not certain that the European States will have the firmness to offer any opposition here. Phrases such as non-discrimination could, in a European system without clearly defined powers, easily lead to the paralysis of the European Community. Here a high degree of single-mindedness and determination on the part of the Member States of the European Community will be necessary. Whether para. 13 in the Paris Communiqué, which envisages 'a concerted and constructive contribution' by the Community to the Member States to the Conference on Security and Co-operation in Europe, is adequate for this purpose may be doubted.

What applies to European politics in general, may have particular relevance for German politics. The latent antinomy between the goal of European integration and German re-unification was scarcely clarified in 1958; it is equally unclear today, even if it is clear that re-unification can only be understood, in the context of the Treaties with countries of

137

Eastern Europe and with the German Democratic Republic, as a long-term process of gradual *rapprochement* between the two German States. Steps towards such a *rapprochement*, indeed many types of so-called relaxations, can be put forward by the Eastern Side, circumstances permitting, in connection with questions of European integration. Here many questions remain to be answered in the future.

The Paris Communiqué devotes para. 15 to the strengthening of the institutions. Council and Commission are required to put in motion practical measures for the strengthening of the European Parliament's powers of control and the improvement of the relationships between Council and Parliament on the one side and Commission and Parliament on the other. Moreover, the Council contracts to take practical measures to improve its decision-making process and the coherence of Community action. This is all that resulted at top level from the Vedel Report's analysis of the problems.

A closer analysis reveals, however, that more is included in para. 15 than is first apparent to the casual reader.

The most important progress made by the Communiqué is the clear commitment to strengthening the control powers of the European Parliament. This strengthening is seen as being independent of the direct elections envisaged in Article 138 of the EEC Treaty. This is in keeping with the Vedel Report.[6] The Communiqué does not lay down how the control powers of the European Parliament should be exercised. It must be assumed, however, that it is not only the Commission's control that is in question. This assumption is reinforced by the fact that the next sentence goes on to demand not just practical measures to improve relations between Commission and Parliament, but first and foremost between Council and Parliament too. Thus the heads of state or government have recognized the necessity for a dialogue on control between Parliament and the Council as the most important decision-making body of the Community. The confirmation of the decision of the Council of the Communities of 22 April 1970 must be seen in the same light; this binds the Council to set out the reasons which might in any given case cause it to disagree with the Parliament's attitude to decisions which have financial consequences.[7]

The consultation of the European Parliament, which according to the present state of the law is the only participation Parliament has in legislation, is, under constitutional law, part of the preventative control of the legislative bodies of the Community exercised by Parliament. Through consultation it is intended to give Parliament the opportunity to begin the dialogue about the correct decision before final legislation takes place. If this control function of legislation is recognized, it becomes clear that once the need to strengthen control powers is admitted, as it is in the Paris Communiqué, this involves a decision to pay stricter regard to the consultation and its results. This is inevitably seen as a challenge to the

138

Council, to stop paying merely formal attention to the results of consultation, as has in part happened up till now, but to give them real consideration in its decision and give its reasons for any deviation from Parliament's attitude. Even if the Paris Communiqué did not envisage the strengthening of Parliament's legislative powers by a formal amendment of the Treaty, the path already mentioned, and embarked upon when it strengthened its powers of control, seems of paramount importance and corresponds to the arguments in the Vedel Report on the opportunities for practical improvements without any amendments of the Treaty.[8]

National constitutional systems have reached a strengthening of parliamentary powers, in part without formal alterations or political decision-making mechanisms by purely factual consideration of the parliamentary votes. In the same way the European Community could gradually be developed by a strengthening of the control powers of Parliament to a much stronger system based on a parliamentary obtained consensus.

The further improvements, announced in para. 15, mainly concerning questions of procedure, are not therefore of lesser importance. If the Council is thereby challenged to produce practical measures for the improvement of its decision-making process to the coherence of its communal action, this broaches a fundamental problem for institutional co-operation. Without its being specifically stated the question of setting up programmes for certain times and the supervision of their implementation will have to be seen under the label of coherence of community action. Only in this way can the haphazard nature of results, which are a consequence of the present procedure of A-Points, be overcome.[9]

Under the slogan 'improvement of the decision-making process' the problem of majority decisions and with it the practice based on the Luxembourg compromise is at any rate indirectly broached.[10] One can only be pleased that the necessity for further deliberations has been impressed upon the Council from the very highest quarters. In addition, the technical possibilities of improving the decision-making process in the Council, especially those of an organizational nature, have to be tackled on the basis of this challenge.[11]

Following a suggestion made by the German Federal Government, a special paragraph in the Communiqué has been devoted to the Economic and Social Committee.[12] According to this, the Community institutions are invited to recognize the right of the Economic and Social Committee in future to advise on its own initiative on all questions affecting the Community. It is interesting here, over and beyond the institution directly involved, that the method of strengthening the institutions in practical terms (without any formal amendment of the Treaty) through using informal opportunities for influencing the institutions, is explicitly approved by the heads of state or government. Naturally the resolutions passed on the strength of the right of advice of the Economic and Social Committee are not formally binding on anyone, but they can serve as important indications to other community institutions. Perhaps this opportunity of developing its own initiatives can open up new possibilities for the Economic and Social Committee, which has recently spent more of a wallflower existence, and so a canalization of the frequently far too impenetrable European lobby can be achieved.

According to the Communiqué, the 'widest possible' use should be made of Article 235, EEC Treaty, for the purpose of carrying out the tasks laid down in the different programmes of action.[13] This is a further proof of the importance which heads of state or government attribute to practical steps in further development. One will have to wait for this attitude to be reflected in individual cases in the interpretation of Article 235, too.

The Paris Conference set forth clearly the political dimension of European union and alleviated to a certain extent the isolation which in resolutions on the subject of the economic and monetary union had up till then separated this goal from other spheres of state politics. It had already been emphasized previously that the economic and monetary union leads to a common pooling of the most important functions of the modern economic state, functions which are decisive for the prosperity and welfare of the population.[14] This was clearly recognized at the Paris Conference and led to the formulation of principles of material politics, even outside economic monetary matters, which were intended to make the Community a reality. So we find here, after economic and monetary policy has been dealt with, sections on regional policy, social policy, industrial scientific and technological policy, environment and energy policy. However one may describe the amalgamation, which would be the result of such a development, it is certain that it would have an eminently political quality.[15] The revised German Customs Union of 1867–71 seems to us today to be merely a transitional stage in the establishment of the Empire out of its various parts, the North German Federation and the Southern German States. As the sole international alliance, it had at its disposal powers which, for that time, were comparable with those that a Community extended into an economic and monetary union should possess.[16] With its Customs Parliament and Customs Federal Council, it also had an institutional system of a constitutional monarchical character corresponding to the later Empire.

The broadening of the goals for the European Union has something inevitable and is to be welcomed in the sense of a rounding off of Community powers, but also the anchoring of the European Community in the consciousness of the European population. A similar indication is given by the British Prime Minister Heath's request to refer only to a European Community and not to a European Economic Community, in order to make clear that the political aims extend far beyond the economy.

Admittedly, there are also dangers involved in this broadening process. The more vague the European aim is, the stronger is the chance of its

140

constant development to 'relativeness' in the everyday business of European politics. While the European economic and monetary union was to that extent still rather clearly defined, the concept of the European Union needs a factual rethinking, which has not found expression in the Paris Communiqué. It will need great political efforts to find it without losing sight of the concrete aims of the Economic and Monetary Union.

Notes

Jochen Abr. Frowein is Professor of Public Law and International Law at the University of Bielefeld. The essay was originally published in (1972) Europa-Archiv, *pp. 623–632 (c) (Verlag für internationale Politik GmbH, Bonn). The postscript was originally published in* Kölner Schriften zum Europarecht *22 (1973), p. 83 et seq., at p. 99 et seq. Translated by R. M. Ockenden.*

1. The decision was passed in the Council meeting on 8–9 February 1971 and published in an appendix to the press communication (cf. the wording in EA/D 1971, pp. 139–144) was accepted at the subsequent Council meeting on 22 March 1971 with only minor editorial alterations. It is referred to under this date by the Community institutions.

2. On a decision of the Commission of the European Community of 22 July 1971, an *ad hoc* group of independent persons was set up with the task of examining all questions arising from an extension of the powers of the European Parliament. Under the chairmanship of Professor Georges Vedel, Honorary Dean of the Faculty of Law and Economics in the University of Paris, the group consisted of: Jean Buchmann, Professor in the University of Louvain; Leopoldo Elia, Professor in the University of Rome; Carl August Fleischer, Professor in the University of Oslo; Jochen A. Frowein, Professor in the University of Bielefeld; Giuseppe Guarino, Professor in the University of Rome, Paul Kapteyn, Professor in the University of Utrecht; Maurice Lagrange, honorary member of the Conseil d'Etat, Paris; John Mitchell, Professor in the University of Edinburgh; Mary Robinson, Professor in the University of Dublin; Ulrich Scheuner, Professor in the University of Bonn; Andrew Shonfield, Director of the Royal Institute of International Affairs, London; Max Sørensen, Professor in the University of Aarhus; and Felix Welter, honorary President of the Conseil d'Etat, Luxembourg. The group held meetings from 26 October 1971 till 25 March 1972. Its report was published in April 1972.

3. Communiqué (preamble), *The Times*, 23 October 1972, p. 4.

4. Communiqué, para. 16; on the general subject of the European Union, see U. Everling, 'Die Europäische Gemeinschaft auf dem Wege zur Europäischen Union', in EA 1972, p. 791 *et seq.*

5. Communiqué, para. 14.

6. *Bulletin of the European Communities*, Supplement 4/72.

7. Cp. *Die Eigenmittel der Europäischen Gemeinschaft und die Haushaltsbefugnisse des Europäischen Parlaments*, EurParlament 1970, p. 212 *et seq.*

8. *Loc. cit.*, fn. 3.

9. Cp. above page 129.

10. Cp. above page 128.
11. Cp. above page 129.
12. Communiqué, para. 15.
13. Communiqué, para. 15.
14. U. Everling, 'Die Entwicklung der Europäischen Gemeinschaft zur Wirtschafts- und Währungsunion. Ihre Bedeutung für die Verfassungsordnung der Mitgliedstaaten', NJW 1971, p. 1481 et seq.
15. U. Everling, 'Die Europäische Gemeinschaft auf dem Wege zur Europäischen Union', in EA 1972, p. 791 et seq.
16. Cp. E. R. Huber, *Deutsche Verfassungsgeschichte seit 1789*, vol. 3 (1963), p. 632 et seq.

Ernst-Werner Fuss

STRENGTHENING THE POSITION OF THE EUROPEAN PARLIAMENT

With reference to the Vedel Report
and other proposals for the
institutional reform of the Communities

The essay which follows is an attempt to make a contribution to the subject of extending the powers of the European Parliament and strengthening its position *vis-à-vis* the Council of the European Communities. It does not mean that the author is under the illusion that he can convert anything of the existing 'mountain of plans' into something ready for consumption, that is realization.[1] At present (June 1974), there is no expectation that the great intellectual expenditure of these plans will bear fruit in the near future and be transformed into practical politics.

The decisions of the Paris Summit in October 1972 have scarcely brought any progress. Admittedly in Paris the governments confirmed their desire to strengthen the 'powers of control' of the European Parliamentary Assembly. But they confined themselves to the statement that the institutions of the Communities should 'without delay' prepare practical measures to achieve this reinforcement and to improve the relations of both the Council and the Commission with the European Parliament. A sceptical view about this result of the Paris Summit seems to be justified, as it was not outlined by the Conference what exactly was meant by 'powers of control' and by 'practical measures'. So the outcome of the Paris Summit shows very clearly that, for the time being, the governments have very little interest in institutional questions.

The business, the function—in concrete monetary and political co-operation—occupy the forefront; on the subject of institutions there is at the moment a certain wariness in expressing any opinion, and there are even warnings against regarding institutions as cures for all evils.[2]

143

Even if the politicians are silent on the subject at the moment, scholarship has a duty to pursue both examination and analysis. The aim of this essay is very modest. The Vedel Report[3] stands out among the mass of proposals for reform because of its comprehensive character, its concentration of subject-matter and its careful argumentation. Some of its details will be discussed here and commented on in the light of other ideas for reform. In this connection it is worth considering in what way institutional reforms might be set in motion, on the one hand with the prospect of success in view and on the other hand without jeopardizing the constitutional bases of the Community's legal system.

I. Guide-lines for Reform: Democracy and Efficiency

1

It is made clear at the beginning of the Vedel Report, that the group was influenced in making their proposals by two factors in particular, the principle of *democracy* and the criterion of *efficiency*.[4] The group was far from unaware that this inevitably involved a conflict of aims, which certainly ought not to be over-dramatized. In this context it should perhaps be kept in mind that it was the decision to establish an economic and monetary union made by the Council and representatives from the governments of the Member States on 22 March 1971, as well as the provision of the European Communities with their own funds, which gave the initiative for the Commission to commit itself to producing proposals for institutional reform and, as a preparatory measure, to give the *ad hoc* group the task of studying any extension of powers.[5] In contrast to the Werner Report,[6] which did not side-step the problem of institutional reforms, the resolution of 22 March 1971, lays the whole emphasis on functions. As regards anything institutional its sole comment is:

'The institutions of the Community shall be enabled to exercise their responsibilities with regard to economic and monetary matters with efficacy and speed.

The Community policies implemented within the framework of the economic and monetary union shall be subject to discussion and control by the European Parliament'.[7]

It depends therefore primarily on the Council and the governments of the Member States to see that the Community functions exercised within the structure of the economic and monetary union are performed as *efficiently* as possible, while no vital importance is attached to the factor of *democracy*. The Commission too, in its directives to the group,[8] names first and foremost the 'gradual extension of the powers of the Community' and the provision of 'an effective institutional system'. The

144

guarantee 'that Community decisions are taken within a framework of democratic legitimacy' is only mentioned in third place.

In contrast the Vedel group moved the democratic factor into first place and based the necessity for strengthening the democratic element in the Community on the following arguments:[9]

(a) The powers, which the treaties leave largely to the due discretion of the Community institutions, can only be extended with the support of political and social forces.

(b) The logic of the democratic system demands that any loss of legal and actual power suffered by the national parliaments as a result of the transference of jurisdiction to the Community should be made good by an extension of powers at the European level, that is, the powers of the European Parliament.

(c) The expansion of the Community powers means that 'European interest' covers increasingly large sectors of the economic and social life of the Member States. This fact makes it imperative to establish a balance between sectoral interests (for example, the priority of industry or agriculture) and also between national interests. The European Parliament is the institution *par excellence* in which views could be concerted. It seems—in contrast to the Council—ideally suited to secure a wide consensus in a complex system of tensions.

(d) The Parliament is the only Community institution in which the parliamentary oppositions of the Member States have any representation. An opposition which is considered to be a key element in the constitutional system should take priority of place in the list of essential structures both from the efficient and legal point of view.

2

It is not within the author's competence, nor is there space here, to work out the fundamental guide-lines for a theory of democracy or parliamentarianism. Nor is there room for the further discussion, proposed in particular by Hans Peter Ipsen, on the need for, and achievement of, consensus.[10] Nonetheless, some comments on the previously mentioned arguments put forward by the Vedel group are perhaps expedient.

(a) In view of the strict method which the group followed, it ought first of all to be made clear what the author understands by democracy. This seems, however, to be superfluous, since the Report has assembled on page 11 all the important characteristics, which permit a comparative study of the democratic systems of government in the Member States (all power is derived from the people, etc.) In all the detail, however, the group has forgotten the fact that the principle of democracy and the concept of the *rule of law* are very closely inter-related, that they overlap as regards content and in particular that the fundamental preoccupation and aim of both is to preserve and protect the *freedom* of the individual.[11]

145

It follows therefore that in any constitutional evaluation of the European Communities both principles should, if possible, be applied as criteria and that any deficit of democratic legitimacy can perhaps be counterbalanced or at least rendered less harmful, if the rule of law standard is high. As far as the elements of rule of law in the legal system of the Community and the practices of its institutions are concerned, it is possible to vouch for the Community's high standards with a good conscience.[12] It is certainly worth maintaining and extending the high rule of law standards of the Communities. This involves among other things a strict observance of the principle of (expressed and enumerated) powers granted by the treaty and the greatest restraint practicable in applying Article 235 of the EEC Treaty, which will be discussed later.

(b) Admittedly the rule of law in the Communities cannot influence either the *transparency* of the decision-making processes of its institutions or the *participation* of the individual citizen of the Community. Before pursuing, in regard to this point, the idea of a 'compensatory satisfaction of needs', the democratic aim of preserving the liberties of the individual should be stressed. It would certainly be misleading to maintain that the Community institutions have the intention or were even in the position, as a result of a lack of transparency and participation, to restrict or destroy the freedom of the European Community citizen. The successful way in which the European Court of Justice has operated precludes any such development and there is fully justified evidence of the fact that it has proved itself superlatively.[13] Quite apart from this, however, precautions exist to prevent the public exercise of power in the Communities from deteriorating into a dictatorial regime. No process of this sort has ever been observed in the history of international organizations and inter-state communities. The reason for this is that the member states act as guarantors against any such false development.[14] In other words: collective forms of inter-state co-operation are simply not suited to the establishment of a dictatorial regime. Moreover the Community legal system takes measures to ensure that institutional positions cannot be abused for dictatorial purposes by *setting a time-limit* to the terms of office for all institution members.[15] In this way the Community legal system very effectively takes into account the democratic concern for preserving individual freedom.

(c) To bring about or at any rate make possible both *transparency* and *participation* has up till now admittedly devolved mainly on the national political systems and, within these, chiefly on the parliaments of Member States. It should, however, not be overlooked that the national parliaments and political parties take in the main only a verbal interest in the integration process. There can be no question of blame here, since the aim of practical politics is inevitably to obtain and retain power. The dilemma suffered by the representative who has a double mandate—national and European—has often been described. European commitment has as yet little importance as far as power and party politics are concerned. This

146

will, however, be changed at a blow if the planned economic and monetary union becomes a reality and Community institutions decide, for example, on principal elements for drawing up the national budgets, lay down monetary parities or fix the discount rate of the central banks. At this stage at the very latest, parliaments and parties will launch into activities which will ensure them an influence on the forming of the decisions already mentioned. European topics will then play an important role both in parliamentary debates and resolutions and also in the struggle for the voters' favour. Indeed, this can already be seen happening when interests of vital concern to the voters (for instance the agricultural prices policy) are under discussion.

Securing transparency and participation in this roundabout way through the national parliaments is something the Vedel group, nonetheless, do not wish to accept, because the collective character of the decision-making process in the Council of Ministers and the irrevocability of the resulting decisions (this probably means primarily urgent politico-economic and monetary decisions) make any effective control by the national parliaments impossible. Moreover the attempt to establish an effective control of this kind would involve a danger in the national parliaments binding their governments by instructions given in advance, which would also make attempts to reach agreements within the Council even more difficult and laborious than previously.[16] This means that there is a conflict here between the two main factors of democracy and efficiency, which could in fact be resolved by transferring to the European Parliament the power of acting as a medium of consent. In contrast to transparency, which the European Parliament can already promote through its debates and publicity work (although within limitations, since it takes no decisions itself), it can only bring about real participation of the Community citizen, if the European representatives receive their mandate from direct general elections. Direct elections to the European Parliament are, how-ever, for the moment scarcely feasible[17] and the Vedel group rightly stressed that any extension of Parliament's powers ought not to be linked to any particular condition, such as the obligation to introduce direct general elections beforehand. Finally, it is very important, from the view-point of democracy as well as of efficiency, to equip the Community at one and the same time with the new politico-economic and monetary powers envisaged if at all possible and to make the European Parliament a partner in safeguarding the appropriate powers of decision-making. If there should be delays at these various stages, the national parliaments will evolve European activities in the sense already described. In this case, by continuing with the practice of unanimity, the exacerbation of the process of reaching agreement in the Council which was feared by the Vedel group, can scarcely be avoided.

(d) The above considerations alone demonstrate sufficiently that the ad hoc group would have done well to take into account and draw distinctions in their arguments on the need for strengthening the democratic element in the Community, according to whether or not the stage of direct election had already been reached. In fact the persuasive power of their arguments depends upon the contention that only Parliament, through balancing out sectoral and national interests, could guarantee a consensus which would resolve complex tensions and obtain representation for the opposition of minority at Community level. Whether democratic consensus at the European level can resolve the conflict of national interests (and of sectoral interests becoming national ones) is at the moment an entirely open question. It is, however, reasonable to have doubts, so long as no political parties have been formed at the European level and the lack of political, social and cultural homogeneity of the individual nations stands in the way of any being established. It is rather to be expected that national divergencies will spread far more widely within Parliament, as soon as it has to take part in decision-making, but cannot draw support from the legitimacy of an institution directly elected by the people. These divergencies will, moreover, become public, as has been the case for a long time in the Council of Ministers. This would naturally not be in the interests either of integration or of democracy. If it came to the national splits which are feared, the oppositional minority would be irresistibly drawn in their wake and the opposition, which is in fact indispensable for a vital democracy, would not be in the position to offer fruitful alternatives to the policies of the majority.[18]

(e) Was it then right for the Vedel group to change the order of the main criteria chosen by the Council and the Commission and accord democracy priority over efficiency? The answer to this question is admittedly of theoretical rather than practical interest, because conflicts between these two criteria will be the exception rather than the rule—at any rate if the powers of Parliament are extended at the same time as direct elections are set up (if need be nationally). If an unavoidable collision should, however, arise, it is essential to investigate what has been put most at risk at the time in question: the realization of European goals of integration or the aims of the democratic principle. Taking previous development as a basis, this has on the one hand brought integration many times to the brink of collapse through numerous Community crises. On the other hand, it does not provide any threat to the freedom of the Community citizen. It reveals an admittedly regrettable deficit of transparency and participation, which should not, however, be overstressed. Priority can, therefore, be conceded without qualms to the efficient working of the institution. Attention ought therefore to be concentrated on those proposals for reform which aim both to strengthen the position of the European Parliament *and* to improve the decision-making ability and readiness of the Council.[19]

II. Enlargement of Parliamentary Powers

Those of the Vedel group's proposals for reform which deserve especial attention deal with the transfer of legislative powers to Parliament and its participation in the investiture of the President and the other members of the Commission.

1

As regards *legislative powers*, the group starts quite correctly from the viewpoint that the Council's function as a legislative institution represents a fundamental principle of the Community constitution which should remain unassailed. Accordingly, it is suggested that Parliament should take an active part in the Council's legislation. The tried and approved method of integration is by division into several phases which lead to integration[20] and in this case *two stages* are envisaged. In addition, a graded system in the intensity of participation is proposed and the group compiled two lists of legislative matters (Lists A and B).

(*a*) During the first stage Parliament is intended to *codecide* on matters named in list A and gain a greater power of consultation for those matters in list B consisting in the right to ask the Council to reconsider a subject and hence a *suspensive veto*.[21]

List A covers the following matters:

(1) Revisions of the Treaties under Article 236, EEC Treaty, Article 204, Euratom Treaty, Article 96, ECSC Treaty, and the provision of the Community with its own resources according to Article 201, EEC Treaty, Article 173, Euratom Treaty (adaptation of the treaty revision procedure to that provided for by Article 201, EEC Treaty; approval to the unanimous Council decision; then ratification by the Member States);

(2) Implementation of Article 235, EEC Treaty, Article 203, Euratom Treaty, Article 95 (1), ECSC Treaty (the Council decision would take effect only after approval by the Parliament);

(3) Admission of new Members under Article 237, EEC Treaty, Article 205, Euratom Treaty, Article 98, ECSC Treaty (approval by the Parliament is a prerequisite);

(4) International agreements concluded by the Community under Articles 113 and 238, EEC Treaty, and Articles 101 and 206, Euratom Treaty (the international agreement concluded cannot come into force without being approved by the Parliament).

In addition to the power of codecision (for instance, the right of suspensive veto) the obligatory consultation of Parliament is being retained and indeed improved (it is extended to all matters of lists A and B; Parliament is kept officially informed about all proposals submitted to the Council by

149

the Commission, as well as any subsequent modifications made to them; a Council decision which deviates appreciably from the opinion received from the Parliament should be justified in detail). There is *no* provision for a mediation committee or the right of Council or Parliament to take the final decision in the case of agreement not being reached by the two institutions. The group convincingly puts forward the view that mediation is one of the natural functions of the *Commission*, that any exclusion of the Council would destroy one of the basic principles of the Treaties,[22] and that it would scarcely be possible to take away Parliament's right of co-decision with one hand, when it had just been granted with the other.

List B names the matters of Articles 43, 54, 56, 57, 75, 84, 87, 99, 100, 103 (2), 113, 126, and 128, EEC Treaty, Articles 31, 76, 85, and 90, Euratom Treaty, and Article 24, Merger Treaty.

The right of *suspensive veto* which is to be granted to Parliament during the first stage in the previously mentioned matters, the group wishes to see formed in the following way. The Council must refer to the Parliament any decision taken on matters in list B. No decision comes into force, until Parliament has either approved it or had made no comment on it within a month. Should Parliament within this period, with a majority of two-thirds of the votes cast and a (simple) majority of its members (and accord-ing to the rules governing under Article 144, EEC Treaty, the motion of censure), demand that the Council should deliberate once again, then the Council must comply with this request and take a new decision which is then definitive and which immediately goes into force. The Commission's right to alter its proposals as long as the Council has not acted (Article 149 (2), EEC Treaty) is being retained; in this context it is emphasized by the Vedel group that the position of the Commission should never as a general rule, be weakened by the new powers granted to the Parliament.[23] This tendency expresses itself, too, in the fact that preliminary participation of Parliament is not recommended for *measures of application*, which remain rather the preserve of the Commission (or the Council), and can only be submitted to an *ex post facto* control by the Parliament.

(*b*) During the *second stage* (beginning not later than 1978) the aim is to give Parliament the *power of codecision* in all the matters on both lists A and B. At this stage, too, the procedure of previous consultation with Parliament will be retained. The provisions for parliamentary powers of codecision are the same as in the first stage. The legislative initiative remains reserved for the Commission; the possibility open to Parliament to stimulate activity on the part of the other institutions through (non-binding) resolutions, is regarded by the group as adequate.[24]

(*c*) Up till now the *Commission* has made no official comment on the results of the Vedel group's work. In the preamble to the publication of the report it merely states that the report would give the Commission valuable suggestions for its own deliberations and has been compiled by a committee of fourteen members under Professor Georges Vedel in complete independence and sole responsibility.[25] In the context of preparing for the summit conference of October 1972, the Commission indeed expressed its opinion on some questions of institutional reform. From these statements[26] it can be deduced that the Commission, too, distinguishes between two phases.

Without treaty revision there is 'one measure which would revalue rapidly the political role of the European Parliament, and increase the effectiveness of the institutional procedures and democratic control': Parliament should be involved more intensively in the 'institutional process' through the introduction of a *procedure of two readings* to be created by agreement between Parliament and Council and to be used for important legislative bills of a general character (with the exception of urgent measures). The Commission would like the Council, whenever its resolutions diverge considerably from the Commission's proposal and Parliament's opinion, to submit them again to Parliament with a detailed statement of the reasons on which its disagreement is based and only finally taking a decision after a further parliamentary debate. Moreover, the Commission refers explicitly to the Vedel group's proposals for improving consultation procedure.

The Commission regards a Treaty revision as indispensable, if there is any real intention of achieving the planned economic and monetary union by 1980. It wants to be certain that included in the economic and monetary union there are also measures which will strengthen the institutions and which will put Parliament into the position, until 1975 at the latest, *inter alia*, of

(1) *codeciding* on all important matters, which lead to legal acts of general importance and
(2) having the 'last word' in certain specific areas of Treaty implementation (for example, the approximation of laws and the right of establishment), which will—in the Commission's view—be granted Parliament as its due after 1975 according to the law in operation (Article 203, EEC Treaty) as far as establishing the budget is concerned.

In its communication to the Council on the results of the first phase of the economic and monetary union as well as on the measures to be taken during the second stage[27] the Commission has again put forward the idea of two readings. Furthermore the Commission has stressed that in cases of implementation of Article 235, EEC Treaty, a consensus should be reached between the Council and Parliament, if necessary, by help of Commission proposals made after a second reading that reveals an appreciable divergence of opinion.

(*d*) In its preparatory resolution on the Paris Summit of 1972[28] the European Parliament has included several passages on 'improving both the balance between the institutions and their ability to perform their

151

functions'. In doing so Parliament takes up the idea of the 'second reading', demands a suspensive effect for its repeated rejection of a motion (put forward by the Commission?) and asks for the introduction of a right of codecision when international treaties are concluded, new members are admitted, Article 235, EEC Treaty, and regulations with financial consequences are applied. Parliament demands a general right of codecision in passing Community law only for a later date.

(e) Comments on the proposals for reform sketched out above must inevitably be limited for reasons of space. The proposals all have one aspect in common, they all aim at a marked political revaluation of Parliament as soon as possible. The instruments proposed to achieve this, the right of suspensive veto and the second reading, should be barely distinguishable from one another in their practical effects, since the veto only has a part to play when the Council diverges from the point of view taken by Parliament. (It would scarcely have been in accord with the Vedel group's purpose for Parliament to alter its earlier viewpoint after the Council's decision had been taken in agreement with this viewpoint and, so to speak, to make use in this way of its right of veto *against itself*.)

As regards the later stage of reform, the proposals of the Commission and Parliament go far beyond the conclusions of the Vedel group. The Commission requires Parliament to have 'the last word' in several especially important areas[29] by analogy with the admittedly disputed[30] interpretation which it places on Article 203, EEC Treaty. Parliament itself postulates a 'general power codecision' in the case of all normative Community acts. In contrast to both Commission and Parliament, the Vedel group mapped out precisely the matters in which it favoured an extension of Parliament's legislative powers. From the aspect of the principle postulating that legal measures ought to be foreseeable by those to whom they are addressed, this is an important point in its favour. The group also gave a great deal of thought, as to whether it would be possible for *one* institution to take the decision on its own in the event of disagreement between the Parliament and the Council. The fact that this solution has been rejected as irreconcilable with the fundamental principles of the Community constitution is proof of the group's grasp of realities and their clear recognition of the difference between a state constitution and the Community constitution.

It has to be said too in support of the group that it has rejected artificial constructions on carefully considered grounds. This would not in any case solve any conflict of aims which might exist between the principle of democracy and the maxim of efficiency. It is obvious that *any* additional participation by Parliament in the Community decision-making process inevitably involves lengthening this process. It is, however, well-known that at the moment, the most critical delays come not from Parliament but from the Council. It appears by no means out of the question that the Council would come to a decision more rapidly in the future, if it had to put its resolution before Parliament afterwards. For this type of procedure would to a certain extent relieve the members of Council of their burden of responsibility. Moreover the Vedel group envisages time-limits for parliamentary decisions—similar to those that German constitutional law imposes on the Council of Constituent States (*Bundesrat*). There should, therefore, be no complaints that any extension of parliamentary powers would reduce the Communities' capacity for action to an intolerable degree. It is more a question of bringing out into the open what the costs of a 'stronger democratization of the Community system' [31] might or might not be. This is a decision which has to be taken not by the Community institutions but by the parliaments of the Member States, as will be discussed later.

2

In its proposals for an extension of the Parliament's powers of control, the Vedel report sets out realistically from the premise that it is completely out of the question to introduce into the relationship between Parliament and Council the traditional parliamentary system of government. The group aptly describes the absence of any system of Council responsibility to the Parliament as a 'basic datum of the Treaties' and in explanation points to the fact that the Council is made up of national ministers,[32] who are subject, one might add, to the political control of their national parliaments.

(*a*) The Vedel report encourages a development of the practice of Parliamentary questions to the Council, as well as a strengthening of Parliamentary committees,[33] and concentrates for the rest on the *investiture of the President of the Commission*.

To hand over this function to the Parliament alone, the group rightly considers to be incompatible with the institutional relations between Council and Commission, as well as with the position of the Commission with regard to the national governments, which for the very maintenance of its authority necessitate that its members be chosen by the governments.[34] The group would, however, in this matter too, as well as in the case of legislation, hand over to the Parliament the *power of codecision*. The result expected by the group from such a procedure is that the political importance of the Commission would be stressed and the governments perhaps induced to favour the choice of outstanding political personalities. It is suggested that the *choice of the President* of the Commission by the governments should be subject to the Parliament's approval. Moreover, the President invested—and his mandate should be extended from two to four years—should be consulted by the governments on the appointment of the other members so that steps can be taken to form a genuine team strengthened by his governmental and parliamentary investiture.

(*b*) The Commission has endorsed this proposal of the Vedel group.[35] In the resolution mentioned above,[36] Parliament has already advanced far

153

beyond this development and is counting on Treaty revisions for the period from 1975, which would lead to the establishment of one single centre of decision-making; this latter is intended to be able to make decisions binding on all Member States and so acquire the character of a European Government. The investiture of the President and members of the European Government should take place at the beginning of a legislative period for the European Parliament through a conference of heads of states and governments. The European Parliament is to take part in the government's investiture by participating in decisions and retains the right of dismissing the European government. Parliament's ideas on the subject are that the essential participation of Member States in the Community's decision-making process should take place in a *States Chamber*, which shares the rights of legislation and control with the European Parliament by means of a procedure which has as yet to be worked out.

(c) No further demonstration is necessary of the fact that any realization of these proposals put forward by Parliament are equivalent to a complete reorganization of the Community's constitution. In this author's opinion such plans have no chance of being put into practice in the next decade. It is therefore superfluous to take up any particular standpoint here and now.

The Vedel group's recommendation, on the other hand, by its unpretentiousness fits admirably into the well-balanced framework of the whole report. The introduction of codecisive powers of Parliament at the investiture of the President of the Commission is capable in fact of considerably revaluing politically this office, which is acutely vital for any progress towards integration and would thus act as a magnet for outstanding political talents. If it should happen that this project succeeds in being put through, the team chosen after consultation with the President of the Commission should set before both Council and Parliament a *general programme of work*, in which it demonstrates the guide-lines of their policy. In view of the planned economic and monetary union and the new powers to be transferred to the Community within its framework (Community policies), such a declaration of intent could contribute substantially to transparency and at the same time bring about a strengthening in the position of Parliament. The ideal position would be for the Commission's programme to be debated not just by Parliament but also by the Council which would possibly see its way to sanction explicitly the plan of action put forward by the Commission, together with timed programming and advance calculation of the budgetary means available, and take these as a sort of general directive for its own actions. Such a voluntary commitment on the part of the Council would in any case be far more effective than putting into practice the idea that the President of the Council should make a 'government statement' before the Council or the Parliament at the beginning of his mandate.[37]

154

III. The Relationship of Parliament and Council

All the analyses of the present institutional structure and the actual functioning of the Communities[38] are in agreement that the legal and political power of the Council has an almost dominating character and that an institutional imbalance exists to the disadvantage of the Commission and of Parliament. Since the Council's activities take place by and large *in camera* and its lack of determination or perhaps its inability to initiate far-reaching resolutions has already often blocked progress towards integration, any thoughts of reform have to take into account whether the relationship between Parliament and Council could be improved as regards an increase in both legitimacy and efficiency.

1

From among the multiplicity of the relevant recommendations for reform, it is worth singling out Sasse's suggestion of divesting the Council sessions of their secret character by allowing the participation of a parliamentary delegation with full powers of joining in the debate. Moreover, parliamentary clerks should have access to the sessions of the Permanent Representatives and their groups and be able to take part in the discussions putting forward Parliament's viewpoint.[39]

At first sight this recommendation seems both effective and easily practicable and certainly requires closer consideration. Parliament's participation in Council activities and the making public of the Council sessions are two different questions, which admittedly have a thematic point of contact. What the chances are of making a practical proposition of either one or the other cannot be discussed here. The governmental character of the Council and resultant preference for the style of procedure of international diplomacy belong at the present stage of integration to the specific peculiarities of the Community set-up. Just as it is impossible to transfer the principle of separation of powers quite uncritically to the structure of the Community,[40] is it politically and constitutionally imperative to insist upon the Council's conducting its debates and passing its resolutions fully in the public eye? After all, the governments of the Member States also meet *in camera*. Why then should anything alter when they amalgamate in the Council? Perhaps because the Council exercises functions which in the Member States are in fact the prerogatives of the (publicly meeting) Parliaments?[41] If so, then it is rather a question not of altering the Council's style of functioning, but of involving the European Parliament in carrying out the necessary functions (legislation, determination of the budget, etc.).

If one accordingly starts from the point that the defects in the transparency of the Council's functioning have to be borne with, there remains the question of what use the participation of the parliamentary members

155

could be to the Council sessions. Certainly political and technical stimuli might be contributed (if these are not seen as the Commission's sphere of action as far as the Council is concerned) and also a mutually better understanding for both institutions. But could a powerful opposition be exercised in this way and would the legal and political position of Parliament be effectively strengthened? This could scarcely be so, especially as Parliament is not in the position to supervise the representatives acting on its behalf *in camera* and if need be call them to account.[42] It could also well be asked whether the parliamentary administrative officials would really know how to obtain a hearing in the circle of Permanent Representatives and their working parties or whether they would simply be felt to be 'political' foreign bodies.

2

The Vedel group concerned itself with the relationship between Parliament and Council from the aspect, in particular, of whether Parliament could provide a new impetus, if one of the Commission's proposals was making no headway, or even finally threatened to remain stationary in the Council's cumbersome apparatus. Even in this context, the group rightly stresses that there is no question of encroaching upon the Council's prerogatives. A rule which allowed the Council to be bypassed in case of a prolonged inaction, 'would be tantamount of changing one of the basic elements of the Treaties'.[43]

The group recommends, therefore, a procedure of a less binding and more flexible character. When a Commission proposal, on which the Parliament has formulated an opinion, is referred to it, the Council should at the Commission's request indicate the time required to prepare its position. Should the time-limit be exceeded substantially, it is thought that the Commission could bring the situation before the Parliament, if it considers the matter urgent, and according to Parliament's opinion, refer the proposal back to the Council, which would then have to pass the outstanding resolution within the period proposed by Parliament. If the Council did not respond to this proposal, the Commission would be entitled to consider its proposal finally rejected and communicate this to Parliament.

This suggestion of the Vedel group would enable the Commission to pass information to the public through the medium of the European Parliament and make it alert to the fact that a specific project is in danger of collapsing because of the Council's inaction. The success of this procedure depends upon whether public opinion would be activated in this way and would rouse the political forces (in the Member States) to activity. In view of the highly technical nature of most of the Commission's suggestions, this would not be feasible without a considerable use of publicity work. If the Commission risked taking such a bold step, it would have to reckon on the possibility of a radical controversy with the Council. There would be far

156

less risk attached if Commission and Council could come to an agreement in accordance with Article 15, Merger Treaty, that certain projects at any rate, which the Commission regards as especially urgent, could be given a thorough debating in the Council within a certain time-limit (one or two months). Any further debate on the project outside the Council sessions would, on the one hand, have to follow the general lines decided on by the Council, and on the other hand come to an end at a particular time (for instance after six months), in order to be terminated by a final Council decision or at any rate to take a substantial step forward by passing a resolution on the subject of the fundamental differences of opinion, which exist between the Commission and the Member States. The idea that the Council should set itself a time-limit for decisions is naturally not new.[44] Putting the idea into practice could contribute a great deal to improving the efficiency of the Council's proceedings.[45]

IV. Ways of Implementing Reforms

The Vedel group did not regard it as part of its task to make a detailed legal study of the procedure whereby the proposals it has put forward might be realized. At the end of the report it did, however, make a few comments that touch on fundamental aspects and therefore deserve no less attention than its suggestions for the reform of the institutional structure.

1

In these comments[46] there is absolute renunciation of the consideration that institutional reform can be accomplished completely or partly by implementation of Article 235, EEC Treaty, Article 203, Euratom Treaty, and Article 95 (1), ECSC Treaty. Here the author can only add his emphatic agreement. Article 235, EEC Treaty, which is so often referred to in the context of plans for establishing the economic and monetary union, gives the Council extraordinary powers, which extend the enumerated and expressed powers granted it by the treaty. This can be used if it is necessary to achieve one of the Community's aims within the context of the Common Market and if the powers necessary to attain the aim in question are missing from the Treaty. Even the words of the otherwise greatly disputed provision[47] make it clear that it can only be cited in order to aid the Council in making a functional ruling, for which it has been granted no individual powers in the Treaty. The keywords 'action by the Community' and the realization of aims within the context of the Common Market make it abundantly clear that the makers of the Treaty thought of additional *functions* in composing the text and not of a total reorganization of the *institutions*. Without having to go into the debatable question of whether Article 235 empowers the Council to grant itself, or another

157

Community institution, powers for which no provision has been made in the Treaty,[48] it can therefore be stated that there is *no question* of this Treaty regulation being regarded as a legal basis for a reform of the institutional structure. It is worth here mentioning Scheuner's comments on the subject,[49] which reach the same conclusion. And even such a resolute advocate of the application of Article 235 as Ehlermann concedes: 'In the present political climate to advocate the application of Article 235 in the institutional sphere is . . . not only risky but practically foolish.' [50]

2

Some proposals for reform suggest adopting a course of making 'gentlemen's agreements' or 'constitutional conventions'.[51] The Vedel group, which included eminent members such as John Mitchell of Edinburgh and Andrew Shonfield of London, does not use these terms for very good reasons. It prefers to consider the 'establishing practices agreed upon by the institutions concerned' [52] and the establishment of customs.[53]

This course should certainly come into consideration where it is a matter of Parliament's participation in the investiture of the President of the Commission, his re-investiture for the purpose of, in effect, extending his mandate to four years, the presentation of a working programme by the Commission to Parliament and the Council, the Council's voluntary acceptance of keeping to time-limits for decision-making and the intervention of Parliament, if any of the Commission's proposals remain at a standstill in the decision-making apparatus of the Council. After thorough consideration, the Vedel group even arrived at the conclusion that there is no need for any revision of the Treaties before introducing its 'proposed innovations that would allow the European Parliament to exercise, for a short period of time, a sort of suspensive veto on Council decisions'.[54] It may be doubted whether the 'certain limit' envisaged by the group would be observed. Since this suggestion does not affect the liberty of the citizen of the Community, since its aim is a strengthening of the democratic element in the Community, and since it does not alter substantially the balance of responsibility among the Community institutions (the Council is under no obligation to subscribe to Parliament's viewpoint), this innovation may be useful for a relatively short transitional period without any revision of the constitution.

3

A revision of the Treaty is nonetheless indispensable, if there is any real intention of transferring a power of codecision to the European Parliament. In the treaties at present in force you can find no indications even of any legal bases. The constitutional conception, upon which the treaties are at present based, would in fact have to undergo a fundamental alteration.

Such a step needs then democratic legitimacy, even though it is a question of strengthening the democratic element in the Communities. It is worth remembering the very close connection between the idea of rule of law and the democratic principle. Part of the constitutional basis of the Community organization is the delimitation of powers between the Communities and the Member States. The decision whether a stronger democratization of the Community system should be granted devolves, however, not on the Community institutions, but on the parliaments of the Member States. It is unequivocally clear that this fundamental politico-constitutional decision which, as has been advocated here, should go together with the enrichment of the Community powers in the context of the establishment of the economic and monetary union, needs a democratic consensus. This necessity for a consensus can be met through the amendment procedure of Article 236, EEC Treaty, which involves the participation of the parliaments of the Member States.[55]

Notes

Ernst-Werner Fuss is Professor of Public Law, International Law and European Community Law at the University of Würzburg. The essay was originally published in (1972) 7 Europarecht *p. 358 et seq. (Verlag C. H. Beck, Munich). It was revised by the author in June 1974. Translated by R. H. Ockenden.*

1. Agricultural and political jargon has coined, as is well known, the term 'mountain of butter' and similar accumulations. It springs instantly to the mind of anyone looking at the gigantic pile of plans for institutional reform of the European Communities. Sasse, 'Die Zukunft der Verfassung der Europäischen Gemeinschaft', in *Europa-Archiv* 1972, p. 87 *et seq.* (p. 100, note 22) names some sources. The plans drawn up by politicians and party bodies are documented by Hans Herbert Götz, 'Neue Pläne für ein demokratisches Europa', in *Frankfurter Allgemeine Zeitung*, 24 May 1972, No. 118, p. 12. See, too, the suggestions of the *Bildungswerk Europäische Politik* of May 1972 for the reform of the institutions of the European Community, *Europa-Archiv*, 1972, D 339 *et seq.*, Scheuner, 'Bestandsaufnahme und Prognose zur Fortentwicklung des Europäischen Parlaments', *Zeitschrift für Parlamentsfragen* 1973, p. 496 *et seq.*; Purnot, 'De positie van het Europese Parlement (Het rapport Vedel)', *Politiek Perspektief* 1972, p. 40 *et seq.*; and Schöndube, 'Wünscht die Kommission ein ohnmächtiges Parlament?', *Europa Union* 1973, No. 8, p. 2.

2. See the statement of the Gaullist representative at the European Parliament: 'Pour eux (the institutionalists), la potion magique, ce sont les institutions!' (European Parliament, Verhandlungen, Vorläufige Ausgabe, Session of 5 July 1972, p. 165).

3. Report of the Working Party examining the problem of the enlargement of the powers of the European Parliament: 'Report Vedel', *Bulletin of the European Communities*, Supplement 4/72. German members of the working party: Ulrich Scheuner and Jochen A. Frowein.

4. 'Report Vedel', p. 11 *et seq.*

5. 'Report Vedel', p. 7.

6. Report to the Council and Commission on the realization by stages of economic and monetary union in the Community: 'Werner Report', Supplement

to *Bulletin* 11/1970 of the European Communities, p. 12 *et seq.* (independent centre of decision for economic policy, Community system for the central banks based on organisms of the type of the Federal Reserve System in the United States). See also p. 17 *et seq.* (organs during the first stage).

7. J.O. 1971, No. C 28, p. 2; 'Report Vedel', p. 17.

8. 'Report Vedel', p. 8.

9. 'Report Vedel', p. 32 *et seq.*, 36 ff.

10. Ipsen, *Europäisches Gemeinschaftsrecht*, 1972, p. 1040 *et seq.* (and in this volume, p. 231 *et seq.*). For the opposite point of view see Sasse, 'Die Krise der europäischen Institutionen', in *Frankfurter Allgemeine Zeitung*, 24 May 1972, No. 118, p. 11; cf. also Nassmacher, 'Demokratisierung der Europäischen Gemeinschaften', *Europäische Schriften des Bildungswerk Europäische Politik*, Vol. 29/30, 1972; Scheuner, 'Verfassungsprobleme der Wirtschafts- und Währungsunion', *Integration* 1971, p. 145 *et seq.* (and in this volume, p. 66 *et seq.*); Ehlermann, 'Sachkompetenzen und Organverfassung der Gemeinschaft', *ibid.*, p. 162 ff; Zuleeg, 'Die Anwendbarkeit des parlamentarischen Systems auf die Europäischen Gemeinschaften', EuR 1972, p. 1 *et seq.* (and in this volume, p. 110 *et seq.*); Nicolaysen, 'Gemeinschaftsverfassung im Zeichen der Wirtschafts- und Währungsunion', *Integration* 1971, p. 90 *et seq.*; and Neunreither, 'Bemerkungen zum gegenwärtigen Leitbild des Europäischen Parlaments', in *Zeitschr. f. Parlamentsfragen* 1971, p. 321 *et seq.*

11. So Article 18, subs. 1 and Article 21, section 2, subs. 1 of the German Federal Constitution emphasize appropriately the *liberal* democratic system.

12. Cf. Fuss, 'Rechtsstaatliche Bilanz der Europäischen Gemeinschaften', in *Recht und Staat, Festschrift für G. Küchenhoff zum 65. Geburtstag*, 1972, II, p. 781 *et seq.*

13. Sasse, *loc. cit.*, fn. 10; Ehlermann, 'Problèmes institutionnels actuels de la Communauté', in *Cahiers de droit européen*, 1972, 3, pp. 255–271; and Nicolaysen, 'Der Gerichtshof, Funktion und Bewährung der Judikative, EuR 1972, p. 375 *et seq.*

14. Even precisely those Member States which in their internal constitutional structure have a tendency towards (presidial) dictatorship. Another question is the hegemonial ambitions of any individual Member State and even those states with optimal democratic infrastructure are not immune to this temptation. An apparently different view is found in Ipsen, *op. cit.* (fn. 10), p. 1046 *et seq.*

15. Ipsen, *op., cit.*, (fn. 10), pp. 1041 and 1043 (and in this volume, p. 182 *et seq.*, on pp. 233 and 235). With regard to membership of the Council of Ministers the tacit prerequisite of a time-limit in the Treaties is confirmed in what actually happens. Who would wish to maintain that a long-term membership of the Council could provide a spring-board for the establishment of a dictatorship?

16. 'Report Vedel', p. 33.

17. There is no need for further comment here on the projects for direct elections.

18. Cf. Ipsen, *op. cit.* (fn. 10), p. 1043 (and in this volume, p. 182 *et seq.*, at p. 235).

19. See below Section III, 2.

20. Ipsen, *op. cit.* (fn. 10), p. 1022 *et seq.* (and in this volume, p. 182 *et seq.*, at p. 217).

21. 'Report Vedel', p. 39 *et seq.*

22. This is overlooked by Gert Meier, 'Die Organe der EWG im Stadium der Wirtschafts- und Währungsunion', NJW 1972, p. 1593 *et seq.*, at 1595.

23. 'Report Vedel', p. 47.

24. 'Report Vedel', p. 48 *et seq.*

25. 'Report Vedel', p. 7.

26. Contribution by the Commission to the subject: 'Strengthening the Institutions and Progress of the political Union' of 25 May 1972.

27. KOM (73) 570–D (definite) of 19 April 1973, p. 30 *et seq.* Cf. also the document KOM (73) 1000–D of 6 June 1973, on the strengthening of the budgetary powers of the European Parliament. As for the latter topic see Kapteyn, 'The European Parliament, the Budget and Legislation in the Community', *Common Market Law Review* 1972, p. 386 *et seq.*

28. On 7 July 1972: J.O. 1972, No. C 82, p. 26 *et seq.*, pp. 27/28.

29. This proposal was not upheld in the document of April 19, 1973.

30. Cf. 'Report Vedel', p. 54 *et seq.*

31. Contribution by the Commission, *loc. cit.* (fn. 26), No. III.

32. 'Report Vedel', p. 57.

33. Cf. the suggestion of the *Bildungswerk Europäische Politik* (fn. 1) No. III: strengthening of the organization of Parliament through the setting up of an expert service, establishment of 'Royal Commissions' and an increase in the number of hearings.

34. 'Report Vedel', p. 58 *et seq.* Cf. Frowein, 'Zur institutionellen Fortentwicklung der Europäischen Gemeinschaften', *Europa-Archiv* 1972, p. 623 *et seq.* (p. 624).

35. Contribution by the Commission, *loc. cit.* (fn. 26), No. 5. But one does not find this proposal in the Commission paper of 19 April 1973 (fn. 26).

36. *Ibid.* (fn. 27).

37. Suggestion of the *Bildungswerk Europäische Politik, loc. cit.* (fn. 1), Section 2. The 'Report Vedel', pp. 77/78, refers to the importance that it would have 'for the effective functioning of the Community's institutions that the Parliament, Commission and Council should between them establish agreed programmes of work, covering fairly long periods, with clear time-tables and regular joint reviews.'

38. Cf. e.g. 'Report Vedel', p. 22 *et seq.*; Sasse, *loc. cit.* (fn. 10).

39. Sasse, *loc. cit.* (fn. 10); similarly Sereni, 'L'avenir de la Démocratie Européenne', in *La Fusion des Communautés Européennes au lendemain des Accords de Luxembourg.* Colloquium organized at Liège on 27–29 April 1966, 1967, p. 127 *et seq.* (142).

40. See Sachsse, *Die Kompetenzen des Europäischen Parlaments und die Gewaltenteilung in den Europäischen Gemeinschaften,* Frankfurt thesis, 1971.

41. On the weakness of the French Parliament's position, cf. Ehlermann, *op. cit.* (fn. 10), p. 170.

42. Zuleeg, *op. cit.* (fn. 10), p. 10 (and in this volume p. 110 *et seq.*, at p. 119).

43. 'Report Vedel', p. 77.

44. Cf. Sasse, *op. cit.* (fn. 10); 'Report Vedel', p. 77; suggestions in the *Bildungswerk Europäische Politik, op. cit.* (fn. 1) No. 5.

45. This problem, which has an important place in almost all reform plans, cannot be dealt with here, lying as it does outside this more narrow subject.

46. 'Report Vedel', p. 81 *et seq.*

47. Cf. Ferrari Bravo-Giardina in Quadri-Monaco-Trabucchi, *Trattato istitutivo della Communità Economica Europea, Commentario,* Vol. III 1965, Article 235, p. 1699 *et seq.*; Hans-Peter Gericke, *Allgemeine Rechtssetzungsbefugnisse nach Artikel 235 EWG-Vertrag,* 1970; Graf Henckel von Donnersmarck, *Planimmanente Krisensteuerung in der Europäischen Wirtschaftsgemeinschaft,* 1971.

48. For a contrary view which leaves out of consideration the delegation of powers to the Commission for the implementation of the rules laid down by the Council, according to Article 155 EEC Treaty, see Fuss, *op. cit.* (fn. 12), p. 791.

49. *Loc. cit.* (fn. 10).

50. Ehlermann, *op. cit.* (fn. 10), p. 167.

51. Suggestions of the *Bildungswerk Europäischer Politik, loc. cit.* (fn. 1) No. I; Ehlermann, *op. cit.* (fn. 10), p. 171.

52. 'Report Vedel', p. 81.

53. 'Report Vedel', p. 84.

54. 'Report Vedel', p. 83.

55. Hans Peter Ipsen, *op. cit.* (fn. 10), pp. 1045 and 1049, has pointed out—in fact in connection with the supplementation of Treaty aims—the relevance of assent in any modifications made to the Treaty (see also this volume, p. 182 *et seq.*, on p. 235 and p. 238).

Gert Nicolaysen

THE EUROPEAN COURT: ITS WORK AND ITS FUTURE

A Review

I. The Judiciary in the Constitutional System of the Communities

1. Critical Appraisal

In spite of all the criticism that the Court of Justice has drawn on itself as regards certain of its judgments, its procedure and style, as regards what are in fact details, it has an indisputable function as an 'integrating' institution, as Hans Peter Ipsen has described it.[1] This fact is all the more striking, the more the defects of both Council and Commission handicap the decision-making process.[2] While the Europeans put their hopes on summit conferences outside the organization (whose initiative and effectivity weakens down from The Hague in 1969 to Paris 1972 and Copenhagen in December 1973), the Court not only represents continuity but also an increasing activity. It is thanks to the Court of Justice, if the legal system of the Community is intact.

The stages of the development of Community law by the Court to its present state are familiar to the reader.[3] The result is an autonomous legal system, which is intended to give the Community the capacity to act internally and externally, which provides it with fundamental attributes of rule of law and which represents, through its general applicability and through the regular involvement of national courts, an essential element of integration.

The fact that the jurisprudence of the Court is favourable to the Community[4] has resulted in there being some discussion about the position of the Court of Justice in the constitutional system of the Communities. It did not need that spectacular reaction to the judgment in the European

163

Road Transport Agreement case[5] to make the problem clear. The anonymous author in *Le Monde*,[6] who caused a widespread sensation with his castigation of the judgment was not, in fact, saying anything that had not been said before. He reproached the Court of Justice with showing lack of respect for the Treaty by an '*arrêt politique*' and imputed to it the ambition of trying to elevate itself into a kind of Supreme Court for Europe. In doing so, he only dramatically brought to a head what constitutional courts have always had to listen to and what had even already been said to the Court of Justice in more restrained form.

2. *Comparisons*

(*a*) The Supreme Court of the United States of America was the first target for such attacks. The phrase 'government by judiciary' was coined[7] to describe its interpretation of the 14th Amendment to the US Constitution as a mandate for comprehensive legal control.[8] The phrase has gained popularity in the formula '*gouvernement des juges*'.[9] The status of the Supreme Court's jurisdiction as far as public life in the United States is concerned is in everyone's mind at present[10] and discussion on the subject is far from over. It is being carried on in particular in the Court itself, as is shown by frequent dissenting opinions.[11]

(*b*) The parallel debate on the German Federal Constitutional Court—which was recently revived through its judgment on the Treaty between West and East Germany on December 21st, 1972—often refers to Carl Schmitt's words, that the consequence of an expansion of judicial review on to subjects that are probably not justiciable would be 'not so much a juridicalization of politics as a politicization of justice'.[12] This is the formula with which critics in the Federal Republic characterize the prominent position of judicial control.[13] The Federal Constitutional Court early defended itself against such criticism with the remark: 'It is in any case incorrect to maintain that political decisions are placed in the hands of the court.'[14] Its decisions are legal decisions and therefore a function of the Third Power, insofar as they are reached by methods of legal interpretation,[15] but in their effects they are in many ways political.[16]

(*c*) The attack launched in *Le Monde* perhaps appears in a different light, if it is considered from the French perspective of the Third Power, which even today has no subsequent legal control of the constitutionality of laws.[17] This explains some comparisons between the French Conseil d'Etat and the US Supreme Court which characterize even the former as the '*juge qui gouverne*'.[18] This verdict is obviously based on the assumption that the Conseil d'Etat has evolved over and above the written law a system of fundamental principles, to which it subjects France's public life as a sort of political philosophy for the nation.[19]

(*d*) It is not surprising that the limits of judiciary are discussed in relation to international judicial power also. Very much in the same way as the German Constitutional Court, the International Court of Justice early established that, quite apart from the political relevance of a treaty text, its interpretation is a legal matter.[20] In spite of this, it remains doubtful whether, for example, there are not disputes which of their nature are unsuitable for decision by the courts[21] and whether even in international organizations a comprehensive legal control can be attained by a sufficiently complete 'legalization' of the resolution of conflicts.[22]

3. The Discussion on the Court of Justice

Some arguments on the functions and limitations of the Court of Justice should be considered here. The invocation of the US Supreme Court did not happen for the first time in the pages of Le Monde. The comprehensive monograph by Colin bears the title: Le gouvernement des juges dans les Communautés Européennes.[23] Its contents do not entirely correspond to its title: the Court of Justice is certainly seen to have played a decisive role in Community politics, but, as Colin says, has nonetheless remained very cautious (prudente) in carrying out its task of interpreting the Treaties.[24] If the title were therefore intended to voice a fear rather than a reality, the author could have found it confirmed now in the European Road Transport Agreement judgment as criticized in Le Monde.

In his farewell address to the Court of Justice after fifteen years' experience, the former President Hammes states that the control of governmental and constitutional functions by the Court of Justice embodies a 'political coefficient'. He therefore sees the Court of Justice in such cases more in an advisory role and suggests making allowance for this by giving the Court of Justice the additional power of submitting an expert report.

The quotations can be multiplied further. For instance, the delicate problems of delimitation between the political and economic discretion of the Council and the legal control of the Court of Justice are also stressed;[26] the importance of the Court of Justice's political role as regards the further development of the institutional system is recognized;[27] and as regards the judgment in the European Road Transport Agreement case doubts are making themselves heard also outside France: legal action by the Commission against the Council could contribute to the frustration of the Community executive, as to whether the course of politics should not have been followed;[28] in certain instances, so it is said, the Court of Justice impressed more by the consistent way it seeks integration than because of its legally verifiable closeness to the text.[29] Elsewhere the Court's adherence to fixed limits is again endorsed; it is said not to rule, but to carefully guide the institutions in a definite direction favourable to the Community,[30] and to keep to the classic role of a court, which is active but with a certain restraint and in the lee, so to speak, of the political powers.[31]

The work and influence of the Court of Justice—as well as the phenomenon of European integration as a whole—has aroused particular interest in the United States. Stuart A. Scheingold[32] has undertaken the attempt to assess its administration of justice according to the 'functional theory' of

165

jurisprudence, by trying to follow up in every case the motives of the Court and its judges. In doing so, he sees as a particular obstacle to the real function of the rule of law the political forces, to which the Court of Justice has to give in from time to time in order to survive.[33] In contrast A. W. Green[34] investigates in particular the influence the Court's jurisprudence has on promoting integration and this he finds completely confirmed by his case-studies.[35]

This extract from the mass of quotations on the subject of the Court of Justice shows the complexity of both problems and opinions. In the following paragraphs three questions are selected as a contribution to this discussion.

4. Integration as Principle of Law and as Mandate

Ipsen has demonstrated that the guarantee of the Communities' functional ability is a fundamental principle of Community law. In the Bensheim Report of 10 July 1964,[36] this was the essential element in establishing the primacy of Community law over national law, which the Court of Justice followed in the Costa v ENEL case of 15 July 1964.[37]

Ability to function as a *legal* principle goes back to the definition of the Treaties as an *instrument of integration*. The establishment of the Communities, the integration of the national economies and the functioning of the Common Market are the aims which underlie the Treaties. The implementation of these aims is either being carried out or is projected in the Treaties' individual provisions. 'Integration' in this sense—as the run-through of the catalogue of Treaty aims demonstrates—is certainly in itself a many-faceted and complex finality and provides a decided contrast with the vagueness of undefined omnicompetence of the national state. Integration is therefore capable, as a binding and guiding principle, as a law of action, of being also an element in the *legal system* of the Communities. The protection of the law which is assigned by the Treaties to the Court of Justice (Article 31, ECSC Treaty; Article 164, EEC Treaty; Article 136, Euratom Treaty) includes therefore also the guarantee of integration, in so far as this is compatible with the functions and powers of the judiciary.

Integration and a functioning Community as maxims of the administration of justice mean primarily a mandate for the Court of Justice to construe Community law accordingly. The interpretation of Article 189 (2), EEC Treaty, as 'the constitutional norm of the Community',[38] in order to deduce the priority of Community law, offers a concrete example of this.

Inimical to Community law, therefore, is the restrictive administration of norms which are conducive to integration, in particular their restriction in favour of the sovereignty of the Member States.[39] Naturally the contractual rights of the Member States are also part of the Treaties and the Court of Justice can in no way bypass them, as long as they are firmly rooted there, i.e. in the Treaty. The Court, however, must start from the premise that *in doubt* they only extend so far as not to impair the effectiveness of any Community action sanctioned by the Treaty. If this is seen as a 'weighing up' [40] then only as far as the unequivocal result of putting the functioning of the Community before the sovereignty claims of the Member States.

The principle of ability to function does not absolve the judge from obedience to the content of the Treaties and the properly enacted secondary law.[41] His task is simply the development of law to the greatest possible efficiency, not its correction.[42] Arguments developed in the American discussion about functional theories of jurisprudence are not applicable here, if they accuse their opponent of disregarding valid law, because he allows political and social aims to take priority over this law.[43] The Common Market is *not* intended to function as the majority of judges consider desirable and expedient, but as prescribed by the Treaties, in the most efficient way, however, and by utilizing all possibilities, which have a basis in law. Personal convictions of members of the Court of Justice that are favourable to the Community may be worthy of our sympathy and practically useful, but they can be no substitute for the legal basis of a Community orientated judiciary.

The fact that the aim of integration is embodied in the Treaties as a legal maxim avoids the possibility of its being understood as a weapon to clear away all obstacles indiscriminately. Once they are made part of the legal system, the aims are also subject to the limits of the legal system. The interests of the Member States have already been mentioned; the rights of the citizen of the Common Market should not be overlooked in this context. In the actual Treaties they are considered at many points[44] and entrusted to the protection of the Court through the right of bringing individual actions. No-one would wish to see integration as an end in itself. The recognition of the Common Market, as a means to an end can, too, find support both in the articles dealing with aims and in the preambles.

The jurisdiction of the Court gives graphic expression to this relation of generally formulated Treaty norms to the individual position of citizens of the Market in the decisions on the direct applicability of Community law. Since the case Van Gend & Loos of 5 February 1963[45] the direct applicability is based on the argument that not only the Member States but individuals too are subjects of the legal system of the Community and that Community law ought therefore to grant individuals rights just as it imposes duties on them.

The Court took a further step when it formulated explicitly that the general principles of the Community legal system, which the Court has to protect and guarantee, include fundamental rights of the person.[46] One very characteristic phrase is that the guarantee of such rights should indeed be supported by 'the common constitutional traditions of the Member States' but should also 'fit into the structure and aims of the Community'.[47] These statements make clear the way in which these legal positions too are deduced out of the Community legal system. The principle of integration did not evolve in the form of decisions out of subjective wishful thinking. Equally, these rights do not spring from a nebulous impetus of rule of law outside Community law and so they must adapt themselves to the particular peculiarities of this legal system.

5. Lacunae in Community Law and General Legal Principles

(a) *Interpretation*. The Treaties are more or less artificial products. Conceived *ad hoc* in negotiations with definite aims in view, they are the opposite of a legal system that has evolved gradually. By and large, they lack the substructure of a legal theory such as the Courts and legal scholarships have evolved in 'old' legal communities. Their elements can in part be attributed to the model of the legal figures of Member States;[48] others, as for example, the directive according to Article 189 (3), EEC Treaty, are new creations evolved in accordance with the particular aims of the organizations.

The interpretation of Community law must leave out of account the very differing sources of its rules: Community law has emancipated itself from its origins and follows its own laws. This does not prevent the interpreter reflecting on and comparing national legal solutions of relevant problems.[49] The result has, however, finally to be drawn from the text, from the systematic position and purpose in Community law. This thesis ought not be in serious doubt any more, although no lawyer entirely escapes the danger of looking for models in his own country's law.

(b) *Filling the lacunae in law*. The judiciary is faced with a related problem, when Community law leaves lacunae, which make it impossible to decide an actual disputed case without first filling them. The long-established practice of the European Court, which has in general found basic approval in all the literature on the subject, is to delve back into the general legal principles of the legal systems of Member States.[50] This is in fact applying a method, prescribed by Article 215 of the EEC Treaty for the investigation of the legal bases of the Community's non-contractual liability.[51] These suggestions come under discussion particularly where it is a question of extending the constitutional guarantee of individual rights under Community law.[52]

This procedure for establishing the law is all the less problematic, the more the principles in question remain general ones. General statements on elements of legal guarantees, on bona fides or the prohibition of discrimination are easier to prove as being common to Western Europe, than for instance the rules for repealing administrative acts benefiting individual,[53] for the retroactivity of legal acts,[54] let alone for the liability of the Community.[55] With regard to such cases, a theoretical foundation of practice is necessary, which the Court itself does not give. Its results can at the same time make clearer which is the task of judiciary within the system of institutions of Community law.

168

What is doubtful is the legal basis or justification for transferring legal principles valid in the Member States to Community law. Since apart from the case of Article 215, EEC Treaty, their validity in the Community is not decreed by the Treaty, this validity would have to stem from other sources. It is also doubtful, and this holds good for Article 215, EEC Treaty, too, what definition of general and, in particular, 'common' legal principles holds true, especially the number of unanimous solutions and the degree of unanimity. The questions are inseparable, as will become clear later.

With regard to the need for a practical application of the method, the second question urgently requires an answer. The question is posed when the individual legal systems have different rules to put forward, whether they gradually diverge or whether they are opposed, whether there are groupings among them or individual solutions. The case of other countries joining could show that the question of the grounds for validity does not simply spring from theoretical curiosity. A permanent dependence of common rules accepted as Community law on their origin in the individual states would necessarily place all the solutions in question, as soon as the legal position circumscribed as 'common' altered with the entry of further states, the legal systems of which would have to be included in the co-operation.

Such problems grow until the method is impracticable, the more strongly a connection or influence from the dogmas of the Member States is accepted.[56] Therefore the *immediate* validity of national legal principles, possibly in their character as national law, would be no practicable solution, even if there were complete unanimity. Equally unsatisfactory are all those solutions which would wish to achieve the result by arithmetical formulae, for instance by establishing a lowest common denominator of national legal systems or by adopting the solution of a numerical majority.

The necessary elasticity, which is the only means of reaching practical conclusions, offers instead the modern method of *evaluative* comparative law such as Zweigert in particular advocates.[57] It empowers the Court to adopt the best among the existing national solutions which in doubt is the one corresponding most closely to the aims of the Treaties. If the solutions are of equal value in this sense, then the Court has a free choice between them.

It is evident that in applying the common maxims of law two principles might come into conflict with one another: on the one hand the influence and the claims to validity of the legal concepts of the Member States and on the other hand the demands of the legal system of the Communities. The argument of common character suffers in this context from a double weakness: as a reason it has to have recourse to the rather metaphysical viewpoints of earlier concepts of homogeneity and to the less practicable assertion that the Community system of law has its basis in the national legal system and therefore 'inevitably' in their common principles of

169

structure and law.[58] Secondly, it must fail in the matter precisely in the precarious case where there is a lack of common character.

The method of evaluative comparative law focuses therefore with great clarity on the standpoint of the usefulness of the different solutions. As far as it is concerned, the national legal systems have first and foremost the function of model kits; they demonstrate tried and tested possibilities for the regulation of the questions which arise, and there is therefore no need to justify their consideration. This application of the method fits in fact perfectly in the other aims, which have already been attributed to it: to present ideas to the national legislature and to take on preparatory work for the approximation of laws.[59]

It follows from these ideas that the evaluation of the 'common legal principles' of the Member States must be considered as a creative act of jurisprudence.[60] The Court of Justice does not simply apply the law to the concrete case, but by its judgment it brings Community law out into the light, under which it is then applied. In doing so, it is not completely free: it is closely tied to Community law, into the framework of which the solution has to fit. In addition, the practicability, suitability and common sense of the solutions of the Member States, struggle for their adoption by Community law. The danger of judicial arbitrariness[61] does not therefore exist. The danger for the security of law [62] lies in the nature of things and cannot be reduced by any particular method.

Gand, the General Advocate, is quite right, therefore, to point to the creative role of jurisprudence[63] and to infer from Article 215 (2), EEC Treaty, a mandate to the judges to decide the scope of non-contractual liability: 'This is a comparative and creative legal task.'[64] As far as the law of liability is concerned this function follows from Article 215, EEC Treaty. In other cases of lacunae in the Treaties, it will have to be taken as implicitly included. As the law-making institutions are under certain circumstances authorized to act beyond their explicit powers (Article 95, 1, ECSC Treaty, Article 235, EEC Treaty, and Article 203, Euratom Treaty), the Court of Justice, too, within the limits of its judiciary function can complement the system of Community law according to the standard of the principles worked out above.

6. Limits of Judiciary

As a constitutional court, there is a danger that the European Court may be drawn into such conflicts between the decisive powers, Member States and institutions, which lie in fact outside the scope of the judicial settlement of disputes. If the judgment fails to be respected, it damages the Court and, therefore, the Community, and the damage is greater than if the attempt at a judicial decision of the dispute had not been undertaken. It is the affair of those involved, especially the Commission, to avoid this by considering very carefully whether it is opportune to bring an action before the Court.

Through the Treaties the relations between the Member States and the institutions have been made subject extensively to legal regulations. It is, therefore, appropriate that they are known as 'legal Communities' and the slogan 'right not might' is a logical consequence of this fact, not simply a well-meaning postulation.[65] The Member States have accepted the legal system of the Treaties, and with the institution of the European Court and its provision with the relevant jurisdiction, the way has been opened for judicial decisions of their disputes within the Communities.

When conflicts can arise, however, which would overtax the Court as Third Power, these are then the cases of wilful damage to Community law. As soon as a Member State consciously takes up a stand against its obligations, it will not change in deference to a judgment. As long, however, as only the interpretation of Community regulations is in dispute, even the lack of any sanction of the judgments according to the Treaties of Rome does no harm. Obedience to them will, moreover, not be refused, if the arts of interpretation are an expression of disapproval of the Treaty obligations, but there is no intention of risking an open breach of the Treaty. The supremacy of the law and therefore the function of the Court presuppose a corresponding willingness of those involved to obey it and end with their opposition.[66] Admittedly, this statement has no legal significance, but it corresponds to actual findings.[67]

Light is shed on these observations by some recent decisions of the Court, which refer to the borderline under discussion. The judgment of 14 December 1971 in the case 7/71 of July 1971[68] decided a dispute between the Commission and the French Republic, the subject of which was the legal interpretation of Article 76 of the Euratom Treaty. Technically, it was a question of the continuing validity of Chapter VI of the Treaty, which regulates the supply of ores, source materials and special fissile materials through the decisive participation of the supply agency. The Commission considered that the French Atomic Energy Commission had infringed some of the provisions laid down in the Chapter, and brought the matter before the Court according to Article 141 of the Euratom Treaty. If this infringement had been politically motivated, then this was not expressed in the arguments brought forward on behalf of the defendants. France accepted the legal challenge and among other things urged explicitly that an unclear legal situation had arisen as the continuing validity of Chapter VI had at the least become uncertain on account of the various possible interpretations of Article 76 (2), Euratom Treaty. The reaction of the Court of Justice in its judgment was analogous: in view of the differences of opinion on questions of interpretation, proceedings according to Article 141, Euratom Treaty, offer the opportunity of ascertaining the precise scope of the obligations of Member States. How far the possible political background of the dispute was thereby successfully settled, only later developments will show.

In a decision of 13 July 1972,[69] the Court had for the first time to adjudicate on a case where its own decision had not been followed. The

171

proceedings dealt with a breach of the treaty in violation of Article 171, EEC Treaty. On 10 December 1968 the Italian Republic had been condemned[70] for infringement of Article 16, EEC Treaty (prohibition of customs duties and charges on exports) because of its imposition of an export charge to protect the Italian cultural heritage. After several warnings of Italy's obligations in accordance with the judgment the Commission delivered an opinion according to Article 169, EEC Treaty, on the grounds of repeated breach of the Treaty, since Italy had neither repealed the relevant law nor had the Italian authorities stopped levying the charges. The Commission's second action followed on 29 August 1971.

In contrast to the case 7/71, the subject of this dispute was of subsidiary importance. The proceedings gained significance from the fact that the principle of the effectiveness of the Court's judgments was at stake. Of course proceedings according to Article 169 of the EEC Treaty cannot be repeated indefinitely. The Commission must nevertheless have promised itself a greater effect from its repeat performance. It was not deceiving itself: at the end of the written and oral proceedings the defendant informed the Court of Justice that the charge would no longer be levied and that its effects would be backdated to 1 January 1962.

The renewed proceedings therefore clearly lent the Court's first judgment the necessary force which Advocate General, Karl Roemer[71] asked for in his final proposals, in view of the 'weak instrument' provided by the procedure for any breach of the Treaty. His point was that 'the authority of the Community's legal system and thus that of the Community itself should not be lessened'. But the Commission's action was only meaningful in a case such as this, in which its success was not prevented by any basic opposition on the part of the Member State. This was shown also by the defence made on behalf of the accused, which pleaded difficulties in the legislative procedure.

The judgment is, moreover, revealing in as far as it proves the necessity for proceedings for breach of treaty in addition to the rule that Community law has priority. It is true that after the judgment of 10 December 1968, the Court had declared Article 16, EEC Treaty, to be directly applicable[72] in a preliminary ruling under Article 177, EEC Treaty, and thus made possible defence within the Member State for those affected by the levy, but Italy did not draw the natural conclusions from this and continued to levy the charge. It was, therefore, not until the Commission took proceedings according to Article 169 of the EEC Treaty that the desired success of a general and retrospective abolition of the forbidden regulation, so that individual protection is superfluous from now on.

As regards drawing limits for the judiciary in the practice of the Communities, those conflicts would be particularly revealing (in addition to the above cases) where the Court was *not* involved because of the limited function of the judiciary. Here the observer is admittedly thrown back on assumptions and can for the rest only quote the phrase formulated by

Joseph H. Kaiser at the height of the Community crisis of 1965–66: 'It has, however, also become apparent, that the political will of the Member States, which is the predominant constituent influence in the Communities, cannot be enforced by legal action.'[73]

Another field, which is not accessible to the Court of Justice, is in fact explicitly closed to it by a provision of the ECSC Treaty. This prohibited fundamentally the re-examination of an 'evaluation of the situation resulting from economic facts or circumstances' (Article 33, s. 1, subs. 2). This means that economic views in general, in so far as the Treaty leaves their formation to the Commission (the High Authority), may not be controlled by the Court. This is not the place to examine the problem more deeply.[74]

II. Future Perspectives for the European Court

Just as crises have affected the Court less than the other Community institutions[75] and have indeed rather emphasized its stabilizing role, so it is in the interests of continuity and stability to hope that any future alterations which will take place in the Communities will not encroach upon the judiciary. In view of the uncertainty of all developments only individual questions can be mentioned here.

1. The Enlargement of the Communities

(a) The organizational alteration in the Court of Justice with the entry of three Members has been kept as small as possible in scope: it now consists of nine judges and is assisted by four Advocate Generals.[76] Just as in the other sections of the Treaties, reformative amendments of the Treaties were not intended to take place as a result of the entry.

(b) The work of the Court could be made more difficult not so much by the increase in numbers of the judiciary, as by the participation of the legal systems of the States that enter in its future activity. It is true that on the subject of Community law nothing is altered fundamentally and it is here alone that the Court has jurisdiction. But to the extent that concepts from national systems of law influence this subject-matter, whether the influence comes from the conception of new laws or from the heads of interpreters and advocates from these States, to this extent the law of the new Member States can also leave its mark in Community law. (See above, Section I, sub-sections 5 (a) and (b).) The encounter, in particular, between Continental law and the legal system of Great Britain, common law and British idiom[77] will take place both in the Court and in the legal profession. Whether this will alter the style of the Court and its judgments, at the moment largely moulded on the French pattern,[78] is something that remains to be seen.

173

2. *Scope of Judiciary*

The general tenor of the judgments of the Court is largely determined by the areas of main Community activity. After the end of the transitional period and the realization of substantial parts of the Common Market, its activity is applied in new areas, which in part are not envisaged in the Treaties or have to be developed beyond the initial stages which are implicit there: economic and monetary policy, social policy, industrial, energy and regional policy, research and technological policy, protection of environment, activation of trade policy, and development aid. The Treaties themselves have become pointless in various parts; it is less their fulfilment than their further development which now provides the central point of interest.

It is already easy to realize that, in this way, the whole range of instruments at the disposal of the Communities is being altered. For example, the final communiqué from the conference of heads of state and government issued from The Hague in 1969 became in subsequent years an independent source of knowledge for the Community authorities. The sketches for policy drafts, the plans to be laid down as regards time and content, are reflected in resolutions, declarations of intent,[78a] decisions which appear side by side with the legal acts provided for in the Treaty. The decisions of the Representatives of Governments of the Member States meeting in Council (that is, not real Council acts) become more frequent, the possibilities for supplementary legal acts according to Article 235 of the EEC Treaty could attain[78b] greater importance, in part Treaty amendments seem absolutely necessary.

The law-making institutions of the Community, and among them the Council in particular, appear in an altered perspective in view of these functions. In addition to the implementation of the Treaties and the execution of their terms, creative plans have to be drawn out of them, on which a preliminary decision legally binding either not at all or only in general options like the statements of aims in the Treaties or the Hague communiqué has to be made. International agreement which has to precede supranational decision and which up till now was usually documented through the Treaty, has now to be worked out.

It is impossible here and now to follow up all the consequences for the Communities' constitutions.[79] The Court might similarly be affected by them, if it had in future to pass judgment in the areas mentioned and will thus be confronted with changed forms of legislative activity. It might be that it would have to come to terms with these new forms of action, the legal quality of which, as Community law, will be indisputable. The questions of planning law which arise in national discussions could also come up within the Communities and would have to be answered by the Court if for instance it were to be accessible to the victims of planning or if it were otherwise a question of the binding force and amount of confidence of Community legal projects. Where standards are no longer provided by detailed provisions of the Treaty, actions have to be measured against the articles stating general aims or against general 'principles of law', in particular where it is to protect the Common Market citizen; questions of powers and procedures could reach greater importance than previously.

3. Reform of the Court

No consideration of future perspectives for the Court should end without at least mentioning the numerous desires for reform which have been constantly expressed over the last twenty years of its existence. As the point of concentration for such ideas it is worth mentioning the conference on 'Ten Years of Jurisprudence of the Court of Justice of the European Communities', which took place in Cologne in 1963. Especially important was the question: Is it advisable to alter the terms of legal protection? This is answered affirmatively by Zweigert, in particular.[80] The same question appears in scarcely differing forms at the 46th Conference of German Lawyers (46. *Deutscher Juristentag*) in Essen in 1966 with a comprehensive report by Carl Hermann Ule[81] and papers by B. Börner and H. Matthies, as well as an extensive discussion.[82] Moreover various earlier judges of the Court have expressed their desires for reform in critical terms, for instance O. Riese,[83] C. L. Hammes[84] and W. Strauss.[85]

The present does not seem a favourable time for a reform of the constitution of the Court. If I am not deceived, the demands for it have become less strident recently, although it is difficult to say whether this is because the need for reform has lessened or whether frustration has spread among its advocates. It may be that in an enlarged Community some of the inadequacies will be more apparent. Thus an increased burden of work could make providing some relief for the Court of Justice unavoidable. Also the necessity for more intensive concentration of national jurisprudence on Community law could require an improvement for the preliminary ruling procedure according to Article 177, EEC Treaty, by means of extending the obligation of the national courts to refer to the European Court.

All demands for improvements in procedure and in the motivation of judgments must of necessity pale before complaints about inadequate guarantees for individual protection by the law through the Treaties themselves, if such complaints are justified. Yet the necessity for an amendment of the Treaty can only be established on the basis of the jurisprudence of the Court that treaty provisions referring to legal protection ought not to be interpreted restrictively.[86] Nonetheless the Court itself does not always seem to follow this prescript. In the economically and legally highly relevant case of the 'competitor's action' (Eridania case[87]) the Court declared that when the Community subsidizes selectively individual undertakings 'only if special circumstances existed' could the individual person, who could prove the measure was having an unfavourable effect on his position in the market, take up an action under Article 173. The still insufficiently clarified prerequisites for actions from the 'directly' and

175

'individually' affected state of the plaintiff demand a special and broad interpretation. This is especially true when the Community executive itself—and not only through the intermediary of the Member States—intervenes in the market relationships. For the 'national' legal protection, which is possible when Community law is executed by the Member State authorities, is in this case not available.

On the other hand some criticism of the legal protection system of the Treaties goes back to an isolated consideration of the Community's legal protection. The implementation of the Treaties, however, takes place in intensive collaboration of national and international authorities, as has repeatedly and impressively been worked out in recent times.[88] Co-operation between legal systems conditions the collaboration of the judiciaries. So, in particular, legal protection against a general norm of Community law, which as a general rule cannot be directly attacked by the individual before the Court of Justice, can only be attained by a complaint before the national court against a national implementation of the norm through an individual act. This admittedly presumes that the national judges are prepared, as Ipsen asked them to be in his closing lecture at the 45th German Lawyers' Conference,[89] 'to give due attention to European law and to take it seriously as common law for Germans'. This means above all: recognizing the direct internal applicability within a state and the primacy of Community law, about which possibly the European Court has supplied binding information through a preliminary ruling according to Article 177, EEC Treaty.[90]

Notes

Gert Nicolayson is Associate Professor of Public Law and European Community Law at the University of Hamburg. The essay was originally published in Europarecht 7 *(1972) pp. 375–390. It was revised by the author in May* 1974. *Translated by R. M. Ockenden.*

1. *Europäisches Gemeinschaftsrecht,* 1972, no. 15/24 *et seq.*
2. See Ipsen, *op. cit.,* no. 54/70 *et seq.*
3. Cf. Ipsen, *op. cit.,* no. 15/26.
4. Cf. O. Riese, 'Über den Rechtsschutz innerhalb der Europäischen Gemeinschaften', EuR 1966, p, 24 *et seq.*, 26. The Court of Justice had 'endeavoured to reach an interpretation of the Treaties which would promote the development of the Communities'. Cf. also further examples given by T. Oppermann, 'Deutsche und Europäische Verfassungsrechtsprechung, Vergleichende Gedanken zur Judikatur des Bundesverfassungsgerichts und des Gerichtshofes der Europäischen Gemeinschaften', *Der Staat* 6 (1967), p. 445 *et seq.*, p. 463 *et seq.*; an interpretation of jurisprudence from the point of view of its effectiveness in promoting integration is given by Andrew W. Green, *Political Integration by Jurisprudence,* Leyden 1969.
5. Judgment of the Court of Justice on 31 March 1971 in the case 22/70, 1971 (10) CMLR p. 335 *et seq.*; also Sasse, 'Zur Auswärtigen Gewalt der Europäischen

Wirtschaftsgemeinschaft', EuR 1971, 208; Fuss, 'Die Befugnis der Europäischen Wirtschaftsgemeinschaft zum Abschluss völkerrechtlicher Verträge mit Drittstaaten', DVBl. 1972, 237; von Arnim, 'Die Vertragsschliessungskompetenz der Europäischen Wirtschaftsgemeinschaft in der Rechtssprechung des Europäischen Gerichtshofes', AWD 1972, 215.

6. *Le Monde* of 27 April 1971, p. 19 *et seq.*: 'La Cour de Justice de Luxembourg a-t-elle outrepassé ses compétences?' Cp. the comments by Sasse, *loc. cit.* (fn. 5), and von Arnim, *loc. cit.* (fn. 5), p. 221.

7. L.B. Boudin in the *Political Science Quarterly*, 1911, quoted from Jean-Pierre Colin, *Le gouvernement des juges dans les Communautés Européennes*, 1966, p. 12 (fn. 10).

8. Cf. C. Schmitt, *Der Hüter der Verfassung*, 1931, p. 14; Colin, *loc. cit.* (fn. 7), p. 12 *et seq.*

9. According to Edouard Lambert in his book, *Le gouvernement des juges et la lutte contre la legislation sociale aux Etats-Unis*, Paris 1921.

10. Cf. for instance Hans A. Linde, 'Zeitgemässe Reform aus zeitloser Verfassung. Der U.S. Supreme Court als politischer Motor gesellschaftlicher Entwicklung', DöV 1969, 299.

11. Cf. the evidence given by Klaus Hopt, *Die Dritte Gewalt als politischer Faktor*, 1969, pp. 202, 208, *et seq.*, with many other proofs. For a German examination of the political question of the Supreme Court see Fritz Wilhelm Scharpf, *Grenzen der richterlichen Verantwortung*, 1965; from the vast literature on the Supreme Court, see R. H. Jackson, *The Supreme Court in the American System of Government*, 1957; O. Kirchheimer, *Political Justice. The Use of Legal Procedure for Political Ends*, 1961; A. M. Bickel, *The Least Dangerous Branch. The Supreme Court at the Bar of Politics*, 1962; on justiciary and the economy see H. Ehmke, *Wirtschaft und Verfassung*, 1961.

12. *Der Hüter der Verfassung*, *loc. cit.* (fn. 8), p. 22.

13. Cf. for instance Werner Weber, *Spannungen und Kräfte im westdeutschen Verfassungssystem*, 3rd ed. 1970, p. 29 *et seq.*; cf. too Helmut Rumpf, *Regierungsakte im Rechtsstaat*, 1955, p. 19 *et seq.*

14. BVerfGE vol. 2, p. 79; see also Leibholz, 'Der Status des Bundesverfassungsgerichts', in *Das Bundesverfassungsgericht 1951–1971*, 1971, p. 39.

15. Leibholz, *op. cit.* (fn. 14).

16. Viz. Bachof, 'Der Verfassungsrichter zwischen Recht und Politik', in *Universitas* (21), 1966, p. 137; P. Wittig, 'Politische Rücksichten in der Rechtsprechung des Bundesverfassungsgerichts?', *Der Staat* 8 (1969), p. 137; an interesting comparison between the Federal Constitutional Court and Court of Justice of the European Communities is drawn by T. Oppermann, 'Deutsche und europäische Verfassungsrechtsprechung', in *Der Staat* 6 (1967), p. 445.

17. Colin, *op. cit.* (fn. 7), p. 14; the 1958 constitution simply introduced a control *a priori*. Cf. now also L. Philip, *La portée de contrôle exercée par le conseil constitutionnel (à propos de la décision du 27 décembre 1973)*, in: (1974) Révue du droit public et de la science politique, p. 531.

18. M. Rivero, 'Le Conseil d'Etat, un juge qui gouverne?', in *Dalloz Chronique*, VI, 1951, *doctrine*, p. 6.

19. Cf. too, Colin, *op. cit.* (fn. 7), p. 15 *et seq.*

20. *C. I. J. Recueil* 1947–1948, p. 61; in the South West Africa case, *Rec.* 1966, p. 47 *et seq.*, the Court refused to follow political principles which had no basis

in law. The correction or revision of treaties was not in its view a matter of interpretation.

21. For the opposite view see Gerhard Hoffmann, 'Die Grenzen rechtlicher Streiterledigung im Völkerrecht', in the *Reports* of the *Deutsche Gesellschaft für Völkerrecht*, Vol. 9, 1969, pp. 1, 25 *et seq.*

22. A more cautious view is given by I. Seidl-Hohenveldern, *ibid.*, p. 70 *et seq.*; cf. also Scheuner, in the discussion on p. 123 *et seq.*

23. Paris 1966 (fn.7).

24. *Op. cit.* (fn. 7), p. 513.

25. 'Gedanken zu Funktion und Verfahren des Gerichtshofs der Europäischen Gemeinschaften', EuR 1968, pp. 1, 5 *et seq.*

26. Pescatore, 'La Cour en tant que juridiction fédérale et constitutionnelle', in *Zehn Jahre Rechtsprechung des Gerichtshofs der Europäischen Gemeinschaften*, KSE Vol. 1, 1965, p. 519 *et seq.*, p. 536.

27. Bebr, *Judicial Control of the European Communities*, 1962, p. 243.

28. E.-W. Fuss, *loc. cit.* (fn. 5), p. 243.

29. Sasse, *loc. cit.* (fn. 5), p. 226.

30. Ferrière, *Le contrôle de la légalité des actes étatiques par la Cour de Justice des Communautés Européennes*, 1969, p. 135.

31. Th. Oppermann, *loc. cit.* (fn. 4), p. 451.

32. *The Rule of Law in European Integration. The Path of the Schuman Plan*, New Haven and London 1965; see too *The Law in Political Integration. The Evolution and Integrative Implications of Regional Legal Processes in the European Community*, Cambridge, Mass. 1971; here the integrating effect of Article 177, EEC Treaty, is examined.

33. *Op. cit.* (fn. 32), p. 284.

34. *Political Integration by Jurisprudence*, Leyden 1969.

35. Cf. the summary on p. 493 *et seq.*

36. In 'Aktuelle Fragen des europäischen Gemeinschaftsrechts', 29. Supplement to ZHR, 1965, p. 1, esp. pp. 17, 20, 25.

37. Case 6/64, 1964 (3) C.M.L.R. p. 425 *et seq.*, p. 455 *et seq.*; cf. also H.-J. Rabe in 'Aktuelle Fragen', *op. cit.* (fn. 36), p. 113 *et seq.*

38. Ipsen, in 'Aktuelle Fragen', *op. cit.* (fn. 36), p. 26.

39. Cf. the evidence in H.-J. Rabe, *Das Verordnungsrecht der EWG*, 1963, p. 130 *et seq.*

40. Similarly Zuleeg, 'Die Auslegung des Europäischen Gemeinschaftsrechts', EuR 1969, p. 106.

41. So the opinion of P. Ulmer can be endorsed that a 'legally creative further development of Community law *contra legem*' is not permissible, as he demonstrated in the cartel jurisprudence of the Court; see 'Europäisches Kartellrecht auf neuen Wegen?', AWD 1970, pp. 193, 198.

42. Cf. also the decisions of the International Court quoted above in fn. 20.

43. A. W. Green, *op. cit.* (fn. 4), p. 464 *et seq.*, in his dispute with Scheingold.

44. Cf. Ipsen, *Europäisches Gemeinschaftsrecht, op. cit.* (fn. 1), no. 41/55 *et seq.*

45. Case 26/62, 1963 (2) C.M.L.R. p. 105 *et seq.*, p. 129 *et seq.* Cf. also E. Grabitz, 'Entscheidungen und Richtlinien als unmittelbar wirksames Gemeinschaftsrecht, EuR 1971, p. 1 *et seq.*, with reference to further cases (fn. 2) and bibliography (fn. 4).

46. Case 29/69, 1970 (9) C.M.L.R. p. 112 *et seq.*=EuR 1970, p. 39, with a note by Ehlermann, *ibid.*

47. Case 11/70, Rspr EuGH, Vol. XVI, p. 1135 (German text); cf. Ipsen, *op. cit.* (fn. 1), no. 41/42.

48. Cf. P. Becker, *Der Einfluss des französischen Verwaltungsrechts auf den Rechtsschutz in den Europäischen Gemeinschaften*, 1963.

49. Cf., e.g., B. Börner on the delimitation of general and individual decisions in the ECSC Treaty, in *Die Entscheidungen der Hohen Behörde*, 1965, p. 107 *et seq.*

50. Cf. the detailed exposition of H. Lecheler, *Der Europäische Gerichtshof und die allgemeinen Rechtsgrundsätze*, 1971; further examples in P. Pescatore, *Die Menschenrechte und die europäische Integration*, and *Integration* 1969, pp. 115/116.

51. Ipsen, *op. cit.* (fn. 1), no. 5/17 *et seq.*

52. Ipsen, *op. cit.* (fn. 1), no. 14/22, Zieger, *Das Grundrechtsproblem in den Europäischen Gemeinschaften*, 1970.

53. Cf. Consolidated Cases 7/56, 3/57–7/57; *Recueil de la Jurisprudence de la Cour,* vol. III, p. 81 *et seq.*; Case 14/61, 1963 (2) C.M.L.R. p. 73 *et seq.*, p. 96; on the same subject Lecheler, *op. cit.* (fn. 50), p. 76 *et seq.*

54. Lecheler, *op. cit.* (fn. 50), pp. 90/91.

55. See the exposition of the problem given by Heldrich, *Die allgemeinen Rechtsgrundsätze der ausservertraglichen Schadenshaftung im Bereich der EWG,* 1961.

56. This is the conclusion of the work written by Heldrich which is also reflected in his essay, 'Art. 215 Abs. 2 des Vertrages über die EWG. Ein Irrweg zu europäischer Rechtseinheit', JZ 1960, p. 681.

57. Rabels-Zeitschrift 28 (1964), p. 610 *et seq.*; 'Les principes généraux du droit des Etats Membres', in *Droit des Communautés Européennes,* 1969, p. 441 *et seq.*, esp. No. 1203; Fuss, 'Rechtssatz und Einzelakt im Europäischen Gemeinschaftsrecht', NJW 1964, 946; Fuss, 'Grundfragen der Gemeinschaftshaftung', EuR 1968, 356; Ipsen, *op. cit.* (fn. 52).

58. Thus Lecheler, *op. cit* (fn. 50), p. 186.

59. Cf. Zweigert, 'Rechtsvergleichung' in Strupp-Schlochauer, *Wörterbuch des Völkerrechts,* Vol. III, 1962, p. 80 *et seq.*

60. The former president of the Court Donner has already pointed this out: 'Il ne crée certainement pas le droit communautaire du néant, mais, en regard aux divergences des différentes doctrines juridiques des six Etats membres, le juge doit, dans une certaine mesure, devenir créateur de droit'; *Le rôle de la Cour de Justice dans l'élaboration du droit européen,* 1964, p. 11.

61. Lecheler, *op. cit.* (fn. 50), p. 191.

62. Lecheler, *ibid.* (fn. 61).

63. Consolidated Cases 5/66, 7/66 and 13–24/66, Rspr. EuGH, vol. XIII, p. 367, and vol. XV, p. 339 (in German).

64. Rspr. EuGH, vol. XIII, p. 367 (in German).

65. W. Hallstein, *Die Europäische Gemeinschaft* (1973), pp. 31 *et seq.*

66. Cf. von Simson, 'Der politische Wille als Gegenstand der europäischen Gemeinschaftsverträge', in *Festschrift für Otto Riese,* 1964, p. 83, 94.

67. Cf. Ipsen, *op. cit.* (fn. 1), no. 4/26.

68. Case 7/71, 1972 (11) C.M.L.R., p. 453 *et seq.*

69. Case 48/71, 1972 (11) C.M.L.R., p. 699 *et seq.*

70. Case 7/68, 1969 (8) C.M.L.R., p. 1 *et seq.*

179

71. Rspr. EuGH, vol. XVIII, p. 541 (in German).

72. Case 18/71, 26 October 1971; 11 (1972) C.M.L.R., p. 4 *et seq.*

73. 'Das Europarecht in der Krise der Gemeinschaften', EuR 1966, pp. 4, 19; see also fn. 67 above on the same subject.

74. I have discussed this point elsewhere.

75. Joseph H. Kaiser, *op. cit.* (fn. 73).

76. Articles 17 and 18 of the Acts of Accession, with Article 9 of the Resolution of the Council of 9 January 1973, on adoption of documents concerning the accession of new Members to the Communities, Official Journal L 2/1 of 1 January 1973, and the Resolution of the Council on the increase of the number of Advocates General, *Official Journal* 1 2/29 of 1 January 1973.

77. Ipsen, *op. cit.* (fn. 1), no. 54/55; further evidence in G. Nicolaysen, *Die Erweiterung der Europäischen Gemeinschaften*, in *Kölner Schriften zum Europarecht,* vol. 15, 1972, p. 101, note 22.

78. Ipsen, Note on cases 106 and 107/63, EuR 1966, p. 60.

78a. Cf. the Court's judgment 9/73 of October 24th, 1973, on the effect of the Council's decision of March 22nd, 1971, on the gradual creation of an economic union. The Court held that this decision has no legal effects which Community citizens can quote before the Court. Cf. (1974) *Europarecht*, p. 36 with notes by G. Nicolaysen.

78b. Referring to the cases where the powers provided for by the treaties do not suffice for carrying out the tasks laid down in them, the Paris summit conference agreed that 'it was desirable to make the widest possible use of all the dispositions of the treaties, including Article 235 of the EEC treaty' (cf. *The Times*, October 23rd, 1972, p. 2).

79. Cf. E. G. U. Scheuner, 'Verfassungsprobleme der Wirtschafts- und Währungsunion', in *Integration* 1971, p. 145, and in this volume, p. 66 *et seq.*; Claus Dieter Ehlermann, *Sachkompetenzen der Organverfassung der Gemeinschaft, ibid.,* p. 162; G. Henckel von Donnersmarck,' Planimmanente Krisensteuerung in der Europäischen Wirtschaftsgemeinschaft', *Planungsstudien*, vol. 8, 1971— where see also p. 92 *et seq.* on government conferences as a means of projecting plans to subsequent data, and on decisions and resolutions adopted by the Representatives of Governments of this Member State meeting in Council, and also E. Millarg, *Die Anwendung des Rechts der Europäischen Gemeinschaften in Dänemark, Grossbrittannien, Irland und Norwegen,* EuR 1972, p. 179 *et seq.*, p. 181 *et seq.*

80. *Kölner Schriften,* vol. I, 1965, p. 580 *et seq*; see also the joint paper by G. Geisseler, p. 559, and M. Lagrange, p. 606.

81. Vol. I of the *Verhandlungen des 46.* DJT 1966, Part 4.

82. Vol. II, Part G, of the *Verhandlungen, 1967.*

83. 'On legal protection within the European Communities', EuR 1966, p. 24.

84. 'Gedanken zu Funktion und Verfahren des Gerichtshofs der Europäischen Gemeinschaften', EuR 1968, p. 1.

85. 'Abschied vom Gerichtshof der Europäischen Gemeinschaften', EuR 1970, p. 303.

86. Case 25/62, 1964 (3) C.M.L.R., p. 29 *et seq.*, p. 46 *et seq.*

87. Case 10 and 18/68, 10 December 1969, Rspr. EuGH vol. XV, p 459, p. 482=EuR 1970, p. 161, with note by Nicolaysen, p. 165. The case 134/73 of January 15, 1974, in which the plaintiff complained against his exclusion from

certain subsidies, did not clarify any questions concerning the so-called competitor's action; cf. (1974) *Europarecht* no. 2 with notes by G. Nicolaysen.

88. Cf. for instance the records of the Berlin Conference (1970) of the Fédération Internationale de Droit Européen (FIDE) on 'Gemeinschaftsrecht und nationale Rechte', *Kölner Schriften zum Europarecht,* vol. 13, 1971.

89. Ipsen, 'Der deutsche Jurist und das europäische Gemeinschaftsrecht', in *Verhandlungen des 45. DJT,* vol. II/L, 1964, L 27.

90. Fundamental opposition to Community law still appears in a resolution of the Administrative Court of Frankfurt of 14 July 1971 (AWD 1971, p. 541) according to Article 100 of the German Federal Constitution, in which the jurisdiction of the German Federal Constitutional Court on Community law is accepted and the existence of equivalent guarantees of legal protection in the Communities is simply denied. It is characteristic that in its own words the Administrative Court 'believes it has found the real reason for the contradictory opinions in the different, even purely politically conditioned, attitudes to the EEC.'

Hans Peter Ipsen

CONSTITUTIONAL PERSPECTIVES OF THE EUROPEAN COMMUNITIES

I. Limitations on Perspectives and Forecasts

The making of the Community is a process of development of indefinite duration. The Treaties do not provide for their expiration. Even the fifty-year period of duration of the ECSC can hardly be considered otherwise. The aims of the Treaties in spite of the complexity of their wording, are inadequate. This is also true, from the point of view of perspectives, for the draft of a system of Community Government, appropriate procedure, institutions capable of development and the creation of a final form. The Communities are not able to draft, let alone establish, on their own a system of action or a constitution for the future, as is provided in the Treaties—and the Treaties are at present the only available basis for the Communities. Although they are in a position to do so, the fact that the Member States (apart somewhat from France) in principle question their own traditional system of government just a little, in spite of continuous unavoidable need for reform is no alibi for the Communities. For they, primarily, unprejudiced as they are since they are new, and not the States, have the opportunity to develop new, more effective and adequate methods than were handed down by the States of the nineteenth century! It is their duty to seize this opportunity, because of the responsibility transmitted to them in the sphere of the economic and social policy of the industrial society for which our national constitutions have become shaky.[1] It is not the political system of the States which can provide a model for the Communities but rather is it the Communities which are suited like a catalyst to bringing about a change in the State structures and have already done

182

so in some spheres.[2] It is true that the States are the creators of the Communities; their Governments decide ultimately in the Council the Community policy, the States insist in view of their personality in international law on remaining masters of the Treaties. But this recognition cannot remove the existence of the Communities as their creations and the reality of their effectiveness. And from that it follows that responsibility for the future devolves on them. It is thus proper, when looking for perspectives of a constitutional policy, to inquire into the means and forms which the Communities possess in their *pouvoirs constitués* for their own constitutional evolution although the States endeavour to retain the *pouvoir constituant* for themselves.

If the political system of the Communities is to develop towards the goal of integration without, by ill-considered analogy, consenting themselves with the reception of State structures and their inadequacies, it needs well thought-out plans. They must avoid the defects of national constitutions and at the same time provide for the best possible organization and democratic legitimacy of the Communities as regards surpassing States and fulfilling public tasks on a larger scale.

The scientific theory of all pertinent disciplines is required to meet the situation. It can hardly be maintained that this theory and the related empirical research have already attained even partially the 'stage of maturity'[3] even though theory and research into the creation of international communities and regional integration is generally more advanced. An outline of the efforts undertaken towards a theory of the Communities considered according to different disciplines, methods and intensity of forecast will show this. The observations of lawyers, social scientists and economists are to be considered in this connection by way of example.

1. COMPETENCE AND METHODS FOR A POLITICAL THEORY FOR THE COMMUNITY

A

Political theory of the Community requires co-operation of disciplines. In this respect it has been, for a long time, lacking and not least in Germany, because here lawyers and economists took up their subject earlier and more intensively than political scientists and sociologists.

In the field of economic theory, to take one example, Hans R. Kramer has undertaken to draw up a system of 'forms and methods of international economic integration' (1969). His methodology assists concept shaping in the EEC Treaty, helps with legal forms of co-ordination and combining the formation of institutions with applied methods of integration. In his description of the integration data he considers the elements of space, sectors and State functions, the constitutional relevance of which, for the Community law is as significant as for its critical analysis and future development.

The plan for an economic and monetary union has led to various proposals for the necessary changes in the constitution of the Communities, their institutions and procedure. The research work of Hans Möller, in particular his analysis of international economic organizations ('*Internationale Wirtschaftsorganisationen*') which appeared as long ago as 1961 based on the experiences of the OEEC has sketched the outline of the 'synopsis' in which the Communities have a special place. However economic theory has so far not provided the plan of a Community going beyond the actual demands of an economic and monetary union. But then this does not belong to its tasks.

B

Public law monographs on the decision-making process in Community law (Heinz Wagner 1965) and on the principle of 'functional integration' (Andreas Sattler 1967) have developed elements of the political theory of the Community as a prerequisite or result of the research on their actual theme. Two German conferences for University teachers of constitutional law (Erlangen 1959, Kiel 1964) have dealt with the relation of the German constitutional law to the Community powers and the maintenance and change of democracy and rule of law in the Communities. In the space of only five years between these collective efforts of German constitutional theory lies a significant advance in knowledge. It has led from a basically introverted 'navel contemplation' to an open approach with regard to a new integration style and its catalytic repercussions on the national constitution. This change, assisted by the judgments of the Luxembourg Court, has penetrated in important questions into the German Constitutional Court and from there into further counts. On the question of a merger of the three Communities and its constitutional perspectives, it has been mooted in Germany whether the 'democracy clause' of Article 138 (3), EEC Treaty, in its attempt to assimilate the parliamentary form of government in the Member States can evoke credibility and claim chances of realization and whether the development of the constitution has not been prejudiced by its premature enactment in a form which appertains too much to a State.[4]

C

On the whole the efforts of the German theory of constitutional law have not yet joined the main discussion of method and substance, which the American political and economic theory in particular offers. The fact that the German social scientists were to that extent until recently unconcerned has more serious grounds: they had not at all recognized the community process as a subject of their discipline. Even at the end of 1969 Heinrich Schneider[5] had stated:

If one were to say that the interest of German political science is comparatively narrower (than that of German law), it would be very much an understatement. Integration politics have until now never featured in the list of subjects of a conference of the German Society for Political Science.

It did not appear there until the end of 1971, and the Munich World Congress of Political Scientists in early autumn 1970 did not include any German contributions in its working group on 'European integration'. Hans-Peter Schwarz[6] has therefore aptly spoken of methodology as 'the Cinderella of integration research' and thereby implied that the step-parents were primarily the German social sciences. He has finally fruitfully begun with his 'critical essay on the methods of European Integration' to work towards a methodology, the first after Heinrich Schneider.

D

This essay provides the requisite relationship with the theories of integration of American social scientists. They investigate the 'possibilities, stages of development and dynamics of an integration of national states into larger political units' and use concepts of function and structure to describe processes of integration, the working of which in the framework of the European Community process provides the empirical basis of a speculation on the perspectives.[7] It is not a question here either of an exposition of these theories of integration or of their critical evaluation or of their adequacy or application on the constitutional policy of the Communities. All that is intended is to indicate that such a constitutional theory pursued by lawyers in Europe and especially in Germany, may not ignore this model team research into precedents of regional integration or reject it *a limine* by a 'judgment of dismissal' as has been largely the case until now.

Karl W. Deutsch[8] and his school have analysed the establishment of greater integrated units particularly on the basis of historical precedents and have inferred from this laws of the process of integration. The German constitutional development to the foundation of the empire also features as material for consideration. The case studies of Amitai Etzioni[9] are based on historical comparison. Whilst the successful American federation into the USA has been analysed, as Schwarz[10] points out, analyses of contemporary interest, drawing comparisons with important state integrations of the last century (Belgium, Switzerland, Germany, Italy, Canada and Australia) and those of our own century have not been undertaken except by Deutsch and his school. The catchword of Pompidou's 'confederation', which is difficult to understand, and was probably so intended, demonstrates sufficiently how much such studies are needed.

The theory going back to David Mitrany[11] of the supranational functionalism and its empirical examination by Ernst B. Haas[12] and Leon N.

185

Lindberg[13] conducted in respect of the integration process of the EEC reveal by their methodology and perspective aspects the tendencies and contrasts in the continental European discussion, especially in German constitutional theory,[14] which have become discernible with regard to the Communities and the future of their constitutional policy. The constitutionalists can see the Community developing automatically only into a European federal state, because the national principles and values have to prevail in the Community process by reason of a kind of 'isonomy' effect. The functionalists of various shades on the other hand see in the gradual 'supranationalization' of the former state functions an adequate method of integration without the formation of a new state. They regard as essential the 'dismembering' of former state functions and their integration in decision-making institutions of the Community, the activities of which through the so-called spill-over effect cause more and more functions to succumb to the process of integration. Certain periods of the making of the European Community confirm this variant of neo-functionalism.

In the light of this polarity between constitutionalism and functionalism the 'democratization' clause of Article 138 (2), EEC Treaty, can be understood in a constitutionalistic sense as non-binding 'bowing before the spirit of the time',[15] as perhaps the insertion in the French Government Declaration of 9 May 1950, which called the ECSC 'the first stage of the European Federation'. For Jean Monnet who knew and believed in Mitrany functionalism probably intended by that 'only the European dressing to a project in the sense of Mitrany'.[16] In view of this polarity, which the American methodological dispute makes clear, the Erlanger conference for University teachers of constitutional law in 1959—at least as regards the delivered papers—and likewise Andreas Sattler's book (in spite of its title *Functional Integration*) are to be classified as constitutionalists. The so-called 'Kiel Wave' of the conference for University teachers of constitutional law in 1964 emancipated the German theory from several constitutional shackles. But its positive effect has nevertheless remained limited (in particular in the attempt to give Community power a legitimate basis), and *Grundbegriffe des Beschlussrechts* by Heinz Wagner (1965)[17] could in spite of its auspicious introduction (in particular p. 8 *et seq.*) not overcome, in its consideration of the constitutional perspectives, the position, that his diagnosis had recognized very aptly for the community situation still determined by de Gaulle. For his view based on U. W. Kitzinger, that it is not a question of 'making super states or supranational states out of national states but rather to take over the functions of the national state' (p.10), that the Communities are 'common instruments of the states for solving problems, which could be solved neither in the state framework nor in the loose forms of earlier alliances and treaties' (p. 9), and his truly apt proposition that what is required for the present is 'maintenance, expansion, and best possible development of functional integration' (pp. 8/9) is, in the last analysis, not vindicated in the parts of his book concerned with constitutional policy. Nothing shows this contradiction more clearly than his words on the question of the precedence of Community law (p. 34): 'absolute precedence of Community law over the law of the Member States cannot be considered as legally desirable'.

(*aa*) International functionalism as a theory of action[18] is intended as a method of securing peace across the borders in the large areas of the industrial society. It is as a strategy for peace a product of the experience after the war and its field of application becomes to such a degree greater in which the states operate redistribution and supply machineries, and become welfare states and their administrations become welfare administrations. It is concerned with functions 'signifying the same as economic, social and administrative tasks and needs, which can best be satisfied by international collaboration'.[19] They are, in simpler words, public tasks which are no longer within state competence. But it is essential even according to the functional theory, that this presupposes the unanimous political decision of the Member States. Therefore the functional integration can take place on the consensual basis of this political decision within the framework of the treaty-based regulations largely in a process of a technical self-determination. Thus is explained the fact that the question of the form of the organization entrusted with such functions need not be a primary object of this theory: 'form follows function'. That is indeed quite an abstract and abbreviated concept which in its approach concerns more the breaking down of the state than the construction of the future form.[20] But it has the force of the antithesis to constitutionalism, which with its 'isonomic' claim, is essentially hegemonic.

The undertaking, no longer by the state, of public tasks, that is, their admission into the sphere of the Community can automatically lead to the similar admission of further tasks and the establishment of links between the Community and other tasks which the states had retained. Therefore neo-functionalists—going beyond Mitrany's technical self-determination—see in the spill-over effect of this kind the chance and the expectation of the gradual political evolution of the Community, which thus becomes a new *raison d'être* of the Member States'.[21] But whether that leads to a new rivalry between them and the Communities and thus to a relapse into nationalism, or whether the Communities in that way progress towards federation, neither functionalists nor neo-functionalists can answer and the lawyer who applies their method on constitutional politics would do well in his turn to refuse to give an answer.

The comprehensive analysis of this process, which would come nearer to an answer, has not yet been made. To make it lies primarily in the province of the economics and sociology. For this the determination of appropriate indicators is necessary under the application of which probability models of regional integration processes could be developed.[22] The manner in which economic theory and social sciences join together for this remains to be discussed.

187

(*bb*) Constitutionalism has obviously determined and accompanied the beginnings of the Community process so far as concerns the political determination of its objectives in the Treaties and their evaluation at least in the Federal Republic.[23] Constitutionalism considers the federal form of government not only as a useful element of peace but also as the necessary form of regional unions. Here the principle holds 'function follows form', which means, the Community process has the aim of creating a federal or similar state structure homogeneous to the constitutional structures and systems of government of the Member States.

In this sense the problem of structural homogeneity between the constitution of the State and that of the Community has for a long time been discussed from a 'constitutionalist' standpoint. Although as such it has been resolved, it is still of importance in such matters as the question of priority between national and Community law and in the claim of assertion over Community powers of fundamental rights enshrined in national constitutions. Above all, it influences 'unconsciously' the demand that Community institutions and decision-making should be provided with a parliamentary legitimacy. Article 138 (2), EEC Treaty, provides the legal basis for it.

In the end stage of integration the constitutionalist method agrees with the apparently inescapable drive towards a federation of the Community. It urges the greatest possible haste and shortening of phases without critically examining the non-legal preconditions. Thereby it fails to appreciate a specific trait of the Community process and its constitution, for the Community process is basically an open system.[24] In its own effectiveness and in its co-operation with, and the influence of, its Member States it presents itself as much more open and amenable to future developments than the constitutional system of the national state which insofar, is still 'closed'. Constitutionalism is therefore on that account, already a political theory which is not adequate for the Community process. For it has a conservative effect *per se*, and does not have the necessary dynamic element, which a new progressiveness doing justice to new needs and tasks, requires as a basis for the legitimacy of decision-making institutions and processes.

E

Methods of analysis are a precondition and basis of all forecasts considered relevant to constitutional policy and are therefore indispensable to lawyers. As far as European integration is concerned these methods have been developed and tested in the Member States[25] but above all in American economic theory and social sciences. Economic and social processes have been thereby studies, and not only with regard to their correspondence to the political integration.[26] The explanation of their course and direction served at the same time to determine the political stage of integration and possible advances.

To be sure, these overlapping analytical comparisons have shown differences between the aims of integration and their assessment, and also about the 'worth' of economic integration in a European Community policy,[27] the suppression and silence about which can cause only harm.

Reference only can be made to the exposition and application of American theory in order to examine its usefulness from the constitutional point of view, particularly as it embraces a wider field of international and intersystem-relations. Thus, for example, the range of approaches and means applied by Karl W. Deutsch and his school is extremely broad: it extends from a theoretical frame of reference and hypotheses, which are examined with the help of test cases, ascertainment of data or qualitative descriptions, to discussions about their interpretation and evaluation with the object of determining anticipated integration processes in order to help political decision-making. It is, of course, the task of non-legal disciplines to judge the evidence value and reliability of interviews with members of elites, representative opinion polls, press comments or the like. For the purposes of a theory of constitutional policy, only their results could be useful. Whether and how far they appear relevant is then the responsibility of constitutional policy. The same holds for the relevance of certain transactions (tourist travel, student exchange, correspondence, etc.). Exchange of goods, capital movements, inland mobility, the interlocking of trade, the share of foreign trade, gross social product afford measurements and instruments of measurement, the summary of which in an index of relative acceptance (R–A index)[28] permits conclusions as to the state and tendencies of the process of integration, economic or not. These diagnostic means of the economic sciences appear more capable of evaluation from the constitutional policy point of view than those of the social sciences, for they can be calculated and tested, meeting thus an essential legal requirement.

Such methods come nearer to the aims of a Community theory (valuation and cognition), and to a constitutional policy for the Communities which try to deduce particular characteristics and elements of the process of integration from economic data and measurements. This is done for instance by basing suggestions about the distribution of power between national and supranational decision-making and control bodies, on the varying use of gross social product by the national states or the Community exerting their respective taxation and budgetary powers. Such an argument is based on a comparison with the degree to which contractual delegations of power or national reservations are made use of. Similarly an adequate method is to compare the various sectors of practical policy and the different powers for their implementation.

This is the course adopted by Lindberg and Scheingold in *Europe's would-be polity* (1970), in addition to politico-sociological methods of diagnosing the Common Market citizen's attitude towards the Community, the national state, and their readiness to consent. They thus convey

189

insights[29] into the development of integration within the framework of the Treaty, the regression from integration, the stages of integration based only on statically administrative work, the setback from these positions as a result of infringement of the Treaty rules of objects as well as into the appearance of a new type of integration impetus independent of decisions in the framework of, or about the Treaties. The knowledge of such facts provides the basis for judging the application of the Treaty, the secondary Community law, the case law and the practice of the Council and Commission, from the point of view of constitutional policy. This method has been applied in case studies[30] of agricultural and transport policy, customs union, the energy (coal) sector and their crises. Such studies make it possible to look at the structure of the Treaties from the constitutional policy point of view and see whether it is suitable or needs revision. With the challenging of a 'permissive consensus',[31] that is the readiness of citizens affected and of political leaders to protect and promote the Community process, the socio-economic method, which seeks to fathom this consensus, encroaches upon the constitutional question of the adequate procedure for obtaining consensus.

2. PERSPECTIVES AND FORECASTS

A review[32] of Karl W. Deutsch's integration theory and its methods, comes to the conclusion that it would have been scientifically more attractive if he

> had developed an independent way of calculating integration and had then applied it over a long period on the R–A index figures for different groups of transactions as well as to the figures, which express the interdependence of the Member States. Since transactions which lead to interdependence and discontinuity are probably not sufficient to explain a great degree of variation in the integration variables, it would have been advisable to introduce as additional classifying variables the aspect of homogeneity and equality, in particular in relation to the power potential and the socio-economic state of development of the Member States and the degree of the politico-ideological agreement among the national leading groups.

(a) Whoever reads these comments on the methods of integration analysis,[33] understands analysis as a precondition of every perspective and forecast, and moreover properly assesses the sources of danger, which lie in the inference from analysis to forecast, will have to accept that there are limits to the practical use of perspectives and their consideration from the constitutional policy point of view. Critical caution is indicated and rightly often demanded, and not only (which alone is of interest here) in respect

190

of its conceivable reliability and usefulness for the Community theory and its constitutional policy. Scepticism enters more and more the longer the period over which the forecast of constitutional policy extends. The economic and monetary union policy extends over a period of ten years. That exceeds, as far as economic policy is concerned, the medium term planning period, the integration steps for which Deutsch[34] puts at from three to five years and calls ten years a long-term process. Perspectives of constitutional policy would like to, and should reckon with longer periods. However, in the community process functioning at first as an economic integration they are set against shorter phases, the course and effect of which provide the basis for the regulation of newer and more adequate authorities and decision-making procedures. Thus the gradual allocation of budgetary powers to Parliament through the Budget Treaty over a period of ten years is one side of this process, and the question of its effect on the position of Parliament in the constitutional system of the Community is the other side. From this it follows that economic and social perspectives of such periods of time can scarcely supply satisfactorily the constitutional theory of the Community with the forecasts it needs, and this means that reservations must be made as to their usefulness. Scientifically therefore, what Katharina Focke[35] states with regard to the European options after the Hague Summit, is indeed more probable:

It would be much too early today in the middle of a dynamic process of development of the Community to describe or determine how the end stage—if there is ever an end stage—is to appear.

Meanwhile, passivity is not thereby commended to the politician,[36] and a scientific Community theory is not thereby exempt from the task of thinking out at least the next foreseeable phases of development.

(b) Whether intuition, political instinct or ideology are better motivations and driving forces for a Community policy is difficult to discuss here. But there is no doubt, that, for a Community theory and constitutional policy seeking legal forms, any method is to be preferred which provides results without relying upon such motivations and driving-forces—even if it turns out so useful or harmful that as a rule a political form cannot take shape without them. In this situation a theory of Community policy can not do without even the most scanty analysis, which the social and economic sciences can offer even by debatable methods. Every interdisciplinary study meets inevitably with reservations. It is, however, indispensable because doing without an 'integrated' Community theory means ignoring suggestions and checks, which should at least be examined. This holds true, for example, as has aptly been remarked,[37] for Ernst Haas's approach and Scheuner's concept of the Communities' prefederal character, for Lindberg's categories of functionalism, and the styling of the Communities in this book as 'purpose-bound organizations' ('*Zweckverbände*'). In any

191

case such comparison of models between the disciplines helps to 'take the ideology out of research approaches', and that alone would be worth the effort.

II. The Aim

1. Community and State Aims

(a) The contractual legal bases of the community process (*Vergemein-schaftung*) determine its aims, its tasks and the means to realize the aims and fulfil the tasks. 'Aims' and 'tasks' in these regulations embrace different aspects of the same subject matter. Therefore, taken together, they permit conclusions as to the complexity of the 'aim' of integration conceived in the Treaties. The aims are set out in the preambles to the Treaties.

The aims contained in the EEC Treaty are a process to an ever closer union among the peoples of Europe, the furtherance of their welfare, their freedom and peace. The Euratom Treaty strives for peaceful progress and the furtherance of the prosperity of the peoples. The community process in respect of the basic industries is for the ECSC Treaty a contribution of an organized Europe to the maintenance of world peace, the furtherance of prosperity, and the foundations of institutions for a broader and deeper community among long-divided and rival peoples.

The objects in the preambles to the Rome Treaties fall behind those of the ECSC Treaty, which sees, in a 'broader and deeper Community . . . a direction to a destiny henceforward shared' by the peoples of the Community.

(b) The language of the preambles to the Treaties in no way falls short of the traditional style of state constitutions in choice of words and pathos. It is scarcely consistent with the sober provisions on institutions and procedure of economic integration. The objects of the preambles are, however, of little use insofar as they do other than postulate or promise progress towards prosperity and freedom. For to that extent they repeat only what economic integration means according to the nature of the Treaties: the exclusion of the non-peaceful means among the Member States to secure internal peace in the Communities insofar, of course, as treaties are capable of doing this. Whether European integration is capable of contributing to world peace, is outside its conception, at least as far as it is a question of objects for which the Community has powers. Only the kind of conception of the preamble in the ECSC Treaty (of an organized Europe and a broadening and deepening of the Community) comes within the sphere of development of actual community policy. That the subsequent Rome Treaties have to that extent less binding preambles can indicate scepticism as well as the political situation at the time of the conclusion of the Rome Treaties.

192

(c) If the Communities are conceived as the means to attain the aims and objects pursued by the peoples of the Member States, that is, instruments, the Treaties and their preambles nevertheless proclaim no aims directed to the dissolution of the states. Understanding the Communities as instruments does not appear, therefore, so far as the Treaties are concerned, as it is said of the liberal theory and as it is essential to the Marxist doctrine, as a 'step on a way, which, as men hope, leads them to a society without state'.[38] On the other hand it follows from the instrumental understanding of the community process, that it obviously cannot do without the provision of aims and objects: even if it is true,[39] that the state cannot be attached to certain aims and objects because it must deal appropriately with each task and situation, the Communities require an object and their functioning is likewise limited by their aim. For they are organizations pursuing one or several objects, not all purpose organizations as the states which still have competence in everything. In the acceptance of this lies also the confirmation of the fact that, furtherance of prosperity, freedom and maintenance of peace, as the preambles to the Treaties describe them, express no appropriate and adequate aim for the community process. For they are in no way different from the conceivable objects of a state. The fact is not thereby overlooked that the distributive power in the modern industrial society makes him attractive who possesses it—thus the states further their own maintenance so long as they possess it, and they jeopardize it when they transfer this power to the Communities.[40] But no matter who possesses it the aim of the distributive power remains the same.

(d) There are many considerations for giving European integration an ultimate aim: the establishment of a European 'nationalism', a European centre of power within world politics, an economically and rationally perfect mechanism or—in the manner of a still unwritten philosophy of integration—an institution securing in the best way possible a dignified human life.[41] All these are outside the Treaties and are, at most, speculations and drafts of constitutional policy. Hitherto the aim of the Community has been limited to the establishment of institutions and the setting up of procedures[42] seeking to secure that public tasks of a broad economic nature, which are not state tasks any longer, are fulfilled as well as possible. Other aims, which appear possible for the Community to pursue, can only be state aims pursued, even though inadequately, by state institutions and in state procedures. Public tasks as such do not change in the integration process, but the manner in which they are fulfilled does.

Whether empirical political science or philosophical political theory is capable of developing a theory of Community aims which attributes intrinsic value to the Communities, cannot be discussed here. In this book no attempt of that kind is made. The Treaties, which are the basis for the present integration, can for the time being only be understood as regards their aims, as instruments providing for the better fulfilment of public tasks which can no longer be taken care of by the states.[43]

2. Progress towards the Aim

(a) The organization of the states of the industrial society, which make up the Community, is overburdened. They stand before the alternative of diminishing their state character or changing their organization and functions.[44] The Community process, which they have undergone, shows clearly that they have opted for change: integration is supposed to offer in its institutions and procedure better stabilization of the order, which the welfare state maintains, than can the national states. Whether that has succeeded and will continue to succeed depends today on whether the conditions for the setting up of the economic and monetary union are fulfilled and the measures necessary for their realization in the next decade are taken. In view of the decision to change it is only logical the Werner report should content itself in describing the aim of the economic and monetary union with the sentence: 'It must make it possible to secure growth and stability in the Community, to strengthen the contribution of the Community to the economic and monetary balance in the world and to make a stability block out of the Community'.[45] The next Community aim, thus described, requires certain decisions regarding institutions and procedure, which set the Community in motion by equipping its institutions, competences and administration. But the Communities will not thereby be transformed into goals in themselves, the objects and aims of which distinguish them from those of their Member States.

(b) As opposed to the aim of the economic and monetary union, the aim to merge the Treaties within a certain period has been postponed. Whether the merger has the character of an independent aim in the present context is doubtful. The answer depends on the form of merger. Only if it goes beyond a technically legal consolidation of the Treaties and merger of the three communities, and represents progress towards integration, including the economic and monetary union, could it have any relevance as regards aims. But even a merged single community, which has the institutions and procedures for realizing the economic and monetary union, will not thereby become an all-purpose organization but it will limit itself to public tasks fulfilled formerly by the Member States.

(c) The start made with the next aim of an economic and monetary union has not prevented the Member States of the Community from jointly endeavouring to allocate other state tasks outside the responsibility for economic output. Insofar as it has taken place with a view to a development towards a 'political union' (which is not inherent in the Community, but which is associated with it and arises out of the membership position of the states), it has received its most recent impetus in the Hague Summit Conference of December 1969. Where No. 15 of the Hague final communiqué refers to the end stage as the United States of Western Europe, the phrase refers to a political programme rather than a legal development.

The study committee under the chairmanship of the Belgian, Davignon, recommended on the application of the foreign ministers, regular consultations on foreign policy. These recommendations led to the resolution of the foreign ministers in their conference in Viterbo on 29 May 1970 to meet together twice a year for consultations on all important questions of foreign policy. The so-called Davignon Agreement was concluded on 27 October 1970. Since then, consultations have regularly taken place.[46] Just as the European Parliament stressed the relation between the creation of the economic and monetary union and the aim of political unity,[47] so this is emphasized in sections I and V of the second part and section I of the fourth part of the Agreement: insofar as the works of the foreign ministers have any effect on the activity of the Community, the Commission is requested to give an opinion, and with reference to the new Member States the connection is stressed between belonging to the Community and participating in activities, which shall make possible progress towards political unity.

The actual subject matter of the consultations is not specified. In the last analysis they are only intended to intensify the solidarity of the Member States. Section I of the second part describes as aims of the co-operation:

> to secure a better mutual understanding of the major problems of international politics by regular information and consultation, to help to harmonize points of view, to co-ordinate attitudes and, where it seems possible and desirable, to adopt a common policy and thereby strengthen solidarity.

For want of guidance as to matter and, therefore, determination of aims, it is limited, in relation to the general aim of integration, to endeavouring by means of procedural rules to harmonize foreign policy and to obtain the participation of the Community institutions in this, insofar as they are affected.

This procedure does not contribute to the aim of a 'political union'. Neither as regards the Treaties nor in the procedure itself, which minimizes the participation of the institutions, is progress secured towards a political community process in a manner relevant to constitutional policy.[48] The exclusive conduct of foreign policy by the state remains untouched. No procedure of integration tried out in the Treaty is applied. There are no proceedings or institutions provided by the Treaties for harmonizing foreign policy as there are for harmonizing other policies. The Davignon Agreement is therefore no appropriate instrument for the aim of political union, which the Hague Conference referred to. From the point of view of integration policy it is a preliminary or sub-stage, which in the last analysis, is scarcely distinguishable from traditional methods of foreign policy. This is the method of co-operation, not integration. The agreed regularity of the consultations and the participation of the Commission and Parliament does not basically alter this.

(*d*) It appertains to the efforts of such disciplines, which are scientifically

195

concerned with the conditions and strategies of a European policy for peace, to determine the role and possibilities of economic integration in this policy.[49] In particular they are concerned with the factors and structures of the states of the Community and those of COMECON to ascertain the conditions of a possible *rapprochement* of the two systems. There cannot be deduced from the structure of the Communities securing peace whether technical, in this sense non-political and functional, co-operation between the Communities and the states of the East block can be relevant to the policy of peace. For the basic political decisions and homogeneities which exist in the Communities and among their members, and which make possible economic integration, are lacking between the Community and COMECON. The fact that the USSR has not recognized the Communities is the external expression of the difference in the systems.[50]

The explanation of this is that foreign policy is not an object of integration. Whether the intersystem position of the Communities can be an object of discussion or decision in the consultations of the foreign ministers is a matter of major foreign policy, the question of the European security conference and developments in world politics. The Communities, themselves, are powerless in this respect. Insofar as economic integration can contribute towards securing world peace[51] it is not due to the object clauses in the Treaties or their fulfilment. Peace can, however, possibly be furthered by foreign trade. Since trade policy is in principle, under Article 113, EEC Treaty, subject to Community co-ordination, this fact makes possible intersystem relations which can work in favour of peace. However, the emphasis given in the preambles to the aim of maintenance of peace was not intended by the Treaties to have any particular relevance in foreign policy. It also seems that it cannot be otherwise from the constitutional policy point of view so long as the Communities are not responsible for foreign policy.

3. The Need for an Aim

(*a*) The making of the Community is a process. Although the Treaties are not for a fixed period or—as the ECSC Treaty with its fifty-year period—are at least established without any political time limit, they express no ultimate aim of the process. What, so far as integration is concerned, if not expressed in the Treaty, is expected and hoped of it and by others is tacitly ruled out, is not, at any rate, an object of the constitution of the Communities. Even the wording of the preamble to the ECSC Treaty, which could be cited as coming nearest this, are limited to the conception of an organized Europe, a broadening and deepening of the Community, which in its turn provides an institutional basis for this. Even they describe elements of the process and no ultimate aim. The Community process in the field of law has no model and no other stated aim of the process of integration than its own development.[52] The same is true of the Treaty of Accession of 22 January 1972.

This shows integration and its manner of proceeding as regarding it against its 'nature' to provide aims of integration from a beginning to ultimate union, because integration aims for an 'open' order as the manner of taking Community decisions and fulfilling tasks which are no longer within the competence of the state.

Whether the Treaties must forthwith or thereafter provide an ultimate aim, depends, from the constitutional policy point of view, on whether the Community process is not capable meaningfully of pursuing its present set aims further without the timely establishment of an ultimate aim. And with every further progress in expanding the Treaty—as by starting the economic and monetary union—the question arises again as to whether in its legal shaping a simultaneous provision of an ultimate aim is necessary or whether its omission does no harm or is even desirable.

The Schuman Plan and its judicial embodiment in the ECSC Treaty were, as a first phase of integration, accompanied by the political idea of a future federation. This idea—if in different nuances—is always finding new champions. The concept of the ultimate aim as being European federation belongs here—as well as the most ambivalent idea of a confederation. In situations of special significance for integration—such as during great crises and most recently before the decision to join by the British House of Commons—the ultimate aim has played an important role in the argument and discussion. In the discussion it was partly also assumed that the integration process as it is given legal form in the Treaties, prejudices the ultimate aim, although the Treaty itself obviously does not stipulate any such ultimate aim.

(b) None of these points of view is correct: neither that of a present need of an ultimate aim to be contained now in the Treaties, nor that the Treaties tacitly prejudice already such an ultimate aim. The present Communities law, its institutions and procedure are sufficient regulations for the immediate aims fixed in the Treaties. Their development, if desirable from the constitutional policy point of view, is possible by amending the Treaty. Such amendment will be necessary for the economic and monetary union. A treaty formulation, such as the Davignon Agreement aims at, would serve this kind of development. An article on the lines of Article 113, EEC Treaty, could deal with foreign policy too. Such a development of aims and steps of integration seems adequate and practicable from the constitutional policy point of view, without saying more about the ultimate aim than the present Treaties, namely nothing. The task of treaty formulation in the next phases can only be, under consideration of the actual stage achieved in the realism of aims, to stipulate now aims and action, and to provide for the necessary institutions and procedure in the manner of Article 8, EEC Treaty.

At least today—at a time in which the ten-year plan for an economic and monetary union needs a legal frame and the Treaties know of no aim in the sphere of policy yet—there is from the point of view of constitutional policy no need for an ultimate aim to be written into the Treaty. Already in 1960 this thesis was advocated:

> European integration is developing as various units and so can it continue for a long time. One can only suspect what the end result will be; but it may not be quite off the mark to prophesy the establishment of a so far unknown pluralistic political structure. Such a structure could very well permit the nations concerned to maintain to a very large extent their identity, whilst at the same time they are included in organizations which transcend the national level.[53]

That may be so and may be what will happen. Things could also develop differently. Integration proceeds and the process of economic integration, which has so far existed for two decades, occupies a very short time in relation to the historic process of creating and changing a state. For this reason and because of its special character there is everything to be said for keeping the ultimate aim open and for refraining from prejudicially fixing any such. A dialectic constitutional policy seems therefore adequate. It is based on a fluctuation between the determination of aims for the immediate future, the provision of adequate institutions and procedures, the realization of these aims, the fixing of new aims and new institutions and procedures until finally a certain renewal of aims amounts to the determination of an ultimate aim, or to the statement that this aim has been attained, — according to the preamble to the ECSC Treaty—the foundations for integration have been laid, 'which will give direction to a destiny henceforward shared'.

(c) The question of an ultimate aim naturally remains open with regard to constitutional policy which is pursued outside and beyond the task of a legal framing—whether by politicians, political scientists, publicists or by anyone else. This is, however, not the place for discussing that. Only so far as concerns the question of the ultimate form of the Community as a problem of a unit and structure is its discussion appropriate from the legal point of view.

III. The People

1. Community without a Community Nation

The Community law disseminates and extends the equality of people in the Community as regards public authority. It furthers the equal treatment of the alien Common Market citizen and the national of the Member State. At the same time it disseminates and extends the freedom of people in the Community by breaking down the frontiers between the Member States which impede freedom. Freedom of movement and freedom of the worker are effects of this kind which most directly concern the individual. The other freedoms of the Common Market and the equality clause of Article 7, EEC Treaty, ensure these effects for large areas of participation in the economy.

The protection of equality and freedom in the economic sphere which the national state seeks to secure in order to limit social inequality and to restrain its abuse[54] is given over to the Community within the ambit of the transference of state sovereign rights. Although the basic distinction between state and society was called in question by reason of the growing interaction between state functions and social processes, the state-society relation has experienced no change solely by reason of the integration process. For the Common Market citizen remains primarily a member of the society of his state. Legal aims and forms of integration have no social dimension.[55] The legal formula is apt here: persons in the Community continue to be nationals of the Member States, their grouping of political participation continues as such national participation, their interests, customs of behaviour and consciousness continue to be directed to the social life in the states and not to the Community and the decision-making process of its institutions, the formulation of Community interests and the consensus to public Community authority. Article 137, EEC Treaty, meets these circumstances when it refers to the assembly of 'representatives of the peoples of the States brought together in the Community.'

It is true, an alien Common Market citizen is provided with a position in a foreign Member State which exempts him from the law applicable to aliens. He overcomes in his economic capacity the claim by the state, based upon nationality, to determine exclusively the meaning of 'nation'. Meanwhile: the fact that Community law changes the status of Common Market aliens, and transforms the citizens of all Member States into Common Market citizens, does not mean that it can change the basic relationship between the individual societies and their Member States, let alone that it can form a Community society in relation to the Community as such that is in the sense of creating a European society by integration. Whether as a consequence of guaranteeing equality and freedom under Community law social relations and structures will also be integrated into Europe is difficult to determine or forecast by legal methods. The disciplines of the social sciences are endeavouring to throw some light on this. Their results could be relevant for shaping legal policy as well as for the question of the institutional development of the Assembly, its election and its powers.

2. Group Interests and Group Organization

From the constitutional policy point of view integration is concerned much less with the individual and his particular interests and much more with the interests of groups and their formation, that is the organization of groups. A model of society based on the 'addition of individuals' no longer accords with the recognition 'that today most people feel that they belong no longer directly to society but only via groups and associations.'[56] A process of integration, which primarily considers the subject 'economy' and people as participants of economic events, must all the more necessarily take into consideration such a model of group society as economic interest in the modern industrial society is *per se* and primarily directed to groups and produces groups. According to these standards the groupings of people existing in the Member States can be described and assessed variously from the integration policy point of view according to their interests and status of organization.

(*a*) The supreme and primary grouping of people in the Community, namely that of peoples into nations, can be left out of consideration for several reasons. In so far as the Community constitution has decided and in the establishment (and expansion) of the communities deemed, that the states integrate certain sovereign powers of their organization with the element of their people. From the point of view of constitutional policy a change in the areas transferred, institutions and procedures of the Community process and the consensus machinery could be considered, as well as, in the last analysis, the form of the integrated unit and thus the dissolution of the national grouping possibly in order to enable the formation of a new political unit, a European nation. Meanwhile this ultimate question is outside all relevant constitutional policy, both present and for a long time to come. The basic decision of the Community process, its present status and foreseeable progress permit only to take as a basis the grouping into national states as expressed in the Community regulations on the position of the Member States. The suggestion of *The Times* to further integration by the introduction of a European community citizenship on 22 January 1972, the day of the signing of the Act of Accession, was effective publicity, but politically simply unreal. On the other hand: the position of the state cannot be disregarded either for the legitimacy of the Community process itself or for its future form.

Because this is so, the question does not arise from the constitutional point of view whether by means of an appropriate legal framework the peoples of the Member States could or ought to be integrated into one European nation. The integration process *per se* can contribute towards the removal of historic rivalries between Member States (Germany/France), the renewal of old alliances (France/Great Britain), or make possible changing coalitions of states, which conflict with historical experience. The Treaty provisions referring to procedure and hard decisions to be arrived at do not exclude such events even though they put limits on their possibilities of development. The great crises of integration show, however, that the states of the Community always revolt against such limitations.

In the language regulations of the Treaties on the one hand and their practical implementation on the other, factors arise which have always been relevant to the concepts of people and nation and only recently in

Belgium have jeopardized the unity of the nation. The language discussions relating to the British accession, and the French concern for the language privilege and the English-Scandinavian influence in the Community[57] illustrate also that the grouping of people into nations does not lead to an integration impetus and cannot be used to that effect. Even the fact that the French language prevailed hitherto as the Community tongue cannot be regarded as a positive contribution to European integration.

Religion, race,[58] level of culture, sense of history and other factors serving to group peoples and build nations can only affect integration in a negative sense. Integration does not emphasize such national characteristics as faith, loyalty and patriotism. There can simply be no question of a corresponding 'integrated' attitude of people of Member States in the sense of a growing loyalty to the Community or 'European patriotism'. To this extent people who feel ties to their state and are at all capable of such feelings have probably remained indifferent to the Community—for this reason this attitude cannot be regarded as positive from the constitutional policy point of view. It is, therefore, idle to expect that direct elections to the Assembly would considerably contribute to the creation of a Community sense. What has been worked out by modern social scientific methods should not be overvalued and should only with the greatest caution be taken into account in constitutional policy.

On the whole, the further development of Community law, in so far as it concerns the relationship of the individual to the public authorities, can continue to reckon with peoples of the Member States and with societies which are aware of a relationship to these states.[59] It remains the task of social sciences to show whether this fact is inherent in the matter or is due to a failure of integration policy and of those who assume responsibility for it in the states and communities: whether nothing more has been demanded of the politically conscious citizen in the Member States, whose attitude is decisive, than to approve or put up with decisions of his political leaders instead of placing him, the citizen, whether he approves or disapproves of integration, before such decisions.[60]

Whether the same holds true for the articulation and orientation of the interests and organization of social groups cannot be answered with the same certainty and it is up to the social scientists to make the necessary research, and their results should be considered from the constitutional policy point of view.[61] This has been done with regard to generation-determined attitudes, the desire of certain social classes in the peoples of the Community, for emancipation, with regard to the organization of economic interests, and—in the forefront of organized political representation— the development of European political parties. Such analyses permit conclusions about the relevance of social groups and their effect on the further prospects of the integration process.

(b) For all further assessment of social group interests and their organization in the forefront of a building of a political opinion the attitude of the different generations is of importance. It is therefore legitimate for social scientific analyses and reviews of methods[62] to have devoted their special attention to empirical investigations to this question. They are entitled to similar attention from the point of view of constitutional policy, even if the fact is taken into account, that the interchange of young generations in group organizations of an economic or political nature and in professional associations can immediately lead to changes in consciousness and attitudes, which influence the result of the analysis. The Commission has appreciated the significance of the question. The discussion organized by it of 12–14 June 1970, 'Youth and the European Community'[63] had in its opinion 'the most significant result . . . the confirmation of the desire on the part of youth for a greater participation in the work of European unification, which in future will have to be taken into account'. The course of the conference and even the composition of the delegations taking part 'from the most important political, trade union, peasant and student youth organizations, which were legally active in the six countries' do not exclude scepticism on two accounts: first whether the course permitted conclusions to be drawn in respect of the attitude of European youth in general, because the silent majority were not represented or articulate in this manner; secondly because the generally critically-orientated, ideological attitude of this generation towards the state and economic structures of the industrial society and the general adoption of their technocratic and undemocratic perfectionism into the Communities suppressed or hindered the requisite rational discussions of constitutional policy. For these reasons a constitutional policy of the Communities is exposed to a large degree in the estimation of the young and younger generations to such problems, with which the process for forming opinion has to contend in the larger Member States. Only to the extent that they are overcome in the context of the Member State can a Community constitutional policy hope that these problems will not have the effect of putting obstacles in the way of integration.[64] Disenchantment with the state and an anti-state attitude based on this kind of ideology, as at present, will not give any impulse to the Community process as tendencies to the dissolution of the state, but clearly will hinder such a process because

now among the generation of twenty-year olds an opposition begins to form against the idea of European unity. Supporters of the concept of Europe will in future have to defend themselves not only against champions of undiminished national sovereignty, but also against the growing group of those who demand other economic structures and a new policy of integration in the name of a 'Europe of realities'.[65]

(c) This attitude is supported by the assertion that a balancing of the European policy does not contribute 'to the freeing of people and the release of their capacities'; integration has thus not maintained itself as a 'strategy of emancipation' but has functioned as 'management of a crisis'.[66] The demand based on this—and with it the requisite conceived aim of properly shaping the constitutional policy of the Community process—is to remove the evil of industrial society, which within the state characterizes the 'system of everyday life', by integrating social policy. It finds the distribution of power in the economy and society existing in the Member States in ever less accord with democratic conception brought into even more disharmony by economic integration. It finds this disharmony in integration moreover additionally increased, because the lack of democracy within the state, already regarded as considerable, is intensified further in the Community institutions and proceedings.[67] It must—to use a simplified expression—be taken into account, that the opposition to 'late capitalism' shows itself as opposition to integration, because this is billed as a 'late capitalistic' system of power.

Social policy diagnoses and constitutional reviews of this kind will not be gone into or discussed further here. They are nevertheless to be taken into account. For constitutional policy of the formation of Community law cannot proceed from the good and secure position of the constitutional order of the Member State. It must take into account the need for reform within the state. Thus it is true that in case and to the extent that there is such, as is maintained,

> the decisive source of error . . . this side of the Community [is]: it is subject to the conditions, under which European politics is conducted, in the governments, parties, associations, in the publicity, ultimately in the antipolitical everyday life . . .[68]

At least all perspectives of a constitutional policy of the Communities must take into consideration the condition of the constitution of the Member States and remain conscious of the fact that the Community process has an important chance of legitimizing itself in compensating for the constitutional defects of the states by its own form of constitution.

(*d*) The representation of organized interests within the Community process is canalized in Community law in the direction of committees. The representation of interests in this manner opens neither a second way of democratic consent nor is it capable of replacing such. This follows from the provisions on the limited participation in the decision process of the Community organs and as a matter of practice from the manner of the personnel and its effectiveness. The fact that the Europeanization of the organization of interests has made progress,[69] but has not overcome the fundamental national foundation, contributes to the further causes of this unsatisfactory situation. An effective shifting of the representation of interests into the stage of integration, its 'supranational change',[70] has so far not taken place. Organized interests have certainly to an increasing extent found their bearings as far as integration is concerned.[71] But in

203

that the process of decision of the Communities is determined by the Member States and the distribution of powers leaves the states the disposition over welfare administration, pressure groups are more effective in the national parliament and in national bureaucracies than at the Community level. Therefore from the constitutional policy point of view the integration of organizations of interests depends much less on their own supranational organization and much more on where the decision is made upon the interests, which they pursue. The integration effect of the construction of European organizations depends functionally on the distribution of powers. From this it follows that increasing committee participation in the Community decisions can only be relevant in this functional dependency.

(e) The same holds true for the formation of political interests in the political parties. An integration of political parties, in a way relevant to the Communities, has so far not taken place.[72] Constitutional policy perspectives must take this fact into account for the proper provision of institutions and procedures as well as for new forms of democracy. A European party system, for which a perfect parliamentary system in the Communities is required,[73] seems quite unreal not only in the foreseeable future. It basically presumes the transformation of the Member States into 'self-governing bodies' of the Communities, in which the powers would be limited in the manner of the Federal Republic over the *Länder* in German constitutional law.

The history of the Europeanization of the political parties,[74] which will not be given here, confirms this relationship. The same holds true of the attempt to form a European party, which can scarcely be regarded as a genuine formation of a party, but rather as an organized demonstration of the Europe idea. The fact that the zeal of the party politicians engaged as members of the Assembly can so easily be lost on their home parliaments and their integrating effect there for many reasons is to be regarded as only very small,[75] is consistent with this situation. As regards constitutional policy the important question posed by Article 138 (III), EEC Treaty, remains, therefore, as to whether the representative effectiveness of the delegates to the Assembly can be increased by their direct election, as is obviously presupposed by the Treaties. On this there are well-founded doubts.

3. Integrative Groups

In the chapter 'Federating Europe—but how?' a theory of methods of European integration, such a combination of forces, 'which initiates, coordinates, and provides the impetus for processes of political integration' is described as a 'federator'.[76] In theories worked out from historical, comparative, strategical and tactical considerations there appear in this role as possible federators (a) a state recognized by other states as the leader, (b) a hegemonic power exercising compulsion, (c) a state outside the federation, promoting it, and (d) groups which co-operate politically and socially in the inter-state area, as well as groups upon which supranational institutions and organs, approved of by the governments of states, are based.

The term 'federator' has a prejudicial effect on a constitutional policy considered in a legal context, because it is directed to a federation as the ultimate form of integration. It has therefore no place here. For the constitutional perspectives considered cannot reckon or at least cannot yet reckon on federation as the ultimate form of the community process within their time-span. The content of this characteristic of an integrating group of forces is meanwhile applicable if people are considered for their effectiveness for the community process as groups. Such integrative groups are of interest for constitutional policy outside party and interest organizations too, because they do not act in functions specifically related to the Community, of their interest in the integration process shows itself as a contribution to the formation of public opinion. Their exposition and evaluation is indeed no task for the lawyer nor directly for a theoretically-founded legal policy. Meanwhile it is proper, in order to do justice to both, to be aware of their existence and effect, in so far as the progress of social sciences concerning 'federation' makes possible.

(a) 'The central problem for any method of integration lies in marrying the "external" forces with the work of the government, in such a way that radical reorganization is possible.' In so far as these forces are represented in human groups, their views and their articulation in organization and forming of public opinion, they can almost take on the effect of the sovereign will. This favours integration, if political parties directly influence the setting-up of institutions and the parliamentary process to this effect. According to present ascertainable facts this approach is today still and for a long time to come mainly a matter for the national state and is regulated by national constitutional law—it is not integrated and not open under Community law. Forces coming from outside, i.e. not constituted or regulated by the state, which can neither be organized in party groups and programmes, can by reason of their elite quality have an integrating effect as vanguard or key groups. There could be a pure and sublimated 'European idea' at work here but it would be the exception and not the rule. 'Europeanism' is a very vague term which means something different for different groups and the common denominator of the doctrines which motivate the process of integration is very ineffective.[78] There still is an 'undeniable weakness'[79] in the feeling of a European solidarity, rooted in Christian humanism and history, and included in many plans of a European unity. The legal construction of integration until now, its course and its need to shape legally the next stage are doubtless not calculated to strengthen these feelings and to provide integrating possibilities for elite groups.

The social scientific methods of elite opinion research[80] have aptly taken these points of view into account and where this did not happen, their results must be regarded very cautiously. Empirical research in this way has not only the difficulty of selecting the questions, but also of selecting those to be questioned (with the danger of selecting oneself), the qualification of those selected according to successful actual participation in decisions and finally assessment of the result.[81] Insofar as research into public opinion is concerned, of elite opinions essential for the development of public opinion and of constitutional policy tasks of integration, is based on practical experience, this must be checked against the criterion of the degree of organized group participation, i.e. the political prospects of achieving the set aim with the help of political parties and other groups.

(b) An integrative group can, as far as its interests are concerned, be attributed to a general European integration interest, as an abstract concept of Europe: the bureaucracy engaged in the process of integration in the Community institutions and (if less effectively) in the Member States insofar as summarizing them in a generalizing way is not already 'prejudiced' for integration in an objectional manner. The 'official' of the administrative union called 'Community', continually participating by reason of his profession in the day-to-day process of integration, can replace the concepts of state, state quality, and sovereignty through daily experience with supranationalism 'and he will be inclined to take the mythology of the principle of supranationalism'.[82]

It depends on such experiences of the bureaucratic class whether this inclination will be felt to be strengthened or disappointed, and on its quality whether the development of their attitude reveals an integrating effect. On this 'the process of learning' described from the social scientific aspect can be relevant, which extends from expert officials over interest organizations of both levels and their experts to 'national receivers' of advantages and disadvantages. And this process can have an integrating effect, according to its content and influence, on the national authorities, which make decisions on the Community process and give them legal shape.

IV. The Subject Matter

1. The Subject Matter of the Community is also Politics

(a) The 'subject matter' of the community process, in the language of the object clauses of the Treaties, their 'task', is neither positively nor negatively conceived of in terms of the political. This is for several reasons: the political cannot specify the sphere of a particular sovereign activity. It is not a category of subject matter but the intensity degree of a contact or stress relationship.[84] To concede that there exists an area of political subject-matter would mean the exclusion of a homogeneous field of public tasks with their possible conflicts, and their specific assignation to the political. This condition cannot be fulfilled. It is therefore not only vain but

206

misleading to discuss whether the matters with which the Communities have to deal appertain to politics or not, whether commitment to the economy in the broadest sense takes them out of politics and would leave politics to the Member States, and whether the Communities need to be made political to bring integration a step nearer to its ultimate aim.

The strict distinction between matters of economic and political integration is fiction, which avoids reality and threatens to lead, or has led already, to false conclusions with regard to the methods of integration. Political integration has already begun, for the transition from economic to political integration takes place gradually and continually.[85]

Not only does the third part of the EEC Treaty (Article 85 *et seq.*) itself speak of the 'Policy of the Community', of the economic, conjunctural, trade, social, agricultural and transport policy. Subjects are thereby aptly indicated, which in complete agreement with general terminology refer to public tasks, which, in their performance and as potential fields of conflict, all appertain to the political. They cannot therefore be described as apolitical, 'only economic', depoliticized, technological or anything else, because other fields proper to politics—such as foreign, defence and security policy—are not matters for the Communities but are the affairs of the Member States.

The distinction still—between 'non-political' (and therefore still incomplete) Communities on the one hand and Member States and their governments on the other hand as possessors of 'political monopoly',[86] thus does not fit the distinction between the affairs of the Communities and the affairs of the states. It merely means that important 'areas of politics' (such as particularly foreign and defence policy, but also others, economic such as monetary policy, and non-economic as cultural policy), are not integrated and on the other hand that the Member States have retained political decision in these matters whether they should be subjected to the community process or not.

An assessment, meaningful for constitutional policy, of the state of integration established by law, of its automatic spill-over effect, and its desirable completion by the transfer of further policies, can therefore be made, as to which fifteen to twenty sectors of practical politics and to what degree important decisions are taken at an integrated level or are left to the Member States. Such an assessment[87] can tell more, and more reliably, about the political content of the Communities' 'affairs' and their 'need for politics' and also about questions of legal policy for which legal regulation is possible and desirable, than general references to the lamentable 'depoliticization' of the Communities and a 'political monopoly' of the Member States.

(*b*) The community process, according to the objects clauses, has made the economy in the broadest sense, its affair, after the objective 'defence and security' had proved a failure and 'political monopoly' of a so-called political Community had proved unrealistic. A decision to expand the field of the Community was made with the plan for an economic and monetary union, which is connected still with 'economy' in the broadest sense but extends into a field of politics, which can no longer be assigned to economy, via the budget policy into the internal affairs and what is today called social policy, via the monetary policy into the foreign affairs. Doubtless this decision means a step in politicizing integration and a corresponding diminution in the still existing so-called 'political monopoly' of the states in so far as these legally give up their claim to be responsible for certain services. The question[88] whether the decision to establish an economic and monetary union represents a qualitatively different and higher level of integration for the Community than the decision to set up the customs union and common market at the beginning of integration is hardly sound. As regards integration policy nothing is more important than the beginning. The question of the qualitative distinction of the Community in the new state of economic and monetary union has its justification particularly in relation to the structure of the Community, and this in the scope of politics for which it is responsible in relation to the Member States and according to the importance of its own internal and external policy.

2. The Ambit

A scale of values in politics, which in the traditional manner gives precedence to foreign and defence policy is not justified under Community law. First because all Member States on account of their present existing ties outside the Community no longer or only within limitations dispose of a 'political monopoly'; secondly because economic and social policy at least for the Member States in their industrial society has come into the area of 'high politics'.[89] To the extent that economic and social policy after the completion of the customs union and common market can become part of 'high politics' in the development of the economic and monetary union, the Community will be 'politicized' in the relevant sense of the word in relation to the states. If the task of the 'social realization' of the state of the industrial society in future is less important than its 'technical realization',[90] and this process must be held within bounds, the Communities rather than the individual states will have the capacity to guide it.[91] Here also their increasing politicization is shown. The description of the ambit in question may make this clear.

(a) One can see from it that the essential tasks of the Community in the economic and monetary union are not completely of a new kind. This is true of the monetary policy on account of the duty already existing to co-ordinate and consult (Article 107, EEC Treaty), of the 'conjunctural' policy (Article 103), of the tasks of trade policy and regional policy, which are fulfilled by the Community to a varying degree as regards management, programming and secondary law. The new structure of the Community requires in its end stage a more intense community process, in particular on the monetary policy with its effects on the national monetary and credit policy, in the short-term economic policy and regional policy. This community process increases in the sphere of monetary policy with the simultaneous integrated central bank organization to the exclusion of national monetary policy. Moreover, with control of national budget policy, integration penetrates the substance of what should be called today 'major' internal policy. With the establishment of budgetary key data which limit the budgetary volume, influence investments and consumption, restrain loan policy, and in general influence in the Community's favour the sovereign decision-making (which is made possible in Germany through Article 109 (III, IV) of the German Federal Constitution and the Economic Stability Act of 8 June 1967), 'a decisive centre of national control . . . [would be] taken away from the states and transferred to the Community', and 'the situation of the individual states' would be 'substantially modified'.[92] This 'loss of freedom of action which economic and monetary union means for the states' already exceeds 'the purely economic and utilitarian sphere'.[93]

(b) The limits of state planning and management of the economy according to the 'requirements of the overall economic balance' which Article 109 (II) of the German Federal Constitution postulates, are drawn in the same way from the constitutional point of view by the freedom to combine and the autonomy of the two sides of industry. The integration step towards the economic and monetary union with its intensifying and extension of the Community's subject matter does not embrace this sphere of wage, labour and social policy, whereby a limit is placed on the Community's planning and management and scope is left to the national social forces. When the Werner Report (III) foresees co-ordination, it presupposes progress towards integration in social policy, the attainment of which by legal provisions at least is neither secured nor even conceivable. Here the integration of tasks of monetary and financial policy, which must necessarily be undertaken in a 'policy mix' can give rise to complications, because the 'conceptions of the desirable economic growth and attainable price stability'[95] in the individual Member States are not sufficiently homogeneous on account of their differences in internal and social policies. Symbolic in this respect are Articles 222, EEC Treaty, and 83, ECSC Treaty, with their guarantee that the system of property ownership in the Member States shall not be prejudiced, that the states strive to assert their sociopolitical autonomy and that, insofar, some last limitations remain on the Community process.

(c) Effects in the classical field of foreign policy must arise from the Community's trade policy and the community process in respect of monetary policy by the establishment of full convertibility of the currencies and the integration of the central bank system. In this manner and in a way inherent in the Treaty, elements can be included in the integration

209

process, which the Member States have reserved until now as foreign policy which they co-ordinate outside the Treaty. The fact that the integrated undertaking by the Community of tasks of trade and monetary policy, which shows the Community as capable of acting as a unit, is of important relevance for foreign policy, is shown by the reactions of the USSR and USA—on the one hand the Russian concern regarding the Community's trade policy (and not only regarding this) and on the other hand the American attitude to this and to a uniform EEC monetary policy. The connexion with the question of European representation on the security conference is obvious. From the neo-functionalist point of view this is a true spill-over effect. Insofar as this concerns the tasks and interests of Member States, which can no longer be regarded as 'politically neutral and technical spheres', the question of the form of the Community arises, in particular after the continued existence of the states at the same time as a supranational organization with an increasingly political role.[96]

3. *The Condition of the Subject Matter*

The condition of the subject matter assigned to the Communities must be assessed variously. It is clarified in relation to the tasks of constitutional policy in particular by the debit side of the stocktaking.

(*a*) Programme intensity and time planning in the Treaties have been shown to be an appropriate method of realizing the aims. This holds true primarily for the establishment of a customs union, the organization of the agricultural market and the Common Market. However, compliance with the stipulated periods in the Treaty is no guarantee that the regulations of the Treaty were or are adequate, that all secondary Community law required by the Treaty has actually been issued, and that the conditions obtaining as a result of fulfilment of the Treaty might not be deficient and needing to be changed as a result of unforeseen and unforeseeable circumstances. That redress by altering the Treaty is disproportionately more difficult (and therefore impracticable) than changing a national law in need of reform, shows the rigidity of integration, which can only to a limited extent be corrected under Article 235, EEC Treaty.

The debit side of the stocktaking provides examples for this from various fields: the organization of the agricultural market has proved most sensitive to monetary developments. New foundations of a structural policy are necessary for its reform. Its condition shows that the provisions of the Treaty are inadequate or at least their application has been defective. Whilst the customs union and the common customs tariff *vis-à-vis* other states exist and on the whole function satisfactorily, the structure of the Common Market gives evidence of sensitive gaps and in particular in the realization of individual 'market freedoms'.

(*b*) Stagnation exists in the sphere of regional policy and technology, controversy about the theoretical models of industrial policy incompatible with the Treaty, destruction in the field of research of the Euratom

Community by reason of the absence of a long-term programme, and only punctitious and very limited, delayed and hesitating progress in transport policy. The fact that the Commission received a mandate to negotiate with the Vienna Atomic Agency over the inspection agreement provided by the Test-Ban Treaty,[97] cannot throw light on the condition of Euratom control. France, who did not sign the Test-Ban Treaty, is partly out of its reach. The fact that the European Court has held that France has broken the Treaty,[98] does not improve the situation. Whether the late reconstruction of the social fund can, under adverse conditions, do justice to the demands of an integrated labour market, remains to be seen.

The catalogue of failures, arrears and defects requiring correction with regard to the tasks of the Community is not exhausted by these. Their extent will be recognized the more clearly in relation to the defects in the decision-making process and those of an institutional nature, to which defects in substance are partly to be traced back—for which reason the proper method of remedying a substantive defect in many spheres is less a matter of dealing with the substance than providing the procedure. A critical stocktaking of the subject will indeed, though this is often not recognized, hardly be able in the Communities' sphere of operation to employ standards other than those used for judging the fulfilment of public tasks in the Member States. It is true that economic integration, which aims to supersede the state in practice by claiming to do the job better, is subject to greater criticism than in the state. But the matter with which it is concerned is no different for the Community than for the states, which have transferred responsibility for it to the Community.

(c) The subject is in addition characterized and complicated by initiatives to deal with tasks, which are not as such foreseen in the Treaty, but which, however, arise in the Member States and which become relevant to the Community by reason of their connexion with the subject. This is true, to name actual examples, of the protection of the environment,[99] which each Member State deals with differently in the light of its system of property ownership, and which can seriously affect competition with its diverse, onerous demands. This is also true of the necessary co-ordination of national measures for the control of drugs,[100] because these after the establishment of freedom of movement could still be regarded as inadequate. Both tasks characterize the relationship between the Community's tasks provided by the Treaty and new state tasks, on the whole between the continually changing and unlimited nature of public tasks, the necessary fixing of the Community's tasks by the Treaty law on the one hand and the equally necessary need to adapt to the circumstances on the other.

V. The Territory

1. The Community Process as a Horizontal Territorial Expansion of Limited Powers

Human life depends on facts of space. The geographical situation and historical, economic and social movement in relation to territory fill the 'cultural space'[101] and make 'territory' in the sense of 'state territory' an element of the character of the state.[102] The state character in relation to this territory means exclusive sovereignty within a limited territory and is conceived of vertically from an organization point of view.

> Today we should introduce as a model a further dimension, the horizontal . . . Not unlimited sovereignty in a limited geographical territory but limited sovereignty in an unlimited geographical territory or better: in a geographical territory, which is congruent with the geography of a problem.[103]

In this sense the Community process is a horizontal organization overlapping territory, which surmounts the national general authority limited as it is to territory, and deals with a limited number of tasks in an area, which exceeds and supersedes the individual national boundaries. The territorial boundaries which are placed on the community process do not depend only on the 'geography of a problem'. Otherwise there would be too much to be said for a world-wide community process of important public tasks.[104] The territorial limitation of integration of such comprehensiveness, as the European Communities display, depend on many factors, the problems of which cannot be posed in a geographical context. They require the consideration of all the other factors, which determine the position of the Community in relation to its narrower and wider environment.

All together they determine the question of the expansion of the Community by accession, the territorial ramifications by associations, preference agreement, trade agreements, the position of the Community vis-à-vis other European states with regard to territory, to other regional communities, and to the Great Powers, eastern and overseas. Their ascertainment and assessment is important from the constitutional point of view for the position and development of the Communities—whether in the sphere of trade, monetary or technological policy, to name only contemporary tasks of the Community. Their significance increases with the increasing 'politicization', in particular with the steps towards integration of the foreign and defence policy. To ascertain, systematize and assess the factors determining the territory of this complexity and relevance from the constitutional point of view, is beyond legal competence and therefore can find no place here. In its limitations all that can be considered here from

212

the constitutional point of view is the manner of legal structure by which the territorial orientation of the Community takes place and is open to change.

Out of the territorial boundaries of the Community process and its protection against the outside, arise dangers of a prohibitive and protectionist attitude. A one-sided introversion of the Community law can accordingly have a harmful effect. It is in the interest of its further development to open itself to a new structure even if it is not exactly indicated in the Communities. The territorial expansion by the accession of states with their own legal systems can help in this respect. It necessitates a broad comparison of laws, the confrontation with so far untouched legal spheres and unconsidered legal systems.

2. The Treaties' Field of Operation

(a) The Treaties determine, using different phraseology but agreeing in content, their sphere of application in Europe and in such territories outside Europe, which are dominions of the Member States. The fact that Berlin provides a special territory as regards their application and that the division of Germany as regards trade has led to an opening up of the territories of the Communities vis-à-vis the non-member German Democratic Republic (East Germany), is expressly taken into account in the Treaties. The making and further development of Treaty relationships between the two Germanys can necessitate or lead to a changed Community legal structure. It will not be able to follow a general model of the Community relationships with state trade countries.

(b) The association relationships, varying in their structure, mean no territorial enlargement of the Communities, but rather relationships of the Communities with external states partly on a permanent basis, partly with a view to subsequent accession, so that the Communities as such remain untouched in their territorial status quo. The participation of such associates in the Community aims can become critical from the legal policy point of view if they, according to a treaty, aspire to a full membership at the end of a certain period, but when this final stage arrives, they no longer fulfil the necessary constitutional conditions, which obtained at the time of association (e.g. Greece). Obstacles may exist to new associations for such reasons (e.g. Spain). Nevertheless this last gives rise to fewer constitutional policy problems than that of states already associated and aiming to accede.

(c) In others, territories lying outside the Member States or their regional connections, the Communities function by means of international treaties without possessing or establishing powers relating to the territory. The Communities are effective here, because they represent an economic power in a horizontal form, which over-reaches the territorial boundaries of the Member States, and which without integration and at the level of the individual state, would not be relevant. Although the Communities

213

make use of, and must make use of, international law in this outside territory, the legal structure can take on special characteristics because of its contents specifically related to the Communities. Its systematization as 'Community external law' can also be useful for legal policy.

The primary territory for such spreading abroad are the remaining EFTA countries after the accession of some of their members to the Communities. Insofar as they have and seek to maintain a neutral status, their joining presents special questions of legal structure, which must take into account the relationship of the neutrals to third countries. In any case special relations arise here to the Communities.

Secondly there arises a further field affected, namely those states and groups of states (outside the associates) with which the Communities have preferential relationships. In the declaration of the extraordinary ministerial conference of the Special Commission for Latin American Coordination (CECLA) in Buenos Aires on 29 July 1970,[105] twenty two Latin American countries expressed the intention of having close relations with the Communities. The latter have offered preferential treatment to India and Pakistan. Cuba, Formosa and state trade countries are waiting to be incorporated in a preferential system. The number of preferential agreements with Mediterranean countries increases.

Thus there are already a total of fifty eight countries which have special relationships with the Communities or are preparing to establish them. 'Is there here an almost closed regional block from the polar circle to the northern boundary of South Africa?'[106]

(d) The Communities as a narrower field of influence of integration and in their territorial ramifications represent a reality of world politics. Its effect is primarily economic, but on that account not unpolitical. The attitude of the USA, which is becoming increasingly critical, and that of the USSR, which came to recognize the Communities as a 'reality', are a reaction against these effects of the Communities. It affects the Communities as such in their lack of competence in foreign policy, and the Member States as countries running their own national foreign policy. A constitutional policy of the Communities must logically be directed to its own capacity to act in foreign policy as a single body, at least insofar as Community questions are concerned. A common trade policy requires wider understanding than Article 113, EEC Treaty, has so far received,[107] and appropriate instruments.

3. Enlargement of the Territory by Accession

After the decisions already taken in 1971 and 1972,[108] the Communities as from 1973 enlarged territorially by the accession of three new Member States.[109] The Communities will be altered in their position and structure particularly by the accession of the new Member State, Great Britain. This is not so in a legal sense, because Great Britain is bound by the 'acquis communautaire', and its position will be no different from that of other Member States. However, the accession of Great Britain could in particular cause the restraints in the Community decision-making process which already exist and the perceptible defects in its legitimacy to increase and deepen. This is particularly true of the rules of voting and the implementation of the majority principle and likewise the entry of a Member State aware of the importance of parliament into the parliamentarily 'lame' Communities with France as a still unparliamentarily ruled Member State.

The task, nevertheless outstanding, of reform and further development of the decision-making process and the democratic consensus is thereby more urgent, although its solution is not more simple.

(a) There were four principles on which the negotiations for the accession of Great Britain, Denmark, Norway and Ireland were conducted and which led to the signing of the Treaty of Accession of 22 January 1972:[110] The acceptance of the existing Community law, the possibly necessary adaptation to this law by transitional provisions under time limitations, the undisturbed further development of the not yet enlarged Communities during the negotiations, and the settlement of all questions of the accession in the negotiations before the signing of the Treaty of Accession. A five-year period from the date of accession is provided as a transitional period, i.e. from the beginning of 1973 to the end of 1977. It is shortened or prolonged in certain respects. Already since the middle of November 1971 and until the coming into force of the Treaties of Accession the acceding countries exercised an influence on the Community decisions by a specially-agreed procedure for consultations and information.[111]

Until the middle of 1977 the common external customs will be extended over the enlarged territory of the Community by a planned reduction of the internal customs in five stages. Beginning on 1 April 1973 and thereafter on 1 July in the years 1974–77 the internal customs between the old and new Member States are reduced by stages of 20%. On 1 January 1974 there followed the first step to assimilation of the external customs by 40%. Further steps of 20% each, will follow at the beginning of the years 1975, 1976 and 1977. Customs quotas (for thirteen products) assist the transition into the customs union. The adoption, too, of the organization and regulation of the agricultural market takes place gradually, in Great Britain until the end of 1977.

(b) The negotiations for accession were conducted between the Communities (not between the individual Member States) under the leadership of the presidents of the Council at the time (Germany, France and Italy) and the countries wishing to join. The bases of the negotiations by the Communities were resolutions passed by the Council, which (in contrast to the abortive negotiations of 1961/3) made possible a uniform and united representation of the Communities. These were prepared by the Commission and continually adapted during the negotiations to the changing circumstances by new proposals. The documents of Accession were signed by the representatives of the former and new Member States and by the president of the Council on behalf of the Communities after the dispute as to the participation of the Commission in the signing had been resolved in this way.[112]

(c) The Treaty of Accession (for the EEC and EAEC) and the Council decision (for the ECSC) comprises the basic decision as to the enlargement of the Communities, regulations on the principles of accession, the technical adaptation of the secondary law, transitional measures for particular economic spheres and their coming into force. Annexes and protocols complete the Treaty structure. The act of Accession has changed the Community Treaties, the Merger Treaty and the Budget Treaty. An authoritative 'consolidated text' of the Treaties, taking account of all amendments and infringements, did not exist during the negotiations. This surprised not a little the British negotiators with their respect for written law.[113]

(d) With the enlargement of the Communities the heterogeneity of the legal systems affected by the community process increases.[114] The six founding states belong to the continental legal family and the Roman-Germanic legal circle. The new members belong to the common law and Northern legal circle and even these circles are only partially embraced in the acceding states. As regards approximation of laws and the determination and maintenance of general legal principles, there are here both difficulties and opportunities of mutual fecundation.

VI. Time

Time is an instrument of the process of integration, a characteristic of legal regulation and its introduction. It is an autonomous dimension, a rhythmical element, a factor determining aims, a measurement of the stages of planning and a means to compel decision. In its function, dimension and legal relevance as a means of sanction, its role belongs to the constitutional policy perspectives and aims at delimiting the dimensions of such perspectives.

1. The Function of Time
The regulation of the programme and stages of the Treaties, the secondary law and other Community measures are scanned by measurements of time and the provision of periods. They are also applied in the law relating to the organization and the formation of policy and to the delimitation by stages of authority between the institutions of the Community and those of the Member States. The time factor is a structural element of Community law for the acceleration of the integration stages foreseen in the provisions, and for compelling decision in a timed series of phases. It is

significant in many ways, the systematization of which remains still to be done.[115] Review and examination clauses for which periods are fixed affect integration policy. The three-year clause of the Merger Treaty, conceived of as such a function, did not achieve its aim because an integration task of a higher level, namely the solution of the questions of accession, claimed priority. In the accession procedure timing is necessary for the proper transition into the *aquis communautaire*, and experience teaches that they are not of less significance than substantive decisions.[116] The question of the fishing reservation concerning Norway's accession was basically a question of the limited or unlimited duration of the accession.

In this diversity of functional application the time factor is a structural element of integration law, which is distinguished by its dynamic character, conceived in terms of progress from national law, especially constitutional law and its static concept.

2. The Dimension of Time

(a) The dimension of time is dependent on the subject and aim of legal regulation. The distinction developed in economic and fiscal planning between short-, medium- and long-term periods has application in Community law for similar purposes. Generally these periods do not extend beyond four years. The great examples of the establishment of the Common Market and the Economic and Monetary Union operate with periods of twelve and ten years, which seem to be adequate for 'creating an integrated system'.[117] This period should represent conceivably the longest period for the realization of an aim which is directed to the integration of a partial system and thereby a large integration step. This means from the constitutional point of view that regulations about institutions, powers and decision-making as legal instruments of such major acts of integration must take these periods into account. As regards time, they must neither anticipate nor prematurely prejudice. Without laying down fixed decisions especially institutional ones which can be avoided, they must remain open to review, adaptation and revocation by new regulations, which for their part could be adequate for the new aim for a new ten year stage of integration. Every long-term provision in the whole sphere of procedure in the widest sense, which according to its intent and form is unchangeable, can be an obstacle to the adequate provision for a further stage of integration. This means no renunciation of a permanent, normative realization and assertion of basic principles of integration, but it does require, with regard to legal policy, a starting point in the system, which within these principles remains open to a flexible legal development capable of adaptation and open to review.

(b) While this is and must remain so, all speculation on time about the final state and its form is out of place and captious. The fact that the Treaties of Rome—as distinct from the fifty-year ECSC Treaty—do not stipulate their duration is relevant less for the lasting quality of the community process expressed therein as for doing without a final aim. It expresses aptly (as far as the measure of time is concerned) the unforeseeable endlessness of the integration process and its likewise unforeseeable form. At a time in which just two decades of the process have elapsed, a third decade painfully conceived and its instruments not yet decided, there can be no serious and exacting constitutional policy perspectives as to the time and form of the end condition of integration. Two decades of the integration process and all economic and political precedents and courses of this period in the Member States, the Communities and their worldwide politico-historical 'context' show the irreality of end perspectives conceived from the constitutional policy point of view. Whether increasing integration leads to a condition, which results in an 'abolition of the time factor',[118] because the attained condition maintains itself simply as the final condition, is likewise a question lying beyond the limits of constitutional consideration. This holds true, moreover, in respect of various similarly considered points of view:

(aa) Insofar as the integration process remains limited to public tasks and interests, which are functionally and not—as in the case of states— universally orientated, an end perspective even in a time dimension can do without 'an end condition similar to that of a state as a static standard'.[119] Even the spill-over calculation of this model, whereby integration in a sector releases that of another, in order to satisfy or compensate for the constraints of the subject, can leave the question of the end point open so long as there is integration functionally in the direction of a 'multi-object organization' and not universally in an all-purpose organization.

(bb) Consideration that the progress of integration reaches—or has already reached—a point of no return, provides end perspectives of limited value. The impossibility of return cannot primarily be derived from the precepts of the Treaties to remain loyal to the Community in the terms of the Treaty and not to break the Treaty by seceding. The impossibility of return is not a legalistic consequence, but the consequence of economic entanglement and the inescapable inseparability from the compactness of integration, that is, weighing the interests between the advantages of integration and the disadvantages of disintegration.[120] In addition or alternatively, secession can appear to be ruled out by the agreed Community procedure, and the Community system as such.[121] From the constitutional policy point of view, however, this presupposes that Community power is based on democratic consensus, to a degree satisfying the standards of the Member State. Constitutional history does not show clauses prohibiting secession to be all that secure: their impotence has been demonstrated as regards federal full integration.

If even fully-developed federations are not safe from disintegration, then it appears still less likely that a process of integration between autonomous states must proceed according to the laws of some historical determinant, which ought to lead the 'unfinished state' [Hallstein] to its completion.[122]

(c) In any case, from the constitutional policy point of view neither the end condition after a particular period nor the establishment of a prohibition on secession for a certain term can be legislated for, so that it has a higher legal effectiveness than the Member State status established by treaty and the constitution of the Community. If Community law takes into account 'shear points' in its phases,[123] namely the inertial compulsion to further stages of integration beyond those immediately planned, as has arisen now in the transition to the economic and monetary union, then a decision is required at the end of each period. Whether it is taken or not depends not only, but nevertheless partly, on the sanction with which Community law connects time-limits.

3. Time Sanctions

(a) Reservations regarding decisions or legal consequences, which sanction the time factor, can be related to the completion of a period, the commencement of a period and the turning-point in time. The latest example of this kind is the 'time clause' in section III, no. 9, of the decisions of the Council of 22 March 1971 passed as the first step of the Werner Plan for an economic and monetary union. Thereafter all Community measures passed in the first stage to the end of 1973 shall be effective only then and only to the end of 1975, if agreement has not been reached before the expiration of this period as the substance of further development to the end stage of this union. Here the time clause sanctioning the principle of concurrent implementation of the further planning stages has the effect that Member States favoured as regards monetary policy in the first stage remain favoured without participating in the integration steps of the next stage which are onerous for them. Here the time factor with its threat of sanction has the effect of bracketing the stages together in the ten-year general plan.

(b) The time clause of the economic and monetary union is a refinement of the technique of Article 8 (3) and (4), EEC Treaty, for the establishment in stages of the Common Market. Finding that its different stages have in fact been attained is like finding that planning stages have been attained, i.e. whether the whole set of actions provided by the treaty have been initiated and carried through concurrently (Article 8 (3), EEC Treaty), and likewise whether obligations related to it have been observed. The time clause of the economic and monetary union contains a possible sanction against going back. Its effect will be removed only by the coming into being of an end plan. The time clauses of Articles 8 (3) and (4), EEC Treaty, contain on the other hand that finding that a stage has in fact been attained, effectuates the continuation of the plan. This was in this case sufficient because this continuation was already planned in the Treaty.

From this follows from the point of view of legal policy that the time

219

factor is more in need of sanctions the less a time stage plan already determines all the stages to the end of the plan. This fact permits and confirms at the same time the conclusion that every legal provision of an ultimate end of the Community process as such appears unreal in its present state. For it would be dependent in its total planning on time sanctions of such a kind, that the progress of the stages determined thereby must ultimately be lost in the uncertainty of its entry or non-entry. This conclusion is also justified from the constitutional policy point of view, because a timed, to say nothing of a time-sactioned, cyclic course of the community process is neither calculable nor does it even seem conceivable.[124] Even if the economic courses could run in such cycles, their rhythm should be calculable, and although the subject matter of the community process is essentially economic, it does not follow from that that the community process is cyclical too. For the community process has the economy as a subject matter, but is itself not an economic but a political process of decision.

VII. The Procedure

Under 'Procedure' we understand here the Treaty rules concerning institutions, powers and actions. 'Procedure' thus embraces in one concept, from the constitutional policy point of view, everything concerning the setting up, the powers, and the decision-making of Community institutions for the present and, within the framework of the economic and monetary union, anticipated tasks of the Communities. 'Procedure' in this sense proceeds from the basis 'that the options over the jurisdiction are closely associated with those over the constitution of the institutions (and) . . . both groups of options condition one another'.[125]

All this refers to the decade to the end of 1980 according to the stage plan for the creation of an economic and monetary union in accordance with section 1, No. 1, of the resolution of the Council and the Representatives of the Governments of the Member States of (9 February) / 22 March 1971 which came into force with effect from 1 January 1971.

The review of the legal regulation of the procedure and the reality of its application is a precondition of any consideration from the legal policy point of view of the shaping of procedure to this end and for this period. Therefore, the procedural perspective for the decade, in which the 'process' of the establishment of the economic and monetary union should take place, must take into account the review of the constitutional situation of the Community and the requirements of the adequate future shaping of the Community.

1. The Requisite Procedure for the Economic and Monetary Union

(a) The Werner Report of 8 October 1970 in its conclusions (VII D)

220

'on an institutional level' stated that two Community institutions were required for the end stage of the union (that is, the second stage beginning with the year 1975):

an economic policy-making body and a Community Central Bank System. These institutions must be responsible for fulfilling their tasks, have effective power of decision, and contribute to the realization of the same aims. The economic policy body must be politically responsible to a European parliament.

This governing body would have basic power over the entire Community economic policy, it would in particular be able to influence the budget policy of the Member States, to determine the currency parities, and to co-ordinate the spheres of integration of the economic and social policy (VII H), whereby the reference is to actions 'in increasingly binding forms'. In general the Report (VII B) intends 'that the most important decisions on economic policy at the Community level should be taken and consequently the requisite powers must be transferred from the national level to the level of the Community'. The Werner Report (VII G II) leaves no doubt that the shaping of procedure anticipated by it would have to be made by amending the Treaty in accordance with Article 236, EEC Treaty.

(*b*) The resolution of 22 March 1971 lags behind these requirements: it is true even it foresees a central bank system (I 3), which, while maintaining its own responsibility, would contribute to the realization of the aim of stability and the growth of the Community. Parliament should discuss and control the Community policy in regard to the economic and monetary union—which does not necessarily mean an extension of its powers beyond Article 137, EEC Treaty. The 'economic policy-making body' of the Werner Report is no longer foreseen as an institution. The decision limits itself to the statement: 'The institutions of the Community will be put in the position to carry out their responsibility for economic and monetary policy effectively and quickly.'[126] It foresees (IV) for the formation of procedure not only an amendment of the Treaty in accordance with Article 236, EEC Treaty, but also 'on the basis of the existing provisions of the Treaty' and of Article 235, EEC Treaty, therefore with the possibility of a procedural regulation inherent in the Treaty and related to the existing institutions of the Community.

(*c*) What kind of procedural structure is required for the end stage of the economic and monetary union and what form under the Treaty or on its amendment comes into consideration, cannot be determined simply from the vague concepts of the resolution of 22 March 1971. What must decide this are the concepts of the ultimate aims of the establishment of the union and the views obtained from a critical examination from the constitutional point of view of the applicable law and the realities of its administration.

221

(*d*) Whether and how far and in what form the constitutional postulates in accordance therewith have a possibility of material implementation in due time depends on the sober and apt statement of the Werner Report (VII A): 'the economic and monetary union can be attained in the course of this decade provided that the political will of the Member States, ceremoniously declared at the Hague Conference, exists to realize this aim.' At the beginning of 1972 when this statement is repeated here, no forecast could be given with sufficient certainty as to the existence and extent of this political will. The fact that this is not a task for lawyers is a consolation, albeit a weak one.

2. *The Defects of Existing Procedure*

The obvious defects of existing procedure—to repeat: in the regulations of the Treaty relating to the constitution of the organs, their powers and their actions—are partly in the provisions and partly in the manner and way of their actual administration or non-administration. The review, which has to affirm the defects of integration procedure, refers at the same time to the constitution and to the actual state of the community process. It concerns in essence four complexes: (a) the council, the role of the Member States in it and the role of the Permanent Representatives of the governments of the Member States; (b) the effective failure to apply, contrary to the Treaty, the majority principle in the decisions of the Council; (c) the role of the Commission, which is no longer in accordance with the Treaties and its relation to the Council and the Member States; and (d) the role of Parliament.

Constitutional perspectives and considerations of legal policy for the procedural structure[129] necessary for the establishment of the economic and monetary union must, if they do not take into account these four defects, remain hypothetical if not quite misleading. Constitutional policy for the economic and monetary union must take into account the defects of the community process, which are apparent here, and must try to overcome as far as possible the existing defects when planning the procedural structure.

(*a*) The Council's procedure for reaching decisions is not suitable for the tasks it has to perform in the integration process in accordance with the Treaties. And it does not avail itself of the powers in the manner possible and provided by the Treaties.

(*aa*) It does not synchronize its work with the proposals of the Commission, so it acts often not in time, often without a clear decision, and often not at all by postponing what must be decided. Its procedure is clumsy. Its enlargement by new members from the acceding countries is not a factor calculated to simplify or speed up the procedure. Rather is the contrary to be expected. Integration policy impulses, even only planning in the terms of the Treaty, have to an increasing extent no longer proceeded, as they should, from the Council, but in crisis situations have come

222

into being only *ad hoc*, and therefore unsystematically, by so-called 'summit conferences' of the heads of state or government.

(*bb*) The Council has disregarded the procedural rules of the Treaties—knowingly and systematically since the Luxembourg 'agreement'—and has come to decisions only when there has been unanimity and has tolerated the use of the veto, where according to the Treaties the majority principle should have been applied. The Council has thereby, and also in other ways of a similar effect, assumed 'intergovernmental' characteristics and neglected or infringed the principles of Community law. The Member States have in Community practice assumed a power in the Council, which Community law did not foresee for the Council as a Community institution. A process of renewed nationalism, which is apparent elsewhere too in the Community system, although it has not stopped the legally-ordered process foreseen by integration policy of transferring public functions from national to Community institutions, has hindered, obstructed and delayed it.

(*cc*) The Council in the Committee of the permanent representatives of Member States, which Article 4 of the Merger Treaty expressly recognizes, has at its disposal an 'infrastructure' [128] of growing importance. With its help as a body functioning as a permanent agent of the Council and taking *de facto* substitute decisions, there is on the one hand an 'intermediary' for the Council and on the other hand the 'intergovernmental' [129] mechanism of unanimous decision is duplicated and the relation of the Commission to the Council in accordance with the Treaties is falsified: the Commission is increasingly confronted not any longer with the Council as such, but with the Committee of the Permanent Representatives, and thus its immediate relationship to the Council is restricted by them too.

(*dd*) The Treaties do not regard the Council as a government within a parliamentary system and therefore does not recognize any political control of the Council by Parliament. The beginning of such a system—with the help of the political control of the Commission by Parliament—is rather in the governmental role of the Commission. A political, parliamentary control can in the construction of the Treaty have effect on the Council only indirectly, and at the constitutional level of ministerial responsibility in the Member States, as regards participation in the Council's deliberations. This political control is, however, in the Member States—at least in Germany, where it is in effect established by the 'chancellor system'—not efficient enough.[130] Therefore the importance of the governments in the Council, and through it their position in the whole system of the Community organization, is inflated beyond the limits of the Treaties and the separation of powers is weakened. The renewed nationalism in the Community lies in the strengthening of the power of the governments. Since there is lacking appropriate 'feedback' [131] between the European Parliament, and national parliaments, this disturbance in the balance is not compensated by them.

(b) Since the Luxembourg agreement, unanimity is exacted in the Council's deliberations in breach of the Treaty, insofar as this latter makes majority decision possible and this is prevented by the use of the veto or other practices, or does not take place. Since the majority principle belongs to the elements of the principle of supranational integration, its disregard can neither be minimized nor ignored from the constitutional point of view, so long as the Community process is to be understood as a process of 'supranationalization'. The principle of unanimity fosters the 'inter-governmental' style of decision of the Council and favours a concept of a confederation, which as such is foreign to Community law. This favouring is not lessened by reason of the fact that the Council limits itself to basic resolutions.[132] Certainly 'majority decisions' require an '... advanced stage of integration, because they require from those subject to them a readiness to accept an unwelcome decision'. Meanwhile, the fact that the Community has attained this stage in important spheres and is in the process of exceeding it in important spheres as regards the economic and monetary union, is not only beyond doubt, but established legally in the Treaty and the decision of 22 March 1971. In an enlarged Community the principle of unanimity, and with it the right of veto by any Member State, increases the difficulty of its 'government', because the risk of the veto increases not only with the number of members, but also with the multiplication of interests. This fact is confirmed by all international organizations of that type of confederative structure and their experiences. Only the adherence without delay of the new Member States to the Treaty rules of the majority principle[134] could prevent the Luxembourg Accord from being prolonged in a Paris-London Accord[135] tolerated by Bonn and gradually under-mining the Treaties as a 'constitutional convention'. The assumption,[136] that the majority principle is overtaxed in the Treaties and that the admission of the principle of unanimity is the better view, ignores the political intention of the Member States clearly expressed in the Treaties. If on the one hand it has slackened since the Luxembourg Accord, on the other hand it has been fostered by the unconditional acceptance of the Treaty by the new Member States in the Treaty of Accession and is accepted by these, and if the states desire the progress of the Community process in the economic and monetary union, the application of the majority decision, at least to the extent previously foreseen, must be insisted upon in principle during the establishment of the union. If this did not happen the constitutional policy of the Community would have to bear the reproach of internal conflict in the system. It does not, of course, follow from this that the majority principle regarding the decisions as to stages within the ten-year plan of the union is necessary and politically debatable.

(c) The Commission is the Community institution, whose role, foreseen in the Treaties and practised throughout the transitional period, has become the most questionable.

(*aa*) The reason for this lies first—and certainly not last—in the rank and quality of its members and presidents. There are Member States which have neglected or infringed the self-evident standards of presentation defined in Article 10 of the Merger Treaty. Manipulation based on national proportionality and political selection instead of selection of an elite based solely on ability have taken place to the detriment of the Community—and this also applies to Germany, which at first fulfilled its obligations with regard to the Community process. Defects in the presentation procedure, which later became apparent, have not been corrected, not even when this was required by Article 10 (2), Merger Treaty.

(*bb*) The Commission's monopoly in making proposals as a balancing element in the decision process of the Council has been weakened, if not crippled or broken. One reason for this is the Council's attitude to the proposals of the Commission, which has discouraged the Commission, another is the prior clearing of its proposals with the Member States—this is done on its own initiative but is also encouraged by the Council and Member States.[138] Instead of developing in the direction of a Community government, which in embryonic form it can be seen to be in Community law, the Commission has taken on the characteristics of the secretariat of an organization.[139] The importance of the Commission's bureaucracy diminishes together with the importance of its role.[140] It can diminish further if a national personnel policy and its system of delegation puts obstacles in the way of or—as is at present the case—rules out an autonomous recruitment of personnel by the Commission and an appropriate policy of payment. In its continual confrontation with the Committee of the Permanent Representatives as the assistant of the federal organ of the Community and in the 'mixed deliberations' of numerous committees sent by the governments to the Commission, the latter is exposed to continual influence by the Member States. For a Commission which, even in its personnel policy, is no longer sufficiently self assured nor capable of initiative, this permanent contact with the interests of Member States, which, although materially useful, is precarious for Community policy, has led to signs that the Commission, too, has been converted to nationalism. The consequence of this contact and the weakening of its position against the Council, is the fact that its own decisions—like the proceedings of the Council—are increasingly (and contrary to Article 17 of the Merger Treaty) subject to the unanimity principle.

(*cc*) The Community system with its separation of powers has, under this influence, experienced a double shifting of weight: with the weakening of the Commission, the control over it exercised by parliament has been devalued and with it the minimum amount of democratic effectiveness of control which the Treaties foresee. Control of the Commission has not been lost altogether. But since it is practically exercised by the national bureaucracies in the Committees concerned with the Commission's proposals, it has been transferred to the Executives of the Member States.[141]

225

This has additionally increased the influence of the Executive in the Council and in the Committee of the Permanent Representatives—an influence which was already considerable. A development is thus taking place, which is not planned in the Community constitution, does not accord with Article 138, EEC Treaty, and does not do justice to the national systems of government—at least not the German. If this development is in accord with the French system of government, it has the inadmissible effect, moreover, of favouring *one* Member State.

(*dd*) In general, this change of the Commission's role means a weakening of the interplay in the Community system, which at the same time rests on the duality Council–Commission and the principle of joint formation of policy, according to which an independent Commission as protector and promoter of the public interest of the Community is called upon to face the interests of the Member States. The dual nature of the decision-making levels,[142] which the Treaties provide for in the Member States and the Communities, and seek to realize in the structure and co-operation between Council and Commission, is placed in jeopardy by the loss of tension between a nationally involved Commission and a Council reverted to nationalism.

(*d*) 'The world of the European Parliament is still unscathed.' [148] This may fit a 'contemporary image' of Parliament and meet the promise of Article 138 (2), EEC Treaty. Yet it contains a self-deception. For this image has been drawn after the model of a national constitution without taking account of the criticism of parliament which obtains there, without considering the change in function of parliament in its task of control *vis-à-vis* economic and fiscal planning of modern governments,[144] without taking into account the different nature of a political community system in comparison with a national constitutional system and also without considering whether the Community process does not offer a chance of new concepts of systems and control mechanisms.[145]

(*aa*) Parliament has enlarged its *budgetary powers* within the limits of the Budget Treaty. It has thus partly succeeded in its demands which were put aside during the crisis of 1965–66. From the constitutional policy point of view, it is more important that, in this way, a first step is taken which others may follow than the fact that the budgetary powers are still modest.[146]

(*bb*) Since Parliament in the sphere of law-making possesses under the Treaties neither power of decision nor the prospect of any, and its consultation by the Council is scarcely accorded much respect and does not compensate the lack of law-making power, it is deprived of the essential element of parliamentary power. This is all the more important since the decline in legislative power of the national parliaments caused by Community law is not compensated by a relative increase in powers of the European Parliament. The executive element of the Community system is thus intensified in this manner. The gaps in democracy remain unfilled by Community law and widen at the national level.[147]

226

(*cc*) The merger of control made possible by the present system between the national parliaments and the European Parliament which would not exclude a 'loan' of control over the Strasbourg delegates does not take place or has no special effect. For the European delegates for various reasons do not have sufficient power in their home parliaments. Their European potential remains untapped.

(*dd*) The option of Article 138 (2), EEC Treaty, appears in the meantime unrealistic and even in the possible eventual realization in the form of partially direct elections politically without special relevance. For the essential preconditions of a consenting and representative effect are missing so long as the parties remain unintegrated.

(*ee*) The present system of powers according to Community law, which are available for the development, inherent to the Treaty, in capital movement and in short-term economic and common trade policy, does not even provide Parliament with an effective power of consultation in the decade of the establishment of the economic and monetary union.[148] There is thus lacking here any beginning of development.

(*ff*) Whether the accession of the United Kingdom with its traditional parliamentary practice could contribute to an activation and revaluation of the European Parliament, remains to be seen. For the new Member State too is bound by the limitation on parliamentary power in the Treaties. It remains to be seen whether delegates of the House of Commons in the European Parliament (and vice versa) can and will take on a mutual control function.

(*e*) The normative and practical review of the community system encounters at the beginning, middle and future of the constitution of the Community: doubts about the correctness and appropriateness of its construction, departure from the principles of the constitution in Community practice, and the possibility of the removal of defects and the maintenance of principles in the procedural structure of the economic and monetary union. The task of an accomplished community system also remains to be considered theoretically.[149] A modest constitutional perspective to 1980 can simply refer to constitutional principles indispensable for integration policy, sketch a procedure for their application and indicate the conceivable ways to that end.

3. The Procedural Structure of the Economic and Monetary Union

(*a*) The principles on which the Treaties are based must guide the procedural structure of the economic and monetary union: the principle of integration and the principle of supranationality including the majority principle, at least to the extent so far provided by the Treaties. The principle of democratic consensus and control can even in the economic and monetary union only apply insofar as it is manifested in the establishment of Parliament and in the task set by Article 138 (2), EEC Treaty, and has not become dispensable and replaceable.

227

(b) The organization necessary for the establishment of the union can—with the exception of the Community central bank system—be made available in the existing Community institutions as foreseen by the resolution of 22 March 1971 (13) and was not clearly provided for in this manner by the Werner Report (VII D: two Community institutions, namely a central bank system and an 'economic policy-making board'). No others are necessary to be responsible for economic and monetary policy if only the existing institutions are put into 'effective and speedy' operation. In this respect, for the assertion of the inalienable constitutional principles and for the remedy or prevention of procedural defects which have appeared, changes in the competence of the institutions must be considered.

(aa) Since the realization of the union presupposes the transfer of important economic, monetary and budgetary powers to the Community, the Commission, as protector of the Community interest, must be staffed with the best personnel and its national commitment must be limited. Its co-operation with the Council requires at the same time the re-establishment and strengthening of its initiative to make proposals and a speeding up of the process of decision, short-term economic and monetary policy in the hands of the Community naturally require prompt and energetic decisions. The communication between decision of intent by the Member States and its putting forward in the Council on one hand, and the looking after of the Community interest by the Commission on the other hand[150] should be, whenever practicable, an immediate one as it is the meaning of Article 149, EEC Treaty. From this follows a necessary limitation on the functions of the permanent representatives and likewise that of the committees in which the Commission tests its intentions before deciding on proposals. Rank, weight and effectiveness of the Commission require strengthening. Its immediate relationship to the Council would be able to achieve it. The concept[151] of providing the Commission with subsidiary powers for urgent cases or such, in which the Council does not reach a decision, could, in conjunction with time sanctions, speed the process of decision. In order to maintain the interplay between Council and Commission the former could be given the power of objecting to decisions of the Commission.

(bb) Apart from the basic question of the appropriate consensus and control mechanisms, which is not only inherent to the Treaties, a strengthening of the parliamentary powers can contribute towards the union. This is because the transfer of the sovereign powers in question closes certain areas subject heretofore to the national parliaments' consensus and control, without at the same time opening them to some other control under Community law. The impetus on the part of a Member State to progress towards integration in the sense of a union is not furthered but hindered by the creation of parliament-free spheres. Since the Council is not designed in the applicable community system as a government, and therefore its decision process can less easily be controlled by the European Parliament, and is controlled—if indirectly—only from within the Member States, there are good grounds for a strengthening of the parliamentary powers in relation to the Commission:[152] on the one hand through participation in nominating its members and on the other by more intensive participation in the proposal-making procedure of the Commission. This consideration lies also within the intention of Article 144, EEC Treaty. Whether Parliament should participate in the decision process of the Council appears more doubtful. Variations of the participation (suspensive veto, consent in limited cases) could be grafted onto various decision-processes. Their application presupposes in relation to the Council—more than with regard to the Commission—that the integrated basis of Parliament is extended. The fulfilment of Article 138 (2), EEC Treaty, alone would scarcely suffice for this.

(*cc*) The Committee of the Permanent Representatives, which is an obstacle to the direct relation of the Commission to the Council, is—like the Council—not conceived of as a governing institution of the Community. The strengthening of its position means a weakening of the Commission. For the realization of the economic and monetary union, which represents a decisive integration step with supranationalizing effect, its function can only be in assisting the Council, not in participating independently in the decision process. The French proposal to give its members ministerial rank as 'Ministers for Europe' and making them as such members of the governments of the Member States, is incompatible, if nothing else, with the sectoral variety of the Community tasks and, in Germany, contrary to Article 65 of the Federal Constitution.[153]

(*c*) The community central bank system foreseen in the resolution of 22 March 1971 requires a central bank council of the Community with powers which go considerably beyond those of the permanent committee of the central bank presidents. The resolution endows this body with the monetary powers necessary to 'govern the union' (I 3), which should be prepared by the intensive co-ordination of the monetary and credit policy of the Member States in the monetary committee and in the committee of the central bank presidents (III 5). For the establishment of the central bank council, the question arises of its independence from the other Community institutions, as is foreseen in Germany according to para. 12 (2) of the Federal Bank Act for the German Federal Bank *vis-à-vis* the Federal Government.[154] The Werner Report (VII D) recommends the individual responsibility of the central bank council. It should, however, at least have to take on such a function supporting the Community policy of the Council as the German Federal Bank bears *vis-à-vis* the general economic policy of the Federal Government. In relation to the independent Commission the Council of the central bank must take up a position of co-operation.

4. Legal Forms of Procedural Structure

The legal forms, which come into question for the procedural structure of the economic and monetary union, cannot be uniform, because they refer to different objects.

(*a*) It is obvious that any legal structure, which can be achieved within the existing Treaties, is as a matter of legal policy to be preferred. For every amendment of the Treaty conceals, apart from the danger of loss of time and the failure to achieve ratification by even only one Member State, the so-called 'domino effect': the attempt to use the opportunity of the proceedings to amend Treaty rules which are not open to amendment and this fact in turn unlocks other desires to amend on the part of other interests. Since it is not certain that constitutional principles and institutions of the Treaties will not thereby also be put in question, the attempt to form a structure exclusively within the terms of the Treaty is understandable. Whether it is ultimately in the interests of integration policy, and whether the danger of an amendment of the Treaty is not exaggerated, is not for lawyers to judge. However, it will be found that the perfect procedural structure for the economic and monetary union does not appear possible without some amendment of the Treaties.

(*b*) A renewing—attainable only by amendment of the Treaties—of the aims and objects of the Community is necessary, insofar as those of the economic and monetary union, as expressed in the resolution of 22 March 1971, are not already covered by the given provisions and the appropriate rules with regard to powers. *In nuce* this is the case and namely in Articles 67, 70, 99, 100, 103, 105 and 106, EEC Treaty, in respect of monetary, economic, 'conjunctural', tax, budgetary, trade and regional policy. Meanwhile these regulations cover the programme of the resolution neither subjectwise nor in the intensity of the integration measures, so that an enumeration of aims and tasks expanding the Treaty appears unavoidable. The same holds true of all possible measures for strengthening parliamentary powers and for the establishment of the Community central bank council.

(*c*) The approximation of laws can, as a permanent task under Article 100, EEC Treaty, also be useful for economic policy. Higher stages of integration, such as the economic and monetary union attempt, cannot be achieved by legal approximation, since it is related to the functioning of the Common Market at the particular phase of development at the time.

(*d*) The power given by Article 235, EEC Treaty, to fill lacunae in the Treaty, which so far has been interpreted restrictively, may be open to more liberal interpretation.[156] Even if the realization of the aim presupposed in Article 235, for which the Treaty does not provide the requisite powers, means the broad objects of Article 2 and the establishment of the Common Market and approximation of economic policy is only understood as instrumental, nevertheless the special delegation of Article 235 does not cover the whole range of objects of the economic and monetary union. In particular Article 235, according to the Jurisprudence of the European Court, does not authorize the delegation of decision powers to an organ not foreseen in the Treaty, such as the Council of the Central Bank,[157] so that an amendment of the Treaty would also be necessary to this extent.

(e) Particular elements of the procedural structure can be achieved by informal agreements between the institutions concerned and the governments of the Member States, as for example, certain 'constitutional conventions' regarding the co-operation in budgetary procedure between Council and Parliament.[158] Since such procedure is not bound to forms it remains flexible and is applicable progressively. Limitations are, however, placed on it through the distribution of power among the different institions. Otherwise such procedure is not without its dangers since it can be used or, more exactly, misused for designs inimical to integration. A procedural structure for the economic and monetary union, which seeks to use only this way, cannot therefore be regarded as adequate for the purpose. Political intent, such as the resolution of 22 March 1971 expresses, can be properly realized only by such procedure, which accords with the style of integration.

VIII. The Consensus

The constitution of the Member States of the Community—if in various ways—is based on democratic principles. Their organs of state are office holders, who derive their power and their legitimacy from a mandate from the people, and whose exercise of power is based on the consensus of the people. The question as to the legitimacy of the public exercise of power, which rests with the Community institutions, is a question of consensus that is whether they too 'require' consensus and in what manner it is to be 'provided'.

1. The Need of Consensus

(a) The written Community law has not ignored the question of consensus, but it has neglected it as such or only indirectly taken notice of it.[159]

(aa) It has instituted the Assembly in the likeness of the national parliaments, afforded it powers of advice and control, recruited its delegates from the national parliaments and with the provision of the prospect of general direct elections has intended an integrated parliament of the Community, apparently as a European representation of the people with parliamentary functions. Since community law has so far neither integrated nor given full parliamentary powers to its parliament, this legal basis of consensus for public community power has remained incomplete and unreal. The first extension of parliamentary powers in budget control

231

is important in principle, but not decisively so in practice. Direct general elections remain to be introduced. And even their introduction would not, in view of the lack of integration of the pre-parliamentary sphere, integrate Parliament in the manner which would make it an integrated organ of the Community.

(*bb*) The obtaining of consensus for the office holders of the Community is largely left by Community law to the democratic system of the Member States and as a question of integrated legitimacy it is not answered by Community law.

The members of the Council are as such authorized and responsible according to the law of the Member States. In Community law, the Council as such does not obtain consensus either in its establishment or in its function. Even for Parliament there does not exist any such system *de jure communitatis*. Its increasing participation in budgetary law represents such a system only in the modest level of its powers and within the limits of the available means. In the legislative sphere it is limited to forms of participation, which include neither participation in the decision nor even a right of veto.

The members of the Commission and the Court derive their office, limited as it is to a certain period, from the governments of the Member States and thus their legitimacy from a very indirect mandate from 'the peoples of the states belonging to the Community'. The political responsibility of the Commission to Parliament, which in the practice of the Community shows itself as more effective than would appear according to the law, is limited constitutionally to the extent that the parliamentary powers are themselves limited and Parliament's own mandate is unintegrated. Finally, parliamentary approval of the Commission is sanctioned in Community law only by means of a possible removal from office but not replacement, which is only open to the governments of the Member States.

(*cc*) This picture of an incomplete consensus to community power and its administrators under Community law shows that the 'tracing back . . . to a mandate' from the peoples of the Community, 'the holding of power by the peoples' [160] *vis-à-vis* the Community institutions *de jure* and in practice falls behind the level of consensus which the Member States on their part reach constitutionally. Indeed this picture requires not only retouching but basic and illuminating restoration in the terms of the democratic principle, which the constitutional system of the Community itself undertakes: if the democratic principle requires consensus to power by the people for the purpose of limiting and controlling power and thereby asserting freedom, it is satisfied to the extent that exercise of power by Community institutions is possible only within limits drawn by democratically legitimate rules of law. The Community law's own principle of the limited powers of all Community institutions limits these powers not only in the interests of the Member States but also in accordance with the intention

232

of the democratic principle and thereby it limits also the need for consensus. In the application of the principle of limited powers thus lies a partial answer to the question of consensus: 'Power which does not exist does not need an external control to be consistent with "democracy"' runs the laconic but in principle apt epithet of an American observer[161] of the process of integration.

(b) The censorious statement that the Community process does not enjoy any democratic consensus and the inference that it requires one, which should be established in accordance with the constitutional model of the Member States are widely canvassed.[162] They are partly rooted in the concept, that the Communities must inescapably find their ultimate form in a new state, supranationalism is ultimately capable of taking shape only in a federation with the character of a state and consensus would establish itself only in the manner of state constitutions. Statement and inference rest, without as a rule taking account of this fact, on the presumption that only the consensus system of parliamentary government as it is practised in the Member States is capable of providing the standard for an accomplished Community constitution. The postulate of structural homogeneity or congruence is their precept for all perspectives of the Community process. Whether the political system of the Member States and in particular their parliamentarism in turn are in need of examination and revision, whether their defective developments and shortcomings should be repeated, or whether the exercise of Community power and the Community process as such does not provide and offer the task and opportunity to try to construct a new political system, remains unanswered.[163]

The question has also not been asked as to whether the state procedure for establishing consensus, which offers in parliamentary elections the possibility of a rotation of rule and is based on the dualism between government and opposition, will do justice with these instruments of a competitive democracy to the requirements of the Community system. Should an opposition in the Community process of integration advocate disintegration, particular national interests, or alternatives to the Community policy? There are good reasons for doubting the appropriateness of the model of competitive democracy and for saying that 'the agonizing form of changing party governments, familiar to parliamentary regimes, would be unsuitable for this purpose' and that 'at the present stage of development a European administration cannot take on a party character, but must stand on the common interest of all concerned, on their common consensus'.[164] This consideration suggests that Community offices should be held for a limited time and not be taken back before the end of this time. In any case, the alternative to opt between the unconsidered copying of models provided by state systems and fresh concepts remains unutilized in this manner, and this is primarily true also of the question of consensus.

(c) The answer depends on numerous preliminary questions, which it is proper to meet first, before the need of consensus is considered. How to organize the obtaining of consensus is the concern of constitutional policy. (*aa*) It is due to the consensus defects in the Community system, that economic integration is to an increasing extent exposed to a criticism which expresses itself in the Member States in demands for more democracy, more participation and more equality. Ideological attacks on the constitutional system of the industrial society are transferred to the Community system in 'radical criticism of the legitimacy of functional supranationalism', and integration also will have to take account of the 'radical democrats' of Western Europe 'who reject any bureaucracy and planning'.[165] Those who regard the Community process simply and globally as a process detracting from democracy of a late capitalist concentration of power,[166] cannot be met simply with the requisite logic of the matter, which in any case they do not perceive. They must be answered with arguments and solutions which satisfy the need for consent.

(*bb*) With the taking over by the Community of most important decision-making, as the responsibility for the growth and budgetary policy of the states foreseen by the economic and monetary union in its final stage, the danger grows of national defective developments spreading to the disadvantage of other Member States: not only inflation is susceptible to import, but entire economic processes, which—caused by individual states—have a disadvantageous effect in the Community, will easily within the states be blamed on the national governments.[167] So long as the people of the state consent only to their own national government and look upon it to answer for faulty developments, the state government will be inclined to react with reservation to increasing integration and rather let the credit of the community process be questioned in domestic public opinion than its own. A need for consensus for Community power, which is not met, can thus be the cause of reactions on the part of electors and governments damaging to integration.

(*cc*) Vice versa: the successful undertaking by the Communities of public tasks formerly the responsibility of the state can tempt national powers to claim *vis-à-vis* the electors the fruit of this success for themselves. This is facilitated so long as the citizen elects only his national organs of state and he is not aware of the indirect consensus to the Community power. Paradoxically, the function of the Community institutions and their bureaucracies has not changed from only administrative to one of responsibility based on democratic consensus:

> . . . the more the supranational authorities compensate the diminished capacity for action on the part of the states, and the more successfully they increase prosperity and security, the stronger becomes the national consciousness of the governments, since they try to claim national credit for the success of the supranational authorities. The consequence is that the governments prevent the supranational bureaucracies from acquiring political legitimacy.[164]

234

Agricultural policy provides an example of such effects and precisely in the largest Member States of the Community.

(*dd*) To the preliminary question about evidence of a need of consensus belongs the doubt whether the public tasks, which have achieved or are due for integration considering their nature and manner of performance, at all require democratic legitimacy, and whether from it is 'in the nature of things' that they elude it, and whether it would be an obstacle to their rational and effective performance. Such doubts are nourished by the recognition that the national parliamentary democratic systems have experienced loss of substance *vis-à-vis* imposition of new tasks of the industrial society, which question the appropriateness of the democratic consensus procedure. In the theoretical concept of integration such as that of a functional community process,[169] economic and social matters appear as non-controversial items of unpolitical technicality and foreseeable processes, the nature of which does not require democratic consensus. Such an understanding of the essential Community functions[170] as 'organized growth of knowledge' ('*organisierte Wissensbildung*') overestimates the inherent force of economic and financial planning, and neglects the importance of the political decisions which led to this planning. Nevertheless the substance of the Community tasks contains—and in a higher measure than at the state level—elements of rationality of the aim and planning conditioned by the object, which are as such neutral from the point of view of consensus, because they are capable of political evaluation. There has opened here, as has been pointedly stated,[171] the field of a theory 'of a plebiscite-orientated "telecracy" and enlightened technocracy', which must be thought out anew as regards legitimacy and consensus. As a preliminary question to the need of consensus in Community law, this consideration has primarily the function of a forewarning—namely not to raise the demands of consensus contrary to the nature of the object, but on the other hand not to juggle away its justification by explaining planning and inherent forces, in an ill-considered and false fashion, as the substance of the Community functions.

(*ee*) Where and insofar as Community tasks are determined and limited by legal rules for which democratic consensus has been given, the question of the need for consensus does not arise or is less pressing. This is true in the first place of the aims and tasks named in the Treaties, which in spite of the 'uncertainty' of their 'legal concepts' cannot be rendered valueless as mere 'empty formulae'. The European Court has shown itself capable of proving this reproach unfounded. But 'within that, which is not contrary to the aims of the Treaties and seems possible in law, are there not inconsiderable margins for the political will, that is to say within the magic N-angled figure; and does not the will which asserts itself within these margins require legitimacy?'[172] It would be unreal and, from the constitutional policy point of view, wrong simply to deny these well founded questions. An amendment of the object clauses of the Treaties under

Article 236, EEC Treaty, would make them as precise as possible, and set time limits and sanctions.[173] This explanation does naturally not overlook the fact, that the Community institutions bound by the Treaties to the Community interests, are faced with difficulties of interpretation and application in ensuring that the objectives set out in the Treaties are attained (cf. Article 145, EEC Treaty, as regards the Council) and that the provisions of the Treaties are applied (Article 155, EEC Treaty, as regards the Commission). This is all the more so the more often facts and intentions of economic, monetary and social policy have to be legally regulated under a Community constitution, which is orientated towards an economic and monetary union. All the known complications arise here of determining the interests, the subjects of the interests, the intention and finality of the legal provisions, the probably requisite balancing or favouring of interests, and coming to a conclusion after assessing values and experience. The complications of legally binding the public power of the Community can thus hardly be overlooked, and they are in Community law rather larger than in equally complicated national law. Nevertheless within the limits of what can be controlled and is possible there is democratic consensus for such provisions regarding the aims and tasks[174] not only once but continually. In other words: the legal provision of aims and tasks can cover the need for consensus and the widespread timidity or reluctance *vis-à-vis* the necessary ratification of Treaty amendments relating to the economic and monetary union refuses a possible means of consensus.

(*ff*) The 'supranational overcoming of system', which sought to include the Communities in a theory rejecting all claims of congruence of the state systems, could answer the question of the need of consensus in its manner: a structure which sought 'to bypass the stage of the European party government and to arrive directly at a European presidential system'[175] would require consensus only in a single plebiscite. Such a conception approaches the idea of a 'consular dictatorship',[176] and it could be worth the comparison of constitutional laws and practices as to whether a Member State of the Community has not already gathered experience in developing towards a consular or presidential system. Perhaps such comparison would also show that a national system of this kind, by the very reason of its applicability for the purposes of integration, acquires if not a hegemonic position, so at least a leading role in the Community system. The fact that France even after de Gaulle can assert this role is in this connection worthy of consideration as regards constitutional policy for the Committee.

The presupposition of all such considerations would be a radical review of the principle of representation, the development of a theory of representation orientated specifically on the lines of integration, and establishing that 'the use of independent authorities to perform a specialized task is in no way inconsistent with democracy'.[177] This however belongs to our next question.

2. *Obtaining the Consensus*

The necessary consensus to the Community power and its holders can be provided by traditional procedures of constitutional theory practised in the Member States, and by surrogates of Community constitutional law which result from the nature of the functions of the Community and the process of integration. Finally, it has also been asked whether the Community system is capable of producing from within itself an autonomous consensus procedure.

(*a*) The procedures under Article 138 (3), EEC Treaty, concerning the basis of the budgetary treaty, the practice regarding Parliament's participation in the decisions of the Council and parliamentary control of the Commission are of conventional constitutional law and directed towards congruence of Community and national state system.

(*aa*) The election of Parliament by direct universal suffrage[178]—totally or partially—can further and strengthen the consciousness of consensus in the Assembly itself and in public opinion. The fact that this alone, without sufficient integration of the European party system and of the remaining pre-parliamentary sphere cannot provide consensus of the degree usual to the internal politics of the Member States, is beyond doubt. The implementation of Article 138 (3), EEC Treaty, alone will not ensure adequate consensus.

(*bb*) The effectiveness of direct elections to Parliament as far as consensus is concerned can be increased by enlarging Parliament's powers. Such enlargement without direct elections promotes consensus, but only to a smaller extent. Enlargement of powers comes into question in the legislative sphere, in budgetary law and in the procedure for the appointment and control of the Commission.[179]

Political control of the Commission by Parliament, as a means of providing consensus, cannot achieve the intensity of the parliamentary system and the dependence of Government on Parliament's confidence. For the Commission is shown as a 'stable organ of leadership' in its position defined in Article 10 (2), Merger Treaty, and the basic Treaties as protector and promoter of the Community, and not the object of control in the sense of competing democracy. It cannot be subjected to the party system of rotation of rule between government and opposition.

Parliamentary participation and control in the interlocking decision-making process of the Council and Commission must have regard to the fact that planning, measures and decisions concerning rules and finance of integration are not tasks requiring, and open primarily to parliamentary control but rather parliamentary co-operation. Consensus through Parliament is obtained therefore rather through its original participation in the decision-making process than through subsequent control.

(*b*) The effectiveness of determining aims and tasks in the Treaties as a means of providing consensus—within its indirect efficiency—depends on the political will of the Member States to lay themselves open to the risks

237

involved in amending the Treaties, and to use this opportunity. The Commission is the born initiator of such amendments where the Community interest, as specified by governments, even at the stage of declaration of intent, and the principles of integration require them. There are good reasons why Article 236 (1), EEC Treaty, entrusts not only the governments but also the Commission with this initiative. It depends on the Commission's importance whether it will make proper use of it.[181] An attitude—to be observed there—of tactical *quieta non movere* can be damaging for the energetic development of the economic and monetary union. Amendment of the Treaty to provide new aims should not be underestimated in respect of its relevance with regard to consensus.

(c) All *co-operation* at a Community level between Community institutions on the one hand and state organs and organizations of interests on the other provided for in the Treaties or secondary law or developed in the community practice contribute to the separation and limitation of powers and mutual participation and control, and can in this way be effective from the consensus point of view. It is as a rule neither expressly characterized in such manner nor always so intended by the parties. Task of a comparative empiricism useful from the point of view of legal policy, would be to examine systematically these procedures—under consideration of other worldwide experiences—as to how far they involve consensus, or are capable of providing surrogates of consensus. Modern planning law can provide stimulation in this respect.[182] It would then be the task of social science to examine the role of the Community and national bureaucracies, technocratic elites, independent experts, the function of the different scientific disciplines for the recruitment of the Community personnel and other factors, which give such procedures their personal basis.

(d) 'Insofar as the supranational structures compensate for the diminished national capacities they become conditions upon which the existence of the Member States depend.' [183] Whoever recognizes the truth of this may be inclined to recognize the Communities as containing an autonomous self-consensus arising from the rationality of their undertaking and at the same time conferring thereby legitimacy. There has not been a lack of such ideas in integration theory,[184] whether it be with reference to the positive effects of economic objectivity, to the actual importance of new ways of procedure, which prove successful, or to the simple view of the advantages of maintaining integration as opposed to the disadvantages of disintegration. They can become relevant with regard to the question of consensus when such factors of integration are capable of evoking a growing, approving 'acceptance' attitude *vis-à-vis* the Community process in 'interactions' between citizens, between them and the Community institutions and especially between them and the elites—an attitude which has been described as 'permissive consensus'.[185]

Meanwhile, within the limits of the perspectives of a legal structure for

238

the economic and monetary union and with regard to the political realities of this period and up to 1980, such considerations do not yet count as factors to be taken into account in constitutional policy. The provision of consensus within the framework of the need for consensus remains limited to the procedures and surrogates indicated. It cannot at present be seen in an autonomous legitimacy of the Community process. The possibility may however exist.

IX. The Form

1. The Question

Perspectives of constitutional policy for the Communities are as a rule—and all too often, the tendency to jump to conclusions—directed to the future or ultimate form of the Communities: to their legal unity, as arises or should arise from the legal character of their construction and tasks. Opinions of this kind are based on sequences of integration steps foreseen in the Treaty, that is already formed and phased legally, out of which—nurtured on the aims and intentions expressed in the preambles to the Treaties—a form of the Communities may be inferred growing out of the integration process.

It is in accordance partly with the commitment to integration policy of such views but also partly to their national and historical prejudice in favour of the manner in which people have struggled for national unity, that this form is sought and found as a matter of course as the end stage of the three-phase development: alliance—confederation of states—federal state. These concepts understandably have their representatives especially in Germany who sought for their perspectives additional evidence in the process of the North American unification to a federal state and its theoretical foundations.

The main alternative attitude which is committed to national and historical ties, but also to national self-assertion, and claims if not exactly a hegemonic position, at least a position of precedence, sets limits to this three-phase development: it stops at the second phase of confederation.

So at least should the French confederation formula,[186] highly ambivalent as it is as regards its legal nature, be understood—if it still means something for the future form of the Communities after the French and British statements on the accession and the insistence on the unanimity principle.

What the Community as a Confederation would mean is shown clearly by the confederation plan of the rebel states which had decided in 1861 to leave the United States of America:[187] a constitution conceived of as a treaty between states, continuing sovereignty of the states reaching the agreement, the right of nullification of laws contrary to federal law by individual states remaining in a minority and their right of secession in the event of serious and otherwise insoluble conflict, so that the confederation with its 'power of the union' and its dependence on the 'unanimous will of the Member States' would 'ultimately be continually dependent on the goodwill of its members'.

Considerations of constitutional policy as to the form of the Community may within the limits of such 'basic data'—between federal state here, confederation there—occupy and fructify a political theory of the Community, and be the object of present and future discussion. They can hardly be of relevance to the perspectives considered here and concerning this decade of the intended establishment of the economic and monetary union and some time beyond. There are only two indisputable facts which are of importance here: on the one hand the increasing dismantling of the state due to integration, and on the other the conclusion that the form of the Community is open and should be kept open without prematurely giving it the character of a state or of a kind of state.

2. *The State in the Process of Dismantling*

The Member States of the Community find themselves in a process involving the continual dismantling of their tasks. Its extent and the course of this process are determined by the Treaties and their implementation. The causes and consequences of this process for the state character of the Member States, and the form of the Communities are of a complex nature.

(*a*) The transfer of former state tasks to the Communities and their mutation into Community tasks have resulted in the fact that the universal competence of the states and their monopoly over all things public has ended. The fact that the Communities as legal Communities do not dispose at all (quite apart from having sole powers) of physical power to enforce their decisions—neither *vis-à-vis* their members nor the citizens—and the fact that this monopoly has remained with the states and that the Communities are to that extent dependent on their 'official assistance', is not decisive with regard to the process of dismantling. Much more decisive is the shifting of tasks and responsibility from the states to the Communities whose power and responsibility increase. In this manner the state is 'blown up by its actual functions' [188] and new, no longer state government bodies and legal procedures will be effective in its territory and over its subjects, over which the state will no longer autonomously dispose.

The state, which as a Member State is—jointly with others—the moving force behind and the object of integration, therefore changes its state character. It enters a process of change, which it has itself commenced, and for which it is jointly responsible through forming the Community law and participating in the Community institutions.

(*b*) The degree and amount of the dismantling and the change effected thereby may be capable of being measured and calculated from the point of view of constitutional policy for further stages of integration. Economists and social scientists are endeavouring to develop appropriate

240

methods of calculating these.[189] From the point of view of constitutional law state and Community powers can be compared. The dismantling can and ought to have effects beyond the transfer of powers: on the part of the states, that the importance and regulation of the remaining tasks are varied *inter se*; on the part of the Communities, that the transferred tasks of the state are taken charge of as Community tasks with other intentions and in any case from the point of view of a Community and no longer nationally-orientated policy. So long as the Community system is itself not fully developed and—such as in the process of forming its will or in the manner of obtaining consensus—shows deficits, the functional dismantling does not mean at the same time a complete release of the tasks out of the political system of the states: in particular respects the Community system remains necessarily 'the extension of certain elements of the political system of decision in the Member States'.[190] In this way the dismantling does not develop the full effect intended for the purpose of integration, and the 'extended' influence of the Member States on the performance of integrated tasks—and indeed not only in the Community procedures, in which they participate in accordance with the Treaty—conceals at the same time dangers for integration and possibilities of the state character being 'extended'. The Communities find themselves at present in this 'intermediary state'. The accession of new Member States will not exactly make the passing of it any speedier. On the other hand the establishment of the economic and monetary union can give rise to procedural elements and new institutions, which can increase the dismantling effect European integration has on the Member States.

(c) In any case, sovereignty is no longer the appropriate standard for the existence and quality of the state character of the Member States. A theory of sovereignty, which presupposes its uniqueness and indivisibility, must deny Member States sovereignty. But this leads one nowhere. And therefore the diplomatic play with the concept of sovereignty—as before the British accession in the talks between Pompidou and Heath[191] and likewise in the language used in the debates in the House of Commons[192]—is simply uninteresting from the point of view of Community and state law. Much more decisive is whether the state still has a sufficient sphere of responsibility. Responsibility for foreign policy, defence, home affairs, security and administration of justice, culture and welfare has—in spite of inconsiderable exceptions—in substance remained with the states. State responsibilities in the many aspects of economic and social aims, as for example are defined in section 1 of the German Economic Stability Act, and extended in the social impetus of the present by co-determination (*Mitbestimmung*) and redistribution, are today at the head of public tasks. They are already integrated or are due for integration in the economic and monetary union. This increasingly concerns the substance of responsibility of the states.[193] The further process of dismantling would not only quantitatively but qualitively go deeper than all previous precedents of this kind fulfilled under the Treaty. It is just as little to be doubted that something corresponding would come about with an integration of the sphere of foreign policy defined in the Davignon Report. Since all the Member States already belong to a separate collective system of alliance with regard to defence and security policy, the question increasingly arises for purposes of assessing the process of dismantling, where the substantial weight would soon lie with the states—or their Community.

(*d*) Something like this has been put in the terms whether—and how long—the states will maintain their national 'identity'[194] under integration or whether they will lose it. But this question of identity does not have its answer in constructive forecasts as to the form of the Community. Besides there is hidden by the identity formula, under which the opening of the Community to the United Kingdom has proceeded, at most the rejection of a state-like form of the Community, that is a negative and not a positive statement of its desired form. Dismantling progress towards integration and change of the state character of the Community members raise, however, further on the option that their end result may be 'the establishment of a so far unknown pluralistic structure' and that it is by no means certain or even probable that it would have the form of a state. 'Such a structure could very well permit the participating nations to maintain their identity to a large degree, while they are nevertheless joined together in organizations, which transcend the national level.' [195]

3. Open Form without Prejudice in Favour of Creating a State

From the point of view of constitutional policy it is important that the decisions to be taken in the future towards determining tasks and providing institutions and procedures are not biased by the fixed idea that the Communities ought to be given a 'state character'. The form of the Community should be kept open. This is particularly true after para. 15 of the Hague Communiqué has foreseen considerations 'how progress in the sphere of political union could be best achieved.'[196]

(*a*) The perspectives of a Community constitutional policy set out in the constitutionalist theory of integration and from the point of view of constitutional law represented as a principle of structural homogeneity or congruence are just as misguided as the automatism, conceived as being inherent in the Treaty, bringing about a federal metamorphosis of the Communities. A concept operating 'on the basis of sovereignty' and aiming as a 'European sovereign power', which again culminates in the state character, is not calculated to attach the principle of supranationality, which is inherent in the Community process, to a functional, purpose-bound organization without a state character.[197] It is also unsuitable for keeping such 'values' away from integration, which are given utterance in myths and ideologies. This, however, it needs very much.

But also an automatism of the integration process as advocated by functionalist theories of integration[198] does not satisfy the precept of keeping the form of the Communities open. It is true, the Werner Report states that the economic and monetary union appears to be 'a ferment of the political union without which it could not last'.[199] But appropriately the planning of the economic and monetary union does not contemplate automatic progress but political decision of the Communities as to the second stage. Keeping open the structure of the Community means thus deciding without prejudice and with the possibility of options and excludes automatism, the effects of which are not foreseeable either in its effectiveness or desirability and appropriateness for integration.

(b) In the meantime and for the foreseeable future the understanding of the Communities as purpose-bound organizations leaves their eventual form open. The 'purpose-bound organization' is not necessarily a concept hostile to that of the state, for that, too, would imply prejudice. It is open in its neutrality. It is neither historically nor ideologically nor mythically charged. It is rational and in connection with the principle of supranationality related to that kind of functionalism, which 'constitutes the most effective federator concept of all those that have been tried out in practice hitherto',[200] because it is directed to simultaneous and satisfactory undertaking by the Community of various public tasks of different members of the Community.

Notes

Hans Peter Ipsen is Emeritus Professor of Public Law and European Community Law at the University of Hamburg. The essay is the last chapter of his textbook European Community Law, *Tübingen 1972, pp. 976–1055 (J. C. B. Mohr (Paul Siebeck) Tübingen). Translated by G. Adlam.*

1. Ipsen, 'Verfassungsperspektiven der Europäischen Gemeinschaften', lecture given to the Berlin Law Society, 17 April 1970, p. 20; Warnecke, 'American regional integration theories and the European Community', in *Integration* 1971, p. 17. Footnote 40 refers to two relevant statements of Görlitz, *Demokratie im Wandel* (1965): 'First, that the rhetoric of the European Community uses nineteenth century concepts which no longer have an adequate social, economic and political basis in the present. Second, the Community has failed to recognize this anomaly.'

2. Neunreither, 'Bemerkungen zum gegenwärtigen Leitbild des Europäischen Parlaments', in *Zeitschrift für Parlamentsfragen* 1971, p. 343.

3. Thus Rittberger, 'Westeuropäische Integration—Fortschritt oder Stagnation', in *Politische Vierteljahresschrift* 1970, p. 342, on the social and economic sciences.

4. Ipsen, *Fusionsverfassung Europäische Gemeinschaften* (1969), p. 57; in addition Wagner, *Staat* 9 (1970), p. 267; Ipsen, note 1, *ibid.*, p. 14 *et seq.*

5. Heinrich Schneider, 'Zur politischen Theorie der Gemeinschaft', in *Integration* 1969, p. 23; on the same question: Heinrich Schneider, 'Funktionalismus und europäische Friedensordnung', in *Integration* 1971, p. 67.

6. Hans-Peter Schwarz, 'Europa föderieren—aber wie?' in *Festschrift für Theodor Eschenburg* (1971), pp. 377–445 (and in this volume, p. 1–65).

7. Steven Warnecke now gives a critical review in 'American regional integration theories and the European Community', in *Integration* 1971, pp. 1–20; the notes 3, 7, 8, 14, 17, 20, 23 and 27 refer to the most important works of (*inter alia*) Lindberg, Scheingold, Haas, Hoffmann, and Etzioni. Eva Senghaas-Knobloch reviews Taylor's 'International co-operation today: the European and the universal pattern' (1971) in *Integration* 1971, p. 135. Heinrich Schneider gives a short analysis of the theory of the Constitutionalists, Functionalists and Neo-Functionalists in *Integration* 1971, p. 61 *et seq.* on the occasion of the review of Gerda Zellentin's *Intersystemare Beziehungen in Europa* (1970). This work represents an application of Functionalism. In *Integration* 1971, p. 75, Eva Senghaas-Knobloch reports on the conference held in April 1969 at Madison, Wisconsin, USA, by American social scientists on the theme of their integration researches and their product in the collection edited by Lindburg and Scheingold, 'Regional integration: Theory and Research', in *International Organisation* 24 (1970), pp. 607–1020.

8. Karl W. Deutsch, *Political Community at the International Level* (1954), *Political Community and the North Atlantic Area* (1957); Deutch, Edinger, Macridis, Merrit, *France, Germany and the Western Alliance. A study of elite attitudes on European integration and world politics* (1967).

9. Etzioni, *Political Unification* (1965); *The Active Society* (1968), esp. p. 554 *et seq.*: 'Political Communities'.

10. Schwarz (fn. 6), pp. 377, 378 (and in this volume, p. 1, 2).

11. Mitrany, *A Working Peace System* (1966).

12. E. B. Haas, *Beyond the Nation-state* (1964); 'International integration', in *International Organisation* 15 (1961), p. 366 *et seq.*

13. Lindberg, *The Political Dynamics of European Economic Integration* (1963).

14. Heinrich Schneider refers pertinently to these connections with the observations of Bülck, Ipsen and Kaiser, in *Integration* 1971, p. 67, note 8.

15. Wagner, in *Staat* (1970), p. 268.

16. Schwarz (fn. 6), p. 419 (and in this volume, p. 42).

17. On this see Heinrich Schneider, in *Integration* 1971, 67, note 8: a 'clever but problematical thesis'.

18. See Zellentin, *Intersystematare Beziehungen in Europa* (1970), p. 172 *et seq.*; review by Heinrich Schneider, in *Integration* 1971, p. 61.

19. Zellentine, p. 181.

20. This is criticized by Heinrich Schneider in *Integration* 1971, pp. 68, 69. But the uncertainty and ambiguity of the formula—according to the forms to which functional integrational steps should lead to—is inherent in its meaning: functionalism is in this sense 'open', i.e. a method which does not shackle the final phase as regards what shall arise from the object clauses of Integration.

21. Zellentin, p. 195; Schwarz, *ibid.*, p. 417 (and in this volume, p. 39).

22. Puchala, 'Entwicklung und Strukturen regionaler Integration', in *Integration* 1970, p. 171.

23. Zellentin, 146, p. 181; (also on the following). The remark 175, note 105 ('The propaganda in Germany at the time the European Communities were established was that they would lead to state sovereignty and to national

reunification') completely misconceives, with regard to the question of sovereignty, the extent of Article 24 (1) of the German Federal Constitution.

24. Heinrich Schneider in *Integration* 1969, p. 35, referring to Hermann Heller, *Staatslehre* (1934), p. 55.

25. E.g. *La décision dans les Communautés européennes.* Grands colloques européens de l'Association pour le développement de la science politique européenne (Adespe) organisé par l'Institut d'Etudes Politiques de Lyon (November 1966) (1969).

26. Cf. Schwarz (fn. 6), p. 383 (and in this volume, p. 7).

27. From this Heinrich Schneider draws the pertinent inference (*Integration* 1969, p. 27) that the concepts of the disciplines relevant to economic and political integration needed previous reconciliation of their terms. See the treatment here of the objects (under II) and subject matter (under IV) of the community process.

28. A formula derived from Deutsch, with the help of which he and his school establish smaller effects of integration than on the basis of traditional trade statistics; cf. Heinrich Schneider, in *Integration* 1969, p. 26; Rittberger, *Politische Vierteljahresschrift* 1970, p. 346 *et seq.*; Kaiser, 'Das Europarecht in der Krise der Gemeinschaften', in *Europarecht* 1966, p. 5 *et seq.* has given an example of a diagnosis of the crisis situation of the Communities obtained from the data of economic integration for the purpose of the legal conclusions in regard to their structure and durability.

29. Lindberg-Scheingold (cf. the diagram in *The European Community Political System*, p. 113) use the formula on p. 114: $ds = f[(S+Su)(dD+dL)]+en$, in which d=change, f=function, S=system, Su=system support, D=demand, L=leadership and en=general factor of error. With their help an attempt is made with regard to the processes of political decisions from the 'input' of political demands, political support and leadership, distribution of authority and institutional powers to determine as 'output' the results of decisions, which arise from the working together of these factors. The results of the decisions are more closely determined into whether they represent the fulfilment of basic treaty obligations, narrow or extend them. Recognizable creative further developments of integration beyond the basic treaty obligations represent shining examples of the neo-functionalist model; narrowing of a duty by non-fulfilment signifies a step backwards for integration; fulfilment of the Treaty in only an administrative manner accords with static stability and does not do justice to integration as a process.

30. Lindberg-Scheingold, pp. 141, 182.

31. Lindberg-Scheingold, p. 249.

32. Rittberger, in *Politische Vierteljahresschrift*, 1970, p. 342.

33. Warnecke criticizes American theories of integration (*Integration* 1971, p. 1 *et seq.*) that they use non-historical and apolitical concepts of function and structure to describe the processes of integration. He therefore requires that historical precedents should be taken into account, in particular with regard to the foreign policy of the states, which may be relevant for integration.

34. Cf. the report by Handley (*Integration* 1970, p. 321) on the German Conference of 20 July 1970.

35. 'European policy after The Hague. A new beginning in European integration?' in *Europa-Archiv* 1970, p. 278.

36. Jansen, in *Integration* 1970, p. 213, note 20, states this quite rightly.

37. Heinrich Schneider, in *Integration* 1969, p. 35.

38. Herbert Krüger, *Allgemeine Staatslehre*, 2nd edn. (1964), p. 197.

39. Herbert Krüger, p. 256.

40. Cf. Schwarz (fn. 6), p. 307.

41. Heinrich Schneider (*Integration* 1969, p. 43); cf. note 6, *ibid.*, p. 428: 'absolute non-material values'.

42. Deutsch talks quite unobjectively of the 'development of new methods of regulation of government activity'; cf. the conference report by Handley, in *Integration* 1970, p. 321.

43. Cf. on the one hand: Heinrich Schneider, in *Integration* 1969, p. 44, and on the other hand, note 6, *ibid.*, p. 427.

44. Eichenberger, *Leistungstaat und Demokratie* (1969), p. 14.

45. Cf. Section A under VII. Conclusions in the so-called Werner Report of 8 October 1970, p. D 544; Schweizer, in *Über die Zukunft der EWG* (ed. by Dietz, 1971), p. 21. Eichenberger (*ibid.*, p. 15) refers aptly to the irreversibility of such object clauses according to the 'social law of the favourable effects of irreversibility when influential social groups have achieved supposed or real advancement, relief or protection'; likewise Forsthoff in *Der Staat der Industriegesellschaft* (1971), p. 34. On the question whether 'the consumer paradise desired by the majority' is human and allows non-material human needs to be reawakened, see Eichenberger, p. 15, and Gerda Zellentin, 'Regieren für eine humane Welt-Innen- und aussenpolitische Prinzipien', in *Geniessen-Verteilen-Regieren, Planung für eine humane Welt* (1970), pp. 173, 175. For Heinz Kuby (in *Europa 1970. Bilanz und Zukunft der Europapolitik, Krisenmanagement oder Emanzipationsstrategie*, pp. 23, 57 *et seq.*) it is a question—summarized—of the 'radical change of the daily life', whereas Rupp ('Die Dogmatik des Verwaltungsrechts und die Gegenwartsaufgaben der Verwaltung', in *Deutsches Verwaltungsblatt* 1971, p. 672) is of the opinion that a future generation will 'judge the European Communities more by the state of realization of democratic ideas than by the amount of agreement on economic and price policy'. Thus do opinions differ!

46. Cf. 'Probleme der europäischen Einigung (IV). Neue Entwürfe für die politische Einigung und für den Ausbau der Europäischen Gemeinschaften' (*Europa-Archiv* 1970, D p. 519); the foreign ministers' report (Davignon Report) of 20 July 1970 regarding the possible progress in the sphere of political union (*Europa-Archiv* 1970, p. D 520); consultations of the foreign ministers in Munich on 19 September 1970, and on 13 and 14 May 1971, in Paris; and on 5 November 1971 in Rome; the representatives of the acceding countries were informed on 6 November 1971 at Bracciano, see: *Europa-Archiv* 1970 (Chronological table), p. 258, 1971, pp. 119 and 247. See also the EEC *Bulletin* 12/1971, p. 23; cf. the first of the yearly reports to the Assembly on the development of the work on political union (Debates of the European Parliament, No. 139, 7th session—7–11 June 1971, p. 168); Hansen, 'Politische Zusammenarbeit in Westeuropa. Der neue Ansatzpunkt des Luxemburger Berichts' (*Europa-Archiv* 1971, p. 456); Schumacher, 'Les termes utilisés pour exprimer la notion de formation d'un système politique européen', in *Revue de Marché Commun* 1971, p. 329.

47. Cf. *Europa-Archiv*, D p. 519.

48. Hallstein ('Das freie Europa muss mit einer Stimme sprechen', in *Die Welt*, No. 85, of 13 April 1971, p. 4) states with regard to the confederation initiative of Pompidou and the placing of it within the development of the

Community: 'that is in pleasing contrast to the manner in which the said practice of consultation between the Six (on the basis of the Davignon Agreement)—and not least at the instigation of Germany—has painfully avoided using the machinery of the European Community'. In so far as this refers to a lack of involvement of the Community legal order it is doubtless true. In the same strain: Carstens, *Politische Führung* (1971), p. 263.

49. Most recently—and in German literature practically the first—Zellentin, *Intersystemare Beziehungen in Europa* (1970); Review by Heinrich Schneider, in *Integration* 1971, p. 61; and by Ipsen in *Das Historisch-Politische Buch* 19 (1971), p. 217. Cf further: 'La paix par la recherche scientifique', conference of 5–6 November 1969 of the Centre de Sociologie de la Guerre (Brussels 1970), in part (p. 151 *et seq.*) contained in Buchmann, *La recherche de la paix par le regionalisme international*.

50. At the Seventh International Conference for International Problems in Rockville on 10 October 1971 Hallstein stated that the USSR wanted to hold back recognition of the EEC 'as a trump card for the planned European security conference', although bilateral economic relations and indirect ties already existed with some East Block states via the GATT membership. An obstacle to legal relations between the EEC and COMECON is the fact that the economic organization of the East Block is not a legal entity: cf. *Frankfurter Allgemeine Zeitung* No. 235, 11 October 1971, p. 3.

51. Cf. the review by Heinrich Schneider in *Integration* 1971, p. 67, of Zellentin's *Intersystemare Beziehungen*, pp. 239, 240.

52. Cf. Heinrich Schneider, 'Zur politischen Theorie der Gemeinschaft', in *Integration* 1969, pp. 30–31, with reference to Lindberg.

53. Heinrich Schneider (*Integration* 1969, pp. 30–31; 1971, p. 68) has repeatedly and aptly recalled this thesis by Schocking and Anderson, entitled 'Observations on the European Integration Process', in *Journal of Conflict Resolution* 4 (1966), p. 388. It still holds good and is authoritative with regard to constitutional policy for the making of the Community.

54. Forsthoff, *Der Staat der Industriegesellschaft* (1971), p. 22.

55. Cf. Schwarz (fn. 6), p. 414 (and in this volume, p. 36), referring to Ernst B. Haas, *The Uniting of Europe* (1958) 'who has directed attention to the social dimension of political integration'. The reproach that integration lacks a social dimension has been given new edge from the point of view of social policy—and this clearly critical, if not hostile—since the postulate of democracy in the social sphere has been pursued 'with the object of systematically abolishing privileges in all spheres' (Willy Brandt); cf. (for example) on the one hand Agnoli and Brückner, *Die Transformation der Demokratie* (1967), and on the other hand von Schrenck-Notzing, *Demokratisierung. Konfrontation mit der Wirklichkeit* (1972). Especially revealing in this connexion for economic integration is *Europa 1970. Bilanz und Zukunft der Europolitik. Krisenmanagement oder Emanzipationsstrategie. Neunzehntes Europäisches Gespräch* (commissioned by the Deutscher Gewerkschaftsbund, edited by Karl Braukmann), *ibid.*, in particular the report by Heinz Kuby, pp. 23–44, 57–77.

56. Herzog, *Allgemeine Staatslehre* (1971), p. 69; Görlitz, *Demokratie im Wandel*.

57. Cf. Nass, *Englands Aufbruch nach Europa. Ein erster Überlick über die Beitrittsverhandlungen* (1971), pp. 83–84.

247

58. The fact that 'race' has so far played no part in European integration is explained by the lack of such phenomena as Delbruck's book, *Die Rassenfrage als Problem des Vökerrechts und nationaler Rechtsordnungen* (1971) has legally and sociologically sketched. Whether the accession of the UK with its important legislation on the subject will bring any change, remains to be seen.

59. Cf. Schwarz (fn. 6), p. 406 (and in this volume, p. 29); Zellentin (fn. 45), p. 186; Puchala, in *Integration* 1970, p. 168; and Erler, *Die Krise der Europäischen Gemeinschaften—Europäischer Bundesstaat oder Europa der Vaterländer?* (1966), pp. 25–26: 'So far there is no such European patriotism . . . the European consciousness is certainly the consciousness of a European cultural heritage and common economic ties, but there is still no common political trust and confidence.' This is true even if it could be suggested—as Erler does—that even today there is only a consciousness of the *state*, of which there are several reasons to doubt; cf. Schmölders, *Der verlorene Untertan* (1971), whose system of types of citizen includes only the overestimated, overdemanded, duped, resourceful, fraudulent and renegade citizen. Since these findings have been made from social economic research into behaviour, they must also be considered with regard to the type of 'Common Market citizen'. None such has yet been developed, but jurisprudence should not be blamed for this.

60. On such questions cf. Kuby-Kitzmüller, *Transnationale Wirtschaftspolitik. Zur politischen Oekonomie Europas* (1970).

61. Cf. 'The Evaluation of the investigations of Ernst B. Haas' by Heinrich Schneider in *Integration* 1969, p. 29; Friedrich, in *Integration* 1970, p. 230; Jansen, *ibid.*, p. 204.

62. E.g. Rittberger, 'Westeuropäische Integration—Fortschritt oder Stagnation?' in *Politische Vierteljahresschrift* 1970, p. 342 *et seq.*

63. 'Die Jugend und die Europäische Gemeinschaft', Brussels, 12–14 June 1970, *Documents* (ed. by the Commission); notification from the Commission to the Council with the conclusions from the conference 'Die Jugend und die Europäische Gemeinschaft' of 24 June 1970. 260 participants represented some 200 organizations at the conference. In answering several questions in Parliament the Commission discussed the methods of choice of the participants and made the point that the press reactions to the conference were largely negative due to the manner of the discussions and the leftist nature of the resolutions; cf. questions No. 157/70 (Biaggi MP), 161/70 (Müller MP), 182/70 (Romeo MP) and the answers of the Commission of 15 September 1970 (Amtsblatt C 118, 14, 16 and 18). Cf. also the conference 'Young parliamentarians in the EEC', the third of which took place in Aachen/Bonn on 22–23 November 1971; cf. *Woche im Bundestag* 1971, Nos. 9/10/11, p. 37.

64. On the changes of direction cf. Schelsky, 'Die Strategie der "Systemüberwindung". Der lange Marsch durch die Institutionen', in *Frankfurter Allgemeine Zeitung*, 10 December 1972, pp. 11/12. From Schelsky's earlier book on the 'sceptical generation' to this very apt analysis the march was not especially long —only some twenty years.

65. Gasteyger, Kewenig, Kohlhase, 'Ortsbestimmung der Zukunft Europas', in *Europa-Archiv* 1970, p. 587.

66. Kuby in the report referred to in fn. 55.

67. Kuby, pp. 39, 41.

68. Kuby, p. 35; similarly the Vice President of the Commission, Haferkamp,

before the third conference 'Young parliamentarians in the EEC' on 23 November 1971: a common social policy is necessary 'to balance the power structures, to control economic power . . . and to pursue a common social policy in Europe'; cf. *Woche im Bundestage* 1971, Nos. 9/10/11, p. 37.

69. Neunreither (in *Zeitschrift für Parlamentsfragen* 1971, p. 329) refers to the activity of the Commission, which since 1958 has systematically attempted 'to build up its own net of European interest organizations' to support its role of 'government'—whereas Parliament has failed in that respect, with the result that it has not been of interest to economic associations.

70. Cf. Schwarz (fn. 6), p. 439, fn. 73 (and in this volume, p. 62).

71. A particular example is provided by the eleven agricultural organizations represented in COPA (comité des organisations professionnelles agricole de la CEE) in their influence on the common agricultural policy; cf. Nass, 'Die Träger der Agrarpolitik in der Europäischen Wirtschaftsgemeinschaft', in COPA, *Symposium Europa* 1950–1970; *Liber Discipulorum* edited on the occasion of the twentieth anniversary of the foundation of the European College at Bruges (1971), pp. 249–275. The Union of Savings Banks in the EEC demanded that European interest organizations should have their 'own status', be 'accredited' to all European institutions, and be represented in the Economic and Social Committee to guarantee them the information and access that they have at a national level; cf. 'Nachrichten aus den Europäischen Gemeinschaften', ed. *VWD-Vereinigte Wirtschaftsdienste GmbH*, Frankfurt/Main, No. 239/71 of 10 December 1971 I/4.

72. Neunreither, in *Zeitschrift für Parlamentsfragen* 1971, p. 329, calls the co-operation of parties especially in the groups of Parliament 'the typical example of every benevolent consideration', but refers on the other hand to the comparatively weaker position of the groups and the stronger 'ties' of MPs in their own national assemblies.

73. This is correct: Neunreither, p. 332; cf. Schwarz (fn. 6), p. 428. The exposition by Guy van Oudenhove, *The Political Parties in the European Parliament* (1965), which sketches the position to the end of 1962, needs to be revised; on which see *Les partis politiques et l'integration européenne*, Colloque de Bruges 1969–70.

74. On this and the European movements, European parties, European party, internationals: Schwarz (fn. 6), pp. 393–398 (and in this volume, p. 16 *et seq.*). The latest example of an attempt at a 'European Party Programme' in the decision of the eighth Congress of the social democratic parties of the EEC in Brussels from 28 to 30 June 1971; cf. *Europa-Archiv*, p. D 386. As regards their own community process, item 4 of the programme agrees upon 'close co-operation'. And it must lead to such a structure, 'that binding resolutions can be taken for the socialist parties'. So far this structure has not existed.

75. Schwarz (fn. 6), p. 440, note 81 (and in this volume, p. 62): parliament = an assembly of 'European parliamentary notables'; cf. Neunreither *op. cit.* (see fn. 72), pp. 330–336. Schwarz announces as a Hamburg Dissertation: Peter Reichel, *Der Deutsche Bundestag und die europäische Integration.*

76. Schwarz (fn. 6), p. 385 (and in this volume, p. 9).

77. Schwarz, *ibid.*, p. 384 (and in this volume, p. 8).

78. Heinrich Schneider, in *Integration* 1969, p. 29.

79. Meyer-Cording, 'Die Europäische Integration als geistiger Entwicklungsprozess', in *Archiv des Völkerrechts* 10 (1962), p. 45.

80. On their methods see Rittberger in *Politische Vierteljahresschrift* 1970, p. 343; Puchala, 'Entwicklung und Strukturen regionaler Integration', in *Integration* 1970, p. 180.

81. Rittberger, p. 350, note 16; cf. Neunreither *op. cit.* (fn. 72), p. 338, note 43.

82. Heinrich Schneider, in *Integration* 1969, p. 39.

83. Zellentin, *Intersystemare Beziehungen in Europa* (1970), p. 192, note 153; Puchala, in *Integration* 1970, p. 173.

84. Ipsen, *Politik und Justiz. Das Problem der justizlosen Hoheitsakte* (1937), pp. 231, 234, 239.

85. Janz, 'Führen alle Wege nach Europa?' in *Integration* 1970, p. 187.

86. Gasteyger, Kewenig, Kohlhase, 'Ortsbestimmung der Zukunft Europas', in *Europa-Archiv* 1970, p. 587.

87. It has been undertaken several times. Rittberger in *Politische Vierteljahresschrift* 1970, pp. 352/353, reports on Lindberg, 'The European Community as a political system' (in *Journal of Common Market Studies* 5, 1966/67, p. 356 *et seq.*); and Lindberg-Scheingold provides another indication, *Europe's Would-be Polity* (1970), p. 74 *et seq.*

88. Cf. Scheuner, 'Verfassungsprobleme der Wirtschafts- und Währungsunion', in *Integration* 1971, p. 145 *et seq.* (and in this volume, p. 66 *et seq.*).

89. Lindberg-Scheingold, *Europe's Would-be Polity* (1971), p. 276: 'Moreover, if material well-being is what is most important to a society, it is difficult to agree with Hoffmann, who identifies high politics and salience with such nonmaterial values as nationhood, leadership, and prestige. As one of the principal agents in Europe of mass consumption, the Community under conditions of social homogeneity would be very much a creature of its time.' This may be regretted. But it is the reality, and constitutional policy must take it into account.

90. Forsthoff, *Der Staat der Industriegesellschaft* (1971), p. 32.

91. Kaiser, in *Die öffentliche Verwaltung* 1971, p. 321 (review of Forsthoff's book).

92. Cf. Scheuner (fn. 88) under I 4 (and in this volume, p. 68).

93. Cf. Ehlermann, 'Sachkompetenzen und Organverfassung der Gemeinschaft', in *Integration* 1971, p. 164 *et seq.*

94. Quite right: Scheuner (fn. 88), under I 5 (and in this volume, p. 68).

95. Hankel, Report of 26 November 1971 (cf. fn. 88) under II 2 (3).

96. On this question, see Erler, *Die Krise der Europäischen Gemeinschaften—Europäischer Bundesstaat oder Europa der Vaterländer?* (1966), p. 29.

97. On 29 September 1971; cf. VWD (fn. 71), No. 181/71, of 20 September 1971, II/6; *Bulletin der Europäischen Gemeinschaften* 11/1971, p. 93.

98. Judgment in case 71/71 of 14 December 1971.

99. According to the view of Burhenne, the president of the committee of IUCN (International Union for the Conservation of Nature), German measures for the protection of the environment are prevented by EEC considerations, i.e. on grounds of competition policy (*Die Welt* No. 219 of 21 September 1971, p. 2); on the problem under German law, see W. Weber, 'Umweltschutz im Verfassungs- und Verwaltungsrecht', in *Deutsches Verwaltungsblatt* 1971, p. 806; cf. also the first announcement of the Commission with regard to the policy of the Community in the sphere of the protection of the environment of 22 July 1971,

and the environmental programme of the German Government of 14 October 1971, *Bundestagsdrucksache* VI/2710.

100. On 20 September 1971 on the proposal of President Pompidou the Council resolved to co-ordinate natural measures to contest drugs and to hold an annual exchange of experiences by the competent ministers (*Die Welt* No. 219 of 21 September 1971, p. 2); cf. also the report of Laudrin, member of the European Parliament, 'Über das Erfordernis einer Gemeinschaftsaktion zur Rauschgiftbekämpfung' (session documents 1971/72, Doc. 229/71 of 14 January 1972), and the following debate (*Debates of the European Parliament* No. 145, sessions of 17 and 19 January 1972).

101. The first systematization: Ratzel, *Anthropogeographie* (1882/1891).

102. Opposed to the naturalistic use of space and territory as an element of the Three Elements Doctrine of Georg Jellinek: Herbert Krüger, *Allgemeine Staatslehre*, 2nd edn. (1966), p. 146.

103. Kitzinger, 'Wohin treibt die EWG?', in *Bergedorfer Gesprächskreis* 6 (1964), p. 66. Correspondingly, Hogan, 'Political representation and European integration' (*Integration* 1970, p. 288): 'Under these conditions, the persistence of the nation state has created a discrepancy between political organization and social reality. The jurisdiction of governments has not kept pace with the geographic and functional scope of the activities and conflicts requiring regulation.'

104. Cf. Meyer-Cording, 'Die Europäische Integration als geistiger Entwicklungsprozess', in *Archiv des Völkerrechts* 10 (1962), p. 66.

105. *Europa-Archiv*, p. D 54.

106. Dahrendorf, 'Möglichkeiten und Grenzen einer Aussenpolitik der Gemeinschaften', in *Europa-Archiv* 1971, p. 119; *ibid.*, p. 117 *et seq.*, a survey of the Community's 'influence' and its current development. Cf. Schaetzel in *Europa-Archiv* 1971, p. 859, on the 'new dimensions of the relations between an enlarged European community and the USA'.

107. Dahrendorf in *Europa-Archiv* 1971, pp. 123–124.

108. Date of the history of the negotiations since May 1967: *Nachrichten aus den Europäischen Gemeinschaften*, pub. by Vereinigte Wirtschaftsdienste GmbH, Frankfurt, No. 14/72 of 20 January 1972, I/9–I/12; negotiations were concluded with Denmark on 8 December 1971, UK on 13 December 1971, Ireland on 13 January 1972 and Norway on 15 January 1972 (*ibid.*, I/12). On 28 October 1971 a large majority in Britain (Commons 356 : 244 : 22; Lords 451 : 58) voted for entry; on 18 December 1971 the Danish parliament (with a majority of 141 : 32) authorized the government to sign the act of accession.

109. In two of the applicant countries a referendum was part of the ratification procedure. The result in Denmark was in favour of, and in Norway against, entry.

110. Nass gives an excellent survey of the course of the negotiations for entry (both from the proximity of the participant and the perspective of the whole problem): 'Englands Aufbruch nach Europa', in *Europäische Schriften des Bildungswerks Europäische Politik* 28 (1971); *ibid.*, pp. 21–39 on the principles of the negotiations; Nass, 'Verfahrensaspekte der Beitrittsverhandlungen', in *Europarecht* 1971, p. 379.

111. O.J. 1972 L 73, p. 203 ff: The Community, also, can ask applicant countries to supply information and can consult them about national measures

of Community relevance. Christopher Layton, a British politician and technology expert, was appointed before the British entry to the 'cabinet' of Signor Spinelli, member of the Commission. After the entry he became chief of cabinet.

112. There is an accurate description in Nass, *Englands Aufbruch nach Europa* (1971), pp. 41–63.

113. Nass, p. 26.

114. Cf. the conference of the Society for Comparative Law in Mannheim from 22–25 September 1971; session organized by the Society for European Law on the subject: 'The application of the law of the European Communities in Denmark, UK, Ireland and Norway'. The different reports were published under the main title 'The Expansion of the European Communities', in *Kölner Schriften zum Europarecht*, vol. 18 (1972).

115. Zellentin (*Intersystemare Beziehungen in Europa*, 1970, p. 194) aptly refers to this, cf. Ipsen, *Fusionsverfassung Europäische Gemeinschaften* (1969), pp. 72–74 and note 98; Haeckel, *Der Faktor Zeit in der Verwirklichung der Europäischen Gemeinschaftsverträge* (1965). Gasteyger, Kewenig, Kohlhase, *Ortsbestimmung der Zukunft Europas* EA 1970, p. 584, consider that a common market will function without friction only if the level of integration in all materially connected spheres 'is developed at the same rhythm'.

116. When the Council meeting of 27 October 1970 took up the question of the transitional period for the would-be acceding states, it regarded this as a resolve to get to 'the heart of the negotiations'; Nass, *Englands Aufbruch nach Europa* (1971), p. 75.

117. Deutsch at the Geneva Conference of 20 June 1970; cf. Handley, in *Integration* 1970, p. 321.

118. Deutsch; cf. Handley, p. 322.

119. Heinrich Schneider, 'Zur politischen Theorie der Gemeinschaft', in *Integration* 1969, p. 33, on the integration model of Lindberg; cf. also Zellentin, *Intersystemare Beziehungen in Europa* (1970), p. 193.

120. The Hague Communiqué of 1 and 2 December 1969, expressed in para. 3 such a non-reversibility: 'Entry into the final phase of the Common Market means not only recognizing the non-reversibility of what has heretofore been achieved by the Community . . .'

121. Heinrich Schneider, in *Integration* 1969, p. 34, refers to Max Weber's remarks on the applicability of 'rules of procedure'.

122. Cf. Schwarz (see fn. 6), p. 426 (and in this volume, p. 49).

123. Janz, 'Führen alle Wege nach Europa?' in *Integration* 1970, p. 185. Overcoming such points can represent a 'qualitative step forward'.

124. Zellentin, *Intersystemare Beziehungen in Europa* (1970), p. 194, refers to phases and sequences of the progress of integration and then adds 'cycles', which she rightly puts in parentheses, with a question mark. Her question is clearly to be answered in the negative.

125. Ehlermann, 'Sachkompetenzen und Organverfassung der Gemeinschaft. Rechtliche Folgen einer Wirtschafts- und Währungsunion', in *Integration* 1971, p. 164 *et seq.*

126. Ehlermann, *Verfassungsprobleme* (cf. fn. 94), refers to the fact that between the Werner Report and the decision of 9 February–22 March 1971, Pompidou's concept of a confederation was put to the press conference of 21 January 1971.

127. Reference should be made especially to: Everling, 'Die Entwicklung der Europäischen Gemeinschaft zur Wirtschafts- und Währungsunion. Ihre Bedeutung für die Verfassungsordnung der Mitgliedstaaten' in NJW 1971, p. 1481; in addition Ehlermann, 'Sachkompetenzen und Organverfassung der Gemeinschaft: Rechtliche Fragen einer Wirtschafts- und Währungsunion', in *Integration* 1971, p. 162 *et seq.*; Meier, 'Die Weiterentwicklung des Gemeinsamen Marktes zur Wirtschafts- und Währungsunion—Aufgabe des Integrationsprinzips?' in *Aussenwirtschaftsdienst des Betriebsberaters* 1971, p. 497; Oppermann, 'Währungsunion und EWG-Vertragsrevision', in EuR 1971, p. 130; Nicolaysen, 'Gemeinschaftsverfassung im Zeichen der Wirtschafts- und Währungsunion', in *Integration* 1971, p. 90; see also the reports of Scheuner, Ehlermann, Hans Möller and Haeckel at the Arbeitskreis Europäische Integration Conference of 26 and 27 November 1971. Cf. also the reports of Kramer, Tiemeyer, Herzog, Sautter, Sasse and Frowein at the conference of the Society for European Law in Bad Ems in April 1972 on the development of the Community in the Seventies.

128. Neunreither, in *Zeitschrift für Parlamentsfragen* 1971, p. 337; also Nicolaysen, in *Integration* 1971, p. 93.

129. Ehlermann (cf. fn. 93) under 8 (2).

130. *Ibid.*, under III 4.

131. Neunreither (fn. 128), p. 340.

132. Cf. Everling, in NJW 1971, p. 1485.

133. Meier in *Aussenwirtschaftsdienst des Betriebsberaters* 1971, p. 501; Nicolaysen, in *Integration* 1971, p. 95.

134. Cf. Schwarz (fn. 6), p. 432: much depends on 'whether the principle of majority decisions is successfully and rigorously applied to the Council. If this were so, the Commission's status would be automatically strengthened'.

135. Cf. the declaration of the British Prime Minister, Mr. Heath, in the Commons on 24 May 1971, agreeing with President Pompidou, that maintenance and strengthening of the structure of co-operation in such a community requires that decisions in practice must be reached unanimously when essential interests of one or more members are involved.

136. By Herzog, *Allgemeine Staatslehre* (1971), p. 410.

137. On these requirements cf. Schwarz (fn. 6), p. 432, referring to Hallstein: 'only politicians of ministerial calibre or, even better, members of the government'. There is cause to doubt whether even this standard suffices. In any case Article 10 (1) of the Merger Treaty cannot be taken sufficiently seriously: 'general competence' and 'whose independence is beyond doubt' neither of which is regarded by choosing exact proportions of the different parties. *Vestigia terrent*!

138. Cf. Neunreither, in *Zeitschrift für Parlamentsfragen* 1971, pp. 327, 337.

139. Ehlermann (cf. fn. 93) under 8 (2).

140. Cf. Neunreither (fn. 138), p. 337.

141. Neunreither, *ibid.*, p. 334, describes it as 'one of the most astonishing questions of the development of the Communities so far', that the executive bureaucratic element of the national systems (could) 'represent itself as the political element of the Community, which had to control the "Brussels technocrats".' This fact is less astonishing when it is considered that the decision-making process derives at present its authority from planning and plan execution, and for this requires a new structure of parliamentary control. There is no special cause for surprise that there where such control functions satisfactorily neither

at the level of the community parliament nor at the level of the state parliaments, national executive organs 'fill the gap', which, for their part, are at least led by a politically responsible minister. It cannot be disputed that this fact reveals lacunas in the constitution of the Community; cf. also Neunreither, p. 335.

142. Cf. Scheuner (fn. 88) under 12 b.

143. Cf. Neunreither (fn. 138), p. 321.

144. Meier, cf. fn. 133, *ibid.*, 501.

145. Ipsen, cf. fn. 1, *ibid.*, 20.

146. Cf. Ehlermann (fn. 93) under 8 (3).

147. Cf. Ehlermann (fn. 93) under III 4; Neunreither (fn. 138), pp. 329, 335 and 338.

148. Cf. Ehlermann (fn. 93), III 4.

149. Quite right: Neunreither (fn. 138), p. 343.

150. Schwarz (fn. 6), p. 399 (and in this volume, p. 22).

151. Meier (fn. 133), p. 500.

152. For proposals about this, cf. Ehlermann (fn. 93), III 5.

153. Cf. Meier (fn. 133), pp. 501, 502.

154. Everling, NJW 1971, p. 1485 with note 32; Meirer, fn. 133, p. 502. The expert opinion 'Wege und Irrwege zur europäischen Wirtschaftsunion' of Willgerodt, Domsch, Hasse, Merx, and Kellenbenz (1972) proceeds naturally from the basis that the bank-note system as understood in German Law must enjoy independence.

155. Cf. Ehlermann (fn. 93), p. 5; Scheuner (fn. 88), p. 7.

156. Approving: Ehlermann (fn. 93), p. 5; disapproving: Oppermann in EUR 1971, p. 133; on the interpretation of Article 235, EEC Treaty: von Donnersmarck, *Planimmanente Krisensteuerung in der Europäischen Wirtschaftsgemeinschaft. Funktion und Bedeutung des Art. 235 EWG-Vertrag* (1971).

157. Cf. Ehlermann (fn. 93), p. 6.

158. Ehlermann, *ibid.*, p. 18. In such informal agreements measures could also be taken for making the proposals of the Commission subject to being dealt with within a fixed period in the Council to ensure for instance their renewal submission in time, or to put a time-limit on their being dealt with from the beginning; cf. on this the suggestions of the Commission member Haferkamp in his interview to *Eurpäische Gemeinschaft* 1/1972, p. 12.

159. On the significance of this cf. Schwarz (fn. 6), pp. 433 and 381 (and in this volume pp. 55 and 5): democratic principle in the Member States as a complication for 'every attempt at a federation'.

160. Herzog employs such terms with regard to the democratic principle in *Allgemeine Staatslehre* (1971), p. 208.

161. Hogan, *Representative Government and European Integration* (1967), p. 207; also 'Political representation and European integration', in *Integration* 1970, p. 294.

162. Cf. Janz, 'Führen alle Wege nach Europa?' in *Integration* 1970, p. 192; Rupp, 'Die Dogmatik des Verwaltungsrechts und die Gegenwartsaufgaben der Verwaltung', in *Deutsches Verwaltungsblatt* 1971, p. 672.

163. Neunreither however (fn. 138, p. 343) raises some precise questions: '. . . the European Community, so far as is certain, has already become a decisive catalyst in the development of the parliamentary system in the Member States. If it avows, as at present, a purely decorative function for parliaments, then, in

addition to the material disappearance of decision-making in the national parliaments, theory in time will not have to establish representation and legitimacy anew'.

164. Cf. Scheuner (fn. 88), p. 13 c.

165. '. . . and Communists'; cf. Schwarz (fn. 6), p. 430 (and in this volume, p. 1). On the position of the Communities in the East–West relationship, see above, p. 214.

166. Typical expression: 'The EEC imperialism'.

167. Cf. Kohler-Schlaeger, *Wirtschafts- und Währungsunion für Europa* (1971), pp. 127/128; Zellentin, *Intersystemare Beziehungen in Europa* (1970), p. 196.

168. Zellentin, *Regieren für eine humane Welt* (see fn. 45), p. 185.

169. By Mitrany, 'whose enthusiasm for international co-operation is exceeded only by his aversion to a European federal state'; cf. Schwarz (fn. 6), p. 381.

170. Cf. Ipsen, *Fusionsverfassung Europäische Gemeinschaften* (1969), pp. 64–65, with references in fn. 84 *et seq.*; Nicolaysen, in *Integration* 1971, pp. 99–103; Schwarz (fn. 6), p. 415 (gradualness and clever use of inherent compulsion); Hans Maier, 'Reform in der Demokratie', in *Zeitschrift für Politik* 1968, p. 393, on the difficulties of discussion of reform under these circumstances.

171. Cf. Neunreither (fn. 138), p. 343.

172. Heinrich Schneider, in *Integration* 1969, p. 42.

173. Cf. Ipsen (fn. 170), p. 62.

174. Hans Möller advocated at the conference on 26 and 27 November 1971 (see fn. 88) not to set up the economic and monetary union as a centralized system with new organs but as a decentralized one with a set of principles. In this way the problem of the democratic control of the competent authorities is posed in a simple form: it must simply ensure the maintenance of the established rules, that is that they are observed. The principle has worked in the organization of combines and is now being discussed by experts for the German 'global direction'.

175. Cf. Neunreither (fn. 138), p. 326, note 10. The reflections of Hogan tend in this direction (see fn. 161).

176. Litten, in *Bergedorfer Gesprächskreis,* Protocol No. 37 (1970), p. 20 under No. 21.

177. Hogan, in *Integration* 1970, pp. 289, 295.

178. Cf. Kohler, 'Direkte Wahlen zum Europäischen Parlament. Grundlagen und Probleme der gegenwärtigen Intiativen', in *Europa-Archiv* 1971, p. 727.

179. The independent working-group formed by the Commission in October 1971 is to concern itself with the following questions: participation of parliament in the permanent task forming the constitution of the Community, in the legislative process in all spheres of Community competence, definition of its budgetary powers, its tasks of political control of the government powers of the Community organs, the effects on the relationship between the organs of strengthening the powers, and their connection with direct elections; cf. *Nachrichten aus den Europäischen Gemeinschaften,* Hg. VWD-Vereinigte Wirtschaftsdienste GmbH, Frankfurt, No. 199/71 of 10 October 1971, I/7–8.

180. Cf. Scheuner (fn. 88) under 13 c, 14 also on the following.

181. Hallstein on 3 December 1971, on the occasion of the conferring of the honorary citizenship of Brussels: 'The Commission . . . in a freer development

should be able to fulfil its own tasks of defining the common interest and pursuing it internally in a dialogue with the Council and representing it externally'; cf. fn. 179, VWD *ibid.*, No. 234/71 of 3 December 1971, I/3.

182. Ipsen, 'Introductory remarks on the occasion of the conference of University teachers of constitutional law at Regensburg 1971'; on the co-report of Brohm on the theme 'Die Dogmatik des Verwaltungsrechts vor den Gegenwartsaufgaben der Verwaltung'. VVDStRL vol. 30, pp. 313–316.

183. Zellentin, *Intersystemare Beziehungen in Europa* (1970), p. 195, referring to Max Weber's *'Legitimitätsgeltung rationalen Charakters'* and its validity for the Communities.

184. There are references (especially to Lindberg) in Heinrich Schneider, *Integration* 1969, p. 34.

185. Lindberg-Scheingold, *Europe's Would-be Polity* (1970), p. 294.

186. Declaration of President Pompidou at his press conference on 21 January 1971 (*Europa-Archiv* 1971, p. D 131). Foreign minister Schuman held the view in the national assembly, that this expression would 'perhaps in future be regarded as the first foundation stone of the European confederation'; cf. on this Berger, 'Vor der Wiedergeburt Europas à la Wiener Kongress? Die Europa-Vorschläge Staatspräsident Pompidous', in *Europa-Archiv* 1971, p. 665. With regard to Mr. Behrendt, the President of the Assembly, President Pompidou put forward the view on 10 January 1972 that Europe had for some time to 'tread the path of confederation' before it reaches the goal of a 'federation'. Whereby confederation as a final form was again put in question, if the diplomatic play on words could be taken at all seriously in a legal sense; cf. the report of the speech in VWD (fn. 179), *ibid.*, No. 7/72 of 11 January 1972, I 3.

187. Georg Jellinek, *Allgemeine Staatslehre*, 3rd edn. (1921), pp. 766, 767.

188. Jansen, 'Zur Situation des Westeuropäischen Integrationssystems—Aufriss einer Analyse', in *Integration* 1970, p. 211; likewise (as opposed to Herbert Krüger in DÖV 1959, p. 725) Kaiser, 'Zur gegenwärtigen Differenzierung von Recht und Staat. Staatstheoretische Lehren der Integration', in *Oesterreichische Zeitschrift für öffentliches Recht* X (1960), p. 418, note 16.

189. Rittberger, 'Westeuropäische Integration—Fortschritt oder Stagnation?' in *Politische Vierteljahresschrift* 1970, p. 352.

190. Cf. Neunreither (fn 138), p. 334.

191. Cf. the declaration of President Pompidou to the press in the presence of Prime Minister Mr. Heath on 21 May 1971, *Europa-Archiv* 1971, p. D 275.

192. Declaration of the Prime Minister, Mr. Heath, to the Commons on 24 May 1971, *Europa-Archiv* 1971, p. D 272.

193. Cf. the drastic view of Hogan, 'Political representation and European integration', in *Integration* 1970, p. 297.

194. This expression was used particularly at the time of the Anglo-French negotiations of May 1971 before British entry; cf. *Europa-Archiv* 1971, pp. D 275, 278.

195. Cf. the reference by Heinrich Schneider (in *Integration* 1969, p. 30) to this statement by Schokking and Anderson, 1960. See also: Lindberg-Scheingold, *Europe's Would-be Polity* (1970), p. 309, with reference to Yondorf, *Europa of the Six: Dynamics of Integration*; Erler, *Die Krise der Europäischen Gemeinschaften—Europäischer Bundesstaat oder Europa der Vaterländer?* (1966), p. 28, speaks of 'federal-type "hybrid institutions" ' and thereby wishes to wean the Communi-

ties from the 'type of association of states known traditionally to international law'.

196. *Europa-Archiv* 1971, p. D 44.

197. Of relevance is Heinrich Schneider, *Integration* 1969, p. 39.

198. Kohler-Schlaeger, *Wirtschafts- und Währungsunion für Europa* (1971), p. 120, with other references in note 21.

199. VII B at the end.

200. Cf. Schwarz (fn. 6), pp. 421–422 and 382 (and in this volume, pp. 44 and 6).

P. D. Dagtoglou

HOW INDISSOLUBLE
IS THE COMMUNITY?

According to Article 240, EEC Treaty, and Article 208, Euratom Treaty, the
Treaties of Rome are concluded 'for an unlimited period'.[1] This rule is
generally interpreted—mostly in a rather perfunctory fashion—as a permanency or perpetuity clause, which, while not precluding a dissolution
of the Treaties by common assent, would certainly exclude any right of
withdrawal for the Member States. However, if this interpretation is more
closely scrutinized, it appears less self-evident than is often held to be the
case. The present essay sets out to register a few reservations and doubts
about the prevailing opinions.[2]

I

To begin with, let us look at the way some authors deal with the subject:
Pierre-Henri Teitgen regards the 'unlimited period' clause as proclaiming
the 'principle of permanence'; for him, the permanence of the institution
and the definitive adhesion of its members coincide.[3] An early commentary
to the EEC Treaty, and more recently Hans-Peter Ipsen, conclude from the
unlimited duration of the Treaties of Rome that a unilateral denunciation
is excluded.[4] For Alan Campbell there is no doubt: 'So it is irrevocable'.[5]
By what is, in a way, the reverse approach, Werner Thieme arrives at the
permanency of the Treaties by focusing attention on the absence of any withdrawal clause: 'Since they make no provision for any right of denunciation
their nature is probably that of a perpetual union'. According to Thieme,
the Community, once called into existence, cannot be freely dissolved—

258

even by an *actus contrarius*.[6] Thus, both the perpetuity or permanence of a treaty and the prohibition of withdrawal from it are deduced from each other.

What exactly does this 'unlimited' period of application of the Treaties of Rome mean? In order to answer this question it will be expedient to draw a comparison. The ECSC Treaty of 18 April 1951 was concluded for a period of fifty years (Article 97)—a time-span which was frequently said in the relevant debates in the parliaments of the Member States to be too long.[7] If the Treaties of Rome are to apply 'for an unlimited period', then this phrase means that these Treaties, *as opposed to the* ECSC *Treaty*, are neither confined nor limited to any particular number of years.[8] Even if the Treaties of Rome did not contain the respective Articles 240 and 208, the legal position would still be the same: if a treaty does not stipulate any fixed duration for which it is to be in force, then it must apply for an unlimited period, i.e. for a period of time which has not been determined beforehand.[9]

Articles 240, EEC Treaty, and 208, Euratom Treaty, contain this negative statement, but nothing more positive. In particular, they may not be equated with a perpetuity clause.[10] There is an essential difference in respect of the degree of commitment and obligation between the words 'for an unlimited period' and 'for ever'.[11] It is highly unlikely that the Six, when they reached agreement in 1957 over a far-reaching and unparalleled treaty actually intended at that stage to propose an indissoluble union. The genesis of the EEC offers many examples of the enthusiastic response occasioned by the union of 1957, but no proof that the Community was constituted as a 'perpetual federation' from the very outset. On the contrary, it is scarcely fortuitous that the declaration made in 1953 to the effect that the (unsuccessful) European [Political] Community should be 'indissoluble'[12] is not repeated in the Treaties of Rome. There is some indication that an effort was made to avoid too far-reaching constructions which would not correspond to political reality and which would therefore be prone to failure.

Moreover, no perpetual commitment can be presumed[13] or deduced from any provisions of a treaty,[14] however much they may seem to suggest it. Such a commitment must be expressly formulated. During the course of history precisely this has repeatedly been the case, and in fact invariably so when an irrevocable commitment has been the definite political intention. Thus Article V of the Final Act of Vienna of 15 May 1820 stated that the German Federation was an 'indissoluble union' (*unauflöslicher Verein*). The preamble to the Constitution of the German Empire of 16 April 1871 speaks of an 'eternal Federation' (*ewiger Bund*).[15] Similar examples could be adduced from outside Germany. The Acts of Union between England and Scotland (1706–7) and between Great Britain and Ireland (1800) stress repeatedly that they apply 'for ever after' and 'in all time coming' and even that the respective Unions shall remain binding for parliaments to come.[16]

259

In the same manner, American Constitutions refer explicitly to 'perpetual league' and 'perpetual union'.[17]

The designation of the projected European Political Community as 'indissoluble' goes to show that such declarations of perpetual commitment belong not merely to the dim and distant past.[18] It must also be admitted that this is an apt example of ideological impetuosity and political miscalculation which clearly illustrates that declarations alone can neither replace nor indeed create political realities.

So the unlimited duration of the Treaties of Rome does not of itself permit them to be regarded as a union forever. [19]

II

A further argument is that the permanence of the European Communities must result from their allegedly *federative* character. In the view of Teitgen, the Roman Treaties have been concluded, in the manner of federal treaties (*à la manière des pactes fédéraux*), for an indeterminate period. He is not prepared to make an exception to this, even in the case of the European Coal and Steel Community, whose treaty is limited to fifty years.[20]

One might, of course, adopt the premise that any true federation will be an 'eternal' one.[21] However, it is probable that, in the meantime, the view has generally established itself that the European Communities do not have a federal character (at least, that they have not had it hitherto and will probably not have it in the immediate future). Nor are these Communities examples of any 'quasi-federalism',' functional federalism' or 'partial federalism'.[22] Such conceptions have met with increasing criticism and are, for the most part, rejected today.[23]

A federal interpretation cannot be justified from the history of European integration, either. Hans-Peter Ipsen has quite rightly emphasized this: present Community law provides no conclusive support for a view that the Communities—even after an eventual merger into one Community— might (let alone would have to) undergo an alteration process through the implementation of their constitution and thereby adopt the characteristic features of a federal organization of any type known hitherto. According to Ipsen, it is not even true that the objectives of functional integration will inevitably lead the Community Constitution towards some kind of federal system: 'There is clearly a better case for refraining at the present time from prejudging the next steps towards European integration in terms of some form of federation.' [24]

But if we now reject constructions orientated along federal lines, they cannot be used to substantiate an interpretation of the unlimited duration of the Treaties of Rome as a perpetuity clause. Even less can they be taken further and used in conjunction with this alleged perpetuity clause to substantiate the rejection of any right of withdrawal.[25]

260

This is, of course, not to say that the Treaties of Rome allow any withdrawal. In point of fact, a right of withdrawal under the Treaties is largely rejected, and is only accepted, if at all, on general grounds relating to international law (first and foremost with reference to the *clausula rebus sic stantibus*).[26] The reasons for the rejection on principle of any right of withdrawal bear, in the first instance, on the content of the Treaties, and especially on the fact that the Treaties, while making no provision for any withdrawal, do prescribe certain procedures for their amendment. In addition, there are those who draw attention to the fact that the Founder Members refrained from all reservations relating to withdrawal and they say that new Members are not entitled to make any reservations. To this we may add arguments deriving from the nature of the Treaties and of the Communities themselves. A right of withdrawal is said to be incompatible with the character of the European Treaties insofar as they are 'integrating treaties'. Finally, against a right of withdrawal it is argued that the degree of integration already achieved cannot now be undone. It is to the close scrutiny of these arguments that we must now turn.

III

It is perfectly true that the European Treaties do not make any provision for a right of withdrawal.[27] This is all the more significant in that treaties setting up international organizations do, as a rule, contain rules specifically governing withdrawal (or resignation, denunciation, as the case may be).[28] The treaty regulating EFTA which was founded to some extent as a counterpart to the EEC also recognizes a right of withdrawal for its members (Article 42). Is it admissible to derive a prohibition of withdrawal fom the absence of a withdrawal clause?

How one answers this question depends upon the answer to the further question concerning the legal nature of the Communities and of primary Community law. It is neither possible nor necessary to go into this question here.

The following observations proceed from the premise that the European Treaties were concluded as treaties in international law and that the contracting partners have retained control over these Treaties—as is demonstrated above all by the ratification requirement in respect of amendments, admission of new members and association agreements. The practice of altering the Treaties regardless of the rules governing amendment (cf. the amendment of the treaties through resolutions of the permanent representative of governments[29]), the extended use of the principle of unanimity and the Council's diplomatic style of operation tend to strengthen this conclusion. We shall come back to this later. A consideration of the whole withdrawal question in the context of international law is indispensable on these grounds alone, without prejudice to the character

261

of European Treaty law as primary Community law. Some subsequent observations from the Community point of view will serve to complete the picture.

The question whether the absence of any provision about withdrawal implies either that there is a right of withdrawal, or that withdrawal is forbidden, has often been discussed in international law.[30] In view of the fact that there are numerous treaties making provision for a right of withdrawal but also others which expressly admit of such a right only after some considerable time,[31] or indeed, not at all,[32] it is no easy matter to establish what the actual intention of a treaty really is on this point.[33]

Had the signatories intended to permit or exclude the right of withdrawal, they would have explicitly inserted the relevant provision into the Treaty. One cannot go so far as to deduce a prohibition of withdrawal simply from the absence of any clause in the Treaties of Rome expressly granting the right of such a withdrawal.[34] To be sure, it is not possible to conclude that withdrawal is permissible either, because of the basic principle of international law, *pacta sunt servanda*.[35]

If a treaty passes over the admissibility of withdrawal in silence, this can only mean that the contracting parties were unable to reach agreement on this difficult point, and excluded it from the body of the treaty. It can also mean that the signatories wanted to avoid any provisions regarding withdrawal for psychological reasons because that would have been to admit from the very outset the possibility that the experiment might fail.[36]

Since the subject of withdrawal figures among the most important points of any treaty (so that negligence on the part of the drafters is out of the question), and since the unlimited period of application of the Treaty is insufficient ground for concluding that withdrawal is forbidden, the silence of the Treaties of Rome in respect of the admissibility of a right of withdrawal can in the first instance only mean that the Member States did not intend or were not in a position (because of lack of accord) to regulate this question by treaty. And in all probability they were also reluctant to dampen the euphory occasioned by the unification of Europe with debates about the possibilities of withdrawing: at weddings the topic of divorce is studiously avoided.[37]

Since any regulation also involves obligation, the question suggests itself whether contracting parties not having let themselves be bound (for whatever reasons) have in this regard remained free and are allowed to withdraw.[38] The matter has been extensively discussed with respect to the United Nations Organization, whose Charter (in contrast to Article 1 (3) of the Statute of the League of Nations) does not regulate the right to withdraw. Here, too, a prohibition of withdrawal has been said to follow from the absence of any provision, especially since such resignation is held to contradict the universality of the organization. Some authors have seen in the act of withdrawal, even where there is no express regulation, an inadmissible unilateral termination of contract.[39]

262

The opposite opinion argues that the sovereignty of the Member States can be restricted only through a voluntary renunciation which is made explicit in the Treaty. Rights (like the right of withdrawal) which have not been expressly limited, let alone renounced completely, would remain unimpaired. The principle of universality may be deemed to be negated not only by any right of withdrawal of the Member States but to have been already impaired by the Organization's right of expulsion (UN Charter, Article 6).[40] The right of withdrawal of members of the United Nations was expressly recognized by Committee I 2 of the San Francisco Conference on 25 June 1945.[41]

Notwithstanding this, the affirmation of a right of withdrawal for members of the United Nations does not yet imply the general acceptance of a right of withdrawal for members of international or even supranational organizations, where this right is not expressly granted. Oppenheim and Lauterbach do accept a right of withdrawal where this is not expressly provided for in the case of all such treaties 'as are either not expressly concluded for ever, or are apparently not intended to set up an everlasting condition of things.'[42] The Treaties of Rome are probably to be placed in this category.

Some recent studies confirm Oppenheim and Lauterpacht's view and accept a right of withdrawal where a treaty is silent on this point.[43] Emile Giraud, too, accepts in his report to the Institut de Droit International the existence of a right of withdrawal in a collective treaty making no express provision for such a right: 'In our opinion, in the absence of any provision concerning denunciation, the general conventions can be denounced at any time.'[44] He supports this opinion with, among other things, the practical consideration that it is hardly advantageous to make general treaties which are basically voluntary and open into something like prisons, which, once having entered them, one is never at liberty to leave. Such a rule would largely discourage States from joining in the first place. Furthermore, he fears that a prohibition on withdrawal may lead to the non-application or infringement of the treaty by those States which wish to withdraw. This would be, in his eyes, a greater disadvantage than withdrawal itself; for violations of international law would diminish its authority. He points out further that there are no means of effectively preventing a State from withdrawing, once it has made up its mind to do so.[45]

The majority of the other members of the Commission, however, rejected Giraud's view.[46] In fact, the tendency appears to be to go along with the opposite interpretation,[47] reflected also in the Harvard Draft of 1935,[48] and to reject the presumption of a right of withdrawal. Nevertheless, this probably predominant view admits that some right of withdrawal may be implied in the Treaty or may result from the attitude (even the silence) of the remaining signatory States.[49]

The Vienna Convention on the Law of Treaties of 23 May 1969[50] also

263

makes careful distinctions, and is, in the last analysis, attuned to the intention of the parties and the nature of the treaty itself. Article 56 (1) of the Vienna Convention reads:

A treaty which contains no provision regarding its termination and which does not provide for denunciation or withdrawal is not subject to denunciation or withdrawal unless:

(a) it is established that the parties intended to admit the possibility of denunciation or withdrawal; or

(b) a right of denunciation or withdrawal may be implied by the nature of the treaty.[51]

We shall return to the question whether the intention of the parties or the nature of the Treaties of Rome establish a right of withdrawal.

IV

All European Treaties provide amendment machinery.[52] In this is some- times seen the intention of the parties to keep the Treaties flexible, so that withdrawal is unnecessary, hence unjustifiable, and therefore inadmissible. In general, it is probably true to say that the possibility of amendment does indicate the intention of the signatory States rather to modify the Treaty, than to force Members into withdrawal. But it is also certain that the possibility of amendment cannot, as such, exclude withdrawal altogether; the emphasis is rather on the machinery for permissible amendment which actually is laid down.

Under the Treaties of Rome an amendment can be initiated by the Member States or by the Commission, or else is conditioned by the entry of new members or by association with third States. In all instances the amendment shall enter into force after being ratified by *all* Member States. This unanimity rule affects the legal position of the individual Member States in a totally different way in respect of both basic types of amendment. In the case of the enlargement of the Communities Member States are provided with the maximum weapon (namely a right of veto) for the defence of the welfare of the Community, but at the same time, also for the protection of their own interests against those of States which are not to be granted entry or association. Since a Member State not in agreement with the enlargement of the Communities can effectively frustrate this (by refusing to ratify the necessary amendments to the Treaties), there is never any question of withdrawal.

The situation differs in the case of an amendment instigated by a Member State or by the Commission. Here the principle of unanimity affords maximum protection to Member States favouring the *status quo*, while it is inimical to those favouring change. Proposals for amendment

264

submitted by a Member State depend upon the consent of each one of its partners. The same applies to Article 235, EEC Treaty, and to Article 203, Euratom Treaty, delegating general powers to the Council. Although these provisions require unanimity of the members of an institution of the Community and not of the Member States as such, without becoming a substitute for amendment of the Treaties, the Treaties remain, insofar as they adhere (without exception in this regard) to the principle of unanimity, orientated towards preserving the *status quo* and respecting the sovereignty of the Member States. The accurate appraisal of the Member States as having remained masters of the Treaty[53] does not mean only that they are not bound by amendment procedures.[54] It also means that the autonomy of the Community is limited and is not in a position to undermine the (still very considerable) sovereignty of the Member States without the aquiescence of every single one of them.

Loss of sovereignty by the Member States is largely compensated for, it is true, by the evolution of a further-looking autonomous Community life. However, Treaty provisions which do not fully recognize the autonomy of the Community but rely in the last instance on the sovereign will of every Member State, cannot be used as arguments for the weakening of the legal position of the individual Member States (as is the prohibition of withdrawal), if anything, they illustrate just the opposite. The amendment procedure demonstrates restraint on the side of the Contracting Parties. *To this extent* the EEC and Euratom Treaties do not, when all is said and done, differ very much from traditional treaties in international law. In *this* respect, compared with other international organizations, say the United Nations (UN Charter, Articles 108, 109), the Treaties are more orientated towards the safeguarding of the rights of the individual Member States. It is the individual sovereign Member States who have the last say, not the Community. An amendment machinery of this type cannot be declared incompatible with the right of withdrawal.

Finally, if the fact that a treaty is open to innovation removes all motives for withdrawal, this can hardly apply in the case of the Treaties of Rome where the amendment procedure is orientated towards the *status quo*.

But these views do require a certain qualification: If, and insofar as, a right of withdrawal were to be acknowledged, the admissibility of exercising it would depend upon the prior failure of the machinery for amending the Treaties as provided for in Article 236, EEC Treaty, and Article 204, Euratom Treaty. That is probably the minimum stipulation resulting from the integrating character of the European Communities. The same holds good for the steps taken together by the Member States in the event of the functioning of the Common Market being adversely affected by internal disturbances in a Member State, in accordance with Article 224, EEC Treaty.

265

V

On 28 February 1957, during the Brussels Talks, the German ambassador, Carl Friedrich Ophüls, while at a meeting of the heads of delegations, made a statement on behalf of the Federal Republic of Germany which exceeds the provisions concerning the amendment of the Treaties, as laid down in Article 236, EEC Treaty, and Article 204, EAEC Treaty:

> The Federal Republic proceeds from the possibility that a revision of the Treaties on the Common Market will take place in the event of Germany being re-united.

This statement was repeated in the Bundestag on 21 March 1957 by State Secretary Professor Walter Hallstein, who explained that the formulation 'revision of the Treaties' had been chosen deliberately 'so as to cover all eventualities that may arise in the event of reunification', that is to say, participation, non-participation or participation after the adjustment of the Treaties to the new situation. According to Professor Hallstein, this statement corresponded to the view of the Government of the Federal Republic 'that a reunified Germany must have full political freedom of action regarding international treaties that have been concluded in the past in the name of one part of Germany'.[55] The same remarks are to be found in the written report of the Bundestag's Committee for Common Market and Euratom affairs.[56]

Here the question at once arises whether the fact that the German Government statement did not form part of the Treaties of Rome deprives it of any legal significance. On this point, Professor Hallstein stated in the Bundestag that a formal reservation did not commend itself because it might admit of an *argumentum e contrario* in the case of earlier treaties which had been concluded without such a reservation. It would not, he explained, be necessary to insert this into the Treaty because

> . . . not only was no opposition voiced against it, but on the contrary, our partners in the negotiations expressed the view that the German statement corresponded to something which was at any case taken for granted.[57]

It is indeed true that (as the SPD Member of Parliament, Dr. Arndt, reported in the Bundestag on 21 March 1957)[58] the French Secretary of State, M. Fauré, speaking on 16 January 1957 about this German statement, set at rest the fears of the Assemblée Nationale by pointing out that a reunification of Germany and the terms of such a reunification would have to depend on the approval of France. But it remains a fact, nevertheless, that the binding nature of the German statement on reunification has not

266

been called into question by her partners in the Treaty. On the contrary, it was repeatedly confirmed. Thus we read in the report of the committee on defence of the French parliament: 'The Treaty binds us permanently but is not binding for West Germany which retains its liberty to choose whether to stay or leave on the day of its reunification'.[59]

Thus there is considerable indication that the other signatories of the Treaty have accepted the German statement regarding possible reunification. This is also the important point; for we need not go into the question whether the Federal Government's statement constituted a formal 'reservation' or whether it was a declaration on the binding nature of the Treaties; given the circumstances, the other contracting parties to the Treaty had in both cases to accept that statement.[60]

The picture of the positions of the Federal Republic and of the other signatory States which has just been outlined is reflected equally in the Community law literature. The German standpoint is that, according to the general principles of international law, Germany will, after reunification, be bound to the Treaties establishing the European Communities only if she generally confirms those Treaties or the international legal obligations of the Federal Republic.[61] Nor does the statement meet (where it is mentioned) with any opposition in the Community law literature of the other signatory States.[62]

If one therefore proceeds to argue that the Treaties of Rome apply with the reservation of full political freedom of action for a reunified Germany, then on this ground alone it follows that the possibility of withdrawal has been built into the Treaties at the very time when they were concluded.[63] It is unlikely that the other signatories could be regarded as bound by the Treaty once Germany had decided to withdraw; 'for we are dealing with a Common Market of the Six and not of the Five' which they originally signed, as has been stressed in French quarters.[64]

The interpretation here presented is probably the only one which will reconcile the statement of the Federal Republic, which is to be regarded as accepted by all partners to the Treaty, with the general claim that the Treaties may not be revoked unilaterally.[65] Bentivoglio's suggested compromise, namely to admit for the reunified German State the right of initiating amendments,[66] shows a lack of appreciation both of the possibilities and limits of this procedure and of the significance and range of the reservation regarding reunification. The complete freedom from obligation of a reunified German State is incompatible with the principle of unanimity laid down in the amendment machinery.

Moreover, it is not only in the event of a possible reunification that conflict is unavoidable. It can also arise at the stage of determining *what* exactly may constitute a 'reunification' in the given circumstances and which political plan and machinery may be acceptable for attaining such reunification; and this raises the further question who shall have the right to decide these issues. If the Federal Republic is to be allowed to claim the

267

power to do this (which is a probable assumption), the reservation on reunification takes on other aspects again.

Finally, the conflict referred to is not unthinkable even within the framework of the Federal Republic's present Ostpolitik. The basic question is: How far is the Federal Republic bound, in its negotiations and agreements with the German Democratic Republic, by the terms of the European Treaties? Here we see opening up the whole panoply of problems occasioned by the contradictory statutory requirements of reunification on the one hand and European integration on the other.[67] Attempts to get over this contradiction or at the least to defuse it, like the Federal Government's statement on the definition of the concept 'German national'[68] and the protocol on inter-German trade,[69] remain foreign bodies within the total conception of the Common Market. Moreover, if these attempts took as a point of departure the view of the then Federal Government (as Wohlfahrt/ Everling/Glaesner/Sprung state) 'that Germany constitutes a political and economic unit and that therefore the setting-up of a customs frontier within Germany is not possible',[70] this raises the question how far the new Ostpolitik makes a review necessary on this issue as well.[71]

VI

The incompatibility of withdrawal with the essence of the European Treaties as 'Treaties of integration'[72] or with the concept of a 'Community'[73] is advanced as the decisive ground for rejecting it as inadmissible.

What is more, according to the Vienna Convention (Article 56) the acceptance of a right of withdrawal or termination in respect of treaties which make no provision for this depends also on the nature of the treaty. All the same, it can hardly be convincingly argued that just such treaties as are markedly dynamic and, like the European Treaties, directed towards continuous change, can fulfil their purpose only if all their signatories abide by them.[74] Integration is primarily a process. A process of integration also implies a treaty which is in process. Consequently, whether withdrawal is (legally speaking) excluded or not depends not on the aim to integrate *in abstracto*, but only on the stage of integration actually reached *in concreto*.

The Treaties set up 'Communities' which differ from traditional international organizations, in particular by the independence of their institutions and the autonomy and authority of their law. This conclusion has been reached many times and it is certainly not necessary to substantiate it yet again in the present context. However, it must be pointed out that neither the extent of the powers transferred to these supranational Communities nor the degree of legal autonomy afforded them by the Treaties permits us to assume for them a 'state-like' structure or even something similar to it which would, *by definition,* preclude any right of withdrawal. This would certainly be the case with a federal state, where a right of secession would exist only if it were expressly provided for by the constitution.[75] But it may be regarded as fairly generally accepted that the European Treaties are not setting up a federal state.[76] It would also be inappropriate to draw a parallel with the German Customs Union—and yet the treaty of 22 March 1833, founding the Deutscher Zollverein, did allow unilateral denunciation (Article 41).

VII

If the will to integrate was not sufficiently strong at the time of signing as to enable perpetuity clauses and others prohibiting withdrawal to be inserted into the Treaties, then it is legitimate to ask whether the development of the European Communities and the stage of integration they have actually attained already amount to having passed the point of no return. It is precisely the way in which international organizations conduct their affairs and the fact that they keep developing which can bring about a *change of meaning* in the text of a treaty. Such change should, inasmuch as it is still compatible with the treaty text, be taken into account in the interpretation of the treaty and, where applicable, it ought to take precedence over the original intentions of the makers of that treaty.[77]

During the fifties it was repeatedly pointed out that the European Communities might develop into a 'state' in the sociological and political sense via the formation of a new community spirit in Europe.[78] On this subject Karl Carstens has made the telling observation that one certainly ought not to exclude this possibility, but that it was a question of a hypothetical future situation: no consequences for the present (1961) could be deduced from it.[79] Thirteen years later there is essentially nothing to add to this conclusion—apart from the sorry realization that European idealism appears to have melted away.

It is clear that this cannot detract from the degree of integration already reached. The entry of the three new Members shows that the European Communities are living organisms (but it has also provided yet another, most impressive, demonstration of the decisive role played by the Member States compared to the position of the Community institutions as such). The important contribution of the European Court of Justice towards a legal integration (especially primacy and direct applicability of Community law) can scarcely be underrated[80] though, in the last analysis, political will cannot be forced by legal action.[81] Nor can the economic interdependence already reached within the European Communities, and the resulting *de facto* difficulty of disengaging from the Common Market, be overlooked—though it is perhaps somewhat exaggerated to speak in this connexion of a 'point of no return' [82] and of political and economic conditions any modification of which would be 'irreversible' and 'inconceivable' or would represent a 'revolution'.[83] At any event, the European Communities have not till now developed a degree of integration such that it might be linked conceptually with indissolubility—although one ought not, of course, to exclude this possibility for the future.[84] To substantiate this thesis would really require a detailed examination of the history and the present state of the European Communities. Within the limitations of this essay, the following remarks will perhaps suffice:

1. A high level of integration will be achieved only if the European Communities enjoy in a generous measure the *autonomy to take decisions*, in the sense of organizational, legislative, executive and fiscal independence. But we are still far from attaining any such goal.[84a] Not only is the European Parliament still powerless,[85] but even the Commission has been drawn up as a relatively weak institution[86] and has remained so.[87] It is interesting to note that, as early as the Bundestag debates on the Treaties, the weak status of the Commission was deplored and it was asked exactly what the significance of a vote of no confidence against the Commission might be, if the real decision-making institution was the Council.[88] To this the spokesman for the Federal Government answered that one could expect the emphasis to shift in practice, because the Commission would build up a panel of experts and technicians to a greater extent than would the Council of Ministers, and this would increase its importance. Furthermore, the fact that the proposals put forward by the Commission would be debated in the Council would strengthen the Commission's standing.[89]

Developments have not fulfilled these expectations. It is not true to say that the Treaties provide for a well-balanced and harmonious interplay between the two institutions instead of which 'the Council has established itself as a centre of gravity and banished the Commission . . . into the role of a satellite'.[90] Quite the contrary: the Council's centre of gravity rests upon the Treaties themselves. The hoped-for shift in equilibrium has not materialized[91]—which is hardly surprising, considering the key position held, just as before, by the individual policies of the Member States. Indeed, for ten years the European Communities were dominated by General de Gaulle who thought in terms of a 'Europe of diplomatic conferences' without any loss of sovereignty for the Member States,[92] and, as a logical consequence of this, described the 'supranational' Commission as a 'technocratic areopagus, stateless, and not accountable for its actions' ('*aréopage technocratique, apatride et irresponsable*').[93]

Some shift of equilibrium has indeed taken place insofar as the Council, which is designed in the Treaties as an institution of the Community, has become to all intents and purposes—as is lamented by those acquainted with the practical running of the Communities—a 'diplomatic conference pure and simple'.[94] Given this state of affairs, the permanency of the Treaty and the prohibition on withdrawal can, and surely ought to be retained as political aspirations and aims. But to derive them from the structure and history of the Community in such a way that they are legally binding seems scarcely convincing.

2. The fact that the Community's autonomy with respect to taking decisions has not developed to the point where it includes by definition the notions of permanency and prohibition on withdrawal, is revealed in the *unanimity principle*, which still prevails in the working of the Communities. In this instance, it is no longer simply a question of frustrated expectations, but of the non-implementation of the programme, as laid down in the Treaties, for the gradual formation of a Community-centred decision-making process.[95]

In the Luxembourg Accords of 29 January 1966, the Member States, at the instigation of France, practically shelved the majority principle. In this context, it is not a question whether that decision and the subsequent practice of acceding to French demands was politically right or wrong— though its political realism at the present stage of integration, at least as regards important decisions, can hardly be doubted.[96] One will probably have to acknowledge its legal character.[97] But above all, this shows not merely that it is still possible to talk of a continuance of the sovereignty of the Member States[98] but that in 1966 those Member States were probably no longer prepared, or at least no longer determined, to go as far with the gradual reduction of their sovereign powers as they had undertaken in the Treaty of 1957.

Despite the Hague and Paris Conferences of 1969 and 1972, it is scarcely possible to support a view that the situation in this respect has changed much since 1966. The positions adopted by the various governments during the recurrent international monetary crises prove rather the opposite. The attitude of the Community and the individual Member States during the oil crisis, and style and results of the Copenhagen Conference of December 1973 have, to put it mildly, disappointed even the most reserved Europeans.

3. A third fact which contradicts this claim lies in the 'democratic deficit' of the European Communities which, in the last three or four years, has repeatedly been deplored.

This is not the place to go into the question of the 'democratization' of the Communities. For the moment it will suffice to state two things. First, with the increasing consolidation and enlargement of the Communities and their sphere of influence, the question of democratic structure, which, rather understandably, was not regarded in the initial stages as being pre-eminent, is increasingly becoming placed in the forefront of discussion. It is no accident, and will probably not remain without repercussions, that in Great Britain the democratic structure of the Communities was viewed as one of the most important questions and was raised and examined with some criticism in the extensive debate on British entry into the Common Market.

Secondly, all parties have come to realize in the meantime that, simply

271

to transfer uncritically some democratic structure appropriate for nation states on to the European Communities would fail to take adequate account of their specific and singular character. There can be no doubt that neither national nor international law is equipped with a set of concepts adequate for dealing with the new phenomenon of the 'community'.

Nevertheless, one thing should be clear: the concept of democracy as the legitimacy for and control of public authority is too basic to apply only to nation states of the traditional type. It must also claim to be valid (though not, it is true, in the sense of a rule of law) for the European Communities. Whether they correspond to its requirements, and to what extent, remains an open question. As a premise, we contend (for reasons which cannot be substantiated in this paper) that the democratic legitimacy of the Communities, while it is not completely absent (as some critics maintain), nevertheless remains rudimentary. In this context, pointing out the inadequacies of democratic legitimacy *within* the various Member States is obviously going to produce different results from state to state, and is in any case poor consolation. These conclusions do not, of course, say anything specific about the legal instruments necessary to ensure adequate democratic legitimacy and control, nor is that the intention here.

Democracy, understood in the sense of legitimacy and control of public authority, is an indispensable basis for any process of integration. For this reason it is impossible for the process of European integration to go beyond a certain point, without adequate democratic legitimacy. This conclusion is not based on an uncritical use of nation-state models and must certainly not be understood as a moral commandment, paying no heed to political realities. To decide when and how democratic legitimacy can and ought to be attained, and to ensure that it is adequate for the needs of the Community, are not legal but *political* questions. But it is certainly the lawyer's duty to point out that adequate democratic legitimacy and advanced European integration are issues which are strictly non-severable. Permanency of the Communities and a ban on any withdrawal from them form part of this stage of the integration process, conditioned as it is by the interdependence of these two factors.

In his *Staat und Industriegesellschaft*, Ernst Forsthoff has drawn attention to the fact that the State is not in a position to limit technological progress according to the dictates of humanity, since the State lacks autonomous power towards the industrial society, as may be seen in the topical example of the destruction of the environment, and since technological progress on the part of that society's active proponents has long since exceeded the limits of the State's jurisdiction. Forsthoff argues from this that the conditions for the effective functioning of an international organization might result from the interaction of these factors, in such a way that that organization might accompany the further progress of technology as an efficient watchdog for humanity.[99]

And indeed, in this context the European Communities represent a valuable entity which must be protected and developed. The lawyer must play his part in this, but he cannot replace the politician. The lawyer's idealism and the self-satisfaction of the 'eurocrat' cannot turn hoped-for developments into hard fact. Quite the contrary: the mysticism of an everlasting and irrevocable union in which some European federalists are quick to shroud their cause has no clear legal foundation, nor does it correspond to the present political realities; its windy superlatives are much more likely to damage the cause of a realistic European integration. This must be borne in mind, especially now, in the new era of the enlarged Communities.

Notes

Professor Dagtoglou is Professor of Public Law and European Community Law at the University of Regensburg and Visiting Professor for European Law at the University College at Buckingham. The essay was originally published in: Festschrift für Ernst Forsthoff zum 70. Geburtstag (*Munich 1972*), *pp. 77–102* (*Verlag C. H. Beck, Munich*). *It was revised by the author in May 1974. Translated by C. J. Wells.*

1. 'Dieser Vertrag gilt auf unbegrenzte Zeit'; 'Le présent traité est conclu pour une dureé illimitée'; 'Il presente Trattato è concluso per una durata illimitata'.

2. The line of questioning taken in the present article—as well as the limited space available—makes it possible to dispense with going into the problems raised by Article 24 (1) of the German Federal Constitution.

3. P. H. Teitgen, 'Objectifs et principes fondamentaux communs aux trois Communautés', in *Droit des Communautés Européennes,* ed. by W. J. Ganshof van der Meersch (Brussels 1969), p. 15 (No. 27) *et seq.,* No. 29.

4. E. Wohlfahrt, U. Everling, H. J. Glaesner, R. Sprung, *Die Europäische Wirtschaftsgemeinschaft—Kommentar zum Vertrag* (Berlin-Frankfurt 1960), p. 616; H. P. Ipsen, *Europäisches Gemeinschaftsrecht* (Tübingen 1972), p. 99 (but see also the subtle interpretation, *ibid.,* p. 1023/1024, and in this volume, p. 182 *et seq.,* esp. p. 216).

5. A. Campbell, *Common Market Law,* Vol. II (London 1969), No. 2284.

6. W. Thieme, *Das Grundgesetz und die öffentliche Gewalt internationaler Gemeinschaften,* VVDStRL, Part 18, p. 50 *et seq.* (72).

7. Cf. the vol., *The Debates on the ECSC Treaty in the National Parliaments,* ed. by the Common Assembly of the ECSC, Research and Information Department, Luxembourg, February 1958, p. 37 *et seq.*

8. Cf. also the plain statement made by the Member of Parliament, Dr. Mommer, on 28 June 1957 in his report within the framework of the written report of the Bundestag's Committee for EEC and Euratom (2 BT—Dr. 3660, p. 14 *et seq.,* 18): 'In contrast to the period of application of the ECSC Treaty, which is limited to 50 years, the two new Treaties shall apply for an unlimited period.'

9. Numerous treaties setting up international organizations contain no regulation concerning their period of application (e.g. the Council of Europe, OEEC, OECD, EFTA, etc.). It is assumed in the secondary literature, without exception,

273

that these treaties apply for an unlimited period; see R. L. Bindschedler, *Rechts-fragen der europäischen Einigung*, Basle 1954, pp. 135, 177, who can stand for many others.

10. Likewise L. M. Bentivoglio, in R. Quadri, R. Monaco, A. Trabucchi, *Trattato Istitutivo della Communità Economica Europea*, Vol. III, Milan 1965, Article 240, Note 1, with reference to further literature; P. Soldatos, 'Durée et dénunciation des Traités de Rome' (*Revue de Droit International des sciences diplomatiques et politiques* 4 (1969), p. 257 *et seq.*) (258) also denies the European Communities any perpetuity even if only because of the kind of political union being aimed at; but whereas he does not accept any 'perpetuité' for the Communities, he recognizes that they have 'permanence'. This distinction (also found in E. Giraud—see next fn. below) is in my opinion erroneous and misleading; in the present article no attempt is made to distinguish between permanence and perpetuity.

11. Cf. Emile Giraud, in *Institut de Droit International, Onzième Commission, Modification et terminaison des traités collectifs.* 'I. Exposé préliminaire présenté par M. Emile Giraud', Geneva 1960, p. 69: 'On s'accorde à dire que les conventions générales ne sont pas perpétuelles mais qu'elles ont une durée illimitée ou indéfinie, ce qui n'est pas du tout la même chose'.

12. Article 1, subsection 3, of the revised draft statute of the European (Political) Community, as passed by an *ad hoc* Assembly on 6 October 1953 (H. von Siegler, *Dokumentation der Europäischen Integration*, Vol. II, 1961, p. 73).

13. Ch. Rousseau, on the other hand (*Principes généraux du droit international public*, vol. I, Paris 1944, p. 586, note 1) concludes from the lack of any provision concerning the period of application of a treaty that it applies in perpetuity ('perpetuité'). In the same author's *Droit international public*, vol. I (Paris 1970), this conclusion is, as far as I can see, not repeated.

14. So the application 'for an unlimited period' ('durée illimitée) is interpreted, by Ch. Rousseau, *Principes* (fn. 13), for instance, as meaning that the Treaty applies in perpetuity (but again, this statement is not repeated in his *Droit international public*, fn. 13).

15. Admittedly, it was a matter of dispute in the secondary literature whether the preamble to the treaty, and consequently the perpetuity clause, had any legal validity. For: Robert von Mohl, *Das deutsche Reichsstaatsrecht*, 1873, p. 23; Max von Seydel, *Staatsrechtliche und politische Abhandlungen*, 1893, p. 97 (but cf. p. 34), and *Commentar zur Verfassungsurkunde für das deutsche Reich*, 2nd ed., 1897, p. 19; Eugen von Jagemann, *Die deutsche Reichsverfassung* 1904, p. 29. Against: Philipp Zorn, *Das Staatsrecht des Deutschen Reiches,* vol. I, 1895, p. 58; Paul Laband, *Das Staatsrecht des Deutschen Reiches,* vol. I, 5th ed. (1911, reprint 1964), p. 90; Gerhard Anschütz, *Die Verfassung des Deutschen Reiches von 11 August 1919*, Kommentar, 14th edn. (1933, reprint 1965), Introduction, p. 2. But it was generally accepted that the German Empire was indissoluble.

16. On the relationship of this binding agreement to the British doctrine of parliamentary sovereignty, see with reference to the British membership of the European Communities J. D. B. Mitchell, *British Law and British Membership*, EuR 1971, p. 97 *et seq.* (102).

17. Article 2 of the New England Confederation of 19 May 1643 between Massachusetts, New Plymouth, Connecticut, and New Haven; Preamble to the Articles of Confederation of 9 July 1778.

274

18. Cf. above, fn. 12.

19. Even those authors denying any right of denunciation accept that the Communities may be dissolved at any time by the unanimous action of all parties through an *actus contrarius*. Cf. H. Brunner, in v. d. Groeben, v. Boeckh, *Handbuch für Europäische Wirtschaft*, vol. 10, IA 67, Comm. on Article 40, p. 137 *et seq*. (137); L. M. Bentivoglio, *loc. cit.*, note 2; N. Catalano, *Manuel de Droit de la Communauté Européenne*, 2nd edn. (Paris 1965), pp. 117, 623 *et seq.*; Fr. Rigaux, 'Nature juridique des Communautés', in *Droit Européen*, No. 49 *et seq*. (93 *et seq.*); P. Soldatos, *loc. cit.* (fn. 10), pp. 258, 259; likewise, regarding the ECSC Treaty: K. Carstens, 'Die kleine Revision des EGKS-Vertrages', ZaöRV 21 (1961), p. 1 *et seq*. (8 *et seq.*); W. Thieme, *loc. cit.* (fn. 6), p. 72, takes a different view. According to Article 54 of the Vienna Convention of 23 May 1969 on the Law of the Treaties, 'The termination of a treaty or withdrawal of a party may take place: . . . (b) at any time by consent of all the parties after consultation with the other contracting states.'

20. P. H. Teitgen, *loc. cit.* (fn. 3), No. 29.

21. Cf. Carl Schmitt, *Verfassungslehre*, 3rd ed. (1928, reprint 1965), p. 367; E. R. Huber, *Deutsche Verfassungsgeschichte seit 1789*, vol. I, 2nd edn. (1957), p. 660.

22. As was often assumed to be the case, especially in the earlier German works on European Community law (Germany is the only member of the Six with a federal tradition); see the detailed bibliography in Fr. Rigaud, *loc. cit.* (fn. 19), No. 49 *et seq*. (87).

23. See the bibliography given by Rigaud, *ibid.*, No. 88; cf. also BVerfGE, vol. 22, 18 October 1967, p. 293 *et seq*. at p. 296: 'The Community itself is neither a state nor a federal state.'

24. H. P. Ipsen, *Verfassungsperspektiven der Europäischen Gemeinschaften*, (1970), pp. 8, 10, and *Europäisches Gemeinschaftsrecht* (1972), p. 183 *et seq.*, 1050/1051, 1054/1055 (and in this volume, p. 182 *et seq*. at p. 239 and p. 242).

25. As a matter of fact, the Soviet Federal Constitution of 10 July 1918 confers the right of withdrawal on each Member State (Article 17).

26. For bibliographical references, see P. Soldatos, 'Durée et dénonciation des traités de Rome', *loc. cit.* (fn. 10).

27. Article 224, EEC Treaty, also provides no legal basis for a secession right of the Member States; H. P. Ipsen, *loc. cit.* (fn. 4), p. 242.

28. Cf. N. Feinberg, 'Unilateral Withdrawal from an International Organization', in XXXIX (1963), *The British Yearbook of International Law*, p. 189 *et seq*.

29. Cf. H. P. Ipsen *op. cit.* (fn. 4), p. 468 *et seq*.

30. Cf. on this subject monographs by N. Singh, *Termination of Membership of International Organizations*, London 1958 (also the review by H.-J. Schlochauer in 62 (1961), *Arch. VR* p. 242 *et seq.*) N. Feinberg, 'Unilateral Withdrawal from an International Organization', *loc. cit.* (fn. 28), pp. 189–219; P. Soldatos, 'Durée et dénonciation des Traités de Rome', *loc. cit.* (fn. 10), pp. 257, 270.

31. According to Article 13 of the North Atlantic Treaty, only after twenty years; according to Article XII, para. 3, of the Treaty about the Western European Union, only after fifty years.

32. These are the treaties with a perpetuity or indissolubility clause (see above).

33. Cf. the much-quoted comments of J. L. Brierly, *The Law of Nations*, 6th ed. (Oxford 1963, unaltered reprint 1967), p. 330 *et seq*.

34. But this is the view held by L. M. Bentivoglio, *loc. cit.* (fn. 10), p. 1743 (note 3), though admittedly in accordance with the rules of constitutional interpretation.

35. But G. Cansacchi, 'Les éléments fédéraux de la CGE', in *Mélanges en l'honneur de G. Gidel* (Paris 1961), p. 93 (as quoted in P. Soldatos, *loc. cit.* (fn. 10), p. 263, fn. 39), does draw such a conclusion—although he does indeed remark that a withdrawal, while legally admissible, would be problematical in practice.

36. Cf. R. L. Bindschedler, *Rechtsfragen der Europäischen Einigung*, p. 42 *et seq.* On the reasons for not adopting a withdrawal clause, see Emile Giraud, *loc. cit.* (fn. 11), p. 66 *et seq.*

37. P. Soldatos, *loc. cit.* (fn. 10), p. 261 *et seq.*, sees behind the silence of the Treaties the desire to keep Member States from withdrawing (dissuader). L. M. Bentivoglio, *loc. cit.* (fn. 10), p. 1743 (note 3), who is referred to by Soldatos, goes still further—see above.

38. This kind of reasoning is thoroughly familiar in civil law; according to the constant jurisprudence of the German Federal Court of Justice (BGH), permanent legal relationships can be denounced *bona fide* provided that there are no statutory or contractual clauses relating to denunciation (BGH NJW 1951, p. 836; BGHZ vol. 29, p. 172; vol. 41, p. 108). In particular, from a company set up for an indefinite period withdrawal is possible at any time (BGB § 723, HGB § 123). This ruling goes back to classical Roman law; cf. Gaius (*Institutiones* III, 151): 'Manet autem societas eo usque, donec in eodem consensu perseverant. At cum aliquis renuntiaverit societati, societas solvitur.'

39. Cf. among many others: H. Kelsen, *The Law of the United Nations— A Critical Analysis of its Fundamental Problems* (London 1951), p. 123 *et seq.*; N. Feinberg, *loc. cit.* (fn. 28), esp. p. 212 *et seq.*, with reference to further literature.

40. Cf. particularly L. Oppenheim, H. Lauterpacht, *International Law*, vol. I, 8th edn. (1955, 8th reprint 1967), p. 411 *et seq.*; cf. again N. Singh *loc. cit.* (fn. 30), p. 88 *et seq.*, 92 *et seq.*; cf. also K. Doehring, 'Internationale Organisationen und staatliche Souveranität', in *Festgabe für Ernst Forsthoff*, 1967, p. 105 *et seq.* (118 *et seq.*).

41. UNCIO *Documents*, vol. 7, p. 267, Doc. 1086, I 2 77, cited by N. Feinberg, *loc. cit.* (fn. 28), p. 200.

42. Oppenheim/Lauterpacht, *loc. cit.* (fn. 40), p. 938.

43. N. Singh, *loc. cit.* (fn. 30), p. 102 *et seq.*; E. C. Hoyt, *The Unanimity Rule in the Revision of Treaties—A Re-examination*, The Hague 1969, p. 78 *et seq.*

44. E. Giraud, *loc. cit.* (fn. 11), p. 69. Giraud considers the expressions 'traités' and/or 'conventions collectives' and 'conventions généraux' as synonymous (pp. 1, 11); he designates them 'traités-lois' (p. 2 *et seq.*) and attributes the treaties which set up organizations to them as well (p. 17).

45. E. Giraud, *ibid.*, p. 71. On Giraud's last point see also W. von Simson, 'Der politische Wille als Gegenstand der europäischen Gemeinschaftsverträge', in *Festschrift Otto Riese* (Karlsruhe 1964), p. 83 *et seq.*, at p. 94; M. Zuleeg, 'Die Kompetenzen der Gemeinschaften gegenüber den Mitgliedstaaten', JöR 20 (1971), p. 1 *et seq.* (63/4).

46. Cf. *Institut de Droit International, Onzième Commission, Modification et terminaison des traités collectifs* II, 'Rapport présenté par M. Emile Giraud' (Geneva 1961), p. 18 *et seq.* The dissenting members were Sir Gerald Fitzmaurice,

Wilfred Jenks, Charles Rousseau, Gaetoni Morelli, and Henri Rolin; Paul de Visscher gave a differentiating answer; Bohdan Winiarski concurred with Emile Giraud.

47. Cf. among many others: Lord McNair, 'La terminaison et la dissolution des traités', Recueil des Cours (Académic de Droit International), vol. 22 (1929), p. 459 et seq. (531), and also The Law of Treaties (Oxford 1961), p. 510 et seq. (511 et seq.); P. Guggenheim, Traité de droit international public, vol. I, Geneva 1953, p. 115; Sir Gerald Fitzmaurice, 'Report to the International Law Commission', Documents of the United Nations, A CN 4 107, 15 March 1957, and also in the vol., Modification et terminaison des traités collectifs, II (see previous fn.), p. 75 et seq. (79 et seq.); G. Dahm, Völkerrecht, vol. III (1961), p. 130; D. P. O'Connell, International Law, 2nd edn. (London 1970), p. 266; Ch. Rousseau, Droit international public, vol. I (Paris 1970), p. 213; cf. also the authors mentioned in the previous footnote.

48. Article 34, Draft Convention of the Law of Treaties (A.J.I.L., vol. 29, Supplement, p. 1173 et seq.): 'A treaty may be denounced by a party only when such denunciation is provided for in the treaty or consented to by all other parties . . .'

49. Cf. the 'Commentary on Article 34 of the Harvard Draft', in A.J.I.L., vol. 29 (1935), Supplement, p. 1173.

50. Published in ZaöRV 29 (1969, pp. 711–760; cf. Shabtai Rosenne, The Law of Treaties—A guide to the Legislative History of the Vienna Convention (Leyden/New York 1970).

51. The Vienna Convention also concerns treaties establishing organizations (Article 5). This probably means that the distinctions drawn between 'organizational' and 'non-organizational' treaties (cf. N. Singh, loc. cit. (fn. 30), p. 85 et seq.) or between 'institutional' and 'normative' treaties (cf. N. Feinberg, loc. cit., fn. 28, p. 191, note 1) or between 'treaties of a constitutional character' and other types of treaty (cf. E. C. Hoyt, loc. cit., fn. 43, p. 52 et seq.) are not accepted. Cf. also R. Bernhardt, Die Auslegung völkerrechtlicher Verträge, insbesondere in der neueren Rechtsprechung internationaler Gerichte (1963), p. 187.

52. ECSC Treaty, Article 35, III, IV, 96; EEC Treaty, Articles 236, 237 II, 238 III; Euratom Treaty, Articles 204, 205 II, 206 III.

53. Thus Jerusalem: Das Recht der Montanunion (1954), p. 16 et seq.; E. Wohlfahrt, U. Everling, H. J. Glaesner and R. Sprung, Die Europäische Wirtschaftsgemeinschaft, Kommentar zum Vertrag (1960), Article 240, note 2 (610 et seq.); U. Scheuner, 'Die Rechtsetzungsbefugnis internationaler Gemeinschaften', Festschrift for A. Verdross (Vienna 1960), p. 229 et seq. (237); K. Carstens, loc. cit. (fn. 19); J. H. Kaiser, 'Das Europarecht in der Krise der Gemeinschaften', EuR 1 (1966), p. 4 et seq. (23).

54. Cf. Jerusalem, loc. cit. (fn. 53), p. 16 et seq.; Wohlfahrt, Everling, Glaesner, and Sprung, ibid., p. 610 et seq.

55. 2. BT-200. Sitzung, Sten. Ber., vol. 35, p. 11332 (A, B); cf. in addition the Bulletin of the Press and Information Service of the Federal Government, No. 122 of 9 July 1957, p. 1154 et seq.; AdG 1957, p. 6331 A.

56. 2. BT-Drucks. No. 3660, p. 11.

57. 2. BT-200. Sitzung Sten. Ber. vol 35, p. 11332 (B), cf. also 2. BT-Drucks. No. 3660, p. 11

58. 2. BT-200. Sitzung, Sten. Ber., vol. 35, p. 11372 (B).

59. *Parliamentary Paper* No. 5367 (quoted by Wohlfahrt, Everling, Glaesner, and Sprung, *loc. cit.* (fn. 53), Article 127, No. 5).

60. Cf. Article 20, para. 2, of the Vienna Convention concerning the 'Acceptance of and objection to reservations' in the so-called 'restricted multilateral treaties' (like those of the European Communities); on this, see St. Verosta, 'Die Vertragsrechts-Konferenz der Vereinten Nationen 1968/69 und die Wiener Konvention über das Recht der Verträge', ZaöRV 29 (1969), p. 654 *et seq.* (680 *et seq.*). Cf. also Article 56, para 1, No. 1, of the Vienna Convention ('A treaty which contains no provision regarding its termination and which does not provide for denunciation or withdrawal is not subject to denunciation or withdrawal unless: (a) it is established that the parties intended to admit the possibility of denunciation or withdrawal . . .').

61. Wohlfahrt, Everling, Glaesner, and Sprung, *loc. cit.* (fn. 53), Article 240, note 2.

62. Cf. for example, L. M. Bentivoglio, *loc. cit.* (fn. 10), note 2, pp. 1742–1743; Teitgen, *loc. cit.* (fn. 3), who holds the view that the European Communities represent a federal type of integration, excludes the possibility of any reservation whatsoever—without, admittedly, touching on the reunification problems.

63. In this much, we are not dealing with a case of the application of the *clausula rebus sic stantibus*, as P. Soldatos, 'Durée et dénonciation des traités de Rome', *loc. cit.* (fn. 10), p. 268 *et seq.*, feels; for the *clausula* only arises in the case of circumstances unforeseen at the time when the treaty was concluded (cf. Article 62 of the Vienna Convention: '. . . which was not foreseen by the parties . . .'; on this see J. A. Pastor Ridruejo, 'La doctrine "rebus sic stantibus" à la Conférence de Vienne de 1968 sur le droit des traités', *Schweizerisches Jahrbuch für internationales Recht* XXV (1968), p. 81 *et seq.*, esp. p. 88 *et seq.*). On the other hand, any appeal to this clause is out of the question 'if the parties have provided for the possibility of later modifications at the outset' (G. Dahm, *Völkerrecht*, vol. III, 1961, p. 151) and/or 'if it can be shown that, at the time the treaty was concluded, the parties had already actually taken account of the particular eventuality and had tacitly started from the assumption that in this case the treaty should lapse' or be 'revised' (I. Seidl-Hohenveldern, *Völkerrecht*, 1965, no. 284, 76 *et seq.*). This is precisely the position in the case of the Federal Republic of Germany's statement regarding the reunification of Germany and the attitude of the other Member States.

64. Thus, the French Secretary of State, M. Faure, speaking in the Assemblée Nationale on 16 January 1957 (quoted in 2. BT-200. Sitzung, Sten. Ber., vol. 35, p. 1132, A).

65. Also pointed out by Secretary of State, Walter Hallstein, in the government statement of 21 March 1957 before the Bundestag. (2. BT-200. Sitzung, Sten. Ber., vol. 35, p. 11329 D).

66. L. M. Bentivoglio, *loc. cit.* (fn. 10), p. 1743, note 2: '. . . there seems to be no doubt that, in the circumstances described, the new unified German state will be legitimately entitled to initiate a revision' ('. . . non sembra dubbio che, nelle indicate circonstance, il nuovo stato tedesco unificato sarebbe legittimato ad iniziare una procedura di revisione').

67. On this contradiction, see K. Doehring, *loc. cit.* (fn. 40), pp. 122–124.

68. BGBl. 1957, II, p. 764; cf. GG, Article 116.

69. Protocol on inter-German trade and related questions of 25 März 1957 (BGBl. 1957, II, p. 984).

70. *Loc. cit.* (fn. 51), Article 227, note 5 (p. 586).

71. Cf. Chr. Tomuschat, 'The two Germanies', in *Legal Problems of an Enlarged European Community* (1972), p. 154 *et seq.*, at pp. 159–161; cf. H. P. Ipsen, *op. cit.* (fn. 4), p. 1017 (and in this volume, p. 182 *et seq.*, at p. 212).

72. E. M. Winterhagen, *Die Revision von Gründungsverträgen internationaler und supranationaler Organisationen*, Frankfurt 1963, p. 35 *et seq.*; P. H. Teitgen, *loc. cit.* (fn. 3), class mark 29, p. 17. Regarding the ECSC, cf. K. Carstens, 'Die kleine Revision etc.', *loc. cit.* (fn. 19), p. 4, with reference to further literature.

73. The line of argument in the case 6/64 (Costa *v.* ENEL) 15 July 1964, CMLR 3 (1964), p. 425 *et seq.*, at p. 455, does not, as it happens, refer directly to the issue of withdrawal, so that P. Soldatos' reference to it (*loc. cit.*, fn. 10, p. 263) is not appropriate.

74. Cf. the preamble of the EEC Treaty: 'Determined to lay the foundations of an ever closer union among the peoples of Europe . . .'; cf. also the preamble to the ECSC Treaty.

75. Cf. H. Nawiasky, *Der Bundesstaat als Rechtsbegriff* (1920), p. 98; Hans Kelsen, *Allgemeine Staatslehre*, 1925 (unaltered photo-mech. reprint 1966), p. 225.

76. See above under II.

77. Thus R. Bernhardt, *loc. cit.* (fn. 51), p. 168 *et seq.*, 187 *et seq.*

78. In the Federal Republic of Germany particularly: Fr. Jerusalem, *loc. cit.* (fn. 53), p. 16 *et seq.*; H. Mosler, 'Der Vertrag über die EGKS', ZaöRV 14, (1951/52), p. 1 *et seq.* (37 *et seq.*, 44 *et seq.*); W. Thieme, *loc. cit.* (fn. 6), p. 50 *et seq.* (71).

79. K. Carstens, *loc. cit.* (fn. 19), p. 7.

80. On the integrating role of the European Court see M. Lagrange, 'The Court of Justice as a factor of European Integration', AJCL 15 (1965/66), pp. 709–725; H. J. Schlochauer, 'Der Gerichtshof der Europäischen Gemeinschaften als Integrationsfactor', in *Festschrift für W. Hallstein* (Frankfurt 1966), pp. 430–452; A. W. Green, *Political Integration by Jurisprudence—The Work of the Court of Justice of the European Communities in European Political Integration* (Leyden 1969).

81. Cf. J. H. Kaiser, 'Das Europarecht in der Krise der Gemeinschaften', EuR 1 (1966), p. 4 *et seq.*, at p. 19.

82. Cf. H. P. Ipsen, *loc. cit.* (fn. 4), p. 158 (but see also p. 1024 and in this volume, p. 218); Maurice Flory ('Irréversibilité et point de non-retour', in *La décision dans les Communautés Européennes*, ed. by the Institut d'Etudes Européennes; Université Libre de Bruxelles 1969, pp. 439–451) argues that the point of no return will be reached at a time not predictable by the political science but certainly not before a federal constitution establishes a legal point of no return.

83. Such is the view of N. Catalano, *loc. cit.* (fn. 19), p. 623; cf. also Rigaux (fn. 19), p. 95.

84. W. von Simson, 'Der politische Wille als Gegenstand der Europäischen Gemeinschaftsverträge', in *Festschrift für Otto Riese* (1964), p. 83 *et seq.*, points out on p. 97 that an irreversibility builds up gradually. But even so there is no kind of automatic development in this (as in any other) direction. Time alone will not make integration irreversible.

84a. For a short account see *P. Dagtoglou,* European Communities and Constitutional Law, (1973) 32 C.L.J. pp. 256 *et seq.,* at pp. 262 *et seq.*

85. The Treaty of 22 April 1972 has broadened the budgetary powers of the European Parliament (as from 1975) but has not decisively changed its position in the constitutional system of the Community. The Vedel Report is still at the discussion stage. Especially British parliamentarians campaign in Strasbourg for a reinforcement of the position of the European Parliament through procedural changes.

86. Even from the very beginning, the Commission within the framework of the EEC and Euratom Treaties has been provided with more limited powers than has the High Authority of the ECSC—a fact which makes the merger of the Communities more difficult.

87. Cf., for instance, E. Steindorff, 'Europäische Wirtschaftsgemeinschaft', in Strupp/Schlochauer, *Wörterbuch des Völkerrechts* (1960), vol. I, p. 479 *et seq.* (482); G. Balladore Pallieri, *Diritto internazionale pubblico,* 8th edn., Milan 1962, p. 602; M. Panebianco, in R. Quadri, R. Monaco, and A. Trabucchi, *Trattato istitutivo della C.E.E.,* vol. III (Milan 1965), p. 1115 *et seq.* (1140); Otto Harnier, *Kompetenzverteilung und Kompetenzübertragung zwischen Rat und Kommission unter Berücksichtigung der Einsetzung von Hilfsorganen im Recht der EWG,* Diss. Saarbrücken (1970); cf. also the comments of some of the connoisseurs of the practical working of the Communities: Wieland Europa (Ralf Dahrendorf), in *Die Zeit,* 9 and 16 July 1971; Christoph Sasse, 'Die Zukunft der Verfassung der Europäischen Gemeinschaften—Überlegungen zu einigen Reformkonzepten', EA 27 (1972), p. 87 *et seq.*; Sasse, 'The Commission and the Council—Functional Partners or Constitutional Rivals', (in this volume, p. 89 *et seq.*); K. H. Narjes, *Die Zeit,* 21 January 1972, p. 3. A different view is taken by, among others, H.-W. Daig, in V. D. Groeben, V. Boeckh, *Handbuch für Europäische Wirtschaft,* vol. 2, IA 62, preamble to Articles 155–163, esp. p. 3 *et seq.*; L. Cartou, *Organisations européennes,* 3rd edn., 1971, no. 67 (p. 63 *et seq.*); E. Noël, J. Amphoux, 'Les Commissions', in *Droit Européen,* no. 514 *et seq.* (597 *et seq.*); R. Pinto, 'Structure générale' (of the EEC), in *Droit Européen,* no. 1671 (1676).

88. This is the view of the member of the Bundestag Dr. Lenz (cited in the report of the member of the Bundestag Dr. Mommer, 2. BT-Dr. 3660, p. 15 *et seq.*). This is probably one of the reasons why the European Parliament has not yet made use of these powers which it has. The other reason may well lie in the over-drastic character of such a measure, which does not do justice to the many levels and the flexibility of political life.

89. Quoted in the report of the member of the Bundestag Dr. Mommer, 2. BT-Dr. 3660, p. 14 *et seq.* (16).

90. Thus Christoph Sasse, *Die Zeit,* 14 January 1972, p. 38.

91. To this extent one cannot agree with the opinion of H.-W. Daig, *loc. cit.* (fn. 87), pp. 4, 8, that the powers of the two institutions are carefully balanced in relation to each other. And the thesis of Peter Baduras, too, 'Bewahrung und Veränderung demokratischer und rechtsstaatlicher Verfassungsstrukturen in den nationalen Gemeinschaften', VVDStRL, vol. 23 (1966), p. 34 *et seq.* (pp. 71, 101: thesis 19), that the basic philosophy of the division of power principle is put into practice in the EEC by the balance between the Council and the Commission, as well as by that between the Council and the European Court of Justice, can be adequately supported neither in the Treaty itself, nor in its practical application.

92. L. Cartou, *loc. cit.* (fn. 87), p. XLV.

93. In his press conference of 9 September 1965, in Charles de Gaulle, *Discours et Messages—Pour l'effet, Août 1962–Décembre 1965* (Paris 1970), p. 372 *et seq.*, on p. 379.

94. To use the expression of K. H. Narjes, chef du cabinet of the former President of the EEC Commission, Walter Hallstein, *loc. cit* (fn. 87).

95. EEC Treaty: Article 8, III–VI, in comparison with Article 148, I.

96. Cf. U. Scheuner, *Constitutional problems of the development of the European Community,* in this volume, p. 66 *et seq.*, at p. 77).

97. Holding this view: H. Mosler, 'Nationale und Gemeinschaftsinteressen im Verfahren des EWG-Ministerrates, die Beschlüsse der ausserordentlichen Tagung des EWG-Rates in Luxembourg vom 21 Januar 1966', ZaöRV 21 (1966), p. 27; likewise K. Doehring, *loc. cit.* (fn. 40), p. 122; J. H. Kaiser, *loc. cit.* (fn. 53), speaks in this connexion of a constitutional compromise. Against a legally binding character of the Luxembourg Accords, see H. P. Ipsen, *loc. cit.* (fn. 4), p. 496 *et seq.*, on p. 500.

98. Thus K. Doehring, *loc. cit.* (fn. 40), p. 122.

99. E. Forsthoff, *Der Staat der Industriegesellschaft—dargestellt am Beispiel der Bundesrepublik Deutschland,* 2nd edn. (1971), p. 168 *et seq.*

INDEX*

*By Gerd Ehlers and Sepp Hingerl